MW00698538

The Rise of Digital Repression

The Rise of Digital Repression

How Technology Is Reshaping Power, Politics, and Resistance

STEVEN FELDSTEIN

OXFORD
UNIVERSITY PRESS

OXFORD
UNIVERSITY PRESS

Oxford University Press is a department of the University of Oxford. It furthers
the University's objective of excellence in research, scholarship, and education
by publishing worldwide. Oxford is a registered trade mark of Oxford University
Press in the UK and certain other countries.

Published in the United States of America by Oxford University Press
198 Madison Avenue, New York, NY 10016, United States of America.

Library of Congress Control Number: 2021932316
ISBN 978–0–19–005749–7

DOI: 10.1093/oso/9780190057497.001.0001

1 3 5 7 9 8 6 4 2
Printed by Sheridan Books, Inc., United States of America

CONTENTS

ACKNOWLEDGMENTS

This book is the product of over three years of research, writing, and discussion. Many people played crucial roles in making this book possible. To start, I want to thank Tom Carothers for his encouragement and support, particularly for the candid feedback he provided at the outset of the project, which forced me to think critically about the scope and purpose of the book. I cannot thank him enough for the generosity of his time. The Carnegie Endowment for International Peace served as a second home to me in this period. I am exceedingly grateful for the friendship and ideas I cultivated from such a dedicated community of scholars.

The backbone of this book is the field research I conducted in Thailand, the Philippines, Ethiopia, and Hong Kong. There are numerous people I'd like to thank who provided contacts, advice, and support for my trips to these places. In Thailand, Janjira Sombatpoonsiri offered ideas about people I should speak to and provided substantive feedback for my chapter. She also introduced me to Benjamin Siritantitham, who served as my eyes and ears on the ground, dil- igently running down meetings and adeptly guiding me through the conges- tion of Bangkok's streets. In the Philippines, Karol Ilagan helped me organize a jam-packed schedule that transported me across vast swaths of metro Manila. In Ethiopia, Brooke Abdu served as my right hand, setting aside his regular responsibilities to set up meetings in Addis Ababa and even accompany me north to Mekele. None of these case studies would have been possible without the generosity of the contacts I reached out to—many of whom chose to remain anonymous—who imparted precious insights on this topic.

I'd like to thank the following individuals who generously participated in my book workshop and provided valuable feedback on my manuscript: Sarah Bush, Shanthi Kalathil, Masashi Crete-Nishihata, Steve Livingston, Adrian Shahbaz, and Jon Bateman. In addition, Yoseph Badwaza, David Timberman, Irene Poetranto, Michael Nelson, Brian Wampler, Isaac Castellano, Nisha Bellinger, Michael Allen, Steve Utych, and Ross Burkhart generously took time to review and offer comments on select chapters. I'm exceptionally grateful for their suggestions and advice.

Many of the ideas in the book developed out of an article I published in the *Journal of Democracy* examining the impact of artificial intelligence technology on political repression. I am grateful to Marc F. Plattner and Larry Diamond for their comments and advice.

The bulk of this book was written while I served as the Frank Church Chair of Public Affairs at Boise State University. I never would have found the time or space to develop my ideas for this project without the support of the university community. I am especially grateful to Garry Wenske, Chase Johnson, Corey Cook, Bob Kustra, and the members of the Frank Church Institute board, for bringing me to Boise and for serving as my esteemed colleagues. Special thanks go to Brian Wampler, with whom I was able to hash out vexing problems and obstacles while single-tracking through the Boise foothills.

This book would not have been possible without the generous support of several institutions and foundations. Kizito Byenkya from the Open Society Foundation saw the promise of the book early on and helped shepherd critical resources to support my field research. Boise State University and the Carnegie Endowment for International Peace provided additional financial support, allowing me to organize workshops and to attend key conferences in the discipline.

Thanks to Oxford University Press and Dave McBride for supporting this project through all phases of publication.

A note of thanks to Ida Rothschild, whose diligent editing immeasurably improved the clarity and readability of the manuscript.

And a final enormous thanks to my family:

To my parents, whose commitment to opening my eyes to the wider world sowed the seeds of my interest in international relations, which indubitably led me down the path to writing this book.

To my brother, who has been my intellectual sparring partner for most of my life and has influenced how I think and see the world.

To my wife Elizabeth, for her belief in the book and her steadfast support throughout the writing process. I cannot thank her enough for the innumerable sacrifices she made to allow me ample time to research and write this manuscript.

To my children, Caleb and Louisa, who bring me hope every day and reaffirm my belief that we have an obligation to keep trying to make the world a better place.

Introduction

In 2017, I began to think seriously about digital repression. I had just completed a three-year stint at the US State Department overseeing democracy and human rights issues for Africa. After my departure, I suddenly had much more time to reflect on emergent trends and over-the-horizon issues. I began to hear about a new form of repression taking place in Xinjiang, China. Chinese authorities were systematically harnessing digital technology to persecute millions of citizens in ways I had never encountered before. I started digging into the matter further. What I uncovered was chilling.

Under the leadership of a regional party secretary named Chen Quanguo, who had gained a reputation in his prior post by pioneering brutal grid-policing tactics in Tibet, Chinese security forces had instituted a police state of Orwellian proportions. Authorities, I learned, were collecting mandatory DNA samples in order to build a genetic database for the region's entire ethnic Uighur population. The police were monitoring all electronic communications: text messages, social media posts, phone calls, and visited websites. Checkpoints had been established at every border crossing to track who was coming and going in the province, and to record specific information, including SIM card numbers, license plate registrations, and passports. In public squares, ubiquitous cameras equipped with facial recognition capabilities and powered by advanced algorithms kept watch over Xinjiang's towns and cities.[1]

The developments in Xinjiang were shocking. They also raised a slew of questions. Did such digital monitoring represent the new face of repression? Were Chinese authorities exporting these technologies and tactics to other governments to enable them to persecute their citizens? How did Xinjiang's surveillance and censorship repression strategy relate to other digital strategies such as Internet shutdowns or online disinformation campaigns against domestic opponents? I started to grasp that what was happening in Xinjiang fit a broader pattern of repression taking place around the world. China was not an exception

The Rise of Digital Repression. Steven Feldstein, Oxford University Press (2021). © Oxford University Press.
DOI: 10.1093/oso/9780190057497.003.0001

but part of a larger trend, where autocrats increasingly turn to digital technology to augment and sharpen their programs of repression.

These insights became the rationale for the book—to investigate and make sense of a new model of repression that is profoundly shifting the coercion paradigm.

This book is first and foremost about how governments repress—how autocratically inclined leaders are deploying new digital methods to reinforce their power, shape political narratives, counter dissent, and push back against mass protests. My purpose is to contribute to the current understanding of the goals, motivations, uses, and drivers of digital repression strategies. I do not wish to leave the mistaken impression that technologically advanced tools have fully upended the balance between citizen and government. Rather, I believe that the political landscape is marked by an ongoing struggle between multiple sets of actors (including private companies), and that many factors contribute to determining whether protest movements or opposition challengers will gain power or whether repressive leaders will prevail. This aligns with Ronald Deibert and Rafal Rohozinski's "access contested" construct for cyberspace, in which they describe an "increasing struggle for superiority and the competition for power, influence, and control."[2] While this book focuses on the digital repression side of the equation, there are many innovative tools, ideas, and strategies that civil society groups and opposition movements are successfully implementing to counter autocracies. The news is not completely gloomy even if it is frequently discouraging. I will discuss countervailing strategies in the final chapter of the book.

I chose to focus on state-led digital repression because it represents a swiftly evolving area that remains understudied. There is still a significant amount we do not understand about these trends. Quantitative data remains scarce, and rigorous case-study research is also limited. Yet significant developments are rapidly occurring, many of which bring major policy repercussions. Governments like China's are deploying digital strategies that signify elemental shifts in how states wield power. Gaining a better understanding of the logic and trade-offs behind these tactics and methods is imperative. We should also recognize that governments are no longer on their heels when it comes to confronting civic movements online. They have adapted and are using new tools to strengthen their hold on power. Shedding light on the costs and benefits of these tools will provide an important contribution to our understanding of authoritarianism.

The broader political landscape in which digital repression is unfolding is worrisome. Democracies worldwide are undergoing a troubling period of retrenchment. There is a growing consensus that the world is experiencing a "third wave of autocratization."[3] For the first time in nearly 20 years, autocracies outstrip democracies: 92 countries or 54 percent of the world's population currently live under authoritarian rule.[4] Researchers from V-Dem estimate that 2.6 billion people, or 35 percent of the world's population, are living through autocratization, a process inverse to democratization in which political rights and freedoms are increasingly limited. Such countries include liberal democracies like the United States, flawed democracies and hybrid regimes such as Brazil, India, and Turkey, and autocratic states like Thailand and Venezuela.[5] In their book on political polarization, Thomas Carothers and Andrew O'Donohue describe how "new and old democracies alike are confronting a daunting array of internal and external challenges, from the crumbling of public support for long-established political parties and the swelling popularity of illiberal politicians to the growing assertiveness and influence of authoritarian powers and ideas across borders."[6]

As I was completing this book, the world was in the full grasp of the coronavirus pandemic. While it is too early to predict the long-term political effects of the virus, current indicators are troubling. Governments around the world have turned to digital tools to fight the virus's spread. While many governments have legitimate reasons for deploying contact-tracing apps or using location-monitoring technology to track infections, there are increasing reports of privacy violations and human rights abuses.[7] As states expand their use of digital tools, there has not been a concurrent dialogue to delimit protections, safeguards, and standards of use. Many states have categorically refused to set limits regarding how long they intend to use these tools or for what exact purpose. It is conceivable that for governments in places such as Russia, China, Thailand, or Turkey, heightened surveillance measures are here to stay.

Before I delve into the book's key arguments, it is useful to describe how the digital ecosystem operates, as well as discuss why leaders choose to repress in the first place. The following two sections elaborate on these ideas.

How the Digital Ecosystem Operates

One major change wrought by the Internet is an increase in the "pervasiveness of information."[8] The scale and availability of data that is instantly available to users is unparalleled. When political crises erupt—such as mass protests in Egypt or violent crackdowns in Venezuela—real-time videos, tweets, and posts about these events are not only rapidly disseminated internally, but also promptly transmitted around the world, helping to shape public opinion almost instantaneously. Users have broadcasted Facebook live streams of police brutality in Chicago, uploaded geotagged recordings to YouTube of barrel bombings in Syria, and generated global reactions to election protests against President Evo Morales in Bolivia or street battles between university students and the police in Hong Kong.

These social and political changes are, in part, due to changing global network structures. Past information systems relied upon broadcast networks (information disseminated from a central node to multiple receivers, such as televisions or radios) or peer-to-peer networks (phone conversations with a limited number of participants). Both network forms are highly susceptible to government interference and control. But in addition to proliferating two-way broadcasts and expanding peer-to-peer communication, the Internet opened up hybrid channels of communication via social media. This development has fragmented the state's ability to monitor and regulate citizen communication and was responsible for the initial outpouring of optimism regarding liberation technology's potential to counteract autocratic regimes.[9]

History has recorded many prior instances of communications breakthroughs that have generated social change and political upheaval. The invention of the printing press, telegraph, and radio broadened our access to information and expanded our ability to reach mass audiences; paradoxically, these inventions also "facilitated the rise of the centralized state and prompted the movement toward censorship."[10] Internet technologies are currently provoking an intense period of disruption. Citizen activists were the first to recognize and exploit the potential of information and communications technology (ICT) to foster rapid political change. But governments have caught up; at this point, activists' first-mover advantages have largely dissipated. Repressive regimes have been hard at work devising counterstrategies to blunt the democratizing impact of Twitter revolutions and Facebook movements, reinforcing Melvin Kranzberg's observation that "technology is neither good nor bad, nor is it neutral."[11] Kranzberg's point is that just as civil society actors shape technology to suit their needs, governments (or private companies for that matter) make design decisions that preference certain objectives over others. We see this clearly in the divergent design choices of companies like Wikipedia (openness and collective control), Facebook (monetization of user data tied to profit incentives), or WeChat (monetization of user data plus embedded censorship).

The initial breakthroughs provided by digital technology were to increase the pervasiveness of information, to empower ordinary citizens to become both content receivers and producers, and to usher in new forms of multiway communication. Autocratic leaders reacted to these developments with hostility. Their efforts to manipulate and control how citizens use these tools—and their attempts to exploit this technology to their political advantage—lie at the heart of this book.

In order to understand specific conditions that facilitate state use of digital repression, it is helpful to sketch a basic outline of the digital ecosystem. While each country possesses a unique constellation of interconnected actors,

I generally focus on three groups: states, civil society and opposition actors, and the private sector.

For the state, laws and regulations provide the framework to harness ICT's potential and enact digitally repressive policies. A major gap in the liberation technology argument was its failure to recognize the central role of states, particularly in authoritarian contexts, in establishing and expanding Internet infrastructure. This role enabled states to exploit ICT in support of their priorities, even as digital technology also permitted challenges to government authority.[12] Specific measures can take the form of intelligence laws, which grant state security agencies wide-ranging surveillance powers; censorship directives, which provide legal authority for the state to suppress dissent; or ICT regulations, which authorize government control over key infrastructure (e.g., telecom ownership, Internet exchange points). Many governments have set up national ICT policy institutions to oversee digital technology issues, such as Thailand's Ministry of Digital Economy and Society, the Philippines' Department of Information and Communications Technology, or Ethiopia's Ministry of Innovation and Technology. These institutions are broadly responsible for safeguarding cybersecurity, implementing national broadband plans, setting standards for cloud computing, ensuring data privacy, authorizing necessary ICT procurement, and implementing relevant ICT laws and policies (although regulations vary by country). Underlying these technocratic goals is a more fundamental objective: monitoring, regulating, and controlling how individuals in their respective countries use Internet technologies.

National ICT policy institutions work closely with law enforcement and security agencies to implement policies. Police departments have created cybercrime units with sophisticated surveillance capabilities to monitor social media chatter and hold transgressors accountable. Prosecutors who work with ministries of justice charge individuals with crimes based on directives from the leadership group. In the Philippines, for example, prosecutors have filed eleven cases in fourteen months against online journalist Maria Ressa, one of Duterte's notable critics. Regimes often deploy intelligence and national security agencies to spy on opponents and carry out operations against political rivals. For instance, in Ethiopia, intelligence services frequently arrested online bloggers and independent journalists, authorized under the country's 2009 Anti-Terrorism Proclamation.[13]

A more recent development is the rise of state-sponsored social manipulation and disinformation strategies. Deibert and his colleagues describe the emergence of "third generation controls," with governments moving beyond censoring or filtering content to advancing propaganda and counterinformation strategies (in addition to employing surveillance) in order to discredit and delegitimize opponents.[14] Government involvement, often through a national information

agency or even the office of the president, ranges from directly implementing social manipulation actions (state executed) or coordinating with external actors
to propagate attacks (state sponsored), to instigating attacks while maintaining
an "arm's-length distance" (state incited), to signaling their endorsement of anti-
opposition trolling narratives to like-minded supporters while refraining from
directly engaging (state endorsed).[15]

The second stakeholder group I consider are political opposition figures, civil
society actors, and ordinary citizens who may be persuaded to join them. Such
groups promote a range of objectives befitting their heterogeneity. Some organizations are narrowly focused on challenging the ruling regime and competing
for political power. Others focus more broadly on advocating for political
liberties and human rights. Scholars Nils Weidmann and Espen Rød emphasize
two significant types of actors: activists and potential dissenters: "*Activists* are
individuals who advocate for a political cause, usually against the government.
To pursue this cause, these activists attempt to mobilize *potential dissenters* in the
population."[16] Weidmann and Rød argue that governments focus on preempting
core political activists while also attempting to deter a larger group of potential
dissenters from joining those activists.

In addition to these two groups, governments also attempt to control information producers (journalists, bloggers) who can influence support in favor of
a particular side. Even in the Web 2.0 era, professional journalists still matter.
People look to journalists to assess the credibility of new information and to provide signaling about the regime's legitimacy. This role helps explain why trend
lines are escalating when it comes to state violence against journalists. Reporters
Without Borders' 2020 world press freedom index warns about "growing hostility and even hatred towards journalists" resulting in "more serious and frequent
acts of physical violence."[17] If journalists were no longer politically relevant, state
authorities wouldn't waste time trying to silence them.

The third stakeholder group is comprised of private sector actors. These
companies run social media platforms, supply sophisticated surveillance technology, and provision censorship filtering equipment. In many countries,
private telecoms oversee broadband and mobile networks. Some firms are
wholly private enterprises that operate separately from government control.
Other companies, such as China's Huawei, have opaque ownership structures
that potentially include controlling interests from government authorities.[18]
In countries like Thailand and Myanmar, which feature aggressive censorship and surveillance efforts by state agencies, US social media platforms have
offshored decision-making responsibilities to their California headquarters,
thus insulating local employees from foreign government pressure campaigns.
International companies that run national mobile networks face trickier
situations. Norway's Telenor, for example, owns mobile networks in Malaysia,

Bangladesh, Pakistan, Myanmar, and Thailand.[19] Telenor is obligated to respond when Pakistan demands an Internet shutdown, Bangladesh requests user data, or Thailand seeks to implant network interception devices. But acceding to government demands likely results in Telenor violating Norwegian regulations and also contravenes international law.

Other companies have fewer problems cooperating with repressive governments. Chinese technology companies have a particularly poor reputation in this regard. Researchers from the Citizen Lab have documented, for example, how Chinese social media platforms WeChat and Weibo have installed pervasive censorship and surveillance controls in order to "comply with government regulations on content controls."[20] This has resulted in the tracking, storing, and filtering of millions of user messages and posts both within and outside of China. Chinese companies that fail to implement such controls face heavy fines or even government suspensions. As a general rule, tech companies based in democracies tend to implement higher ethical standards and push back more assertively against repressive policies. Companies based in autocracies, whether national telecoms, Chinese firms, or Russian cybersecurity outfits, operate with few constraints when it comes to cooperating with human rights-violating regimes. But exceptions abound. In September 2020, US technology company Sandvine found itself in the news for providing deep packet inspection technology to Belarusian authorities so they could block websites and messaging apps to suppress election protests. In response, Sandvine's chief technology officer declared, "We don't want to play world police. We believe that each sovereign country should be allowed to set their own policy on what is allowed and what is not allowed in that country."[21] These are precisely the type of "cyber sovereignty" arguments China, Russia, and Iran consistently make.[22]

A valid question might be whether the "corporate surveillance" business model employed by many tech companies bears responsibility for enabling the mass exploitation of personal data, expanding states' ability to undertake surveillance, and promulgating a global epidemic of disinformation.[23] There is little doubt that algorithms from Facebook, Twitter, or YouTube have contributed to the poisoning of informational discourse worldwide. In countries such as the Philippines, many argue that Facebook is culpable for abetting Duterte's populist campaign to suppress critics and spread falsehoods about his rule. In addition, some critics argue that the deliberate constriction of informational choices by algorithms designed to provide a running list of like-curated items has led to the creation of filter bubbles, if not "mass propaganda" facilitated by tech platforms.[24] These concerns are troubling and point to substantial supply-side defects that companies must tackle and for which regulators must hold them accountable (more on these concerns in Chapter 8).

But the spread of online disinformation is equally dependent on individuals who are expressly interested in circulating bad information, sowing discord, and promoting their political agendas—in other words, disinformation is also a demand-side problem. As technologist Samuel Woolley has observed: "To address the problem of computational propaganda we need to zero in on the people behind the tools. Yes, ever-evolving technology can automate the spread of disinformation and trolling. It can let perpetrators operate anonymously and without fear of discovery. But this suite of tools as a mode of political communication is ultimately focused on achieving the human aim of control."[25] As this book will argue, digital repression is an adjunct of political repression. And political repression remains a distinctly human enterprise.

Why Do Leaders Repress?

What particular benefits do leaders get from adding digital repression tools to their arsenal—beyond the advantages they already accrue from conventional repressive tools? To answer this question, it's helpful to review why leaders repress in the first place.[26]

Autocracies use a range of strategies to maintain power. As a first-order tactic, autocratic leaders rely heavily on *coercion* to maintain political order, keep internal and external rivals at bay, and ensure political survival. Rulers must cultivate security forces that will tamp down popular challenges while simultaneously ensuring loyalty that is sufficiently coercive to preempt internal threats. As a result, violence becomes an inherent part of the authoritarian political landscape. As scholar Milan Svolik argues, "The lack of popular consent—inherent in any political system where a few govern over the many—is the 'original sin' of dictatorships."[27]

But coercion alone is insufficient to keep most regimes in power. A second important characteristic of most autocracies is the use of *co-optation*, which involves inducing opponents to join your side or convincing allies to stay in your camp through the provision of specific benefits. Party loyalty has proven to be an especially strong mechanism for maintaining an autocracy because it leads to incentives that "encourage sunk political investment by their members."[28] Authoritarian parties successfully exploit "opportunism and career aspirations" among their members in order to create a stake in the continuation of the regime.[29] While co-optation strategies can be deeply effective, there are limits to their utility. For one, co-optation becomes increasingly expensive to sustain relative to repression. Even if an autocrat can successfully co-opt relevant elites, the majority of the population will still be left outside the tent without access to equivalent benefits or opportunities.

Thus, a third "pillar" of autocratic regimes comprises strategies of *legitimation*. Many autocracies persist not only by threatening or buying off would-be challengers, but by cultivating popular consent for, and societal approval of, their application of power. Scholars such as Johannes Gerschewski contend that coercion and co-optation strategies are insufficient without also seeking to "guarantee active consent, compliance with the rules, passive obedience, or mere toleration within the population."[30] Legitimation can be rooted in socioeconomic factors (e.g., sustained economic growth used by the CCP to validate its authority) or can stem from ideological foundations.

Finally, scholars have also documented the emergence of "hybrid regimes," or "*competitive authoritarianism*."[31] These states occupy a nebulous zone between fully autocratic and partially democratic. In these regimes, "Formal democratic institutions are widely viewed as the principal means of obtaining and exercising political authority. Incumbents violate those rules so often and to such an extent, however, that the regime fails to meet conventional minimum standards for democracy."[32] In such "diminished" authoritarian contexts, autocratic leaders exploit the trappings of democracy in order to perpetuate their rule.[33] While they might hold elections, they rig them significantly against challengers by denying media coverage, stealing votes, and using ruling party machinery to mobilize supporters. They frequently harass and intimidate journalists and government critics to diminish opposition support. Such regimes face a crucial dilemma: "On the one hand, repressing them [opposition groups] is costly, largely because the challenges tend to be both formally legal and widely perceived (domestically and internationally) as legitimate. On the other hand, incumbents could lose power if they let democratic challenges run their course."[34] Thus, in addition to offering limited political competition, these regimes also deploy a mix of coercion, co-optation, and legitimation to stay in power.

No matter how successfully autocrats implement co-option strategies, limit political competition, or seek to bolster their legitimacy, they still must rely on political repression (and, by extension, violence) to stay in power.

But the type of threat a regime faces also matters. As Svolik has established, autocrats confront a fundamental problem: how to manage the majority of citizens excluded from power while also tamping down challenges from within the ruling coalition.[35] During the Cold War, military coups were the most common means for autocrats to leave office, comprising 48.6 percent of authoritarian exits. But in the post–Cold War era (1989–2017), trends have changed; the most common causes of leadership exit are now electoral losses or popular revolts. Exits through coups currently make up only 12.9 percent of total departures.[36] This change indicates that the most serious threats today, at least when it comes to autocratic survival, stem from public discontent—manifested through demonstrations on the streets or rejections at the ballot box.[37] Thus, for most autocrats, building coercive apparatuses to guard against external threats—rather than deterring potential coups—is in their best interest.

Coercive institutions designed to preempt external threats look very different from those intended to block insider challenges. As scholar Sheena Greitens has posited, leaders concerned with insider threats create "fragmented and exclusive organizations," while those preoccupied with popular challenges establish "unitary and inclusive ones."[38] What is the difference? Fragmented and exclusive organizations are designed to maximize loyalty and are built with less regard for intelligence collection or analysis. Such organizations are also inclined to carry out higher levels of violence. Conversely, unitary and inclusive institutions emphasize "preemptive, discriminate, and targeted forms of repression."[39] They feature enhanced intelligence capacity and incentives that diminish the likelihood of using violence. They are, therefore, natural institutions for adopting digital repression techniques.

Can leaders design institutions to address both types of threats? Generally, no—given that the very traits that make one type of organization uniquely effective against insider coups are the same attributes that make it vulnerable to popular revolts.[40] The choice of institution—based on a leader's perception of threat—goes a long way toward determining how they will govern and what methods of repression they will choose.

Steven Levitsky and Lucan Way have offered a similar perspective when describing two essential forms of coercive state capacity: high-intensity and low-intensity coercion. High-intensity coercion entails visible acts of violence against known figures or large groups—such as the mass killings of protestors, violent suppression of democratic institutions, and assassinations of opposition leaders and critics.

Low-intensity coercion involves less visible but systematic actions to monitor and repress opposition activity. Such actions include "extensive surveillance of opposition, short-term detainment by police, harassment of opposition and its financial backers by tax and other regulatory agencies, crippling libel and other suits against opposition leaders and media, beatings of opposition activists by informal thugs tied to the incumbent, and restriction of employment and other career opportunities for those with known oppositionist views."[41] Not surprisingly, techniques of digital repression fall squarely in the low-intensity category.[42]

Levitsky and Way also contend that a state's ability to carry out low-intensity coercion is reliant on "scope and cohesion." Scope refers to the state's effective reach across its territory and into society, while cohesion refers to the level of "compliance" within the state bureaucracy. They note that scope is particularly critical for carrying out low-intensity coercion, observing that "systematic surveillance, harassment, and intimidation of opponents require an infrastructure capable of directing, coordinating, and supplying agents across the national territory."[43] Without sufficient scope, carrying out digital repression is a hard—if not impossible—task.

If we bring together Svolik's problem of autocratic control (insider threats vs. popular challenges), Greitens's theory of coercive institutions (fragmented/exclusive vs. unitary/inclusive), and Levitsky and Way's theory of coercive state capacity (high-intensity vs. low-intensity coercion), we can conclude the following:

- Autocrats face two main threats: insider challenges and popular protests.
- In the post–Cold War era, popular protests are greater threats to autocratic survival than coups.
- Preempting popular protests requires creating unitary and inclusive coercive institutions with strong intelligence capabilities that can deter protestors and opposition activists.
- Such governmental systems rely on low-intensity coercive tactics—surveillance, opposition harassment, legal persecution, and short-term detentions—to maintain power.
- Digital repression techniques directly align with low-intensity coercion, providing a significant advantage to autocratic regimes.

Accordingly, digital repression strategies provide unparalleled capabilities to monitor personal communications, disrupt political organizing, and manipulate public conversations. They are also far less obtrusive than conventional, more violent tactics. As a result, regimes that pursue digital strategies run a lower risk of undermining their legitimacy (e.g., inciting public backlash by using violent tactics) while still accomplishing their political control objectives.

It's important to emphasize that repression is not limited to autocracies. Democracies, particularly illiberal regimes, also carry out repressive policies. But across the board, autocracies repress more frequently and with more severity than democracies. Even in illiberal democracies and hybrid regimes (which lack the same liberal political traditions as advanced democracies), repression is still costlier for leaders to pursue; coercion threatens to create a presumption of illegitimacy, raising the likelihood that citizens will vote the incumbent out of office.[44] When it comes to the application of digital techniques, the same logic holds: autocracies are more likely than democracies to use digital tools to reinforce regime survival. But as I explore later, this rule applies more strongly for certain digital tactics than others.

While digital repression enhances the state's capacity to quash external challenges, it doesn't always succeed in preempting popular protest or promoting stability. The reason is that many of these techniques are dual use. As much as digital tools assist governments in monitoring opponents, censoring communications, or manipulating political narratives, such tools can also help civil society and opposition actors lower barriers to collective action by facilitating leaderless coordination, pushing back against government narratives, and exposing state brutality in real time (as witnessed in Sudan and Iran in 2019).[45]

Main Arguments

I approached writing this book with two basic questions in mind: What is digital repression: how do you define it? And how frequently are states employing these tools? Determining what constitutes digital repression and how the different categories of digital technology relate to one another was challenging. Are these mostly surveillance and censorship tools? Are other techniques, such as disinformation, also relevant?

To answer these questions, I reviewed leading scholarship and interviewed numerous experts to test different propositions. I scrutinized material from digital rights groups and research outfits like Freedom on the Net, Privacy International, the Citizen Lab, Oxford Internet Institute, Access Now, Data & Society, Harvard's Berkman Klein Center, the Electronic Frontier Foundation, Human Rights Watch, Amnesty International, Article 19, and many others. I empirically tracked state deployment of digital tactics through media reports and news articles, and I organized them into databases. I subsequently developed a taxonomy of digital repression comprising five broad areas: surveillance, censorship, social manipulation and disinformation, Internet shutdowns, and persecutions against online users for political content.

I then turned to the second question: how frequently are states using these tools? I found that a wide range of governments are deploying digital tactics on a regular basis, and that government usage of these techniques is rapidly increasing. For example, one of the sources I initially examined regarding global patterns of disinformation was Samantha Bradshaw and Philip Howard's inventory of social media manipulation. They revealed that the number of countries featuring information-manipulating campaigns has soared—from twenty-eight countries in 2017 to seventy countries worldwide by 2019.[46] Similarly, Freedom on the Net's 2018 report, subtitled "The Rise of Digital Authoritarianism," cautioned that a combination of online disinformation, state propaganda, expanding censorship, and automated surveillance had resulted in eight consecutive years of declining Internet freedom. Particularly worrisome, the report underscored that of sixty-five surveyed countries (representing 87 percent of global Internet users), eighteen governments had adopted Chinese artificial intelligence (AI) and facial recognition technologies to confront political threats.[47] The sheer number of countries adopting this technology and integrating it into government repression strategies came as a surprise.

A critical question then arose: Do these digital techniques represent something fundamentally new and distinct in the arsenal of repression? Or is it more accurate to consider them extensions of traditional repression?

The more I looked into this issue, the less I was convinced that digital methods represented a paradigm shift in how governments enact their repressive agendas. Instead, I saw clear overlaps between traditional coercive strategies—detentions, torture, beatings, extrajudicial killings—and digital variants. One of the first issues I investigated was whether a relationship existed between digital repression and political systems of government. It seemed obvious that authoritarian systems would naturally be disposed to adopt digital repression strategies, but I wasn't sure whether state capacity or a country's technological development would be determinative. I anticipated that the most likely candidates for high levels of digital repression would be authoritarian countries with substantially developed technological infrastructures—such as Saudi Arabia or China. It turns out I was only partially correct. Both Saudi Arabia and China rank among the most digitally repressive countries in the world. But they are joined by states such as Turkmenistan, Iran, Tajikistan, Venezuela, and Syria. While some of these governments feature high levels of technological capacity, others have weak economies and underdeveloped digital infrastructures. One aspect they all have in common, however, is a high level of authoritarian governance. No democratic state ranks near the top of the digital repression list—not even illiberal democracies. Put simply, the more authoritarian a government, the higher the likelihood it is relying on digital repression techniques to reinforce its political control.

But while all authoritarian countries digitally repress, my research showed that they digitally repress in distinctive ways. Some countries rely primarily on tactics that require little technical expertise, such as Internet shutdowns or arrests of online users posting unfavorable political content. Unsurprisingly, many such countries exhibit lower levels of technological capacity. Other countries have invested significant resources in surveillance systems or sophisticated censorship filtering techniques. These governments have expended considerable resources purchasing facial recognition cameras, predictive analytic packages, and intrusive malware programs. In other words, digital repression strategies in autocratic states are not monolithic. While an advanced society like China has the capabilities and resources to institute an elaborate Orwellian system in Xinjiang, few other countries can replicate these actions. Instead, they opt for alternative digital strategies that reinforce their repressive agendas but reflect capacity and resource constraints.

Digital strategies offer many advantages over more coercive alternatives. They are less likely to produce a public outcry than violent crackdowns. And they are less prone to generate international condemnation or pressure to cease their deployment. But they also come with a cost. One constraint I began to notice was a phenomenon experts term the "dictator's digital dilemma."[48] Regimes that choose to repress using digital tools face a trade-off between deriving gains from political control versus sacrificing economic benefits that come from allowing citizens to make full use of digital technologies. For instance, when Iraq cut off Internet access nationwide for eleven days in 2019 to quell escalating political protests, this action came at a steep cost. Analysts estimate that the economy suffered over $2.3 billion in losses due to the shutdown.[49] Therefore, regimes must carefully weigh the pros and cons of pursuing a particular digital strategy— none of them are cost free in terms of the resulting spillover effects. Thus, these considerations become another factor that shapes how and when a regime chooses to use its digital repression tools.

While autocracies predominate in their use of digital repression, democracies sometimes engage in it as well. Particularly in illiberal democracies—such as the Philippines, India, Kenya, Hungary, or Brazil—states are quick to deploy online disinformation and manipulation tactics against their political opponents. In fact, several democracies (Colombia and Brazil, for instance) rank among the highest users globally of social manipulation and disinformation tools. This observation points to another insight: relatively open political systems are not antidotes to digital repression. Instead, those countries might substitute one type of repressive technique (disinformation) over others (Internet censorship, obtrusive surveillance). The exceptions to this rule are liberal democracies, which have higher rule-of-law standards and more accountable governance institutions. In those countries, digital repression remains a rarity.

I then turned to questions of diffusion. Which countries and what companies are supplying these technologies? What role are Chinese companies playing in proliferating advanced repressive tools to autocratic and illiberal regimes across the world? I landed on two insights.

First, while there is little dispute that Chinese firms are a significant supplier of digital tools used for repression, I uncovered scant evidence that regimes that are not otherwise inclined to employ these tactics have begun doing so at China's behest. Instead, other factors appear more relevant in determining whether a particular government is engaging in digital repression, such as political environment, intelligence and security capacity, and levels of social media penetration (and corresponding online dissent).

Second, I found that companies based in democracies were just as active as Chinese firms in selling repressive technology to illiberal and authoritarian regimes. In Ethiopia, for example (detailed at length in Chapter 6), analysts have documented how Israeli, Italian, German, and US firms provided spyware to the Ethiopian government to assist its repression program.[50] During a research trip to the country, I met with Tekleberhan Woldearegay, the former director of Ethiopia's Information Network Security Agency (INSA), which is responsible for most of the state's digital repression activities. When I asked him about the level of Chinese influence during his tenure at INSA, he smiled and said, "Always the Americans think we're working behind the door with the Chinese. Never. That's a completely false perception." Instead, he explained that Ethiopia "bought technology from Israel, from Italy, even from Germany, including from America. Also from China. Always to protect our country to create a secure environment. We were searching the best technologies from every part of the world."[51] I received similar responses from security and intelligence officials in Thailand and the Philippines.

Finally, I returned to a foundational question: given governments' rapid adoption of repressive digital tools, are these techniques fundamentally tilting the playing field in favor of authoritarian leaders against their civic and political opponents? I found that the answer is mixed. In states that feature extensive repression supported by high-capacity institutions (and where civil society and government oversight are comparatively weak), digital technology can have a transformative effect on a regime's ability to achieve its political agenda. In other cases, where governments either have insufficient capacity to take advantage of digital tools—or in democracies, which have built-in safeguards to mitigate the impact of digital strategies—the effect of these techniques is more limited. More precisely, in high-capacity coercive countries, digital repression tools not only reinforce existing repression, they can potentially transform the state's ability to track political opponents, monitor dissent, quash protest movements, and consolidate political control. But in lower-capacity countries, acquiring digital tools does not bring the same transformative effect. These tools require specific elements: disciplined security forces that coordinate and communicate across units, a coherent command-and-control structure that enforces adherence to organizational objectives, and highly trained personnel able to analyze, interpret, and act on relevant information. Where regimes lack these ingredients, the impact of digital tools noticeably diminishes.

What can we conclude from these insights?

Digital repression is a growing trend and represents a serious threat to civil society groups and opposition figures around the world. Policymakers must take it seriously. Digital repression is also more nuanced and complex than it might appear at first glance, encompassing a range of tactics and tools wielded differently by regimes depending on the circumstances. While authoritarians rely far more heavily on digital repression techniques than democracies, democratic leaders are also prone to exploiting these tools, sometimes at higher levels than their authoritarian counterparts. China plays a critical role as a model for how state deployment of digital repression can effectively control its citizens. China is a major proliferator of repressive technology, but pinpointing China as a primary driver of digital repression in individual countries overstates the case. Finally, I maintain that in certain countries, digital technology is having a transformative effect on repression; this impact, however, is highly dependent on state capacity and regime type.

Plan of the Book

The research design of my book incorporates a multimethod approach.[52] In an emerging field like digital repression, where basic concepts are still being developed and data collection methods are nascent, I have chosen to supplement quantitative analysis with qualitative fieldwork.

In Chapter 2, I begin by laying out a conceptual framework for digital repression and identify five principal digital repression techniques. I then examine how leaders confront the "dictator's digital dilemma," and to what degree digital technology is transforming the balance between governments and their opponents. I also assess China's responsibility for driving the global spread of digital repression.

In Chapter 3, I present pooled, cross-national, time-series data, drawn from the Digital Society Project, to provide insights into trends associated with digital repression.[53] This approach allows comparisons across a number of variables, including countries, regions, regime types, political liberties, private liberties, physical violence, and digital repression capacity. It also allows me to probe key questions raised in the book: Which countries are deploying digital repression techniques and how prevalent is their use? What is the relationship between regime type and digital repression? How does the deployment of individual components of digital repression differ in democracies versus autocracies?

In the following three chapters, I present country case studies for Thailand, the Philippines, and Ethiopia. Chapter 4 examines how Thailand deploys digital repression techniques to advance its political agenda. Thailand's situation offers insights into how an autocratic state with a history of censorship and political suppression has adapted to the new digital environment. The Thai government adeptly pairs information controls with traditional repressive methods, giving the state potent capabilities to control dissent. Thailand also demonstrates how digital repression is born from and develops out of internal factors—external actors only have limited influence in shaping the state's digital strategies. Chapter 5 focuses on the Philippines, particularly examining how Duterte has implemented a unique strategy of social manipulation and disinformation to advance his political objectives. This chapter discusses democratic backsliding in the Philippines, explores the meaning of Duterte's political ascent, and investigates three principal drivers of digital repression in the country. Chapter 6 turns its focus to Ethiopia, discussing the meaning of political change in the country and the impact of Abiy's reforms in the context of digital repression. It examines the government's Internet shutdown strategy, rising levels of social manipulation and disinformation, as well as ongoing surveillance and censorship concerns. Finally, the chapter looks at China's influence in Ethiopia and considers whether Chinese actions have enabled repression in Ethiopia.

I selected the book's three country case studies based on representativeness and dimensions of interest. First, I looked for regime diversity. According to V-Dem's regime rankings, Thailand ranks as a closed autocracy, the Philippines stands between an electoral autocracy and an illiberal democracy, and Ethiopia is considered an electoral autocracy.[54] Moreover, each has a distinctive political trajectory. Under the leadership of President Rodrigo Duterte, the Philippines is in the midst of severe democratic backsliding. Ethiopia is undergoing a precarious political transition under President Abiy Ahmed. As for Thailand, while it held elections in 2019 to transition out of military junta rule, the electoral process was deeply flawed, indicating a continuation of Thailand's autocratic status quo.

Each country also displays a notable intersection between repressive political strategies and digital technology. For the Philippines, Duterte has navigated a delicate balance, aggressively manipulating the country's information ecosystem while refraining from pursuing censorship or surveillance tactics that would run afoul of the country's political traditions. In Thailand, the regime has pursued a sophisticated censorship-and-surveillance strategy that has kept authorities firmly in control while maintaining economic growth and technological development. Ethiopia's government is undergoing an unsteady transition from years of political repression. It has discarded some elements of its digital repression program (surveillance), has continued to rely on other techniques (Internet shutdowns), and is witnessing the emergence of new tactics (information manipulation and disinformation). Finally, I sought regional diversity in the case studies, intending to represent at least two distinct areas of the globe.

I offer the case studies in chronological order based on the timing of my research visits. I traveled to Thailand and the Philippines during the spring of 2019. I visited Ethiopia almost a year later, during the winter of 2020. Each case study features multiple sets of interviews from a broad array of stakeholders: government officials, civil society actors, academics, researchers, private sector companies, technologists, and journalists. These interviews include individuals directly responsible for implementing digital repression strategies, persons who have supplied advanced technology to repressive regimes, and those who have suffered the consequences of these tactics.

The book's final two chapters touch on broader issues. In Chapter 7, I investigate a specific set of technologies—AI and big data—and their relation to repression. I provide a working understanding of how states deploy these instruments and why they have become a boon for autocratic leaders. I also present a global index of AI and big-data surveillance, measuring the deployment of this technology in 179 countries. In Chapter 8, I present ideas and solutions for how civil society and democracies can fight back against digital repression trends, discussing strategies civil society groups can use to raise the costs of repression associated with the dictator's digital dilemma. I also examine roles and responsibilities of companies in relation to digital repression. Finally, I review strategies that civil society groups can adopt to counter the proliferation of digital repression tools provided by authoritarian states like China and Russia, and I discuss policy implications of the COVID-19 pandemic.

Notes

1. Steven Feldstein, "How Artificial Intelligence Is Reshaping Repression," *Journal of Democracy* 30, no. 1 (2019): 40–52.
2. Ronald Deibert and Rafal Rohozinski, "Contesting Cyberspace and the Coming Crisis of Authority," in Ronald Deibert et al., eds., *Access Contested: Security, Identity, and Resistance in Asian Cyberspace* (Cambridge: MIT Press, 2011), 21.
3. Anna Lührmann and Staffan I. Lindberg, "A Third Wave of Autocratization Is Here: What Is New about It?," *Democratization* 26, no. 7 (October 3, 2019): 1095–113, https://doi.org/10.1080/13510347.2019.1582029.
4. Anna Lührmann et al., "Autocratization Surges—Resistance Grows: Democracy Report 2020," Varieties of Democracy (V-Dem), University of Gothenburg, 2020, 9.
5. The full list of twenty-six autocratizing countries identified by the V-Dem researchers includes the United States, Czech Republic, Hungary, Burundi, Bulgaria, Venezuela, Yemen, Benin, Tanzania, Burkina Faso, Serbia, India, Bolivia, Brazil, Ukraine, Bangladesh, Romania, Zambia, Turkey, Nicaragua, Croatia, Thailand, Poland, Mali, Paraguay, and Comoros. Lührmann et al., "Autocratization Surges—Resistance Grows," 12.
6. Thomas Carothers and Andrew O'Donohue, eds., *Democracies Divided: The Global Challenge of Political Polarization* (Washington, DC: Brookings Institution Press, 2019), 1.
7. Several researchers and rights groups have compiled useful trackers to provide a global snapshot of digital measures countries are taking in response to COVID-19. See, for example, Samuel Woodhams, "COVID-19 Digital Rights Tracker," *Top10VPN*, May 7, 2020, https://www.top10vpn.com/news/surveillance/covid-19-digital-rights-tracker/; "Tracking the Global Response to COVID-19," Privacy International, April 26, 2020, https://www.privacyinternational.org/examples/tracking-global-response-covid-19.
8. Nils B. Weidmann and Espen Gellmuyden Rød, *The Internet and Political Protest in Autocracies* (New York: Oxford University Press, 2019), 16–18.
9. Weidmann and Rød, *Internet and Political Protest*, 17–18.
10. Larry Diamond, "Liberation Technology," *Journal of Democracy* 21, no. 3 (2010), 71.
11. Melvin Kranzberg, "The Information Age: Evolution or Revolution?," in Bruce R. Guile, ed., *Information Technologies and Social Transformation* (Washington, DC: National Academy Press, 1985), 50.

12. Michael L. Miller and Cristian Vaccari, "Digital Threats to Democracy: Comparative Lessons and Possible Remedies," *International Journal of Press/Politics* 25, no. 3 (2020): 8.

13. "Ethiopia Country Profile," Freedom House, 2015, https://www.justice.gov/eoir/page/file/917171/download.

14. Deibert et al., *Access Contested*; Ron Deibert et al., eds., *Access Controlled: The Shaping of Power, Rights, and Rule in Cyberspace* (Cambridge: MIT Press, 2010); Ron Deibert et al., eds., *Access Denied: The Practice and Policy of Global Internet Filtering* (Cambridge: MIT Press, 2008).

15. Carly Nyst and Nick Monaco, "State-Sponsored Trolling: How Governments Are Developing Disinformation as Part of Broader Digital Harassment Campaigns," Institute for the Future, 2018, http://www.iftf.org/fileadmin/user_upload/images/DigIntel/IFTF_State_sponsored_trolling_report.pdf.

16. Nils B. Weidmann and Espen Geelmuyden Rød, "The Internet and Political Protest in Autocracies," *Oxford Scholarship Online*, September 2019, https://www.oxfordscholarship.com/view/10.1093/oso/9780190918309.001.0001/oso-9780190918309.

17. "2020 World Press Freedom Index," Reporters Without Borders, 2020, https://rsf.org/en/2020-world-press-freedom-index-entering-decisive-decade-journalism-exacerbated-coronavirus.

18. Christopher Balding and Donald C. Clarke, "Who Owns Huawei?," *SSRN*, April 17, 2019, https://papers.ssrn.com/sol3/papers.cfm?abstract_id=3372669.

19. "Dtac, Thailand," Telnor Group, 2018, https://www.telenor.com/about-us/global-presence/thailand/.

20. Jeffrey Knockel et al., "We Chat, They Watch: How International Users Unwittingly Build Up WeChat's Chinese Censorship Apparatus," Citizen Lab, May 7, 2020, https://citizenlab.ca/2020/05/we-chat-they-watch/#part-1---background.

21. Ryan Gallagher, "U.S. Company Faces Backlash after Belarus Uses Its Tech to Block Internet," *Bloomberg*, September 11, 2020, https://www.bloomberg.com/news/articles/2020-09-11/sandvine-use-to-block-belarus-internet-rankles-staff-lawmakers?sref=QmOxnLFz.

22. For example, in a joint letter to the UN General Assembly in 2015 regarding an international code of conduct for information security, China and Russia declared that the "policy authority for Internet-related public issues is the sovereign right of States, which have rights and responsibilities for international Internet-related public policy issues." Letter from the Permanent Representatives of China, Kazakhstan, Kyrgyzstan, the Russian Federation, Tajikistan, and Uzbekistan to the United Nations General Assembly, "Developments in the Field of Information and Telecommunications in the Context of International Security," A/69/723, January 13, 2015, https://digitallibrary.un.org/record/786846?ln=en.

23. There is a growing literature that apportions substantial blame to Big Tech for advancing a business model heavily reliant on behavioral manipulation and data exploitation in order to generate exorbitant streams of revenue. See, for example, Tim Wu, *The Attention Merchants: The Epic Scramble to Get Inside Our Heads* (New York: Vintage Books, 2016); Ronald J. Deibert, "The Road to Digital Unfreedom: Three Painful Truths about Social Media," *Journal of Democracy* 30, no. 1 (2019): 25–39; Shoshana Zuboff, *The Age of Surveillance Capitalism: The Fight for a Human Future at the New Frontier of Power* (New York: Profile Books, 2019); David A. Kaye, *Speech Police: The Global Struggle to Govern the Internet* (New York: Columbia Global Reports, 2019); Tarleton Gillespie, *Custodians of the Internet: Platforms, Content Moderation, and the Hidden Decisions That Shape Social Media* (New Haven, CT: Yale University Press, 2018); Zeynep Tufekci, *Twitter and Tear Gas: The Power and Fragility of Networked Protest* (New Haven, CT: Yale University Press, 2017); Siva Vaidhyanathan, *Antisocial Media: How Facebook Disconnects Us and Undermines Democracy* (New York: Oxford University Press, 2018); Peter Pomerantsev, *This Is Not Propaganda: Adventures in the War against Reality* (New York: PublicAffairs, 2019).

24. Danagal G. Young and Shannon C. McGregor, "Mass Propaganda Used to Be Difficult, but Facebook Made It Easy," *Washington Post*, February 14, 2020, https://www.washingtonpost.com/outlook/2020/02/14/mass-propaganda-used-be-difficult-facebook-made-it-easy/.

25. Samuel Woolley, "We're Fighting Fake News AI Bots by Using More AI. That's a Mistake," *MIT Technology Review*, January 8, 2020, https://www.technologyreview.com/s/614810/were-fighting-fake-news-ai-bots-by-using-more-ai-thats-a-mistake/.

26. Research on nondemocratic regimes has gone through several different waves of inquiry to answer how autocratic regimes maintain power. Initially, scholars focused on totalitarian systems, a governing structure characterized by a "monistic" center of power and an exclusive and elaborate ideology used as a basis for legitimation. This wave of research lasted from the 1930s to the 1960s. As empirical incidents of totalitarian regimes began to wane, a second research wave sprung up that focused on authoritarianism (distinct from totalitarianism). Scholars heavily emphasized socioeconomic bases for autocratic regimes and developed the concept of bureaucratic authoritarianism. Their core argument was that as certain countries, such as Argentina and Brazil, hit limits in their import substitution strategies, military and business elites became increasingly frustrated with political and economic stagnation. In response, they formed a coalition that established an authoritarian regime based on "economic progress and state order." As opposed to totalitarian explanations, this research wave posited that autocrats needed to rely on factors beyond terror or ideology (namely the provision of economic and social benefits) in order to ensure regime survival. In the 1990s, a new wave of autocracy research, led by Barbara Geddes, revealed that autocratic regimes do not rely exclusively on coercion, but must also incorporate co-optation strategies to manage the difficulties of sharing power with other elites while ruling over the broader population. See Johannes Gerschewski, "The Three Pillars of Stability: Legitimation, Repression, and Co-optation in Autocratic Regimes," *Democratization* 20, no. 1 (2013): 14; Juan J. Linz, *Totalitarian and Authoritarian Regimes* (Boulder, CO: Lynne Rienner, 2000), 70; Barbara Geddes, "What Do We Know about Democratization after Twenty Years?," *Annual Review of Political Science* 2, no. 1 (1999): 138; Jennifer Gandhi, *Political Institutions under Dictatorship* (New York: Cambridge University Press, 2008).
27. Milan W. Svolik, *The Politics of Authoritarian Rule* (New York: Cambridge University Press, 2012), 10.
28. Svolik, *Politics of Authoritarian Rule*, 163.
29. Svolik, *Politics of Authoritarian Rule*, 163.
30. Gerschewski, "Three Pillars of Stability," 18.
31. See Steven Levitsky and Lucan A. Way, *Competitive Authoritarianism: Hybrid Regimes after the Cold War* (Cambridge: Cambridge University Press, 2010); Thomas Carothers, "The End of the Transition Paradigm," *Journal of Democracy* 13, no. 1 (2002): 5–21; Larry Diamond, "Elections without Democracy: Thinking about Hybrid Regimes," *Journal of Democracy* 13, no. 2 (2002): 21–35.
32. Steven Levitsky and Lucan A. Way, "Elections without Democracy: The Rise of Competitive Authoritarianism," *Journal of Democracy* 13, no. 2 (2002): 52.
33. Juan J. Linz, *Totalitarian and Authoritarian Regimes* (Boulder, CO: Lynne Rienner, 2000), 34.
34. Levitsky and Way, "Elections without Democracy: The Rise of Competitive Authoritarianism," 59.
35. Svolik, *Politics of Authoritarian Rule*, 2.
36. The statistics and classification system used to make these determinations are based on data for 1946 to 2010 from Barbara Geddes, Joseph Wright, and Erica Frantz, "Autocratic Breakdown and Regime Transitions: A New Data Set," *Perspectives on Politics* 12 (June 2014): 313–31. Data for the period 2010–2017 has been updated by the author with assistance from Erica Frantz.
37. For an excellent analysis about the ways in which autocrats have evolved new tactics to fix elections in their favor, see Nicholas Cheeseman and Brian Paul Klaas, *How to Rig an Election* (New Haven, CT: Yale University Press, 2018).
38. Sheena Chestnut Greitens, *Dictators and Their Secret Police: Coercive Institutions and State Violence* (New York: Cambridge University Press, 2016), 12.
39. Greitens, *Dictators*, 12.
40. Greitens, *Dictators*, 32.
41. Lucan A. Way and Steven Levitsky, "The Dynamics of Autocratic Coercion after the Cold War," *Communist and Post-Communist Studies* 39, no. 3 (2016): 388.
42. Erica Frantz and Andrea Kendall-Taylor offer a similar breakdown of repression, dividing tactics into two categories: empowerment rights repression, such as censorship and freedom-of-association limitations, and physical integrity rights repression, including

torture, disappearances, extrajudicial killings, and imprisonment. Erica Frantz and Andrea Kendall-Taylor, "A Dictator's Toolkit: Understanding How Co-optation Affects Repression in Autocracies," *Journal of Peace Research* 51, no. 3 (2014): 332–46.

43. Way and Levitsky, "Dynamics of Autocratic Coercion," 388.
44. Jacqueline H. R. DeMeritt, "The Strategic Use of State Repression and Political Violence," *Oxford Research Encyclopedia of Politics,* 2016, http://politics.oxfordre.com/view/10.1093/acrefore/9780190228637.001.
45. See, for example, Clay Shirky, *Here Comes Everybody: The Power of Organizing without Organizations* (New York: Penguin, 2008).
46. Samantha Bradshaw and Philip N. Howard, "The Global Disinformation Disorder: 2019 Global Inventory of Organised Social Media Manipulation," Working Paper 2019.2, Oxford: Project on Computational Propaganda, 2019.
47. Adrian Shahbaz, "Freedom on the Net 2018: The Rise of Digital Authoritarianism," Freedom House, 2018, https://freedomhouse.org/report/freedom-net/2018/rise-digital-authoritarianism.
48. See Philip N. Howard, Sheetal D. Agarwal, and Muzammil M. Hussain, "The Dictators' Digital Dilemma: When Do States Disconnect Their Digital Networks?," Brookings, 2011, https://www.brookings.edu/wp-content/uploads/2016/06/10_dictators_digital_network.pdf.
49. Samuel Woodhams and Simon Migliano, "The Global Cost of Internet Shutdowns in 2019," *Top10VPN*, January 7, 2020, https://www.top10vpn.com/cost-of-Internet-shutdowns/.
50. See Bill Marczak et al., "Champing at the Cyberbit: Ethiopian Dissidents Targeted with New Commercial Spyware," Citizen Lab, December 6, 2017, https://citizenlab.ca/2017/12/champing-cyberbit-ethiopian-dissidents-targeted-commercial-spyware/; Bill Marczak, John Scott-Railton, and Sarah McKune, "Hacking Team Reloaded? US-Based Ethiopian Journalists Again Targeted with Spyware," Citizen Lab, March 9, 2015, https://citizenlab.ca/2015/03/hacking-team-reloaded-us-based-ethiopian-journalists-targeted-spyware/; Bill Marczak et al., "Hacking Team and the Targeting of Ethiopian Journalists," Citizen Lab, February 12, 2014, https://citizenlab.ca/2014/02/hacking-team-targeting-ethiopian-journalists/; and Morgan Marquis-Boire et al., "You Only Click Twice: FinFisher's Global Proliferation," Citizen Lab, March 13, 2013, https://citizenlab.ca/2013/03/you-only-click-twice-finfishers-global-proliferation-2/.
51. Tekleberhan Woldearegay (former director of INSA), interview with the author, February 19, 2020. Tekleberhan's reference to the purchase of German, Italian, and Israeli surveillance technology aligns with independent reporting from the Citizen Lab documenting extensive spyware contracts between Ethiopian intelligence and those same firms. See Marczak et al., "Champing at the Cyberbit"; Marczak, Scott-Railton, and McKune, "Hacking Team Reloaded"; Marczak et al., "Hacking Team and Targeting"; and Marquis-Boire et al., "You Only Click Twice."
52. For a deeper discussion of the advantages of pursuing a multimethod analytic approach, see Gary Goertz and James Mahoney, *A Tale of Two Cultures: Qualitative and Quantitative Research in the Social Sciences* (Princeton, NJ: Princeton University Press, 2012), 144. See also Barbara Geddes, *Paradigms and Sand Castles: Theory Building and Research Design in Comparative Politics* (Ann Arbor: University of Michigan Press, 2003).
53. Valeriya Mechkova, Daniel Pemstein, Brigitte Seim, and Steven Wilson, Digital Society Project Dataset v2, 2020. There is growing interest in analyzing quantifiable data to substantiate key theories and assertions regarding digital repression. Researchers such as Weidmann and Rød (Mass Mobilization in Autocracies Database), Rebecca MacKinnon (Ranking Digital Rights), Samantha Bradshaw and Philip Howard (annual global inventories of social media manipulation), and Freedom on the Net are providing invaluable contributions through their respective data collection and analytic efforts. See Weidmann and Rød, *Internet and Political Protest,* chap. 4; Ranking Digital Rights, https://rankingdigitalrights.org/index2019/; Freedom on the Net, https://freedomhouse.org/report-types/freedom-net.
54. Michael Coppedge et al., "V-Dem Dataset v10," V-Dem Project, 2020, https://doi.org/10.23696/vdemds20.

2

Motivations and Incentives
for Digital Repression

In 2019, Sudan and Iran faced escalating protests that threatened to topple their governments. Both regimes employed similar strategies to try to quell mass protests in the streets. In Sudan, demonstrators had congregated in major cities for six months. Initially, protests were instigated by economic frustrations: rising prices, commodity shortages, and a cash crunch. Gradually, they evolved into calls for greater freedoms and political liberties. In Iran, demonstrators had also taken to the streets in reaction to abrupt increases in the cost of fuel. Again, protests transformed into broader political demonstrations, this time against the Islamic Republic and Supreme Leader, Ayatollah Ali Khamenei. In desperation, both regimes implemented what has become a standard two-part strategy: cut off Internet communication to sap the protests' momentum and prevent citizens from virtual organizing for actual activism on the streets, and then use the ensuing information blackout to commit atrocities to end the uprisings.[1]

Thus, on June 3, 2019, the Sudanese regime instituted a near-total Internet blackout that lasted for thirty-six days and resulting in economic losses exceeding $1.8 billion.[2] In that month-long period, the regime unleashed the notorious Rapid Support Forces (RSF) paramilitary force to terrorize Khartoum residents and slaughter those who dared to continue demonstrating. During one infamous massacre, troops opened fire on a peaceful sit-in outside military headquarters, killing at least 128 people; hundreds more went missing.[3]

Likewise, after three days of swelling protests in Iran, on November 15, 2019, jittery authorities shut down the Internet for eight days. Iranian security forces then exploited this communications blackout to commit serious atrocities. Human rights groups estimate that at least 450 people may have been killed.[4] In one gruesome episode in the southwest city of Mahshahr, Islamic Revolutionary Guards chased a mass of demonstrators to a marsh. After surrounding the

The Rise of Digital Repression. Steven Feldstein, Oxford University Press (2021). © Oxford University Press.
DOI: 10.1093/oso/9780190057497.003.0002

protesters, the guards opened fire with machine guns, killing between forty and one hundred people.[5]

After Internet access was restored in both countries, video footage detailing government atrocities began to surface. The BBC stitched together a live-stream video that documented, minute by minute, a massacre of protesters in Khartoum. Taking video footage from more than three hundred smartphones—individuals kept filming even while soldiers were shooting—they spliced it into one contiguous scene.[6] In Iran, citizens similarly kept their phones recording to document mass shootings by Iranian forces. Hundreds of videos made their way to YouTube, as well as to news outlets and groups like Amnesty International.[7] In Sudan's case, the Internet shutdown and subsequent massacre represented the final death knell of the regime. The country is now in the midst of a delicate political transition to a more representative government. In Iran, massacres carried out during the Internet shutdown seem to have quelled the uprising—at least for now.

Both situations exemplify the way that states have adapted traditional repressive strategies in order to keep up with digital changes that have shifted the way citizens communicate, organize, and protest against the state. Even with new digital variants, repression often remains a distinctly violent enterprise.

Naturally, however, repression takes many forms beyond the heavy use of force combined with Internet blackouts that some governments employ in response to protests. Often it involves quieter methods of surveilling and persecuting political dissidents or opponents. Here too, new digital methods are enhancing the toolbox of repression. For example, in 2016, United Arab Emirates (UAE) authorities contracted with former National Security Agency operatives to hack into smartphones in order to access "phone numbers, emails, passwords, and even track the location of the phones' users."[8] They called the operation Project Raven.[9] While it ostensibly intended to keep tabs on ISIS terrorists, its true surveillance capabilities were trained on political opponents, civil society activists, and independent journalists.

Prominent Emirati activist Ahmed Mansoor became a particular focus of the program. Mansoor was a public critic of the UAE's history of human rights violations and had gone on record criticizing the government's involvement in the Yemen conflict and its persecution of regime opponents (in 2015, Amnesty International recognized his efforts by presenting him with the Martin Ennals Award for Human Rights Defenders).[10] As Citizen Lab researchers documented, he was previously the target of UAE-sponsored spyware attacks from FinFisher in 2011, Hacking Team in 2012, and NSO Group in 2016—representing a stunning outlay of resources targeted against an individual.[11] Project Raven operators used a new surveillance tool known as "Karma" to access Mansoor's personal information—everything from email and text messages, to personal photos, contacts, and phone numbers. Karma was especially sinister because it didn't require that a target click on a link to activate its malware. Instead, Karma granted remote access "simply by uploading phone numbers or email accounts into an automated targeting system."[12] Following a secret 2017 trial, UAE authorities sentenced him to ten years in prison.[13]

The arrival of various digital technologies is bringing new tools, techniques, and dimensions to political repression. At its core, the expanding digital dimension of repressive regimes reflects a fairly simple motivation: states are seeking and finding new ways to control, manipulate, surveil, or disrupt real or perceived internal threats. As case studies for Thailand, the Philippines, and Ethiopia will show, the degree to which governments make use of new digital tools for repressive purposes depends on a range of factors: ongoing levels of repression, leadership, state capacity, and technological capabilities. But their overall reliance on digital repression is premised on a basic political motive: to find an optimal combination of tactics that will preserve and sustain political incumbency.

This chapter explores two principal questions: What is digital repression? And how significant is digital repression—is digital technology changing the balance between governments and civil society?

In addition, I also inquire: How do governments manage trade-offs between advancing digital innovation while maintaining political control? Why do certain states employ digital repression but not others? And finally, what is the role of China in spreading digital repression globally?

I begin by defining digital repression and laying out its five principal components. Next, I discuss how leaders confront the "dictator's digital dilemma" (balancing innovation while maintaining political control). I then address whether digital technology is changing the balance between governments and civil society. I argue that in certain countries, where repression is already ongoing and supported by high-capacity institutions, digital technology can have a transformative effect on political repression. Subsequently, I examine why certain states but not others employ digital repression and offer two arguments: First, governments that rely on repression as a core governing tool are more likely to employ digital repression techniques. Second, both autocracies and flawed democracies deploy digital repression, but they employ distinctive combinations of these techniques. Finally, I explore China's responsibility for globally spreading digital repression and contend that while it has enabled the proliferation of repressive technologies, domestic factors are more important drivers of these tactics.

What Is Digital Repression?

Political repression involves the actual or threatened use of force within the territorial jurisdiction of the state, against an individual or organization. As scholar Christian Davenport notes, such force is intended to impose a "cost on the target as well as deterring specific activities and/or beliefs perceived to be challenging to government personnel, practices or institutions."[14] Such tactics involve applications of state power that "violate First Amendment–type rights, due process in the enforcement and adjudication of law, and personal integrity or security."[15]

Digital repression enhances states' abilities to carry out more traditional forms of repression. *I define digital repression as the use of information and communications technology to surveil, coerce, or manipulate individuals or groups in order to deter specific activities or beliefs that challenge the state.*[16]

Experts have used terms such as "digital authoritarianism," "algorithmic repression," and "authoritarian tech" almost interchangeably to describe what I am designating as digital repression.[17] I believe digital repression is a more accurate description. Unlike digital authoritarianism or authoritarian tech, this designation does not imply a bias toward a particular form of government. Democracies deploy digital repression techniques for a host of reasons without necessarily intending to transform their political systems into authoritarian models. As for algorithmic repression, this term refers to tools that incorporate artificial intelligence, whereas the trends described in this book incorporate a broader set of technologies.[18]

Disaggregating digital repression into its constituent parts offers further insights. I divide digital repression into five categories: surveillance, censorship, social manipulation and disinformation, Internet shutdowns, and targeted persecution of online users. These five techniques are not mutually exclusive; in many instances they overlap. Internet shutdowns are both an instrument of information censorship and a broader method of state control. But as I detail later, each technique draws from a unique set of tools to perform its objectives—which is why I have separated them into distinct categories.

In addition, many techniques rely on specific uses of technology that work in parallel with legal, policy, or regulatory actions. For example, censorship may involve technical filtering of certain social media applications or websites. Yet censorship strategies can also include government enforcement of legal content restrictions, such as with cyber libel laws in the Philippines or with lèse-majesté regulations in Thailand. Table 2.1 presents a taxonomy of digital repression techniques.

Table 2.1

Surveillance	Online Censorship	Social Manipulation and Disinformation	Internet Shutdowns	Targeted Persecution of Online Users
Technologies, systems, or legal directives that enable control through identification, tracking, monitoring, or analysis of individual data or systems	Laws, regulations, or actions undertaken by state authorities to restrict content & limit access to information	Strategies deployed by state or state-sponsored actors to shape narratives & beliefs and to mislead & manipulate users	Intentional restrictions or disruptions of ICT networks or electronic communications rendering them effectively unusable for a specific period of time	Online users persecuted by state authorities as a reprisal for posted political or social activity
Passive surveillance: Internet monitoring, mobile phone tapping, SIM registration, location monitoring, deep packet inspection, network interception, cable tapping, telecom surveillance	Content blocking and filtering	Disinformation	Total Internet shutdowns	Online users charged, arrested, imprisoned, or in prolonged detention
Targeted surveillance: intrusion operations which manipulate software, data, computer systems, or networks in order to gain unauthorized access to user information & devices (spyware/malware)	Social media/ICT apps blocked	Trolling, doxing, harassment	Partial shutdowns (restricted websites, blocked social media access	Online users physically attacked or killed
AI & big data surveillance: facial recognition, intelligent video, smart policing, smart cities/safe cities, social media monitoring	Takedown requests; content removal	Flooding	Throttling, blackouts, slowdowns	
Surveillance laws: supports digital surveillance actions through the provision of intelligence & national security laws, data disclosure, data retention, and data localization directives	Distributed Denial of Service (DDOS) attacks	Automated methods – bots, algorithms		
	Infrastructure restrictions (Internet firewalls; closed ICT infrastructure – e.g., Great Firewall, Halal Net)	Vandalism and defacement		
	Censorship laws & directives: religion/blasphemy, cybercrime, false news/fake news, political/hate speech, lèse-majesté, security/terrorism, copyright infringement, defamation/libel/sedition, indecency/anti-LGBT, financial targeting of groups			

Surveillance

Definitionally, surveillance entails the gathering of information through the identification, tracking, monitoring, and analysis of individuals, data, organizations, or systems.[19] Surveillance can be used for legitimate purposes as well as for coercive purposes. But at its core, surveillance is premised on concepts of power and control. The use of surveillance by governments for political purposes is not new; security services in both democracies and autocracies have traditionally relied on close observation, physical trailing, phone tapping, and house searches. In recent years, state deployment of surveillance has become more pronounced, particularly in the post-9/11 era, leading to the ascendance of what Gary Marx terms "the new surveillance."[20] The new surveillance relies on technical processes to extract or create personal data and is a direct result of the availability of individual transactional data or metadata from new digital technologies that facilitate communication, commercial transactions, political participation, and entertainment.[21]

Government surveillance is not inherently illegitimate. States have legitimate reasons for tracking individuals who may represent different types of security risks. The accepted international standards for lawful surveillance are based on principles of necessity, proportionality, and legitimacy.[22] Is the surveillance measure strictly and demonstrably necessary to achieve a legitimate aim? Does the surveillance restriction represent a proportionate response to that aim? In addition, domestic law should authorize circumstances in which surveillance is appropriate, and these legal regulations should be formulated with "sufficient precision to enable an individual to regulate his or her conduct accordingly and it must be made accessible to the public."[23] Finally, the interests justifying the surveillance action should also be legitimate. Here, there is significant disagreement: while many governments use national security or public order rationales to justify surveillance programs, the line separating legitimate surveillance from abuses of power is purposefully blurry. The UN's Office of the High Commissioner for Human Rights (OHCHR) warns that such laws are often unacceptably vague or overly broad, and that lawful surveillance requires states to "demonstrate the risk that specific expression poses to a definite interest in national security or public order."[24] To guard against abuse, independent oversight should be put in place that empowers judiciaries to authorize relevant surveillance measures and provide remedies when required.

I identify four broad surveillance strategies commonly used by governments: passive surveillance, targeted surveillance, AI and big-data approaches, and surveillance laws and directives.

Passive surveillance represents the first category. Such communications surveillance is made up of hundreds of instruments that directly monitor, collect, intercept, and retain data that has been "communicated, relayed or generated over communications networks to a group of recipients by a third party."[25] This category encompasses everything from mobile phone tapping and location monitoring to network interception and deep packet inspection.[26] The onset of the coronavirus has generated heightened government interest in these techniques. By October 2020, seventy-one countries had deployed contact-tracing apps, thirty-eight countries had introduced digital tracking measures linked to Covid-19, and twenty-seven countries had adopted advanced physical surveillance technologies in response to the pandemic.[27] While it should come as no surprise that authoritarian governments in China and Russia are relying on facial recognition, social media surveillance, mobile phone location monitoring, and QR code systems to confront the virus, many democracies have also employed digital tools to confront the crisis. In India, for example, authorities in Rajasthan publicly disclosed the personal details of those under quarantine. In Karnataka, officials directed all persons under quarantine to send geotagged selfies every hour throughout the day. In major cities like Delhi, officials put up posters on the homes of quarantined patients, revealing their names. The Ministry of Electronics and Information Technology introduced a national contact-tracing mobile app, Aarogya Setu, to monitor users' whereabouts.[28]

The second category consists of *targeted surveillance*—intrusion operations that manipulate software, data, computer systems, or networks in order to gain unauthorized access to user information and devices. Unlike passive surveillance, which targets a wider range of individuals or groups in an undifferentiated manner, targeted strategies involve specific deployments of malware or spyware to collect information.

The Citizen Lab classifies intrusion operations into three distinct models: national in-house operations or advanced persistent threat (APT), repurposed crimeware, and commercial spyware.[29] The first category involves high-capacity state actors, such as the NSA or Chinese actors, who use customized malware and who have a long track record of carrying out campaigns. The second category, repurposed crimeware, is well illustrated by parties involved in Syria's civil war: "These attacks primarily rely on basic Remote Access Trojans (RATs) that are circulated among hobbyists and criminals, but which we have found are deployed for political reasons and—in the case of Syria—in the context of armed conflict."[30] The third category of commercial spyware relies on the acquisition of "commercial lawful intercept products and services that provide actors with turnkey surveillance solutions."[31] Firms such as NSO Group, FinFisher, and Hacking Team are major players in this sector. They provide sophisticated spyware (at high cost) to government clients designed to infiltrate another user's device in order to obtain confidential data or to continuously monitor communications without the information holder's permission. The implantation of spyware relies on a variety of methods, including *social engineering* (psychological manipulation to trick users into revealing information in order to compromise their devices or online accounts) and *spear phishing* (malicious files or links, frequently delivered by email, intended to bait targets into installing spyware that will compromise their devices or accounts). Many tactics have evolved to the point where attackers are able to access a user's smartphone simply by uploading phone numbers or email addresses. As Patrick Howell O'Neill notes, they are "designed to silently infect and invisibly surveil even 'paranoid targets' who might have a high level of digital security awareness."[32]

Experts have documented patterns of official abuse related to intrusion operations in many countries—even in democracies. In Mexico, an investigative collaboration between the Citizen Lab, Article 19, R3d, and SocialTic identified twenty-five infection attempts connected to the government carried out against journalists, lawyers, opposition politicians, and anticorruption activists. At least nine of these incidents have been linked to the NSO Group's Pegasus software.[33] Globally, the Citizen Lab has identified at least forty-five countries where Pegasus operators are carrying out surveillance operations.[34] This includes countries such as Bahrain, Kazakhstan, Mexico, Morocco, Saudi Arabia, and the UAE, which have prior linkages to spyware abuses against civil society organizations. A primary justification for state use of these technologies is that the software is assisting legitimate criminal cases. But as the Citizen Lab notes, "We have found indications of possible political themes within targeting materials in several countries," signifying that the real motivation for their deployment is to track and target political opponents.[35] My own data reveals that at least sixty-one countries worldwide are deploying commercial spyware in support of their objectives.[36]

Harms stemming from these attacks have become so concerning that social media companies have started filing lawsuits against private surveillance companies responsible for proliferating malware. In October 2019, WhatsApp sued NSO Group in US federal court, alleging that the company's spy technology enabled repeated hacking of human rights activists and journalists, leading to irreparable damage.[37]

The third category is comprised of *AI and big-data surveillance*—automated technologies that classify and store data and compare captured information to other data for pattern recognition and prediction purposes. These techniques are used in public facial recognition systems (biometric technology that matches stored or live footage of individuals with images from a database; this technology can also include systems designed to assess aggregate demographic trends via facial recognition and crowd scanning), smart cities or safe cities (networks made up of thousands of sensors that transmit real-time data to manage cities and facilitate public safety), smart policing techniques (data-driven methods used for police response, investigations, and crime predictions), and social media surveillance (machine-driven programs designed to automatically monitor millions of communications for specific keywords or to detect more generalized patterns). Chapter 7 expressly discusses how states are incorporating artificial intelligence and big-data techniques for repressive purposes.

The final category includes *surveillance laws and directives* that provide governments with expanded authority to carry out the blanket collection of metadata or communications content, to monitor or intercept private communications, or to surveil citizens using physical devices (e.g., wiretaps and stingrays). Frequently, such laws mandate that cloud servers or social media platforms store data locally (to expedite local law enforcement access), or they may grant security agencies authorization to access personal data or communications under particular circumstances—often justified on national security or public order bases.

The advent of new ICT surveillance tools has brought further complications. There is more communications data available for government perusal than ever before. The Internet has dramatically expanded the level of transactional data or metadata available about individuals—including websites people have visited, emails and chat messages they have sent, data about social media they have used, and location-tracking and web-tracking information from apps or browsers they have accessed.[38]

Online Censorship

Censorship is another widely used tool by repressive governments. The digital information space has opened up a new domain for censorship, paving the way for the deployment of uniquely invasive techniques. Online censorship involves laws, regulations, or actions undertaken by state authorities to restrict Internet content and circumscribe access to information. Blocking social media sites or ICT applications, forcing the removal of content, and using laws or directives that "punish legitimate online activity" are key indicators of censorship.[39]

Scholar Margaret Roberts has identified three censorship techniques that governments frequently deploy: fear, friction, and flooding.[40] Fear tactics involve "deterring" individuals or the media from distributing, collecting, or creating certain content through the provision of punitive measures—threats, arrests, fines, and closures. Many countries have instituted highly structured legal provisions designed to facilitate content suppression. Such measures range from lèse-majesté provisions in Thailand to defamation laws in Azerbaijan and sedition provisions in Pakistan.

Friction techniques, on the other hand, "act like a tax on information." They raise the costs of consuming information enough to deter large numbers of people from accessing prohibited content. For example, many countries put Internet restrictions in place that block certain websites. An easy circumvention solution is to use virtual private network (VPN) technology, which is commonly available. Yet taking time to download a VPN application, figuring out how to activate it, and then searching for unfiltered sources of information represents enough "friction" to sufficiently deter large majorities of citizens.

For purposes of this book, I categorize flooding in the social manipulation and disinformation category. While flooding provides a censorship function by deliberately drowning out legitimate sources of information, its first-order use is to manipulate existing content.

Another frequently used censorship tactic is distributed denial of service (DDOS) attacks, which intentionally render computer networks or websites inoperative by flooding them with data simultaneously sent from multiple computers. One of the most prominent examples of state use of DDOS is China's Great Cannon. As the Citizen Lab relates, the Cannon hijacks Internet traffic to or from individual IP addresses, "silently programming their browsers to create a massive DDoS attack." The result is a "significant escalation in state-level information control," serving to normalize the widespread use of attack tools to enforce censorship.[41]

A final censorship strategy is to implement infrastructure restrictions, such as setting up closed national Internet networks where government monitors have free reign to restrict content. China's "great firewall" and Iran's National Information Network or "halal net" represent two flagrant examples of alternative, government-controlled systems. Russia has also conducted tests to develop a national network, known as RuNet, featuring a restricted number of access points to the global Internet. It conducted a multiday test of this new system in December 2019.[42]

The COVID-19 crisis has accelerated information controls globally and empowered leaders to arrest, prosecute, and suppress dissent under the aegis of fighting the outbreak. In Myanmar, authorities blocked access to hundreds of news websites, claiming they carried "fake news."[43] In neighboring Cambodia, the government arrested dozens of social media users simply for sharing pandemic information (coincidentally four of them were aligned with the opposition Cambodia National Rescue Party).[44] In Turkey, authorities detained numerous people for sharing "unfounded and provocative" posts on social media relating to the outbreak.[45] The government also used the crisis as an opportunity to push new measures to throttle the bandwidth of social media companies that refused to appoint in-country representatives and adhere to Turkey's politically restrictive content guidelines.[46] Finally in China, authorities used a mixture of censorship (giving specific instructions to websites and social platforms about what news they were allowed to communicate about the virus) and information manipulation (activating fake online commentators to flood platforms with misleading chatter) to reclaim control of the pandemic narrative.[47]

Social Manipulation and Disinformation

While repressive governments have relied on propaganda and disinformation techniques for hundreds of years, new digital technologies are enhancing state capacity to manipulate information and weaponize communication. I use the term "social manipulation and disinformation" to describe state-sponsored tactics intended to shape narratives and beliefs and to mislead and manipulate users. This category contains a number of overlapping terms: misinformation, disinformation, fake news, strategic communications, computational propaganda, information operations, political warfare, and active measures.[48] For our purposes, I identify five tactics that are key components to social manipulation and disinformation: disinformation, trolling and harassment, flooding, automated methods (the use of bots and algorithms), and vandalism. These tactics share a common set of objectives: suppress legitimate information, discredit opponents, and delegitimize public institutions, leading to a loss of faith in political systems.

Disinformation is the intentional dissemination of "false, inaccurate, or misleading information" in ways that "cause demonstrable and significant public harm."[49] A typical example of disinformation occurred during the 2018 Brazilian election. In the lead-up to the October runoff between far-right candidate Jair Bolsanaro and leftist Fernando Haddad, a deluge of images started circulating on WhatsApp (a messaging platform used by 120 million Brazilians). The images showed the name of a purported presidential candidate, former president Luiz Inácio Lula da Silva, next to the number 17. In the Brazilian system, citizens press a number in the voting machine that corresponds to a particular candidate or party. The problem with this recommendation was that Lula was not actually running—he had been disqualified by the courts. The number 17 actually corresponded to Bolsonaro's ticket (Bolsonaro ultimately won the vote count and was elected president). This situation represented only "one of millions of photos containing disinformation believed to have reached Brazilians" prior to voting.[50]

The onset of the coronavirus crisis has led to a rash of disinformation. Many sources are linked to state actors, particularly governments in China, Russia, Turkey, and Iran.[51] Other sources of bad information stem from conspiracy websites or individuals seeking to manipulate the crisis for political advantage. Tech companies have mounted an aggressive response. In one eye-opening action, Facebook, Twitter, and YouTube simultaneously removed posts published by Bolsonaro for including coronavirus-related misinformation in violation of platform rules.[52]

Trolling and harassment involve deliberately posting offensive content online in order to provoke or disrupt conversations.[53] Chinese authorities have relied heavily on trolling techniques to counter protests in Hong Kong. The Facebook pages of two Hong Kong organizations identified with the 2019 demonstrations—Civil Human Rights Front and the Hong Kong National Front—were repeatedly hit with images showing violent protestors and insinuating foreign influence. Thousands of comments were posted linking the CIA to the protest movement and falsely accusing individuals of committing brutal acts.[54] In Cambodia, the *New York Times* reported, authorities posted fake videos on Facebook smearing a prominent government critic, the monk Luon Sovath, for having sexual relations with three sisters and their mother. A state-controlled religious council "defrocked the monk" for violating his vows of celibacy. Fearing arrest, Luon Sovath fled the country, resigning himself to a life in exile.[55]

Doxing is a subcomponent of trolling that involves the public release of personal information in order to compromise individual safety and intimidate people to prevent them from engaging in certain actions. Doxing is a technique used by both protestors and state agents. In Hong Kong, protestors routinely doxed unbadged police officers and posted their personal information online. In one notorious instance, demonstrators tried to derail a police officer's upcoming wedding by disclosing detailed information about the event.[56] Likewise, state authorities also set up an anonymous website, HK Leaks, that targeted approximately two hundred Hong Kong pro-democracy figures, including activists, journalists, and even lawmakers. The site listed their personal details—email addresses, phone numbers—resulting in a deluge of hostile phone calls.[57]

Flooding in the social manipulation context is similar to flooding strategies employed for censorship purposes. This strategy involves promoting competing or distracting information that overwhelms legitimate information sources. Regimes in countries that have advanced disinformation capabilities—like Russia, the Philippines, and Turkey—are adept at flooding strategies. As monitors become aware of critical news stories related to the government, operatives will begin peddling prepackaged counternarratives to state news outlets and social media channels to sew confusion and disarm government critiques. Frequently, this method of manipulation entails co-opting trending hashtags. During the 2011 Syria uprising, state operators tried to flood the hashtags #Syria, #Daraa, and #Mar15—which protesters were using to document the regime's crackdown—with misleading links to scenic photos and sports statistics.[58] More recently, "electronic flies" have become a routine hazard for pro-democracy organizers in Algeria. These "flies" are pro-regime individuals who amplify propaganda, spread false information, or send multiple false reports to social media platforms to deactivate legitimate accounts that belong to opposition activists.[59]

Automated repressive methods that incorporate bots and algorithms are made up of social media accounts that are "operated entirely by computer programs." Such bots are designed to create spikes in engagement for specific messages— whether to promote pro-regime narratives or to spread toxic falsehoods about particular opposition figures.[60] In addition to amplification, bots are also designed to create the impression that a campaign is more "organic" or widespread than it actually is. These bots are now widely used in both democracies and autocracies (in Mexico, for instance, political bots deployed by former president Peña Nieto became so ubiquitous that people began to refer to them as "Peñabots").[61]

Vandalism or defacement involves unauthorized acts such as modifying a website or social media account. State agents carry out this activity to obscure legitimate information on a targeted website or account, as well as for the purpose of harassment or intimidation.

Internet Shutdowns

There is some murkiness when it comes to delineating what exactly constitutes an Internet shutdown versus an associated network restriction like censorship filtering. I use the following definition for Internet shutdowns: activities undertaken by states to intentionally restrict, constrain, or disrupt Internet or electronic communications within a given geographic area or affecting a specific population in order to exert control over the spread of information.[62] A critical component of shutdowns is their time-bound nature. Unlike ongoing filtering activities, shutdowns include fixed beginning and endpoints. Shutdowns are therefore characterized by their alteration of an existing operating state of the Internet. Experts identify six categories of Internet disruption related to scope: national Internet shutdowns, subnational Internet shutdowns, national mobile shutdowns, subnational mobile shutdowns, national shutdowns of apps/service, and subnational shutdowns of app/service (including VoIP like Skype).[63] National shutdowns occur most frequently, followed by subnational mobile disruptions and national app/service disruptions. However, there are prominent examples that buck this trend. India, for instance, leads the world in Internet shutdowns, but the majority of its disruptions are confined to a single city or state (in 2018, India had only one shutdown incident that encompassed more than one state).

Shutdowns also vary by type. Certain shutdowns do not completely block Internet access, but instead employ *bandwidth throttling*—the intentional slowing of Internet service or Internet traffic by an Internet service provider in order to disrupt communications and regular online access. During bandwidth throttling, mobile Internet connections, for example, may be downgraded to 2G, effectively making it "almost impossible to upload pictures, stream live, and share information quickly."[64] Access Now reports at least fourteen cases of throttling in 2019, including in Jordan, Ecuador, Zimbabwe, India, Benin, China, Tajikistan, Kazakhstan, and Bangladesh.[65] Other shutdowns incorporate *Internet blackouts*, which are extreme measures that cut off access to the Internet entirely (national or subnationally), meaning all broadband and mobile Internet connections are severed. In such situations, mobile phone and texting connections are frequently disrupted as well. Finally, shutdown strategies may focus on *blocking specific apps and services*, such as social media platforms or messaging services. In 2019, this practice proliferated with governments blocking Facebook (thirty-eight global incidents), Twitter (thirty-three global incidents), WhatsApp (twenty-three global incidents), Instagram (twenty-nine global incidents), and Telegram (seven global incidents).[66]

The impact of shutdowns varies. Connectivity disruptions sometimes lead to perverse effects, revealing an embattled regime's fragility and precipitating its downfall. As mass protests swept through the Middle East in 2011, for example, President Hosni Mubarak ordered telecom companies to cut off Internet access in Egypt in order to thwart escalating protests. The cutoff, however, served to inflame public sentiment and paradoxically "pushed more people on to the streets" to find out what was transpiring.[67] The shutdown also blinded the regime to the protesters' developing plans and intended gatherings. Thus, the shutdown not only failed to contain protestor momentum, but likely accelerated Mubarak's demise.

Despite growing research about the limitations of Internet shutdowns as a tool of repression, leaders regularly deploy this tactic during crises. In 2019, at least 213 shutdowns occurred in more than thirty-three countries, leading to a cumulative economic cost of approximately $8 billion.[68]

Targeted Persecution against Online Users

The final category of digital repression encompasses targeted arrests, physical attacks, legal charges, prolonged detention, and violence directed against online users—actions described by Freedom House that are intended as a "reprisal for digital expression."[69] Journalists and human rights activists are particularly common government targets.

In 2016, I traveled to the Democratic Republic of the Congo on a diplomatic mission for the US State Department. Under President Joseph Kabila, who had ruled the Congo since 2001, the country was fast lurching toward a constitutional crisis. The facts of the matter were simple: Kabila was constitutionally barred from seeking another term in office. This didn't sit well with him, and he was trying every means at his disposal to remain in power. Kabila had settled on a strategy commonly referred to as *glissement*, or "sliding." Congo's constitutional court had ruled that if an election could not take place on time, then the incumbent would remain in office for an indefinite period. Kabila and his allies were frantically using the levers of bureaucracy to delay the election. Civil society activists grew increasingly frustrated and were planning a mass action they deemed *ville morte*, or "dead city." The idea was to close down the Congo's urban centers—for workers to call in sick, for markets and shops to shut down, and for people to stay at home—in order to show their frustration with Kabila's maneuverings.

The night before *ville morte*, I had dinner with two activists, Bienvenu Matumo and Marc Héritier Kapitene, who were members of an online civic group named Lutte Pour Le Changement (LUCHA). The group was mostly student advocates, and it didn't have a large membership. Yet its activities struck a nerve with government authorities. LUCHA advocated over social media for Kabila to stop flouting electoral laws and to respect presidential term limits. Its members frequently called out government officials for corruption or human rights abuses. Along with other civil society organizations and opposition parties, LUCHA strongly backed *ville morte*. Some hours later, after our dinner had broken up, Congolese police arrested Matumo and Kapitene and whisked them to an undisclosed location. The only clue to their whereabouts was a text message one of the activists sent to a friend at 5:40 a.m. saying "arrested."[70] I learned about their detentions later that morning. It became apparent that security forces had made the arrests in order to send a threatening signal to online activists, as well as to undercut *ville morte*. It would take months of behind-the-scenes diplomatic pressure coupled with public criticism before the Congolese government finally freed Matumo and Kapitene in August 2016.[71]

After watching Arab Spring protests topple one government after another in 2011, autocratic leaders vowed they would not fall for the same tactics. Consequently, by 2016, security forces had retooled their strategies. One of their favored techniques—particularly for governments that lacked more sophisticated capabilities—was to persecute individuals who advocated online for political change. While LUCHA didn't necessarily represent a political threat to Kabila in a traditional sense—it was not running parliamentary candidates or supporting electoral challengers against him—its youthful composition and ability to mobilize scores of student protestors through social media made it a major state target.

Government arrests and detentions are not limited to online journalists or well-known political bloggers. Ordinary citizens are routinely ensnared by state authorities as well, often as a warning to other citizens. In Thailand, for example, the courts sentenced a tour operator and a twenty-nine-year old hotel worker to multiyear prison terms for ill-advised social media postings that violated lèse-majesté provisions.[72]

The Dictator's Digital Dilemma

Digital technology has exacerbated the dictator's dilemma: how can those in power benefit from the economic gains and political advantages (e.g., increased information about public sentiment) that come from a digital society without sacrificing political control?[73] Censorship, for example, allows leaders to regulate information flows and blunt the effect of political opponents, but it can also lead to negative spillover effects. Censorship may signal to citizens that the government has something to hide, thereby reducing its legitimacy. Yet censorship can also motivate citizens to specifically seek out information that has been banned by the regime. Further, censorship may also limit the state's ability to collect "precious information" about citizen preferences—a vital means for states to keep tabs on their citizens. Because governments possess limited means to know how citizens feel about their performance, reducing information could obscure "fixable political problems" and prevent governments from solving them "before they become too significant to overcome."[74] Such potential costs also extend to economic considerations. Governments that constrain digital communications and thereby hamper technological innovation may suffer economic harm as a result, prompting investors to flee to alternative markets.

Governments have devised creative ways to solve this dilemma. No other country has had more success, at present, in confronting this problem than China. Its underlying bargain entails sacrificing personal liberties in exchange for steady economic growth. As long as the economy stays strong, citizens will tolerate diminished political freedoms. Thus, alongside China's economic boom—which has enlarged its middle class by millions of people—the Chinese Communist Party (CCP) has instituted a digital repression agenda incorporating mass web filtering, an expansive surveillance network anchored by facial recognition technology, mass Internet and social media monitoring, and even a mammoth DNA collection program. But China's repression strategy also retains flexibility; it is much more than a monolithic regime of control. Instead, it has pursued what Rebecca MacKinnon terms "networked authoritarianism," where the CCP maintains top-level control but also permits a "wide range of conversations about the country's problems" on social media and websites.[75] This accomplishes three objectives: citizens have an outlet to express grievances (providing a greater sense of freedom), the government can periodically respond to highlighted concerns (demonstrating its responsiveness to public concerns and making citizens feel that their voices are heard), and its authorities gain an effective means to monitor emerging problems and track dissent.

China is an outlier. It can get away with actions that other countries cannot. For example, when the CCP faced resistance from companies like Google, which were reluctant to institute mass censorship controls, it nurtured national alternatives—Baidu, Weibo, WeChat, Alibaba—that would abide by its rules. This led to the creation of a parallel Chinese Internet that not only has flourished in the intervening years, but whose model now poses a direct threat to the original concept. China's market size and sophisticated tech sector have given it the means to solve its digital dilemma. Most other countries lack these options. Instead, they have been forced to pursue alternative strategies to address their digital dilemmas.

One strategy is to rely on carefully calibrated methods of digital control. This could entail retaining state ownership over telecom companies responsible for providing Internet access—as in Ethiopia—and throttling or limiting access when politically necessary. Another tactic is to vary digital investments or shutdowns by region based on political loyalty. In Cameroon, for example, longtime dictator Paul Biya has enacted full-scale shutdowns in the country's restive anglophone region, while maintaining Internet access in the rest of the country, ensuring he retains his base of support.[76] In Thailand, the government pursues an array of Internet controls but is keenly aware of what measures the public will tolerate (and what may go too far). As I discuss in Chapter 4, the Thai state readily blocks websites and uses lèse-majesté or cyber libel laws to suppress dissent, but it stops short of shutting down the Internet; the threat to its digitally reliant economy would be too great and would risk alienating its middle-class base.

A second strategy, one that I will explore in detail in Chapter 5 (Philippines case study), is to forgo information control for social manipulation and disinformation tactics. In other words, keep the information environment fairly open in order not to scare off investment, but use social media channels to relentlessly troll the opposition and flood out criticism of the government. As scholars Nils Weidmann and Espen Rød observe, these approaches operate from a common premise: government control over the Internet is "highly asymmetrical" in relation to opposition activists, providing state authorities with crucial advantages when carrying out their strategies.[77] These examples illustrate how much governments have adapted their digital strategies in the intervening years since the Color Revolutions and Arab Spring protests.

Nonetheless, states do not always succeed in accomplishing their digital repression objectives. While their strategies reduce the odds for successful regime challenges, online protest movements sometimes prevail, as recent cases in Armenia, Sudan, and Gambia attest. How have these movements managed to withstand a generally dismal environment for digital activism? In part, their survival may be due to the discrepancy between short and long-term strategies of digital control. The bulk of the tactics described in this book—except for Internet shutdowns—represent longer-term approaches. Such strategies are designed to establish, over time, systematic state control over key information pathways and communications networks in order to suppress dissent. But this approach does not mean that regimes won't make miscalculations along the way that provide unexpected openings for their opponents. And once protests begin, they are difficult to contain: "Much research points to the importance of the speed with which digital communication travels during ongoing protests."[78] As a result, the best long-term digital strategies can fall by the wayside when luck, opportunity, and momentum come together for protesters.

Even if demonstrators are able to exploit short-term vulnerabilities to accelerate actions against incumbent regimes, overall trends still favor governments. This trajectory represents a considerable shift from earlier pronouncements that liberation technology would be an inexorable force for change. Less than ten years ago, Larry Diamond made the convincing argument that ICT would enable profound democratic connections between citizens and their governments, and would "expand the horizons of freedom."[79] By 2019, Diamond had significantly changed his tune: "Once hailed as a great force for human empowerment and liberation, social media—and the various related digital tools that enable people to search for, access, accumulate, and process information—have rapidly come to be regarded as a major threat to democratic stability and human freedom." He further warned that digital threats today have become much more menacing and powerful: "Democrats worldwide are in a race against time to prevent cyberspace from becoming an arena of surveillance, control, and manipulation so all-encompassing that only a modern-day fusion of George Orwell's *Nineteen Eighty-Four* and Aldous Huxley's *Brave New World* could adequately capture it."[80] With that warning in mind, this brings us to a core question: does digital technology provide decisive advantages to states carrying out repression?

Is Digital Technology Changing the Balance between Governments and Civil Society?

The questions at the heart of this book are these: How much does digital repression matter? Are digital technologies fundamentally tilting the playing field in favor of authoritarian power holders against their civic and political opponents?

I find that the answers vary. In states that feature extensive repression supported by high-capacity institutions (and where civil society and government oversight are comparatively weak), digital technology can have a transformative effect on a state's ability to carry out political repression. In other cases, where governments either have insufficient capacity to take advantage of digital tools, or in democracies which have built-in safeguards that blunt the impact of digital strategies, the effect of digital repression is much more limited.

Digital repression has the greatest impact in countries that feature a significant level of repression, possess high internal coercive capacity, and have civil society institutions and government oversight mechanisms that are relatively weak. Digital tools not only augment existing repression, but can transform the state's ability to track political opponents, monitor dissent, quash protest movements, and consolidate political control. When implemented correctly, they can upgrade surveillance efforts (particularly enhancing online monitoring—where most protest movement activity occurs), allow for targeted, ongoing tracking of political challengers, filter specific content or censor mass amounts of information, and also provide states with an unparalleled ability to manipulate information and to push pro-government narratives.

But in lower-capacity countries, acquiring digital tools does not bring the same transformative repression effect. These tools require certain elements: disciplined security forces that coordinate and communicate across units, a coherent command-and-control structure that enforces adherence to organizational objectives, and highly trained personnel able to analyze, interpret, and act on relevant information. When states lack these ingredients, the impact of digital tools noticeably diminishes.

Some argue that a crucial advantage of digital tools is that they allow governments to rapidly acquire advanced capabilities at an affordable cost—as a substitute for building up extensive cadres of agents to carry out repression. Andrea Kendall-Taylor, Erica Frantz, and Joseph Wright contend that "aspiring dictatorships can purchase new technologies, train a small group of officials in how to use them—often with the support of external actors, such as China— and they are ready to go."[81] This only holds true to a limited extent. In countries like Saudi Arabia or Egypt, which have high preexisting repression capacities and comparatively weakened civil society actors, digital tools substantially enhance repression outcomes. But in low-capacity countries, their effect is modest.

A country like the Democratic Republic of the Congo (DRC) is a good case in point. According to my data, the DRC ranked thirty-first in the world in 2019 for prevalence of digital repression with a GDP per capita ranked 178th globally. In other words, it exhibits a tremendous mismatch between levels of digital repression investment and its poverty rate. But the DRC's digital capabilities are deceiving. The main tools at its disposal are Internet shutdowns and persecutions of online users.[82] The former is a blunt tactic relied upon by weak regimes that lack the capacity to undertake more sophisticated operations. The latter is an adjunct of traditional repression and doesn't require specific technical expertise.

For actions that necessitate higher capacity—carrying out a targeted surveillance or filtering online content—the DRC's capabilities are sorely lacking. Even if the government were to acquire a suite of advanced tools from China, its inadequate infrastructure, disorganized security and intelligence bureaucracy, and lack of trained personnel make it highly unlikely that it could enact a competent digital repression program. Thus, a major factor determining whether digital tools will make a difference is whether a state possesses the requisite capacity to fully use them.

A second factor relevant to digital repression is regime type—whether a country is authoritarian or democratic. Digital tools provide considerable benefits to authoritarian regimes. Such governments have less constraints when it comes to determining which tactics they will use and how they will use them. In contrast, democracies face higher hurdles to adopting digital techniques (digital repression use is rare in liberal democracies, but more prevalent in illiberal democracies). Even in flawed democracies, digital repression brings downside risks and the potential for public backlash, constraining governments' abilities to deploy them. Public sensitivity naturally limits how far democratic governments can go to implement mass surveillance programs or enact information controls. While many illiberal democracies have taken serious steps to constrain civil society—including Hungary and India—their voices still have much more resonance than counterparts residing in authoritarian states. This means that digital repression matters far less—and provides reduced benefits—in democracies. The exception is social manipulation and disinformation. Those techniques help solve the dictator's digital dilemma in that they bring significant repressive impact without sacrificing economic innovation or being perceived to violate political freedoms. The Philippines illustrates how a well-organized state-sponsored disinformation campaign can lead to a sizable—if not transformative—political payoff in a democratic system.

The emergence of AI technology as a digital repression tool raises new questions. As Chapter 7 lays out, AI and big-data technology will further transform models of repression, not only by providing governments with unprecedented capabilities to monitor their citizens and shape their choices, but also by giving states heightened capacity to disrupt elections, elevate false information, and delegitimize democratic discourse across borders. China is showing the world just what these tools are capable of accomplishing. As their unit cost decreases and more countries build capacity to use them, AI-powered tools may prove to be decisive when it comes to enhancing state repression. Because few countries have developed the capacity to implement them at scale, for now we are left to speculate whether AI technology will revolutionize global repression.

Despite the advantages offered by digital technology, we shouldn't underestimate the ability of civil society and political opposition groups to counteract coercive digital strategies. Once political mobilization occurs and protests start in earnest, they are difficult for regimes to contain. As much as digital technology provides repression benefits to governments, it also provides crucial network advantages for escalating protests. This is why notwithstanding considerable digital investments by regimes in Sudan and Algeria, their governments were unable to withstand mass demonstrations in 2019.

Under the right conditions, digital technology can provide decisive, even transformative, repression advantages for governments. But these advantages are not absolute; they can be overridden by a number of factors—state capacity, regime type, and political leadership.

Assessing Costs and Benefits of Digital Repression Tools

Each of the five repressive digital tactics offers a mixture of costs and benefits. Intrusive tactics with increased levels of effectiveness may also generate greater public backlash. Conversely, lower impact techniques may bring limited political advantages. When leaders calculate the relative costs and benefits of pursuing a particular tactic, a country's political system or regime type often plays an important role. Table 2.2 breaks down the associated costs and benefits for three digital techniques commonly deployed by autocracies: surveillance, censorship, and targeted persecution of online users.

Each of these techniques provides tangible benefits for political leaders. These techniques can enable substantial information collection and tracking (surveillance), suppress communication by opponents (censorship), and sideline specific individuals who challenge the government. While effective, these tools also bring complications and potential costs.

Extensive state reliance on *surveillance* is generally frowned upon in democracies unless justified through limited public order and national security exemptions. The potential for public backlash is generally high, but there are exceptions. In particular, when it comes to AI and big-data surveillance, both autocracies and democracies are actively expanding their reliance on those capabilities. As publics become more aware of facial recognition technology, predictive policing algorithms, and safe city networks, this understanding may affect AI's future relevance in democracies. In September 2020, for instance, Portland became the first US city to ban facial recognition technology for all local government agencies as well as for private businesses.[83] The EU is also considering stringent new rules to limit AI's reach and safeguard fundamental rights.

For targeted surveillance, particularly use of commercial spyware, my data shows that autocracies are much more likely to rely on these methods. According

Table 2.2 **Costs and Benefits of Surveillance, Censorship, and Targeted Online Persecution**

	Surveillance	*Censorship*	*Targeted persecution of online users*
Tools	AI and big-data surveillance, passive and targeted surveillance, surveillance laws/regulations	block/filter, content removal, censorship laws, financial targeting	arrests, detention, charges, violence, physical attacks
Purpose	extract information, track opposition movements, monitor dissent, intimidation	suppress dissent and impede opposition communication; intimidation	intimidation, suppress dissent; eliminate opposition activists
Benefits	high impact; advanced digital tools can be cost-effective substitutes for human agents; can be implemented discreetly	high impact—enables state control of the information space; offers a variety of tactics states can deploy	highly effective against targets; chilling effect against opponents
Costs	public backlash; advanced systems require high state capacity and funding outlays; possible reputational damage	public backlash; reputational damage; spillover economic effects; less feasible for democracies	public backlash; reputational damage; spillover economic effects; less feasible for democracies
Which regimes?	Autocracies and hybrid regimes; AI and big data surveillance used by all regime types	Mostly autocratic	Mostly autocratic, some hybrid regimes

to my research (presented in Chapter 3), at least sixty-one governments are using commercial spyware to target political activists, civil society groups, journalists, and other challengers.[84] In 2015, for example, a data breach targeting the Italian private surveillance company Hacking Team revealed that it had sold intrusive spyware to government agencies in Ethiopia, Bahrain, Egypt, Kazakhstan, Morocco, Russia, Saudi Arabia, Sudan, Azerbaijan, and Turkey.[85] The leak verified technical research published by the Citizen Lab showing suspected government clients in these countries.[86] Researchers have uncovered abuses in some democracies as well, such as the 2017 revelation that Mexico's government was using spyware against media figures, public health officials, politicians, and anti-corruption advocates.[87] The benefits of these tools are that they are comparatively discreet and narrowly tailored to impact specific individuals or organizations—heightening their effectiveness. But there can be high costs as well, including public outrage when government use is disclosed. In many democracies, state-sponsored intrusion attacks against political opponents is unlawful (or at least skirt the line of illegality), making them especially risky choices.

To be maximally effective, surveillance generally requires high state capacity along with a substantial resource commitment. These requirements make surveillance most relevant for wealthy autocratic regimes that are less concerned about public backlash and have sufficient capacity to operate advanced systems. Countries such as China, Russia, the Gulf States, Turkey, and Iran are major adopters.

When it comes to *online censorship*, publics in democracies have minimal tolerance. Unlike surveillance, which states can undertake discreetly, censorship tactics are blunter: when information is restricted and certain websites or apps are blocked, users feel the impact right away. Moreover, while there are legal carveouts for surveillance under necessary and proportionality standards, legal exceptions for censorship are much narrower. In most democracies, government censorship is permissible only in situations of imminent harm. As a result, censorship strategies can instigate serious public backlash, and can lead to spillover economic effects—scaring away foreign investment and creating reputational damage. Countries most prone to adopting online censorship strategies tend to be highly autocratic with less concern for reputational damage or public criticism (key examples include China, Turkey, Iran, Russia, and Saudi Arabia).

Targeted persecution of online users, similar to censorship, can be highly effective, but it also brings significant associated costs. This technique is closely linked to traditional repression; it uses imprisonment, prolonged detention, and legal harassment as key means to suppress dissent. While such persecutions occur less often in flawed democracies, they still persist. For example, in the Philippines, a flawed democracy with a tradition of political liberties, the state has intensified its persecution of online critics, including prolonged legal harassment of Maria Ressa, cofounder of the online news site *Rappler*. This technique can lead to extensive reputational damage and high economic costs. Saudi Arabia's online harassment and assassination of journalist Jamal Khashoggi, for instance, brought global outrage and negative economic fallout. Consequently, countries that consistently employ this technique—such as North Korea, Bahrain, South Sudan, Eritrea, Syria, and Turkmenistan—tend to have poor human rights records and high levels of authoritarian control. In contrast with the first set of techniques, the second set of tools (social manipulation and disinformation, and Internet shutdowns) are less contingent on regime type. Table 2.3 provides a side-by-side comparison.

Social manipulation and disinformation represent a unique set of tactics. They have only emerged at scale in the last few years, and their impact is widely felt across regime types. They offer many of the benefits of censorship (such as inhibiting the free flow of information, suppressing dissenting viewpoints) without equivalent reputational or economic costs. Many illiberal democracies, such as Brazil, Nigeria, Kenya, and the Philippines, have deployed

Table 2.3 **Costs/Benefits of Social Manipulation and Internet Shutdowns**

	Social manipulation and disinformation	*Internet shutdowns*
Tools	disinformation, trolling, flooding, false reporting, automated methods	total and partial Internet shutdowns, infrastructure restrictions, app/service shutdowns
Purpose	manipulate information to benefit regime; intimidation; suppress dissent	suppress dissent; quell opposition communication and activity
Benefits	more nuanced way to manipulate information without resorting to censorship; diminished public backlash	high impact when deployed; useful for time-bound crises
Costs	delegitimizes political system; growing public backlash; unknown future costs	blunt tool—high negative externalities; public backlash; reputational damage; spillover economic effects
Which regimes?	All types	Autocracies and some democracies

social manipulation tools to great effect—from spreading misinformation over WhatsApp in Brazil and Nigeria to state-sponsored cyber trolling on Facebook in the Philippines and Kenya.

As the public grows increasingly aware of the negative societal costs linked to disinformation and online manipulation, this technique could potentially foster a backlash. Autocracies rely upon this technique to a greater extent than democracies, but democratic governments are also crucial players in this space. As researchers Samantha Bradshaw and Philip Howard note, "The earliest reports of government involvement in nudging public opinion involve democracies, and new innovations in political communication technologies often come from po-litical parties and arise during high-profile elections."[88]

Internet shutdowns are used by a heterogeneous mix of regimes, although there is a heavy autocratic lean. They are easy to enact, but as instruments of repression, they bring two significant disadvantages. First, they lead to outsized economic impacts: "Because shutdowns impact every citizen in the country, they effec-tively bring commerce to a halt, particularly in high-technology economies."[89] Studies show that shutdowns dampen ongoing economic activity and also gen-erate negative effects that can last for years.[90] Second, Internet shutdowns have the perverse effect of not only disrupting protester communications, but also making it extraordinarily difficult for the government to track what is occurring in the country—such as which groups are mobilizing, how much support they are eliciting, or where they are planning demonstrations. Over an extended period, such shutdowns can lead to significant blind spots for the government and precipitate regime turnover. Newer research also indicates that Internet shutdowns may lead to increased rates of violent mobilization among protesters during blackouts.[91]

My data shows that in 2019, eighteen of twenty-four countries experiencing Internet shutdowns were categorized as closed or competitive autocracies; only six were classified as democracies. While the number of autocracies implementing shutdowns is triple the rate of democracies, it also shows that cer-tain democracies are open to using this tactic.

Why Do Certain States Employ Digital Repression but Not Others?

Digital technology provides new capacities that enhance how states carry out repression. It reinforces existing repression and can also substitute for tradi-tional forms of repression. In closed autocracies that severely limit political freedoms—like China—digital tools enhance the coercive power of the state and reinforce existing repressive patterns. In competitive autocracies with partial liberalization (e.g., Thailand, Uganda, Turkey), digital tools can "fill the gap left by the lack of control over political competition."[92]

Of particular interest is determining why some states choose to adopt certain digital tactics and not others. Does regime type matter? Are autocratic leaders more likely to use certain digital repression techniques than democratically elected ones? I make the following arguments regarding new tools, techniques, and dimensions that digital tools bring to political repression.

First, governments that rely on repression as a core governing tool are more likely to employ digital repression techniques, but this reliance does not translate into straightforward adoption. Autocracies are not homogeneous. They come in a variety of forms, each of which brings significant variations regarding preferred digital repression techniques. As Barbara Geddes has observed, "Different kinds of authoritarianism differ from each other as much as they differ from democracy."[93] Autocratic regimes range from single-party states and military dictatorships to personalist regimes and monarchies. Government deployment of digital tools is therefore contingent on a number of factors: prior levels of repression, administrative capacity, political norms, the nature of regime challenges, and existing digital capabilities.

This heterogeneity suggests that digital repression methods deployed by closed autocracies, such as Turkmenistan (which seek to fully restrict political freedoms and the ability of nonstate actors to organize in any meaningful way), can contrast sharply with tactics used by competitive autocracies, such as Thailand or Zimbabwe (which allow limited political expression while foreclosing genuine political competition).

Second, both autocracies and flawed democracies deploy digital repression, but they pursue distinctive combinations of techniques. While autocracies carry out digital repression programs with greater frequency and robustness than their democratic counterparts, illiberal democracies also undertake distinctive digital strategies in pursuit of their political objectives. Autocrats tend to embrace more coercive measures, such as intrusive surveillance, censorship, and arrests and detentions of online users. In turn, democracies favor subtler methods: manipulating public opinion, trolling opposition members, and distorting factual narratives.

One explanation for this division is that the first set of tactics is closely linked to traditional repressive practices, making them more likely to be adopted by autocracies. Surveillance, for example, has a long pattern of use. Scores of governments have built complex informant networks and sophisticated intelligence apparatuses to keep tabs on citizens. While digital technology provides unparalleled new ways for state authorities to monitor individuals, this is less a paradigm shift than a process innovation. Censorship is also a timeworn tactic; almost as soon as Johannes Gutenberg invented the printing press in the fifteenth century, governments started devising methods of censorship.[94] Likewise, persecuting online users is not, strictly speaking, a digital strategy. Instead, it represents a traditional bureaucratic-legal approach to crushing online dissent by deliberately targeting opponents through detention and imprisonment.

In contrast, the second set of tools lacks the same historical connection to repression. While some might argue that social manipulation and disinformation are just digital variants of propaganda, their scale and impact make them more complex. Social manipulation involves a complicated interplay of censorship (flooding voices critical of the state), surveillance (keeping tabs via social media surveillance about who is saying what against the regime), and the dissemination of false narratives.

Is China Responsible for Driving the Global Spread of Digital Repression?

A final question tackled in this book is how much Chinese technology is driving the global spread of digital repression worldwide.[95] *Many experts and policymakers overstate the impact of China as a global driver of digital repression. While China plays a sizable role in proliferating digital technologies used for repression, domestic factors are more significant explanations for these tactics.*

Chinese technology used for repressive purposes has proliferated worldwide. Major Chinese firms, such as Huawei, ZTE, Hikvision, Dahua, Meiya Pico, Sensetime, and others, are building safe city surveillance projects, peddling high-tech censorship tools, and supplying advanced social media monitoring capabilities to countries around the world. Many of the recipient governments possess troubling human rights records. Cloudwalk's mass surveillance facial recognition project in Zimbabwe and Huawei's string of safe city projects in Pakistan illustrate this trend. They raise concerning questions about the motives behind China's exports—in particular, is the dissemination of these technologies reinforcing, if not driving, the spread of digital repression?

Some policymakers and analysts claim that China is implementing a program of digital authoritarianism designed to establish an alternate model of governance and undercut democratic values worldwide. In May 2020, the White House released a strategy document accusing Chinese authorities of "exporting the tools of the CCP's techno-authoritarian model to countries around the world," thereby "enabling authoritarian states to exert control over their citizens and surveil opposition, training foreign partners in propaganda and censorship techniques, and using bulk data collection to shape public sentiment."[96] Researcher Samantha Hoffman observes that "the CCP's power-expansion effort does not stop at China's geographic borders," but that it "aims to re-shape global governance" and is using technology to attain its objectives.[97]

But a larger number of experts stake a middle ground and maintain that the CCP pursues multiple objectives in the export of its model. Elizabeth Economy, for example, identifies three priorities: convince a growing number of countries to share China's norms and values in order to "garner support for its policies on the global stage"; use the Belt and Road Initiative to reinforce China's development model and promote opportunities for Chinese companies involved in infrastructure or digital technologies; and leverage China's growing influence to "legitimize the Chinese Communist Party at home."[98]

Similarly, Christopher Walker, Shanthi Kalathil, and Jessica Ludwig criticize China's repressive objectives and its harnessing of digital technologies, but acknowledge that China's digital authoritarian efforts alone do not reshape political systems:

> China and other autocracies cannot simply will into existence overseas replicas of their surveillance states. How technologies get used around the world depends on the populations that interact with them, the democratic and rights-based safeguards put in place by individual societies, and the democracies' success at defining and defending their values within international institutions.[99]

Jessica Chen Weiss goes further in her arguments. She notes that while China is subsidizing and selling advanced surveillance packages and censorship technologies, "that is not the same as a dedicated effort to remake other countries in China's authoritarian image." She contends that "neither China nor Russia today is engaged in a messianic effort to topple foreign governments and replace them with ideologically similar regimes." Instead, Xi Jinping's interest is to "create space for autocracy to survive in a system dominated by liberal democracies—rather than forcibly exporting Chinese-style autocracy."[100]

The research I undertook for this book leads me to two conclusions. First, in none of the countries I visited did I encounter evidence of an overt Chinese push to establish an alternate governance model through the export of repressive technology. When I asked whether there was a perception that China was using digital tools as leverage to push for governance changes or for closer alignment with its foreign policy, I received little agreement. Rather, most concurred that the biggest selling point for Chinese technology was its low cost and accessibility—with few strings attached.

Second, I found scant evidence that China is serving as a lead driver of digital repression in particular countries. Instead, other factors appeared more relevant: the country's political environment, its intelligence and security capacity, and its level of social media penetration (and corresponding online dissent).[101] In other words, while Chinese exports of digital tools matter, domestic considerations matter more. In Thailand, for example, despite close ties and geographic proximity to China, the government has been careful not to fully embrace Chinese repressive technology, or to rush to establish mass surveillance systems that resemble China's AI-driven models. While digital repression techniques are a crucial means for the government to counter dissent, it is also cautious about adopting policies that run afoul of its political traditions.

However, just because China's proliferation of authoritarian technology is not directly driving the spread of digital repression in specific countries does not mean that the CCP isn't exploiting digital tools to project greater influence. In this regard, China is pursuing three approaches.

First, its diffusion of digital technology enhances its economic influence and strengthens its political ties to recipient governments. Starting in 2015, Chinese officials began to trumpet the "Digital Silk Road," an adjunct to the BRI focused on Internet connectivity, artificial intelligence, the digital economy, telecommunications, smart cities, and cloud computing.[102] The launch of the Digital Silk Road has been murky, and tangible figures are hard to come by. Nonetheless, reports indicate that China has signed cooperation agreements with at least twenty countries, leading to investments totaling $40 billion.[103] This likely undercounts the global scope of Chinese tech activities. In fact, according to researchers C. Raja Mohan and Chan Jia Hao of the National University of Singapore, Chinese officials claim that as a result of the BRI, over six thousand Chinese Internet companies and over ten thousand Chinese technology products have gone to overseas markets.[104]

Second, China seeks to shape international norms related to digital technology. Its delegations are undertaking an extensive push to promote a "cyber sovereignty" vision of Internet governance. As described by the U.S.-China Commission, this doctrine holds that data and networks "constitute sovereign territory within individual countries' jurisdictions, to be governed according to local laws," even if those regulations come into conflict with international law.[105] China also seeks to increase its influence in global standard-setting bodies, like the International Telecommunication Union (ITU), the International Standards Organization, the International Electrotechnical Commission, and the World Intellectual Property Organization (WIPO)—where it narrowly lost an election to have its own candidate lead the agency, a potential outcome one official described as putting "the fox in charge of the henhouse."[106] The competition over technologies that will define the 21st century matters greatly. There is some debate about whether China's bid to dominate standards bodies is a serious step or misreads how such institutions work. For example, the US-China Commission notes that "Dominance of technical standards underpinning information and communications technologies and other emerging fields is integral to Beijing's ambitions, both to secure global markets for Chinese firms and to shape the norms and values for how emerging technologies are deployed."[107] But other experts push back, arguing that this line of thinking indicates a fundamental misunderstanding about how standards work. Naomi Wilson writes for the Council on Foreign Relations that "International standards are not required rules, laws, or even norms. Companies choose the most appropriate standards for their products, which change with rapidly developing technology. The notion that the Chinese government is going to swindle the world's best engineers into adopting voluntary standards that will shape the technological landscape in China's favor, and continue to do so with every technological change, is a significant reach."[108] Even if China's push in standards bodies will have limited effect, it does show the seriousness in which the CCP is investing resources and capacity into enhancing its technological foundation.

China also shapes tech norms in subtler ways. Many products and platforms put out by Chinese companies, such as WeChat's social app or Alipay Health Code (which classifies users' health status and determines whether they are allowed to travel or enter certain public spaces), are designed to facilitate government surveillance and censorship and implicitly promote an intrusive model of digital governance.[109] Walker, Kalathil, and Ludwig write: "The CCP has been forging an increasingly seamless synthesis combining consumer convenience, surveillance, and censorship. This model is exemplified by such all-encompassing platforms as WeChat . . . which includes politically based content restrictions and lends itself to surveillance (for instance, through selectively required user 'faceprints')."[110]

Third, China uses emulation and modeling to demonstrate to other governments how digital repression techniques can serve their political needs. One primary means is through trainings and exchanges, where the CCP flies in scores of foreign officials to tour Huawei, Baidu, or Tencent headquarters and learn about their offerings. Trainings frequently focus on topics of high priority for the CCP. Freedom House describes a two-week training hosted by Chinese officials to inform BRI member governments how they can better manage their cyberspace security challenges. Visiting officials "toured the headquarters of a company involved in 'big data public-opinion management systems,' including tools for real-time monitoring of negative public opinion and a 'positive energy public-opinion guidance system'"[111]—or in less jargony terms, teaching governments how they can use Chinese technology to surveil their citizens, track dissent, and spread propaganda.

China is not the only country that exports digital repressive tools. Russia is also a major player and warrants discussion. One area of digital repression in which Russia is increasingly active is the provision of disinformation and electoral manipulation services. In Madagascar, for example, a *New York Times* investigation revealed that Russian operatives set up troll factories and created fake Facebook pages to support specific candidates running in national elections. They supplemented digital disinformation efforts with bribes, billboard ads, and television airtime.[112] Likewise, in the Central African Republic, a trusted confidant of Vladimir Putin, Yevgeny V. Prigozhin, has overseen a social media campaign to bolster preferred political leaders and create positive perceptions about Russian influence.[113] While these examples point to growing Russian digital influence, they are a far cry from China's more systematic efforts to provide advanced technology to bolster autocratic repression. Instead, not only do these operations seem to occur opportunistically, but the Russians rarely leave behind residual capacity that recipient governments can later use.

Russia also provides what Alina Polyakova describes as "post hoc" surveillance tools.[114] During the Cold War, the KGB established the "System of Operative Search Measures" (SORM), which Soviet agents mostly used to monitor phone calls. In the 1990s, Russia revived SORM so it could monitor email communication and Internet traffic. SORM essentially operates as a "backdoor" to the Internet, allowing authorities to monitor all data flowing through telecommunications networks and on the Internet.[115] Former Soviet states, such as Belarus, Kyrgyzstan, Kazakhstan, and Ukraine, are key clients of this system, although some governments in Latin America, Africa, and the Middle East also use this technology.

Paradoxically, as Russia upgrades its surveillance capabilities, including adopting more cutting-edge AI-powered tools, it is increasingly relying on Chinese technology. Researcher Valentin Weber notes that "facial recognition cameras in Russian cities use Russian software but run on Chinese hardware," and that Russia's buildout of its 5G infrastructure will potentially fall to Huawei and other Chinese firms.[116] Even in Central Asia, Russia's traditional backyard, Weber observes that "China is becoming the security equipment supplier of choice in the region," with governments "upgrading surveillance equipment and supplying governments with safe city technology to monitor citizens and govern the Internet."[117] This leads to the conclusion that China's influence in the technological domain is far more relevant than Russia's.[118]

Comparing drivers of digital repression for each of the book's country case studies clarifies why internal drivers are more significant determinants of digital repression than external factors. The case studies offered here represent complementary but distinct political contexts, including Thailand (closed autocracy/competitive autocracy), Philippines (flawed democracy), and Ethiopia (competitive autocracy). Chapters 4, 5, and 6 present full findings and analysis. In all three countries, China wields significant influence. But the nature of its involvement and the degree to which it is enabling digital repression varies. Table 2.4 outlines how each country compares.

In Thailand, China supplies abundant technology, an arrangement that has enhanced Thailand's relationship with China's current leadership. At times, Thai authorities have seemingly modeled their digital strategies on Chinese concepts. In 2015, the Thai government proposed creating a "single gateway" that would decrease the existing twelve Internet gateways to one gateway, overseen by state-owned CAT Telecom to enhance content monitoring and surveillance. After a public outcry, the state backed down from its plans. More recently, the Thai government has explored the widespread installation of facial recognition cameras tied to public surveillance systems. While these plans have yet to be implemented at scale, China's mass surveillance techniques have certainly made an impression on Thai authorities. That being said, Chinese-supplied tech remains peripheral to Thailand's core drivers of digital repression. Internal factors play a more significant role in advancing digital repression strategies. Long-standing military-bureaucratic repression, established censorship practices linked to lèse-majesté provisions, and political challenges due to heightened online communication and social media use are much more salient factors linked to digital repression in the country.

In the Philippines, Duterte has sought to align himself with China—representing a break with past precedent (the public at large remains wary of Chinese influence). China has aggressively courted Philippines officials and sponsored "study trips" for an array of senior government officials. The country has announced massive new investments, including a $400 million "Safe Philippines" program—implemented by China International Telecommunication and Construction Corporation (CITCC) and Huawei—that will install twelve thousand advanced surveillance cameras in metro Manila. Duterte even welcomed Xi Jinping to the country for an elaborate two-day state visit in 2018, which led to the signing of twenty-nine separate investment and cooperation agreements.[119] And yet, as in Thailand, the primary drivers of digital repression in the Philippines are internal. By far the most prevalent digital repression tactic in the Philippines is social manipulation and disinformation, something the Chinese have little involvement in (although rumors abound about Chinese slush money being used to lubricate Duterte's disinformation network).

In Ethiopia, its leaders have fostered a close relationship with China, resulting in billions of dollars of investment in modern railways, upgraded highways, hydroelectric dams, stadiums, and modern skyscrapers. This cooperation has naturally extended to technology. Ethiopia's national telecom network was predominantly built by the Chinese company ZTE. As Zhang Yanmeng, ZTE's chief executive officer, crisply put it, "This is the world's only project in which

Table 2.4 Comparative Country-Level Drivers of Digital Repression

	Thailand	The Philippines	Ethiopia
2019 digital repression ranking	51st most repressive globally	50th most repressive globally	33rd most repressive globally
2019 V-Dem Electoral Democracy Score	163rd globally	98th globally	128th globally
Major tools	censorship; surveillance; targeted persecution of online users; limited social manipulation/disinformation	social manipulation/disinformation; targeted persecution of online users; limited surveillance	Internet shutdowns; growing social manipulation/disinformation; decreasing surveillance, censorship
Key drivers	long-standing military-bureaucratic repression; established censorship practices; political challenges from rising online communication	hyperconnectivity and social media use; democratic weakness; illiberal leadership of Duterte	political shocks from 2005 elections and Arab Spring; political reordering under Abiy
Role of China?	Significant actor but not a primary driver of digital repression	Growing presence but peripheral influence on digital repression	Has provided key ICT capabilities, but other countries also supply advanced tech to the Ethiopian state for digital repression

a national telecom network is built by a sole equipment supplier."[120] China's vital role in building out Ethiopia's ICT infrastructure has afforded it influence in shaping the Ethiopian government's key choices, including providing digital capabilities that enable surveillance and censorship. But as with Thailand and the Philippines, it would be inaccurate to attribute the bulk of responsibility for Ethiopia's digital repression to China. Rather, other factors better explain the progression of digital repression in the country: Ethiopia's long-standing politics of control used by its rulers to maintain dominance over the population; fallout from disputed 2005 elections and regime anxiety from Arab Spring protests; and "tectonic shifts" to Ethiopian politics ushered in by the new prime minister, Abiy Ahmed.[121]

The next chapter presents global data on digital repression patterns and sheds light on key questions raised in the book: which countries are deploying digital repression techniques, and how prevalent is their use? What is the relationship between regime type and digital repression? What about the relationship between specific types of repression (violating political liberties, physical violence committed by the state, curtailing private civil liberties) and digital repression? How does the deployment of individual components of digital repression differ in democracies versus autocracies?

Notes

1. See Akshaya Kumar, "Shutting Down the Internet to Silence Critics," Human Rights Watch, 2020, https://www.hrw.org/world-report/2020/shutting-down-the-internet-to-silence-critics.
2. "Severe Internet Outage across Sudan amid Reports of Darfur Paramilitary Attacks," Netblocks, June 10, 2019, https://netblocks.org/reports/severe-internet-outage-across-sudan-amid-reports-of-darfur-paramilitary-attacks-aAwq0oyM. Samuel Woodhams and Simon Migliano, "The Global Cost of Internet Shutdowns in 2019," Top10VPN, January 7, 2020, https://www.top10vpn.com/cost-of-internet-shutdowns/.
3. Samy Magdy, "Sudanese Protests Demand Answers over June Crackdown Deaths," *Associated Press*, November 3, 2019, https://apnews.com/cb039b6869544b8bb5c9655f301c02e8.
4. Ishaan Tharoor, "Iran's Bloody Crackdown Could Mark a Historic Turning Point," *Washington Post*, December 3, 2019, https://www.washingtonpost.com/world/2019/12/04/irans-bloody-crackdown-could-mark-historic-turning-point/?utm_campaign=todays_worldview&utm_medium=Email&utm_source=Newsletter&wpisrc=nl_todayworld&wpmm=1.
5. Farnaz Fassihi and Rick Gladstone, "With Brutal Crackdown, Iran Is Convulsed by Worst Unrest in 40 Years," *New York Times*, December 1, 2019, https://www.nytimes.com/2019/12/01/world/middleeast/iran-protests-deaths.html.
6. "Sudan's Livestream Massacre," *BBC News*, July 12, 2019, https://www.bbc.com/news/av/world-africa-48956133/sudan-s-livestream-massacre.
7. "Iran: Death Toll from Bloody Crackdown on Protests Rises to 208," Amnesty International, December 2, 2019, https://www.amnesty.org/en/latest/news/2019/12/iran-death-toll-from-bloody-crackdown-on-protests-rises-to-208/?utm_campaign=todays_worldview&utm_medium=Email&utm_source=Newsletter&wpisrc=nl_todayworld&wpmm=1.
8. Steven Feldstein, "Can a U.N. Report Help Rein in Expansive and Abusive Digital Surveillance?," *World Politics Review*, July 9, 2019, https://www.worldpoliticsreview.com/

articles/28016/can-a-u-n-report-help-rein-in-expansive-and-abusive-digital-surveillance; Christopher Bing and Joel Schectman, "Inside the UAE's Secret Hacking Team of American Mercenaries," *Reuters*, January 30, 2019, https://www.reuters.com/investigates/special-report/usa-spying-raven/.

9. See also Bill Marczak and John Scott-Railton, "Keep Calm and (Don't) Enable Macros: A New Threat Actor Targets UAE Dissidents," Citizen Lab, May 29, 2016, https://citizenlab.ca/2016/05/stealth-falcon/.

10. "Ahmed Mansoor Selected as the 2015 Laureate Martin Ennals Award for Human Rights Defenders," Amnesty International, October 6, 2015, https://www.amnesty.org/en/latest/news/2015/10/ahmed-mansoor-selected-as-the-2015-laureate-martin-ennals-award-for-human-rights-defenders/.

11. Bill Marczak and John Scott-Railton, "The Million Dollar Dissident: NSO Group's iPhone Zero-Days Used against a UAE Human Rights Defender," Citizen Lab, August 24, 2016, https://citizenlab.ca/2016/08/million-dollar-dissident-iphone-zero-day-nso-group-uae/ ; Morgan Marquis-Boire, "Backdoors Are Forever: Hacking Team and the Targeting of Dissent?," Citizen Lab, October 10, 2012, https://citizenlab.ca/2012/10/backdoors-are-forever-hacking-team-and-the-targeting-of-dissent/.

12. Joel Schectman and Christopher Bing, "UAE Used Cyber Super-weapon to Spy on iPhones of Foes," *Reuters*, January 30, 2019, https://www.reuters.com/investigates/special-report/usa-spying-karma/.

13. "UAE: Free Rights Defender Ahmed Mansoor," Human Rights Watch, April 12, 2019, https://www.hrw.org/news/2019/04/12/uae-free-rights-defender-ahmed-mansoor.

14. Christian Davenport, "State Repression and Political Order," *Annual Review of Political Science* 10 (2007): 2. See also Robert Goldstein's definition: "Political repression consists of government action which grossly discriminates against persons or organizations viewed as presenting a fundamental challenge to existing power relationships or key government policies, because of their perceived political beliefs." Robert Justin Goldstein, *Political Repression in Modern America: From 1870 to 1976* (Urbana: University of Illinois Press, 2001), xviii.

15. Davenport, "State Repression and Political Order," 2.

16. The *Oxford English Dictionary* provides an extensive analysis of the etymological roots to the term "digital." In the 1930s and 1940s, "digital" referred to devices that did not rely on analog instruments but instead relied upon data "represented as a series of discrete digits." More recently, looser meanings have begun to apply. Digital can designate a "computer-mediated counterpart" of an item that exists in the real world (digital shopping), and entire organizations and countries that are seen to "embrace computer technology or the Internet" are now described as digital. For our purposes, "digital" is an appropriate term to describe an ICT-mediated counterpart to traditional repression that is reliant on computer technology and the Internet. "Digital," *Oxford English Dictionary*, August 16, 2012, https://public.oed.com/blog/word-stories-digital/.

17. See, for example, Shahbaz, "Freedom on the Net 2018"; Alina Polyakova and Chris Meserole, "Exporting Digital Authoritarianism," Brookings, August 2019, https://www.brookings.edu/wp-content/uploads/2019/08/FP_20190826_digital_authoritarianism_polyakova_meserole.pdf.

18. Steven Feldstein, "When It Comes to Digital Authoritarianism, China Is a Challenge—but Not the Only Challenger," *War on the Rocks*, February 12, 2020, https://warontherocks.com/2020/02/when-it-comes-to-digital-authoritarianism-china-is-a-challenge-but-not-the-only-challenge/.

19. See Torin Monahan, *Surveillance in the Time of Insecurity* (New Brunswick, NJ: Rutgers University Press, 2010), 8. Portions of this section derive from previously published material by the author, including Steven Feldstein, "Surveillance in the Illiberal State," in András Sajó, Stephen Holmes, and Renáta Uitz, eds., *The Routledge Handbook of Illiberalism* (New York: Routledge, forthcoming).

20. Gary T. Marx, "What's New about the 'New Surveillance'? Classifying for Change and Continuity," *Knowledge, Technology & Policy* 17, no. 1 (2004): 18–37.

21. Marx, "What's New"; Frank La Rue, "Report of the Special Rapporteur on the Promotion and Protection of the Right to Freedom of Opinion and Expression," A/HRC/23/40, April

17, 2013, https://www.ohchr.org/Documents/HRBodies/HRCouncil/RegularSession/Session23/A.HRC.23.40_EN.pdf.

22. Electronic Frontier Foundation et al., "Necessary and Proportionate: International Principles on the Application of Human Rights to Communications Surveillance," March 4, 2016, https://necessaryandproportionate.org/principles.

23. David Kaye, "Report of the Special Rapporteur to the Human Rights Council on Surveillance and Human Rights," A/HRC/41/35, May 28, 2019, https://ap.ohchr.org/documents/dpage_e.aspx?si=A/HRC/41/35.

24. "The Right to Privacy in the Digital Age," Report of the Office of the United Nations High Commissioner for Human Rights, A/HRC/27/37, June 30, 2014, https://www.ohchr.org/EN/HRBodies/HRC/RegularSessions/Session27/Documents/A.HRC.27.37_en.pdf.

25. "Communications Surveillance," Privacy International, February 8, 2018, https://privacyinternational.org/explainer/1309/communications-surveillance.

26. Deep packet inspection technology allows authorities to track communications data (emails, visited websites, published blogs, text, chat groups). When authorities detect objectionable activities, they can block or redirect access to particular sites or services. "Deep Packet Inspection and Privacy," Electronic Privacy Information Center, 2020, https://epic.org/privacy/dpi/.

27. Figures updated through October 13, 2020. Samuel Woodhams, "COVID-19 Digital Rights Tracker," *Top10VPN*, October 2020, https://www.top10vpn.com/news/surveillance/covid-19-digital-rights-tracker/.

28. Pallavi Pundir, "Coronavirus Is Pushing Mass Surveillance in India, and It's Going to Change Everything," *Vice News*, April 6, 2020, https://www.vice.com/en_in/article/qjd9ew/coronavirus-surveillance-privacy-india.

29. Masashi Crete-Nishihata et al., "Communities @ Risk: Targeted Digital Threats against Civil Society," Citizen Lab, November 11, 2014, https://targetedthreats.net/media/1-ExecutiveSummary.pdf.

30. Crete-Nishihata et al., "Communities @ Risk."

31. Crete-Nishihata et al., "Communities @ Risk."

32. Patrick Howell O'Neill, "The Fall and Rise of a Spyware Empire," *MIT Technology Review*, November 29, 2019, https://www.technologyreview.com/s/614767/the-fall-and-rise-of-a-spyware-empire/.

33. John Scott-Railton et al., "Reckless VII: Wife of Journalist Slain in Cartel-Linked Killing Targeted with NSO Group's Spyware," Citizen Lab, March 20, 2019, https://citizenlab.ca/2019/03/nso-spyware-slain-journalists-wife/.

34. Bill Marczak et al., "Hide and Seek: Tracking NSO Group's Pegasus Spyware to Operations in 45 Countries," Citizen Lab, September 18, 2018, https://citizenlab.ca/2018/09/hide-and-seek-tracking-nso-groups-pegasus-spyware-to-operations-in-45-countries/.

35. Marczak et al., "Hide and Seek."

36. Steven Feldstein, "Commercial Spyware Global Inventory," Mendeley Data, v1, 2020, https://doi.org/10.17632/dycfyzj8j8.1.

37. Nicole Perlroth, "WhatsApp Says Israeli Firm Used Its App in Spy Program," *New York Times*, October 29, 2019, https://www.nytimes.com/2019/10/29/technology/whatsapp-nso-lawsuit.html.

38. La Rue, "Report of the Special Rapporteur," 3.

39. Freedom House, "Freedom on the Net Methodology," 2018, https://freedomhouse.org/report/freedom-net-methodology.

40. Margaret E. Roberts, *Censored: Distraction and Diversion inside China's Great Firewall* (Princeton, NJ: Princeton University Press, 2018), 42–43.

41. Bill Marczak et al., "China's Great Cannon," Citizen Lab, April 10, 2015, https://citizenlab.ca/2015/04/chinas-great-cannon/.

42. Lily Hay Newman, "Russia Takes a Big Step toward Internet Isolation," *Wired*, January 5, 2020, https://www.wired.com/story/russia-internet-control-disconnect-censorship/.

43. Mark Mackinnon, "How the Coronavirus Pandemic Is Making Strongmen Stronger, from Hungary to Serbia to the Philippines," *Globe and Mail*, April 6, 2020, https://www.

theglobeandmail.com/world/article-how-the-coronavirus-pandemic-is-making-strongmen-stronger-from/.

44. Human Rights Watch, "Cambodia: COVID-19 Clampdown on Free Speech," March 24, 2020, https://www.hrw.org/news/2020/03/24/cambodia-covid-19-clampdown-free-speech#.

45. Daren Butler, "Turkey Detains 19 People over 'Provocative' Coronavirus Posts," *Reuters*, March 17, 2020, https://www.reuters.com/article/us-health-coronavirus-turkey/turkey-detains-19-people-over-provocative-coronavirus-posts-idUSKBN2140T9.

46. Diego Cupolo, "Turkish Pandemic Plan Raises Concerns over Citizens' Digital Rights," *Al-Monitor*, April 9, 2020, https://www.al-monitor.com/pulse/originals/2020/04/turkey-coronavirus-response-concerns-digital-rights.html.

47. Raymond Zhong, Paul Mozur, Jeff Kao, and Aaron Krolik, "No 'Negative' News: How China Censored the Coronavirus," *New York Times*, December 19, 2020, https://www.nytimes.com/2020/12/19/technology/china-coronavirus-censorship.html.

48. The Rand study "Hostile Social Information" has compiled a useful inventory of terms commonly used in the field. Michael J. Mazarr et al., *Hostile Social Manipulation: Present Realities and Emerging Trends* (Santa Monica: Rand Corporation, 2019), 12–14.

49. "Informing the 'Disinformation' Debate," Access Now, Civil Liberties Union for Europe, and European Digital Rights, October 18, 2018, https://dq4n3btxmr8c9.cloudfront.net/files/2r7-0S/online_disinformation.pdf.

50. Mike Isaac and Kevin Rose, "Disinformation Spreads on WhatsApp Ahead of Brazilian Election," *New York Times*, October 19, 2018, https://www.nytimes.com/2018/10/19/technology/whatsapp-brazil-presidential-election.html.

51. Jonathan Bright et al., "Coronavirus Coverage by State-Backed English-Language News Sources: Understanding Chinese, Iranian, Russian and Turkish Government Media," Data Memo 2020.2., Oxford: Project on Computational Propaganda, comprop.oii.ox.ac.uk.

52. Kurt Wagner, "Facebook, Twitter, YouTube Remove Posts from Bolsonaro," *Bloomberg*, March 30, 2020, https://www.bloomberg.com/news/articles/2020-03-31/facebook-twitter-pull-misleading-posts-from-brazil-s-bolsonaro.

53. Claire Wardle, "Information Disorder: The Essential Glossary," *First Draft*, July 2018, https://firstdraftnews.org/wp-content/uploads/2018/07/infoDisorder_glossary.pdf?x30563.

54. Jane Li, "An Army of China's Internet Trolls Has a Message for Hong Kong Protesters," *Quartz*, July 23, 2019, https://qz.com/1672487/chinas-internet-trolls-target-hong-kong-protesters/.

55. Hannah Beech and Sun Narin, "Threatened by Facebook Disinformation, a Monk Flees Cambodia," *New York Times*, August 23, 2020, https://www.nytimes.com/2020/08/23/world/asia/cambodia-facebook-disinformation.html.

56. D. Lin and Sai Kung, "How Hong Kong Protests Turned Dream Wedding into a Nightmare for Policeman's Bride," *South China Morning Post*, November 23, 2019, https://www.scmp.com/comment/letters/article/3038809/how-hong-kong-protests-turned-dream-wedding-nightmare-policemans.

57. Esther Chan and Rachel Blundy, "'Bulletproof' China-Backed Doxxing Site Attacks Hong Kong's Democracy Activists," *AFP*, November 1, 2019, https://hongkongfp.com/2019/11/01/bulletproof-china-backed-doxxing-site-attacks-hong-kongs-democracy-activists/.

58. Jilian C. York, "Syria's Twitter Spambots," *The Guardian*, April 21, 2011, https://www.theguardian.com/commentisfree/2011/apr/21/syria-twitter-spambots-pro-revolution.

59. The use of the term "electronic flies" in reference to state-sponsored trolls appears to have originated in Saudi Arabia in 2018 and spread throughout the region: "In the Sudan they are called 'electronic chickens,' in Egypt we say 'electronic committees.'" Layli Foroudi, "In Algeria, 'Electronic Flies' Threaten a Protest Movement," *Coda Story*, December 10, 2019, https://codastory.com/disinformation/algeria-election-protest/.

60. Wardle, "Information Disorder."

61. Nyst and Monaco, "State-Sponsored Trolling."

62. See Berhan Taye, "Targeted, Cut Off, and Left in the Dark: The #KeepItOn Report on Internet Shutdowns in 2019," Access Now, 2020, https://www.accessnow.org/cms/assets/uploads/2020/02/KeepItOn-2019-report-1.pdf; Jan Rydzak, Moses Karanja, and Nicholas Opiyo, "Internet Shutdowns in Africa: Dissent Does Not Die in Darkness. Network Shutdowns and Collective Action in African Countries," *International Journal of Communication* 14 (2020): 24.

63. Darrell M. West, "Internet Shutdowns Cost Countries $2.4 Billion Last Year," Brookings, October 2016, www.brookings.edu/wp-content/uploads/2016/10/intenet-shutdowns-v-3.pdf.

64. Berhan Taye, "The State of Internet Shutdowns around the World: The 2018 #KeepItOn Report," Access Now, 2019, https://www.accessnow.org/cms/assets/uploads/2019/07/KeepItOn-2018-Report.pdf.

65. Taye, "Targeted, Cut Off."

66. Taye, "Targeted, Cut Off."

67. "Arab Spring Anniversary: When Egypt Cut the Internet," *Al Jazeera*, January 25, 2016, https://www.aljazeera.com/indepth/features/2016/01/arab-spring-anniversary-egypt-cut-internet-160125042903747.html.

68. Taye, "Targeted, Cut Off"; Woodhams and Migliano, "Global Cost of Internet Shutdowns."

69. "Freedom on the Net Methodology," Freedom House, 2019, https://freedomhouse.org/report/freedom-net-methodology.

70. "DRCongo:YouthActivistsRoundedUpatStrike,"HumanRightsWatch,February23,2016, https://www.hrw.org/news/2016/02/23/dr-congo-youth-activists-rounded-strike#.

71. "DRC: Release of Pro-democracy Activists Cause for Celebration," Amnesty International, August 30, 2016, https://www.amnesty.org/en/latest/news/2016/08/drc-release-of-pro-democracy-activists-cause-for-celebration/.

72. "Thai Courts Give Record Jail Terms for Insulting King," *BBC News*, August 7, 2015, https://www.bbc.com/news/world-asia-33819814.

73. See Philip N. Howard, Sheetal D. Agarwal, and Muzammil M. Hussain, "The Dictators' Digital Dilemma: When Do States Disconnect Their Digital Networks?" Brookings, 2011, https://www.brookings.edu/wp-content/uploads/2016/06/10_dictators_digital_network.pdf.

74. Roberts, *Censored*, 23–24.

75. Rebecca MacKinnon, "Liberation Technology: China's 'Networked Authoritarianism,'" *Journal of Democracy* 22, no. 2 (2011): 33.

76. Abdi Latif Dahir, "Cameroon Has Restricted Internet Access for More Than 150 Days in 2017," *Quartz*, November 27, 2017, https://qz.com/africa/1138529/cameroons-anglophone-ambazonia-region-has-had-internet-restriction-for-150-days-in-2017/.

77. Weidmann and Rød, *Internet and Political Protest*, 31.

78. Weidmann and Rød, *Internet and Political Protest*, 31–32.

79. Larry Diamond, "Liberation Technology," *Journal of Democracy* 21, no. 3 (2010): 70.

80. Larry Diamond, "The Threat of Postmodern Totalitarianism," *Journal of Democracy* 30, no. 1 (2019): 20–21.

81. Andrea Kendall-Taylor, Erica Frantz, and Joseph Wright, "The Digital Dictators: How Technology Strengthens Autocracy," *Foreign Affairs*, March–April 2020, https://www.foreignaffairs.com/articles/china/2020-02-06/digital-dictators.

82. See for example, "Evidence of Internet Shutdowns in DRC amid Election Unrest," Netblocks, December 31, 2018, https://netblocks.org/reports/evidence-of-internet-shutdowns-in-drc-amid-election-unrest-PW80YLAK; "Democratic Republic of the Congo: Events of 2018," Human Rights Watch World Report 2019, 2019, https://www.hrw.org/world-report/2019/country-chapters/democratic-republic-congo.

83. Rachel Metz, "Portland Passes Broadest Facial Recognition Ban in the US," *CNN Business*, September 9, 2020, https://www.cnn.com/2020/09/09/tech/portland-facial-recognition-ban/index.html.

84. See Appendix 3.

85. Cora Currier and Morgan Marquis-Boire, "A Detailed Look at Hacking Team's Emails about Its Repressive Clients," *The Intercept*, June 7, 2015, https://theintercept.com/2015/07/07/leaked-documents-confirm-hacking-team-sells-spyware-repressive-countries/.

86. Bill Marczak et al., "Mapping Hacking Team's 'Untraceable' Spyware," Citizen Lab, February 17, 2014, https://citizenlab.ca/2014/02/mapping-hacking-teams-untraceable-spyware/.

87. John Scott-Railton, "Bitter Sweet: Supporters of Mexico's Soda Tax Targeted with NSO Exploit Links," Citizen Lab, February 11, 2017, https://citizenlab.ca/2017/02/bittersweet-nso-mexico-spyware/.

88. Samantha Bradshaw and Philip Howard, "Troops, Trolls and Troublemakers: A Global Inventory of Organized Social Media Manipulation," Computational Propaganda Research

Project, Working Paper no. 2017.12, 2017, http://blogs.oii.ox.ac.uk/politicalbots/wp-content/uploads/sites/89/2017/07/Troops-Trolls-and-Troublemakers.pdf.

89. Steven Feldstein, "To End Mass Protests, Sudan Has Cut Off Internet Access Nationwide. Here's Why," *Washington Post,* June 13, 2019, https://www.washingtonpost.com/politics/2019/06/13/end-mass-protests-sudan-has-cut-off-internet-access-nationwide-heres-why/.

90. "Despots and Disruptions: Five Dimensions of Internet Shutdowns in Africa," CIPESA, February 2019, https://cipesa.org/?wpfb_dl=283.

91. Jan Rydzak, "Of Blackouts and Bandhs: The Strategy and Structure of Disconnected Protest in India," *SSRN,* 2019, https://papers.ssrn.com/sol3/papers.cfm?abstract_id=3330413.

92. Weidmann and Rød, *Internet and Political Protest,* 139, 142.

93. Geddes, "What Do We Know," 121.

94. Ithiel de Sola Pool, *Technologies of Freedom* (Cambridge, MA.: Belknap Press, 1983), 226.

95. Parts of the proceeding section are taken from previously published material by the author, including Steven Feldstein, "Covid-19 and the Geopolitics of American Decline," *MIT Technology Review,* August 19, 2020, https://www.technologyreview.com/2020/08/19/1006349/covid-american-decline-geopolitics-coronavirus/; Steven Feldstein, "Testimony—Hearing on China's Strategic Aims in Africa," U.S.-China Economic and Security Review Commission, May 8, 2020, https://www.uscc.gov/sites/default/files/Feldstein_Testimony.pdf.

96. *United States Strategic Approach to the People's Republic of China* (Washington, DC: President of the United States, 2020), 5.

97. Samantha Hoffman, "China's Tech-Enhanced Authoritarianism," Testimony before the House Permanent Select Committee on Intelligence, Hearing on "China's Digital Authoritarianism: Surveillance, Influence, and Political Control," May 16, 2019, https://docs.house.gov/meetings/IG/IG00/20190516/109462/HHRG-116-IG00-Wstate-HoffmanS-20190516.pdf.

98. Elizabeth C. Economy, "Exporting the China Model," Testimony before the U.S.-China Economic and Security Review Commission, Hearing on the "China Model," March 13, 2020, https://www.uscc.gov/sites/default/files/testimonies/USCCTestimony3-13-20%20(Elizabeth%20Economy)_justified.pdf.

99. Christopher Walker, Shanthi Kalathil, and Jessica Ludwig, "The Cutting Edge of Sharp Power," *Journal of Democracy* 31, no. 1 (2020): 130–31.

100. Jessica Chen Weiss, "Understanding and Rolling Back Digital Authoritarianism," *War on the Rocks,* February 17, 2020, https://warontherocks.com/2020/02/understanding-and-rolling-back-digital-authoritarianism/.

101. See for example Gadi Wolfsfeld, Elad Segev, and Tamir Sheafer, "Social Media and the Arab Spring: Politics Comes First," *International Journal of Press/Politics* 18, no. 2 (2013): 115–37.

102. C. Raja Mohan and Chan Jia Hao, "China's Digital Expansion and India," ISAS Working Paper No. 32, October 8, 2019, https://www.isas.nus.edu.sg/wp-content/uploads/2019/10/ISAS-Working-Paper-No.-320.pdf.

103. Sheridan Prasso, "China's Digital Silk Road Is Looking More Like an Iron Curtain," *Bloomberg Businessweek,* January 9, 2019, https://www.bloomberg.com/news/features/2019-01-10/china-s-digital-silk-road-is-looking-more-like-an-iron-curtain.

104. Mohan and Hao, "China's Digital Expansion."

105. *USCC 2020 Annual Report,* U.S.-China Economic and Security Review Commission (Washington: US Government Publishing Office, 2020), 110. China's approach to Internet standards and protocols are a good illustration of this priority. As Adam Segal writes, China's objectives to "prevent the flow of information that threatens domestic stability, foster technological independence, and counter U.S. influence" means that China is "increasingly capable and willing to pursue these goals by shaping the global internet rather than only the internet behind the Great Firewall." Adam Segal, "China's Vision for Cyber Sovereignty and the Global Governance of Cyberspace," *The National Bureau of Asian Research,* NBR Special Report no. 87, August 25, 2020, p. 92, https://www.nbr.org/publication/chinas-vision-for-cyber-sovereignty-and-the-global-governance-of-cyberspace/.

106. Colum Lynch, "China Bids to Lead World Agency Protecting Intellectual Property," *Foreign Policy,* November 26, 2019, https://foreignpolicy.com/2019/11/26/china-bids-lead-

world-intellectual-property-organization-wipo/. For a discussion of different types of technical standards and the corresponding design implications for varied devices, see *USCC 2020 Annual Report*, 115–116.

107. USCC 2020 Annual Report, 105.
108. Naomi Wilson, "China Standards 2035 and the Plan for World Domination—Don't Believe China's Hype," Council on Foreign Relations—Net Politics Blog, June 3, 2020, https://www.cfr.org/blog/china-standards-2035-and-plan-world-domination-dont-believe-chinas-hype.
109. Olivia Shen, "Coronavirus and Techno-Authoritarianism," *China Story* blog, May 25, 2020, https://www.thechinastory.org/coronavirus-and-techno-authoritarianism/.
110. Walker, Kalathil, and Ludwig, "Cutting Edge," 130.
111. Shahbaz, "Freedom on the Net 2018."
112. Michael Schwirtz and Gaelle Borgia, "How Russia Meddles Abroad for Profit: Cash, Trolls and a Cult Leader," *New York Times*, November 11, 2019, https://www.nytimes.com/2019/11/11/world/africa/russia-madagascar-election.html.
113. Dionne Searcy, "Gems, Warlords and Mercenaries: Russia's Playbook in the Central African Republic," *New York Times*, October 24, 2019, https://www.nytimes.com/2019/09/30/world/russia-diamonds-africa-prigozhin.html.
114. Alina Polyakova, "Russia Is Teaching the World to Spy," *New York Times*, December 5, 2019, https://www.nytimes.com/2019/12/05/opinion/russia-hacking.html.
115. Polyakova and Meserole, "Exporting Digital Authoritarianism."
116. Valentin Weber, "The Sinicization of Russia's Cyber Sovereignty Model," Council on Foreign Relations, *Net Politics* blog, April 1, 2020, https://www.cfr.org/blog/sinicization-russias-cyber-sovereignty-model.
117. Weber, "Sinicization."
118. One area where Russia remains a global leader is the propagation and dissemination of external influence operations, including disinformation campaigns to manipulate 2016 US elections, as well as a host of European elections and referendums. Those operations fall outside the scope of this book.
119. "Xi Jinping's State Visit to the Philippines," *Rappler*, November 21, 2018, https://www.rappler.com/nation/217087-watch-state-visit-china-president-xi-jinping-philippines-november-2018.
120. Zhao Lili, "Contributing to the Development of Ethiopia with Wisdom and Strength," *ZTE Tech*, June 12, 2009, https://www.zte.com.cn/global/about/magazine/zte-technologies/2009/6/en_414/172517.html.
121. David Kaye, "Visit to Ethiopia, 2–9 December 2019, End of Mission Statement," UN Office of the High Commissioner for Human Rights, 2019, https://www.ohchr.org/EN/NewsEvents/Pages/DisplayNews.aspx?NewsID=25402&LangID=E.

3

Global Patterns of Digital Repression

This chapter presents quantitative data related to a series of questions about digital repression raised in the previous chapter: Which countries are deploying digital repression techniques, and how prevalent is their use? What is the relationship between regime type and digital repression? How might we understand the relationship between specific types of repression (violating political liberties, physical violence committed by the state, or curtailing private civil liberties) and digital repression? How does the deployment of individual components of digital repression differ in democracies versus autocracies?

I present pooled, cross-national, time-series data to explain global patterns of digital repression, and use that data to develop and validate two composite indexes: a latent construct of digital repression and a latent construct of digital repression capacity.

This chapter proceeds as follows: First, I present key insights from the data related to the main arguments of the book. Second, I outline the methodology used to construct the digital repression index, as well as the digital repression capacity index. Third, I present overall findings from the digital repression index—the relationship between regime type and digital repression, highest- and lowest-performing countries, as well as outliers. I also compare digital repression enactment to capacity and investigate differentiations between autocracies and democracies. Fourth, I analyze individual components of digital repression—social media surveillance, online censorship, social manipulation and disinformation, Internet shutdowns, and arrests of online users for political content—and provide explanations for authoritarian and democratic use.

Insights from the Digital Repression Index

The data presented in this chapter confirms three important insights: First, there is a strong statistical relationship between regime type and digital repression.

The Rise of Digital Repression. Steven Feldstein, Oxford University Press (2021). © Oxford University Press.
DOI: 10.1093/oso/9780190057497.003.0003

Second, autocracies digitally repress more than their capabilities indicate, forcing them to make up the gap through external sources or reliance on less advanced digital tools. Conversely, digital repression capacity in democracies outstrips enactment, meaning that democracies opt not to deploy the excess capabilities they possess. Third, not only do autocracies and democracies deploy contrasting digital strategies, but among autocracies there is significant variance regarding which digital methods those regimes choose to implement.

To elaborate on my first point, the data shows a strong relationship between regime type and digital repression. Across the board, autocracies perform worse on all digital repression measurements than democracies, directly supporting the proposition that traditional repression is closely linked to digital repression strategies. I compared levels of digital repression to regime type to confirm the relationship between a country's form of governance and its digital repression score. A simple linear regression reveals a moderately strong relationship between the two variables: 76 percent of the variability of the digital repression index can be explained by the level of electoral democracy. Simply put, electoral democracies rely on digital repression at far lower rates than authoritarian regimes.

I then investigated which specific types of repression were most predictive of digital repression enactment. I tested several different variables: physical violence committed by the state, violations of political liberties, violations of private civil liberties, and civil society repression. *Overall, I found that a government's curtailment of political civil liberties was the strongest predictor of digital repression.*

V-Dem's political civil liberties index includes measurements of media censorship, journalist harassment, freedom of discussion, freedom of academic and cultural expression, political party bans, and civil society repression. All of these factors are closely linked to the same political objectives as digital repression. Interestingly, state reliance on hard coercion—for example, physical violence used against citizens—showed the weakest statistical relationship to digital repression. The likeliest explanation for this weak correlation is that digital repression often serves as a substitute for more violent strategies of political control. Many governments that are dependent on digital repression feature some degree of liberalization—where the state relies less on traditional political repression strategies. Scholars Nils Weidmann and Espen Geelmuyden Rød come to a similar conclusion, finding that in autocracies "with a more liberalized institutional setup" (Zimbabwe, Kyrgyzstan), Internet technology reduced protests more than fourfold compared to Internet controls used in closed and competitive autocracies (Saudi Arabia, China). Weidmann and Rød conclude: "This is ample evidence that Internet technology serves as a substitute for traditional restrictions on the right to organize. While the technology is effectively used by governments in closed autocracies to suppress unrest, the impact is smaller because traditional means of control already play a large role in reducing the threat of protest mobilization."[1]

To expand on my second point, when analyzing the relationship between digital repression and digital repression capacity, the data reveals that *repression capacity lags repression enactment in autocracies, but that this relationship reverses in democracies.* Put simply, autocracies digitally repress more than their capabilities allow—forcing them to make up the gap in other ways, either through external sourcing or by employing lower-capacity digital tools (like Internet shutdowns). In contrast, digital repression capacity in democracies outstrips enactment, meaning that democracies choose not to deploy digital repression capabilities that they otherwise possess.

A key policy implication is that capacity deficiencies can result in autocracies relying on outside manufacturers and service providers to operate the very surveillance, facial recognition, censorship, and social manipulation programs used to repress their citizens. In practice, this can take many forms.[2] The state may choose to hire outside consultants to bolster its in-house capacity to carry out certain digital techniques, such as targeted surveillance. It may employ repurposed crimeware, such as in Syria, to target regime opponents. Or the state may purchase commercial products and services, such as surveillance spyware or facial recognition systems, supplied by international companies. Many of these capabilities are provided by corporations headquartered in democracies, including the United States, Israel, France, United Kingdom, and Japan. As I will discuss in Chapter 8, it behooves policymakers in liberal democracies to consider tightening export requirements related to these technologies. Of course, some repressive governments may choose a simpler route—deploy more rudimentary tools that align with their capacity level (e.g., use Internet shutdowns rather than advanced surveillance techniques).

And to add to my third primary point, when I examine specific components of digital repression to determine how and why certain countries adopt particular digital tactics over others, *I find that not only do autocracies and democracies digitally repress in divergent ways, but among autocracies there is significant variance about which digital methods they choose to implement.*

In general, autocracies are likely to use social media surveillance, social manipulation and disinformation, and arrests of online users for political content as favored techniques. In contrast, most democracies tend to rely on social manipulation and disinformation when carrying out digital repression. Social manipulation techniques showed the smallest gap in use between autocracies and democracies. In this area, democracies ruled by illiberal leaders (e.g.,

Brazil, India, Philippines) display scores that are fairly close to autocracies like Russia and Serbia. Similarly, while Internet shutdowns occur more frequently in autocracies, a number of democracies and hybrid regimes also rely on this strategy. India particularly stands out, with its government leading the world in its number of shutdowns.

The data presented in this chapter clearly supports one of the book's main assertions: overall levels of digital repression are closely related to existing levels of repression. But this pattern does not translate into straightforward adoption of repressive techniques. As I have described, digital repression in autocracies varies from state to state. Government deployment of digital techniques is contingent on a number of factors: state security capacity, political norms, the nature of regime challenges, and technological capabilities.

Constructing the Digital Repression Index

An essential piece of my research design was to identify a way to quantify a country's overall level of digital repression—to describe the extent to which a state is utilizing digital instruments for repression. I required a measurement that would be universal in coverage, incorporating the majority of independent, sovereign entities worldwide.[3] It was also important for this measurement to closely resemble the digital repression taxonomy presented in Chapter 2 by incorporating the five components of digital repression (surveillance, censorship, social manipulation and disinformation, Internet shutdowns, and persecutions of online users). Finding appropriate data from which to construct such an indicator proved challenging.

Eventually, I came across data collected by a new research initiative, the Digital Society Project (DSP).[4] The project uses infrastructure from the Varieties of Democracy (V-Dem) project to provide insights into how digitalization impacts democracies. Like V-Dem, DSP collects expert-coded surveys that are disseminated to country expert coders in order to rate specific observations. DSP offers a range of digital measurements, including the government's capacity to regulate the Internet, degrees of online polarization, levels of privacy protections, and censorship policies. And its data incorporates measurements for 179 country units (essentially all independent political entities worldwide with a population over 250,000). Finally, because DSP's method of data collection follows rules and procedures from V-Dem, there is seamless compatibility between DSP statistics and traditional democracy and governance indicators collected by V-Dem, facilitating cross-comparison.[5]

My digital repression index, which incorporates time-series data for ten years (2010–19), contains eight DSP variables that roughly conform to my digital repression taxonomy:

- Government social media monitoring
- Government Internet filtering in practice
- Government social media censorship in practice
- Government dissemination of false information domestic
- Party dissemination of false information domestic
- Government Internet shutdown in practice
- Government social media shutdown in practice
- Arrests for posting online political content

These eight variables cover most of the issues identified in my digital repression taxonomy. However, one noted gap relates to surveillance. DSP's surveillance variable only measures government social media monitoring; it does not incorporate physical surveillance measurements (such as the presence of public facial recognition systems). In this regard, I have developed a stand-alone AI and big-data global surveillance index that I present in Chapter 7. Table 3.1 shows how the DSP variables align with my digital repression taxonomy.

Aggregating the DSP variables into a composite digital repression indicator provides valuable insights and passes several validation tests. For additional information about quantitative analysis methods used to construct the digital repression index, see Appendix 2. The full country-level digital repression index can be accessed online at http://dx.doi.org/10.17632/rrnz8p6rvw.1.[6]

When I calculated global digital repression scores for 2019, I incorporated an interaction for social media penetration for three DSP variables: government social media monitoring, government dissemination of false information domestic, and party dissemination of false information domestic. My reasoning is that those particular variables are predicated on a government's ability to monitor and/or manipulate communications via social media. The extent to which social media access is either tiny or nonexistent (such as North Korea's minuscule 0.6 percent social media penetration level) affects how much those variables contribute to a state's digital repression strategy.[7] This data is presented in Appendix 1. The data for 2019 can also be accessed online at http://dx.doi.org/10.17632/5dnfmtgbfs.1.[8]

Note that DSP's measurement model aggregates ratings provided by country experts—taking disagreement and measurement error into account. The point estimates are the median values of these distributions for each country-year. The scale of the measurement model variable is typically between −5 and 5, with 0

Table 3.1 **Comparison of Digital Repression Taxonomy and Variables from the Digital Society Project**

Digital taxonomy category	Applicable DSP variable
Surveillance	Government social media monitoring (v2smgovsmmon): "How comprehensive is the surveillance of political content in social media by the government or its agents?"
Censorship	Government Internet filtering in practice (v2smgovfilprc): "How frequently does the government censor political information on the Internet by filtering?" Government social media censorship in practice (v2smgovsmcenprc): "To what degree does the government censor political content on social media in practice?"
Social manipulation and disinformation	Government dissemination of false information domestic (v2smgovsmcenprc): "How often do the government and its agents use social media to disseminate misleading viewpoints or false information to influence its own population?" Party dissemination of false information domestic (v2smgovdom): "How often do major political parties and candidates for office use social media to disseminate misleading viewpoints or false information to influence their own population?"
Internet shutdowns	Government Internet shutdown in practice (v2smgovshut): "How often does the government shut down domestic access to the Internet?" Government social media shutdown in practice (v2smgovsm): "How often does the government shut down access to social media platforms?"
Targeted persecutions of online users	Arrests for posting online political content (v2smarrest): "If a citizen posts political content online that would run counter to the government and its policies, what is the likelihood that citizen is arrested?"

approximately representing the mean for all country-years in the sample.[9] Thus, a country displaying a negative score means that it is performing below the mean for that particular variable (likewise, countries displaying positive scores are performing above the mean for the given variable).

Digital Repression Capacity Index

In addition to evaluating a country's digital repression score, I also sought to measure the government's digital repression capacity. DSP provides capacity measurements that are conceptually separate from a state's pursuit of digital repression in practice. Experts are queried about a state's capacity to carry out certain activities "independent of whether it actually does so in practice."[10] Four DSP variables are relevant to our inquiry:

- Government Internet filtering capacity (v2smgovfilcap): "Independent of whether it actually does so in practice, does the government have the technical capacity to censor information (text, audio, images, or video) on the Internet by filtering (blocking access to certain websites) if it decided to?"
- Government Internet shutdown capacity (v2smgovshutcap): "Independent of whether it actually does so in practice, does the government have the technical capacity to actively shut down domestic access to the Internet if it decided to?"
- Government cybersecurity capacity (v2smgovcapsec): "Does the government have sufficiently technologically skilled staff and resources to mitigate harm from cybersecurity threats?"
- Government capacity to regulate online content (v2smregcap): "Does the government have sufficient staff and resources to regulate Internet content in accordance with existing law?"

These variables apply to two of the five digital repression categories: censorship and Internet shutdowns. They do not provide capacity measurements for surveillance, social manipulation and disinformation, or targeted persecution of online users. However, DSP includes a new variable—government cybersecurity capacity—that applies more broadly. Cybersecurity capacity is relevant as a general-use digital measurement (and not specific to digital repression). Because cybersecurity capacity is closely related, from a skills standpoint, to a state's ability to carry out sophisticated digital strategies, I include it in the index.

2019 data for the digital repression capacity index is incorporated in Appendix 1. Full data from 2010 to 2019 can be accessed online at http://dx.doi.org/10.17632/rrnz8p6rvw.1.[11]

Relationship between Governance and Digital Repression

Digital repression is a function of traditional repression; countries with existing levels of repression are more likely to adopt digital techniques. The digital repression index allows us to test this proposition using variables from DSP and V-Dem. To investigate this relationship, I ran a bivariate regression using V-Dem's electoral democracy index as the explanatory variable and the digital repression index as the outcome variable. I used the electoral democracy index as a proxy for regime type; the higher a country scores on this index, the more closely it represents "the ideal of electoral democracy." The lower a country scores, the more it resembles an autocratic state, lacking meaningful multiparty elections or citizen representation (the min/max range is 0.023 to 0.9).[12]

As the scatterplot in Figure 3.1 shows, there is a close alignment between the two variables: 76 percent of the variability of the digital repression index is explained by the electoral democracy index (see Appendix 2 for regression tables).[13]

I then sought to determine which components of the electoral democracy index are most causally linked to the digital repression index. Is a country's respect for political rights related to whether it will carry out digital repression? What about private civil liberties or civil society repression? To what degree does a state's physical violence—political killings and torture undertaken by the government—influence whether the government will carry out digital repression as well?

I used a pooled time-series random effects model that incorporated four V-Dem variables: political civil liberties (freedom of association and expression),

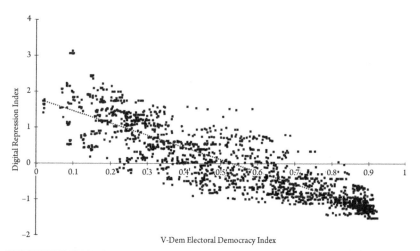

Variable	Min	Max	Mean	Std. deviation
Digital Repression Index	−1.53	3.13	−1.40e-09	0.986
Electoral Democracy Index	0.019	0.924	0.533	0.254
N= 1789; r² = 0.76				

Figure 3.1 Global Relationship between Digital Repression and Electoral Democracy, 2010 to 2019

private civil liberties (freedom of movement and religion, freedom from forced labor, or property rights), physical violence (freedom from political killings and torture), and civil society organization (CSO) repression. The coefficient data is listed in Appendix 2.

The analysis shows that 78 percent of the variability of the digital repression index is explained by the four independent variables. After controlling for each of the variables, the analysis indicates that constraints on political civil liberties is by far the most influential predictor of digital repression enactment. In other words, state violations of political civil liberties— censoring political speech, preventing groups from organizing, restricting academic freedom, or banning political parties, for example—shows a causal relationship to the deployment of digital repression. The analysis shows a much weaker relationship between the other three variables to digital repression (surprisingly, physical violence committed by the state displays the weakest relationship to digital repression measures). Figure 3.2 depicts these results graphically.

This result underscores that there may be a substitution effect between the most coercive forms of state repression (violence committed by the state) and digital repression. While such technology is unquestionably used by closed autocracies to suppress dissent (e.g., reinforcing existing high levels of repression), the impact is more pronounced in competitive autocracies with limited amounts of political liberalization.

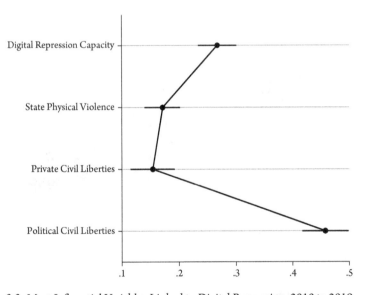

Figure 3.2 Most Influential Variables Linked to Digital Repression, 2010 to 2019

Digital Repression Performance: Which Countries Score Lowest and Highest?

In line with the preceding findings, countries with poor human rights records showed the highest global levels of digital repression. The map in Figure 3.3 provides an overview of the global distribution of digital repression (darker shaded countries display higher levels of digital repression). As a reminder, the measurement model's scale is typically between −5 and 5, with 0 representing the approximate mean for all country-years in the sample. Countries with negative scores, for example, perform below the mean for a given variable.

Certain regions are overrepresented when it comes to levels of digital repression.[14] The two regions with the highest levels of digital repression in 2019 were South and Central Asia and the Near East. In contrast, Europe and Eurasia and countries in the Western Hemisphere showed the lowest digital repression scores. These countries also displayed excess digital repression capacity (particularly in Europe, digital repression enactment significantly lags repressive capabilities). Figure 3.4 provides a regional breakdown.

For countries with the highest digital repression scores, all of them are classified as closed or competitive autocracies, and those evaluated by FOTN all receive "not free" rankings. But there are unexpected variances as well. Digital repression capacity does not fully align with digital repression scores. While China, Iran, North Korea, Saudi Arabia, and the UAE all register high capacity scores, Tajikistan and Syria show lower capacity. Likewise, there is little relationship between digital repression and national wealth. Saudi Arabia, Bahrain, UAE, and China are situated near the top of most global economic indices, while North Korea and Tajikistan fall on the opposite end. Table 3.2 provides a breakdown.

Similarly, countries with the least amount of digital repression in 2019 also align closely to regime type. Other than Iceland and Lithuania, every country is categorized as a liberal democracy. All countries score highly on global economic indicators. But as Table 3.3 shows, they also demonstrate significant inconsistency when it comes to digital repression capacity. Certain countries on the list (Lithuania, Canada, the Netherlands) display low digital repression capacity, while other countries are situated on the high end of the scale (New Zealand and Iceland). This disparity indicates that certain countries with a highly developed industrial base, like the Netherlands, have not prioritized building digital capabilities, whereas other liberal democracies, like Denmark, have acquired advanced digital capabilities but are choosing not to use them.

A number of countries with strong electoral democracy rankings had unexpectedly high digital repression scores. I calculated 2019 residual measurements for every country in the digital repression index (the difference

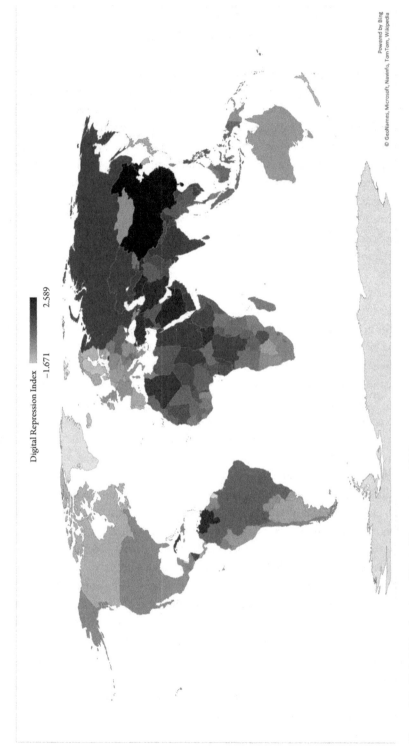

Digital Repression Index

−1.671   2.589

© GeoNames, Microsoft, Navinfo, TomTom, Wikipedia

Powered by Bing

Figure 3.3 Global Distribution of Digital Repression in 2019

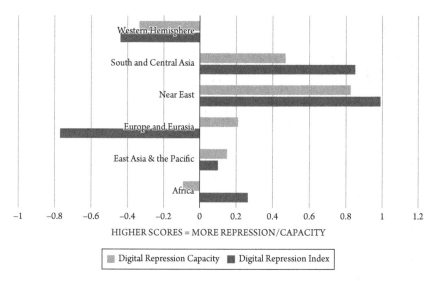

Figure 3.4 Regional Breakdown of Digital Repression and Capacity in 2019

between an observed value and its corresponding predicted value based on the model). India, Mauritius, and Nepal topped the list of countries that diverged most negatively from their predicted values (e.g., India's electoral democracy index score of 0.507 should have resulted in a digital repression score of 0.045; instead, its digital repression score stood substantially higher at 1.213). Brazil is another large democracy with surprisingly high digital repression scores (predicted digital repression score of −0.545 versus an actual score of 0.296). Widespread disinformation disseminated by the populist Bolsonaro government helps explain its poor showing. India's high score is attributable to state censorship and widespread dissemination of false information by political parties. In addition, India also leads the world in state-sponsored Internet shutdowns. Conversely, several countries displayed unexpectedly low digital repression scores despite poor democracy rankings—including Belarus, Eswatini, and Honduras.

Comparing Digital Repression Capacity to Enactment

The second insight from the findings is that digital repression capacity lags digital repression enactment in autocracies; this relationship, however, reverses in democracies. The link between a country's capacity to deploy digital repression and the amount of digital repression a government actually wields brings

Table 3.2 **Countries with the Highest Levels of Digital Repression in 2019**

Country	Digital repression index[a]	Digital repression capacity	V-Dem electoral democracy index	V-Dem regime type[b]	GDP per capita (US$)	2019 defense budget (US$, millions)[c]
China	2.589	1.592	0.083	CA	9,771	181,135
North Korea	2.555	2.501	0.099	CA	–	–
United Arab Emirates	2.199	1.816	0.101	CA	43,004	22,755[d]
Saudi Arabia	1.981	1.662	0.023	CA	23,339	78,400
Turkmenistan	1.945	1.321	0.154	EA	6,967	–
Bahrain	1.913	0.920	0.118	CA	24,051	1,501
Iran	1.800	1.647	0.217	EA	5,628	17,428
Venezuela	1.745	1.009	0.229	EA	–	465[e]
Tajikistan	1.718	0.113	0.166	EA	827	187
Syria	1.681	0.621	0.145	CA	2,033	1,800

[a] Observations: 179. Min: −1.67. Max: 2.59. Mean: 3.02e-09. Standard deviation: 0.983.
[b] CA: closed autocracy; EA: electoral autocracy.
[c] "The Military Balance 2020," International Institute for Strategic Studies, 2020, https://www.iiss.org/publications/the-military-balance-plus.
[d] Figure from 2014.
[e] Figure from 2017.

Table 3.3 Countries with the Lowest Levels of Digital Repression in 2019

Country	Digital repression index[a]	Digital repression capacity	V-Dem electoral democracy index	V-Dem regime type[b]	GDP per capita (US$)	2019 defense budget (US$, millions)[c]
Sweden	−1.671	0.126	0.874	LD	54,608	6384
Denmark	−1.623	0.792	0.9	LD	61,350	4592
Lithuania	−1.588	0.265	0.803	ED	19,153	1065
Finland	−1.508	0.427	0.87	LD	50,152	3999
Iceland	−1.500	1.608	0.85	ED	73191	55
Netherlands	−1.409	−0.067	0.83	LD	53,024	12,097
Portugal	−1.394	0.729	0.87	LD	23,408	2682
Canada	−1.392	0.331	0.866	LD	46,233	18,723
New Zealand	−1.391	1.046	0.873	LD	41,945	2722
Cyprus	−1.380	0.509	0.84	LD	28,159	403

[a] Observations: 179. Min: −1.67. Max: 2.59. Mean: 3.02e-09. Standard deviation: 0.983.

[b] ED: electoral democracy; LD: liberal democracy.

[c] "The Military Balance 2020," International Institute for Strategic Studies, 2020, https://www.iiss.org/publications/the-military-balance-plus.

important policy implications. Overall, a country's digital repression capacity is a poor predictor of its actual use of digital repression. Capabilities on their own do not translate to usage. Statistical analysis (2010–19) confirms the weakness of the relationship between digital repression capacity and its deployment ($r^2 = 0.11$).

Why is this relationship so tenuous? One explanation is that many countries with high levels of digital repression capacity opt not to deploy their capabilities. For liberal democracies, this means that governments with high capabilities (like France or Estonia) also have strong political safeguards and liberal values that mitigate the risk of using these tools for political repression. In addition, as Erica Frantz, Andrea Kendall-Taylor, and Joseph Wright note, "New technologies are useful to governments for a wide variety of reasons, beyond just repressing citizens."[15] Democracies leverage technology for a variety of purposes unrelated to digital surveillance or censorship. Thus, countries topping the digital repression capacity index include repressive stalwarts like North Korea, Qatar, and UAE, as well as technology darlings like Estonia and Singapore.

When we plot global digital capacity against digital repression enactment over a ten-year period, we gain further insights. Figure 3.5 shows that over time, digital repression use and corresponding capacity have risen. This is not unexpected—as dissent has moved online and digital tools have become cheaper and easier to use, a greater number of governments are employing these techniques. Up through 2014, global digital repression capacity lagged deployment. But starting in 2015, global digital capacity started to surpass digital repression deployment—indicating that increasing numbers of countries

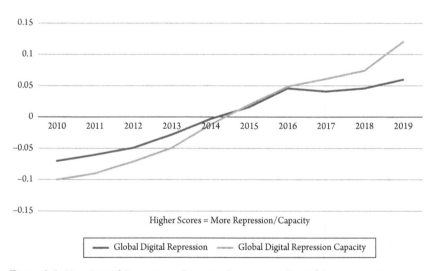

Higher Scores = More Repression/Capacity

——— Global Digital Repression   ——— Global Digital Repression Capacity

Figure 3.5 How Digital Repression Capacity Compares to Digital Repression in Practice, 2010 to 2019

have improved their domestic digital capabilities. This marks a crucial turning point for the spread of digital repression. Technology is getting cheaper and capabilities are becoming easier for less advanced countries to replicate. This progression means that we should expect to see a continued expansion of states' abilities to use sophisticated instruments for repressive political purposes.

Breaking down digital repression and capacity trends by democratic and autocratic regime types yields further insights. Digital repression deployed by democracies systematically lags behind their capacity for digital repression. In other words, democracies have the means to deploy a full array of digital repression techniques but refrain from doing so. Conversely, the deployment of digital repression tools in autocracies continues to outpace domestic capacity. One outcome is that many autocracies turn to external suppliers to close the gap between what they are capable of producing or carrying out and what their programs of repression demand. Presumably, if outside sources of repressive support were curtailed, then digital repression in autocracies might also diminish. That being said, in certain sectors, autocracies appear to be making significant strides in developing national capacity to meet repression demands—such as the degree to which autocracies censor political information by filtering online content. In addition, as technology becomes more affordable, it is only a matter of time before dramatically cheaper products that can facilitate digital repression will come onto the marketplace.

A second outcome stemming from the enactment/capacity gap is that many autocracies choose to deploy lower-capacity tactics, particularly Internet shutdowns, which require less expertise than more sophisticated instruments. Rather than making up their capacity gap through imports, governments instead choose to deploy less advanced tools—a trend that has played out in countries like Ethiopia, Sudan, and Tajikistan.[16]

As policymakers consider different ways to limit the spread of intrusive digital tools, the deployment/capacity gap in autocratic countries means that regulatory approaches like export controls could have a positive impact. At the same time, there is a risk that stringent controls may backfire—they could incentivize autocratic regimes to upgrade their digital repression capabilities, or convince such regimes to turn toward authoritarian suppliers like China or Russia, or simply encourage states to substitute out advanced digital tools for simpler ones.

Unpacking the Digital Repression Gap

If we break down the digital repression index into its component parts, autocratic regimes continue to demonstrate higher levels of digital repression than democracies across the board. Figure 3.6 shows a clear gap between

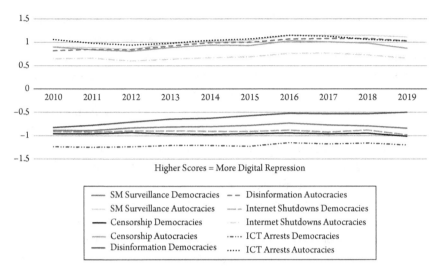

Higher Scores = More Digital Repression

—— SM Surveillance Democracies	– – Disinformation Autocracies
······ SM Surveillance Autocracies	— – Internet Shutdowns Democracies
—— Censorship Democracies	······ Intermet Shutdowns Autocracies
—— Censorship Autocracies	·–··· ICT Arrests Democracies
—— Disinformation Democracies	····· ICT Arrests Autocracies

Figure 3.6 Digital Repression Gap between Democracies and Autocracies, 2010 to 2019

autocratic and democratic states for all five DSP digital repression variables (2010–19).

Autocracies rely most prominently on three techniques: social media surveillance, social manipulation and disinformation, and arresting online users for political content. This trend holds true for much of the entire ten-year period. Strong autocratic reliance on these techniques should not come as a surprise. Arresting dissidents, journalists, and activists for posted online content is closely linked to conventional repression strategies. Extending political persecutions to Internet activities is hardly a stretch for autocratic regimes to enact. Likewise, social media surveillance is not terribly difficult to deploy and it provides an abundance of useful information about political opponents.[17] A multitude of autocratic regimes, from China and Russia to Vietnam and Pakistan are deploying advanced social surveillance capabilities in order to "analyze, evaluate, and categorize millions of social media posts."[18]

In democracies, social manipulation and disinformation represents the most widely used digital repression technique. As the Chapter 5 case study on the Philippines explores, it presents a valuable alternative for illiberal leaders in democracies who may have a limited ability to constrain political liberties. The next most commonly used digital tool in democracies is social media surveillance. While there is a lower likelihood that democracies will rely upon social media surveillance to enact repressive policies, law enforcement agencies are using these techniques with minimal oversight, accountability, or transparency.

As the next sections show, there is significant variance regarding which digital methods autocratic leaders (as well as many democratic leaders) choose to implement. The following sections will examine each of the five primary repressive techniques in turn: (1) surveillance, (2) censorship, (3) social manipulation and disinformation, (4) Internet shutdowns, and (5) arrests of online users for political content.

Surveillance

Government reliance on social media surveillance has increased dramatically in recent years, mirroring the growth of online-based protest movements. Social media surveillance refers to "the collection and processing of personal data pulled from digital communication platforms, often through automated technology that allows for real-time aggregation, organization, and analysis of large amounts of metadata and content."[19] Such surveillance takes a myriad of forms—from government agents individually penetrating closed chat groups to automated programs monitoring millions of communications for specific keywords. Increasingly, the trend is for governments to implement sophisticated programs (often paired with human monitors) to improve their ability to track online-based threats to the regime. Social media surveillance has become such a concern that Freedom on the Net's 2019 report focused primarily on how social media has developed into a "conduit for surveillance and electoral manipulation."[20] An array of both autocratic and democratic countries are aggressively employing social media surveillance strategies.

China, for example, is a global leader of social media surveillance. Chinese firms such as Semptian and Meiya Pico offer state agents powerful capabilities for systematically monitoring texts, chats, posts, emails, and other electronic communications (Semptian, for example, claims its Aegis system presently monitors over two hundred million Chinese citizens—representing a quarter of its Internet users).[21] Likewise, Pakistan signed an $18.5 million contract with US firm Sandvine to build a "nationwide web monitoring system" that relies on deep packet inspection to analyze "all incoming and outgoing Internet traffic" from the country (the same technology Sandvine has also provided to Belarus).[22] Nigeria has appropriated $6.6 million for a "Social Media Mining Suite" and has previously directed the military to track online antigovernment content. Israeli firms Verint and WebIntPro have "reportedly sold similar surveillance software to Angola and Kenya, respectively."[23] In Bangladesh, the government appropriated $14 million to its notorious Rapid Action Battalion to implement "location based social network monitoring system software," and even sent personnel to the United States for specific training in its use.[24] Meanwhile, Kazakh authorities purchased a $4.3 million "automated monitoring tool" to allow government authorities to track political discontent on social media.[25]

Liberal democracies are also getting into the game.[26] While their surveillance activities are less tied to repressive objectives, they still demonstrate troubling aspects. For one, many advanced technologies adopted for surveillance purposes are not yet well understood, contain significant deficiencies, or are highly intrusive. Technologist Roger McNamee describes the problem well: "The flaws of new products like facial recognition and AI are not inevitable; they result from a culture that ships products at the earliest possible moment, without consideration for the impact on the people who use or are affected by them."[27] In addition, the design logic of this technology, whether smartphones or social media platforms, is oriented toward maximizing the collection of user data with little oversight or transparency. Because smartphone apps and phone carriers accumulate a surprising amount of information on a user's physical location and activity on their devices, democratic governments frequently piggyback on market-based surveillance models.

US law enforcement agencies have been especially active in acquiring an assortment of automated technologies to collect and examine personal information. During the Black Lives Matter protests, for example, AI startup Dataminr scanned the contents of millions of social media posts, forwarding crucial information to police departments so agents could track and surveil demonstrators.[28] In early 2020, the *New York Times* documented how a startup, Clearwater AI, scraped billions of personal images from social media sites—Facebook, YouTube, and Twitter—and provided paid services to US law enforcement officials "to solve shoplifting, identity theft, credit card fraud, murder and child sexual exploitation cases."[29] Firms such as Palantir and Israeli company Cellebrite have signed contracts with Immigration and Customs Enforcement and Customs and Border Protection to provide social media search capabilities for individuals of interest.[30] Other democracies, such as the United Kingdom and France, are also ramping up their law enforcement capabilities to monitor the social media communications of millions of individuals.

Autocracies are more likely to acquire and deploy social media surveillance than democracies. A simple linear regression using V-Dem's electoral democracy index as the explanatory variable and DSP's government social media monitoring as the outcome variable shows a moderate fit: 65 percent of the variability of social media monitoring is explained by the electoral democracy index (regression tables for each of the five components are listed in Appendix 2). Nonetheless, among democracies, reliance on social media surveillance is a preferred digital tactic, second only to social manipulation and disinformation. Table 3.4 shows the ten worst-performing countries in 2019 when it comes to levels of social media surveillance, measured by DSP. (Note that I modified the

Table 3.4 Countries with the Highest Social Media Surveillance Levels in 2019

Country	Region	Govt. social media surveillance score	Social media penetration (% of pop.)[a]	V-Dem electoral democracy index	V-Dem regime type[b]	Digital repression global ranking
Qatar	MENA	2.656	0.99	0.091	CA	15
United Arab Emirates	MENA	2.427	0.99	0.101	CA	3
Saudi Arabia	MENA	2.324	0.72	0.023	CA	4
China	EAP	2.061	0.72	0.083	CA	1
Oman	MENA	1.589	0.56	0.185	CA	21
Bahrain	MENA	1.475	0.84	0.118	CA	6
Cuba	WHA	1.420	0.55	0.203	CA	12
Turkey	EUR	1.4	0.64	0.292	EA	11
Venezuela	WHA	1.399	0.42	0.229	EA	8
Singapore	EAP	1.342	0.79	0.398	EA	71

Note: Observations: 179. Min: −1.779. Max: 2.656. Mean: −0.018. Standard deviation: 0.758.

[a] "Complete Report Library," *DataReportal*, 2020, https://datareportal.com/library.

[b] CA: closed autocracy; EA: electoral autocracy.

2019 DSP social media surveillance variable to incorporate an interaction with social media penetration.)

The list elicits few surprises. Three of the Gulf States—Qatar, UAE, and Saudi Arabia—top the list. They are net importers of surveillance technology and are well-known customers of advanced surveillance packages provided by Western firms and Chinese companies. None of the listed countries are classified as democracies, although Singapore stands as an outlier—its overall digital repression ranking is significantly lower than other countries in the table. Democracies with the highest levels of social media surveillance are Mauritius and Colombia (ranked eighteenth and nineteenth respectively). The countries with the least amount of government social media surveillance belong to a standard group of liberal democracies: Costa Rica, Sweden, Iceland, and Cyprus.

DSP does not provide an analytic measurement of physical surveillance measures (such as AI and big-data techniques, which the book examines in Chapter 7), nor does it evaluate governments using targeted surveillance tools. Accordingly, I compiled an inventory of commercial spyware use with a focus on three overarching questions: First, which governments show evidence of procuring and employing commercial spyware against domestic actors? Second, which private sector companies are involved? Third, are the operations being carried out pursuant to a repressive agenda—do they violate "principles of legality, necessity, proportionality and legitimacy in objective?"[31]

To explore these questions, I relied on source material from the Citizen Lab, Freedom on the Net, Privacy International, the Council on Foreign Relations' Cyber Operations Tracker (CFR), and the Electronic Frontier Foundation (EFF). I supplemented this source material with information from major print and news media outlets (e.g., the *New York Times, Reuters, Haaretz, Financial Times*, and the *Wall Street Journal*). Because of attribution challenges and the difficulty of pinpointing intrusion operations within a specified time frame, I aggregated observations between 2011 and 2020.

My data collection and analysis indicate that at least sixty-four countries worldwide employ commercial spyware against domestic actors—typically political opponents, civil society activists, independent journalists, or regime critics. Given the clandestine nature of this tool, this figure may undercount the true number of countries relying on such techniques. The majority of these governments are authoritarian, comprising forty-three countries, or 67 percent of the total. The full table is listed in Appendix 3. It can also be accessed online with corresponding source links at http://dx.doi.org/10.17632/csvhpkt8tm.2.[32]

How does spyware work? In Pakistan, for instance, Amnesty International published a 2018 report documenting a comprehensive, state-sponsored operation targeting civil society networks and human rights defenders "for the purpose of gaining social capital within activist communities and ultimately convincing specific targets to download malicious surveillance technologies and malwares."[33] The operation used four methods of attack: creating a network of fake social media profiles that used social engineering to deliver spyware to targeted activists; using phishing techniques to steal Google and Facebook login credentials from activists; deploying a malware program known as Crimson that would subject activists to "extensive and long-term digital surveillance"; and employing custom-built Android spyware called StealthAgent to "intercept phone calls and messages, steal pictures, and track victims' locations once installed."[34] In a country where civil society is already under extreme duress, such attacks further imperil the activist community.

Leading firms include NSO Group (Israel), Hacking Team (Italy), Cyberbit (subsidiary of Israel's Elbit Systems), FinFisher (part of UK/Germany-based Gamma Group), and Blue Coat Systems (United States). A large number of companies are headquartered in Israel. In a comprehensive global survey of private surveillance companies, Privacy International noted that twenty-seven firms operate out of Israel, giving it the "largest amount per capita, with 0.33 companies per 100,000 people located in Israel, compared to 0.04 in the United States and 0.16 in the United Kingdom."[35] Its companies reportedly account for between 10 and 20 percent of the worldwide cyber market.[36] But it would also be unfair to exclusively single out Israel. The same Privacy International survey identified 528 firms worldwide that provide a range of private surveillance technology, 87 percent of which are based in OECD countries (e.g., the United Kingdom alone is home to 104 companies).[37]

Censorship

Censorship of websites, social media platforms, chat groups, and related forms of electronic communication are well-trodden digital tactics that are heavily influenced by traditional methods of repression. I averaged two DSP variables— government Internet filtering in practice, and government social media censorship in practice—in order to measure levels of online censorship worldwide. Censorship aligns even more closely with regime type; autocracies are significantly more likely to use this technique than democracies. A simple linear regression shows a moderately strong relationship: 68 percent of the variability of Internet censorship is explained by the V-Dem electoral democracy index ($r^2 = 0.68$).[38] Table 3.5 displays countries with the highest levels of online censorship globally.

There are even fewer surprises with this group. All of the countries here are solidly autocratic, with North Korea's despotic regime once again topping the list. Internet penetration levels for this group are low, with a mean of 38 percent.

Table 3.5 **Countries with the Highest Levels of Online Censorship in 2019**

Country	Region	Censorship score (DSP average)	Internet penetration (% of pop.)	V-Dem electoral democracy index	V-Dem regime type[a]	Digital repression global ranking
North Korea	EAP	4.675	No data	0.099	CA	2
Turkmenistan	SCA	3.401	21.25	0.154	EA	5
United Arab Emirates	MENA	3.008	94.82	0.101	CA	3
China	EAP	2.848	54.3	0.083	CA	1
Tajikistan	SCA	2.658	21.96	0.166	EA	9
South Sudan	AFR	2.506	7.98	0.18	CA	13
Equatorial Guinea	AFR	2.467	26.24	0.18	EA	14
Iran	MENA	2.361	60.42	0.217	EA	7
Eritrea	AFR	2.317	1.31	0.071	CA	17
Cuba	WHA	2.277	49.1	0.203	CA	12

Note: Observations: 179. Min: −1.879. Max: 4.675. Mean: −.041. Standard deviation: 1.36.
[a] CA: closed autocracy; EA: electoral autocracy.

This makes some sense given that the best way to control online access is to prevent the vast majority of citizens from logging on in the first place. The democracy showing the highest levels of online censorship is India; it ranks thirty-fifth globally. The countries with the least amount of online censorship are all European democracies—including the Netherlands, Ireland, Sweden, Denmark, and Slovenia.

Social Manipulation and Disinformation

While prior categories of digital repression closely follow regime type (e.g., autocracies rely more heavily on social media surveillance and censorship than democracies), social manipulation and disinformation present a somewhat different result. Autocratic regimes are still likelier to deploy this tactic, but the gap between autocracies and democracies is narrower. I averaged two DSP variables—government dissemination of false information domestic, and party dissemination of false information domestic—in order to assess global levels of social manipulation and disinformation. A simple linear regression shows a moderate relationship: 59 percent of the variability of social manipulation and disinformation is explained by the electoral democracy index ($r^2 = 0.59$).[39] Figure 3.7 graphically displays the extent to which both democracies and autocracies deployed these techniques in 2019. (Note that I modified the 2019 DSP disinformation variables to incorporate interactions with social media penetration.)

As we can see, two democracies in particular, Colombia and Brazil, register higher social manipulation and disinformation scores than most

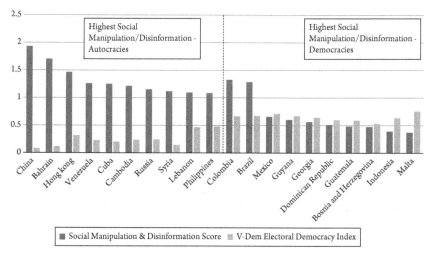

Figure 3.7 Comparison of Social Manipulation and Disinformation Scores for Democracies and Autocracies in 2019

autocracies (due to Bolsonaro's populism and Colombia's history of political conflict). While there remains a gap between autocracies and democracies, it is narrower than for any other digital tactic. In countries like Tunisia, for example, which performs well on most digital governance measurements (ranking 109th globally for levels of digital repression), it is still prone to sizable concentrations of disinformation and misinformation, particularly in conjunction with major events like national elections. Tunisia's 2019 elections featured a deluge of political party and candidate Facebook pages, many of which were "actively involved in spreading political disinformation and sponsored content praising certain parties."[40] A report from the Tunisian Association for the Integrity and Democracy of Elections found that "unofficial Facebook pages with no declared political affiliation or purpose" comprised 38.5 percent of all political messages collected by the survey.[41] This is troubling because unofficial pages are not accountable for what they say, and it is nearly impossible to determine who is sponsoring them: "We do not know whether they are simply run by individuals whose high political conscience dictates that they must get involved during an electoral period or whether there is a strategy behind the creation or the political use of such pages."[42]

In the last few years, a growing number of countries have adopted social manipulation strategies. In their 2019 report on social media manipulation, researchers Samantha Bradshaw and Philip Howard conclude that upwards of seventy countries feature "at least one political party or government agency using social media to shape public attitudes domestically."[43] This development represents a steep rise from 2018, when forty-eight countries displayed evidence of social manipulation, or from 2017, when only twenty-eight countries featured social media manipulation activities. The coronavirus pandemic has further accelerated these numbers. In particular, China, Iran, Russia, and Turkey have taken the lead in disseminating pro-government narratives domestically and anti-democratic messages abroad.[44]

Internet Shutdowns

Internet shutdowns are blunt instruments that are often deployed by countries that lack more sophisticated capabilities to counter mass protest movements, or by leaders anxious to arrest the momentum of escalating demonstrations.[45] As such, Internet shutdowns do not necessarily correlate with states exhibiting the highest levels of repression. Rather, shutdowns tend to be instruments of choice for illiberal or hybrid regimes, such as India, Pakistan, Algeria, and Sudan, or weak regimes with low digital capacity, like the Democratic Republic of the Congo or Yemen.

In 2018 and 2019, India continued to lead the world in Internet shutdowns. Digital rights organization Access Now documented at least 121 shutdown incidences in India in 2019 and 134 shutdowns in 2018.[46] Notably, many of these shutdowns were limited in size and scope. Sixty-two percent of India's 2018 shutdowns were confined to one city, while 36 percent extended to multiple cities but stayed within a single state. Access Now recorded only one shutdown in 2018 that affected more than a single state in the country.[47] India is guided by a statute—Temporary Suspension of Telecom Services (Public Emergency or Public Safety) Rules 2017[14], falling under the 1885 Indian Telegraph Act— that provides legal standards to determine when regulators can order shutdowns. Perversely, this law may actually facilitate recurrent shutdowns in the country. As Access Now observes:

> Countries like India which have laws that facilitate and le- galize shutdowns tend to order more shutdowns. India's current regulations . . . allow temporary Internet shutdowns for "public emer- gency" or "public safety." Such broad and vague grounds for cutting ac- cess can easily lead to misuse or abuse of this shutdown authority, and indeed, year after year, India tops the list globally for the number of disruptions.[48]

For democratic governments that have explicit regulations permitting shutdowns, such guidance may provide sufficient bureaucratic "cover" to jus- tify repeated shutdowns. In contrast, many autocratic governments lack explicit laws governing when shutdowns can occur, and "only rarely provide information about the orders or directive to shut down the Internet, and seldom publicly rec- ognize shutdowns."[49]

Governments in Africa have been especially aggressive in implementing Internet shutdowns, exceeding most other regions. Shutdowns in Africa cu- mulatively lasted nearly eight thousand hours and resulted in $2.1 billion of lost economic activity in 2019—comprising a quarter of total global losses.[50] Jan Rydzak, Moses Karanja, and Nicholas Opiyo observe that three conditions typify Internet shutdowns on the continent. First, states that disrupt network access "are overwhelmingly authoritarian or hybrid regimes." Second, the ac- tors responsible for implementing shutdowns are largely based in the executive branch, and "shutdown orders consistently come from central authorities in the highest echelons of power." This represents a major departure from India, for example, where regional authorities are primarily responsible for executing shutdowns. Third, there is a relationship between a leader's longevity in power and willingness to implement shutdowns—"of the 14 longest-ruling heads of state in Africa as of early 2019, only three—Eritrea's Isaias Afwerki, Djibouti's

Ismaïl Omar Guelleh, and Rwanda's Paul Kagame—had not ordered a shutdown during their time in office, which has ranged from 18 to 25 years."[51]

Overall, autocracies are more prone to deploy Internet shutdowns as a tool in their repressive arsenal. I averaged two DSP variables—government Internet shutdown in practice, and government social media shutdown in practice—in order to measure Internet shutdown levels. The data shows a moderate relationship between Internet shutdowns and regime type ($r^2 = 0.58$).[52]

Methodologically, there are divergences between the DSP Internet shutdown variable and data from other sources, such as Access Now's Shutdown Tracker Optimization Project (STOP). STOP is an event-driven tracker that incorporates quantitative and qualitative data to "record the number of Internet shutdowns in the world in a given year and to characterize the nature of the shutdowns, including their magnitude, scope, and causes."[53] Unlike DSP's measurement, STOP doesn't use an expert survey methodology to determine country performance. Rather, it strives to empirically capture all "recorded instances of shutdowns."[54] Accordingly, STOP provides a valuable empirical window as to which countries display the most shutdown incidences in a given year. But it is less useful in describing the depth, severity, or preemptive impact of shutdown policies.[55] A country with a handful of national shutdowns that have led to inordinate political or financial impact (Iran) ranks higher on DSP's scale than a country featuring numerous shutdowns that are primarily regional (Ethiopia).[56] Likewise, a country such as North Korea, which tops DSP's list, restricts Internet and social media connectivity so thoroughly that it results in the virtual equivalent of a constant, around-the-clock shutdown. Table 3.6 provides a side-by-side comparison of assessments by DSP and STOP data of countries with the most Internet shutdowns in 2019 (shaded countries appear in both indexes).

Another useful shutdown measurement is the NetBlocks Cost of Shutdown Tool (COST). COST estimates the financial harm of Internet shutdowns based on the country, geographic breadth of the shutdown, type of shutdown, and the shutdown length. I incorporated shutdown data from COST and from "The Global Cost of Internet Shutdowns in 2019" report.[57] The ten most financially damaging Internet shutdowns in 2019 are listed in Table 3.7.

An important takeaway from this data is that despite the fact that India leads the world in shutdown incidences, the aggregate cost of its shutdowns (many of which are locally based) lagged behind national shutdowns in Iraq and Sudan. The financial impact of shutting down the Internet, even for short periods of time, is significant. Four countries—Iraq, Sudan, India, Venezuela—registered losses in the billion due to their shutdowns.

Most of these countries have moderate to robust levels of Internet penetration (ranging from 30 percent to 64 percent), which explains why persistent shutdowns bring such high economic costs. Chad stands as the lone exception.

Table 3.6 **Countries with the Most Internet Shutdowns in 2019**

DSP government internet shutdowns		STOP shutdown index	
Country	*Shutdown score*	*Country*	*Shutdown incidences*
North Korea	4.379	India	121
Turkmenistan	3.363	Venezuela	12
South Sudan	3.002	Yemen	11
India	2.697	Iraq	8
Chad	2.66	Algeria	6
Tajikistan	2.655	Pakistan	5
Eritrea	2.527	Ethiopia	4
Saudi Arabia	2.288	Sudan	3
China	2.277	Sri Lanka	3
Gabon	2.238	Iran	3
Bahrain	2.231	Russia	3
Venezuela	2.124	Bangladesh	3
Iran	2.047	Indonesia	3
Burkina Faso	2.007	Kazakhstan	3

Table 3.7 **Most Economically Damaging Internet Shutdowns in 2019**

Country	*Shutdown duration (hours)*	*Cost (millions)*	*Internet penetration (% of pop.)*
Iraq	263	$2,319.5	49.7
Sudan	1,560	$1,866.3	30.9
India	4,196	$1,329.8	34.5
Venezuela	171	$1,072.6	64.3
Iran	240	$611.7	60.4
Algeria	50	$199.8	47.7
Indonesia	416	$187.7	32.3
Chad	4,728	$125.9	6.5
Sri Lanka	337	$83.9	34.1
Myanmar	4,880	$75.2	30.7

With an Internet penetration rate of just 6.5 percent, a scant portion of its citizens benefit from online access. The Chadian government's actions to curtail Internet use is mostly geared toward preempting elite challenges—that is, those who possess sufficient resources to enable online access in the first place.

Arrests of Online Users for Political Content

The final digital repression technique is government persecution of citizens for online political content—the extent to which state authorities arrest citizens for publishing content that runs afoul of government interests or policies. This category of repression displays the highest correlation to regime type; autocracies are substantially more likely to use this technique than democracies. A simple linear regression shows a moderately strong relationship: 74 percent of the variability of V-Dem's arrests of online users for political content variable is explained by the electoral democracy index ($r^2 = 0.74$).[58] Table 3.8 displays the worst-performing countries.

For the first time, Burundi tops this list. It is joined by stalwarts such as North Korea, Syria, Bahrain, and Tajikistan. Democracies that perform the worst on this indicator, such as Senegal, Côte d'Ivoire, and India, display scores that are significantly improved from their autocratic counterparts (for example, Senegal and India score 1.8 and 1.5, respectively).

Conclusion

To summarize, across the board, autocracies display higher levels of digital repression than democracies, indicating that traditional repression is closely linked to digital repression strategies. I began by presenting two composite scores: a latent construct of digital repression, and a latent construct of digital repression capacity. I investigated which specific types of repression were most predictive of digital repression enactment.

Overall, I found that a government's curtailment of political civil liberties was the strongest predictor of digital repression. This finding confirms the idea that in many countries, digital repression serves as a substitute for harder strategies of political control.

Next, when I examined the relationship between digital repression and digital repression capacity, the data showed that repression capacity lags repression enactment in autocracies, but that this relationship reverses in democracies. In other words, autocracies pursue digital repression strategies beyond what their capabilities allow—forcing them to make up this gap, frequently through

Table 3.8 Countries with the Highest Rates of Arrest for Online Content in 2019

Country	Region	DSP online arrests score	Internet penetration (% of pop.)	V-DEM electoral democracy index[a]	V-DEM regime type	Digital repression global ranking
Burundi	AF	3.19	5.59	0.162	EA	35
North Korea	EAP	3.039	—	0.099	CA	2
Syria	MENA	2.947	34.25	0.145	CA	10
Bahrain	MENA	2.738	95.88	0.118	CA	6
Equatorial Guinea	AF	2.728	26.24	0.18	EA	14
United Arab Emirates	MENA	2.717	94.82	0.101	CA	3
Yemen	MENA	2.682	26.72	0.123	CA	16
Tajikistan	SCA	2.364	21.96	0.166	EA	9
Qatar	MENA	2.31	95.94	0.091	CA	15
South Sudan	AF	2.238	7.98	0.18	CA	13

Note: Observations: 179. Min: −2.46. Max: 3.19. Mean: −0.059. Standard deviation: 1.53

[a] CA: closed autocracy; EA: electoral autocracy.

external assistance. Conversely, digital repression capacity in democracies outstrips enactment, indicating that democracies choose not to deploy the excess digital repression capabilities that they possess. The implication of this data is that many autocracies rely heavily on outside suppliers and service providers to operate sophisticated surveillance programs and cyber operations. As a result, it is incumbent upon policymakers to consider whether tightening export restrictions for these technologies is warranted.

Finally, when I examined specific components of digital repression to determine how and why certain countries adopt particular digital tactics over others, I found that autocracies and democracies digitally repress in divergent ways, and that among autocracies there is significant variance regarding which digital methods they pursue. Generally, autocracies are disposed to rely on social media surveillance and arrests of online users as preferred techniques. In contrast, democracies rely on social media manipulation and disinformation—and to a lesser degree on social medial surveillance—when carrying out digital repression.

Notes

1. Weidmann and Rød, *Internet and Political Protest*, 139.
2. Crete-Nishihata et al., "Communities @ Risk."
3. Another index that closely aligns with this project is Freedom on the Net (FOTN). It evaluates sixty-five countries on an annual basis—using expert surveys—on their online freedom performance. But for my purposes, the report has a few limitations. First, while the sixty-five surveyed countries represent 88 percent of the global Internet population, it still leaves crucial parts of the world unassessed. Second, FOTN heavily focuses on Internet-related issues with less emphasis on other digital techniques, such as physical surveillance technologies. Third, only a limited amount of statistical analysis can be undertaken using FOTN variables (in contrast to comprehensive statistical indices available from V-Dem).
4. Mechkova et al., *Digital Society Project Dataset v2*. See also Valeriya Mechkova et al., "Measuring Internet Politics: Introducing the Digital Society Project," Digital Society Project (DSP), 2019; Michael Coppedge et al., "V-Dem Methodology v10," V-Dem Project, 2020; Daniel Pemstein et al., "The V-Dem Measurement Model: Latent Variable Analysis for Cross-National and Cross-Temporal Expert-Coded Data," V-Dem Working Paper no. 21, 5th ed., University of Gothenburg: Varieties of Democracy Institute, 2020.
5. All data from V-Dem is compiled from Coppedge et al., "V-Dem Dataset v10."
6. Steve Feldstein, "Digital Repression Index 2010–19", Mendeley Data, V1, 2020, doi: 10.17632/rrnz8p6rvw.1.
7. The other variables in the index, related censorship, Internet shutdowns, and arrests of online users, do not exhibit the same relationship to Internet access or social media penetration. For example, even if a small percentage of a population has Internet access, this doesn't necessarily mean that censorship or shutdown strategies aren't relevant. In fact, low Internet access may be a direct result of excessive state censorship and network disruptions that discourage households from obtaining Internet access in the first place.
8. Steven Feldstein, "2019 Digital Repression Index", Mendeley Data, V1, 2020, doi: 10.17632/5dnfmtgbfs.1.
9. Mechkova et al., *Digital Society Project Dataset v2*.

10. Mechkova et al., *Digital Society Project Dataset v2.*

11. Feldstein, "Digital Repression Index 2010–19."

12. Michael Coppedge et al., "V-Dem Codebook v9," Varieties of Democracy (V-Dem) Project, 2019, 39.

13. I tested a number of other relationships to the digital repression index as well: GDP per capita, Internet penetration levels, social media penetration levels, technological capacity. None showed statistically significant relationships.

14. For purposes of this book, I use the same country-regional breakdown as the US State Department (https://2009-2017.state.gov/countries//index.htm). One of the main differences between the State Department's classification and regional classifications from other agencies is that the Africa region does not include countries in North Africa (Algeria, Egypt, Libya, Morocco, Tunisia). Instead, these countries are included in the "Near East" region.

15. Erica Frantz, Andrea Kendall-Taylor, and Joseph Wright, "Digital Repression in Autocracies," V-Dem Users Working Paper Series, 2020, https://www.v-dem.net/media/filer_public/18/d8/18d8fc9b-3ff3-44d6-a328-799dc0132043/digital-repression17mar.pdf, 8.

16. Frantz, Kendall-Taylor, and Wright, "Digital Repression in Autocracies," 8.

17. Adrian Shahbaz and Allie Funk, "Social Media Surveillance," Freedom House, 2019, https://www.freedomonthenet.org/report/freedom-on-the-net/2019/the-crisis-of-social-media/social-media-surveillance.

18. Shahbaz and Funk, "Social Media Surveillance."

19. Shahbaz and Funk, "Social Media Surveillance."

20. Shahbaz and Funk, "Social Media Surveillance."

21. Celia Chen and Meng Jing, "What You Need to Know about Meiya Pico, China's Low-Profile Forensics Champion Named in Data Privacy Scandal," *South China Morning Post*, July 9, 2019, https://www.scmp.com/tech/start-ups/article/3017688/what-you-need-know-about-meiya-pico-chinas-low-profile-forensics; Shahbaz and Funk, "Social Media Surveillance."

22. Umer Ali and Ramsha Jahangir, "Pakistan Moves to Install Nationwide 'Web Monitoring System,'" *Coda Story*, October 24, 2019, https://codastory.com/authoritarian-tech/surveillance/pakistan-nationwide-web-monitoring/.

23. Shahbaz and Funk, "Social Media Surveillance."

24. "Updated—amid Crackdown in Bangladesh, Government Forces Continue Spytech Shopping Spree," Privacy International, July 30, 2019, https://privacyinternational.org/long-read/2226/updated-amid-crackdown-bangladesh-government-forces-continue-spytech-shopping-spree.

25. Shahbaz and Funk, "Social Media Surveillance."

26. Parts of this section are taken from previously published material by the author, including Steven Feldstein and David Wong, "New Technologies, New Problems—Troubling Surveillance Trends in America," *Just Security*, August 6, 2020, https://www.justsecurity.org/71837/new-technologies-new-problems-troubling-surveillance-trends-in-america/.

27. Roger McNamee, "Dear Joe Biden: Don't Listen to Silicon Valley," *Wired*, July 9, 2020, https://www.wired.com/story/opinion-dear-joe-biden-dont-listen-to-silicon-valley/.

28. Sam Biddle, "Police Surveilled George Floyd Protests with Help from Twitter-Affiliated Startup Dataminr," *The Intercept*, July 9, 2020, https://theintercept.com/2020/07/09/twitter-dataminr-police-spy-surveillance-black-lives-matter-protests/.

29. Kashmir Hill, "The Secretive Company That May End Privacy as We Know It," *New York Times*, January 18, 2020, https://www.nytimes.com/2020/01/18/technology/clearview-privacy-facial-recognition.html.

30. Electronic Frontier Foundation, "Freedom of Information Act Appeal," May 14, 2012, https://www.eff.org/files/filenode/foia__20120808155244.pdf.

31. David Kaye, "Report of the Special Rapporteur on the Promotion and Protection of the Right to Freedom of Opinion and Expression, David Kaye," Human Rights Council 29th Session (United Nations Office of the High Commissioner for Human Rights), May 22, 2015, http://www.ohchr.org/EN/Issues/FreedomOpinion/Pages/CallForSubmission.aspx.

32. Steven Feldstein, "Commercial Spyware Global Inventory," Mendeley Data, V2, 2020, doi: 10.17632/csvhpkt8tm.2.

33. "Human Rights under Surveillance: Digital Threats against Human Rights Defenders in Pakistan," Amnesty International, 2018, https://www.amnesty.org/download/Documents/ASA3383662018ENGLISH.PDF.

34. "Human Rights under Surveillance," Amnesty International.

35. "The Global Surveillance Industry," Privacy International, July 2016, https://privacyinternational.org/sites/default/files/2017-12/global_surveillance_0.pdf.

36. Hagar Shezaf and Jonathan Jacobson, "Revealed: Israel's Cyber-spy Industry Helps World Dictators Hunt Dissidents and Gays," *Haaretz*, October 20, 2018, https://www.haaretz.com/israel-news/.premium.MAGAZINE-israel-s-cyber-spy-industry-aids-dictators-hunt-dissidents-and-gays-1.6573027.

37. "The Global Surveillance Industry," Privacy International.

38. I used V-Dem's electoral democracy index as the explanatory variable, and Internet censorship as the outcome variable (a composite indicator derived from two DSP variables—government Internet filtering in practice and government social media censorship in practice) for the regression analysis.

39. When running the regression analysis, I used V-Dem's electoral democracy index as the explanatory variable and social manipulation as the outcome variable (a composite indicator derived from two DSP variables—government dissemination of false information domestic and party dissemination of false information domestic).

40. Yosr Jouini, "Ahead of Tunisia Elections, Social Media Was Flooded with Mis- and Disinformation," Global Voices, October 21, 2019, https://globalvoices.org/2019/10/21/how-misinformation-and-disinformation-disrupted-tunisias-2019-elections/.

41. "Monitoring of Electoral Campaigning on Social Media—Tunisia," Democracy Reporting International, September 2019, https://democracy-reporting.org/wp-content/uploads/2019/09/20190911_Tunisia_Social_Media_Monitoring_Report_One_ENG_FINAL.pdf.

42. "Monitoring of Electoral Campaigning," Democracy Reporting International.

43. Samantha Bradshaw and Philip N. Howard, "The Global Disinformation Disorder: 2019 Global Inventory of Organised Social Media Manipulation," Working Paper 2019.2, Oxford: Project on Computational Propaganda, 2019.

44. Jonathan Bright et al., "Coronavirus Coverage by State-Backed English-Language News Sources: Understanding Chinese, Iranian, Russian and Turkish Government Media," Data Memo 2020.2., Oxford: Project on Computational Propaganda, comprop.oii.ox.ac.uk.

45. See, for example, Kumar, "Shutting Down the Internet."

46. Taye, "Targeted, Cut Off."

47. Taye, "State of Internet Shutdowns."

48. Taye, "State of Internet Shutdowns."

49. Taye, "State of Internet Shutdowns."

50. Yomi Kazeem, "Internet and Social Media Shutdowns Cost African Economies over $2 Billion in 2019," *Quartz Africa*, January 16, 2020, https://qz.com/africa/1785609/internet-shutdowns-in-africa-cost-2-billion-in-2019/.

51. Rydzak, Karanja, and Opiyo, "Internet Shutdowns in Africa," 24.

52. I ran a simple linear regression using V-Dem's electoral democracy index as the explanatory variable, and Internet shutdowns as the outcome variable (an average of two DSP variables—government Internet shutdown in practice, and government social media shutdown in practice). The analysis shows that 61 percent of the variability of government Internet shutdowns is explained by the electoral democracy index.

53. "Updates," Access Now, June 12, 2018, https://www.accessnow.org/cms/assets/uploads/2018/06/Read-Me_-How-to-view-the-Access-Now-Internet-Shutdown-Tracker-Jun-2018.pdf.

54. "Updates," Access Now.

55. Another explanation for differences between DSP and STOP rankings is that there is significant clustering in DSP's scale. When standard deviations are incorporated, distinctions between countries in particular clusters become less meaningful—i.e., there is not a meaningful difference between Country X (ranked third worst for Internet shutdowns) and Country Y (ranked fifteenth worst for Internet shutdowns).

56. It is also worth noting that many countries cluster within DSP's margin of error, particularly near the top of the scale, limiting the utility of providing an ordered global ranking for their shutdown variable.

57. Woodhams and Migliano, "Global Cost of Internet Shutdowns."

58. I used V-Dem's electoral democracy index as the explanatory variable, and Internet censorship as the outcome variable (a composite indicator derived from two DSP variables—government Internet filtering in practice and government social media censorship in practice) for the regression analysis.

4

Thailand's Strategy of Control

After five years of military rule, Thailand held national elections in 2019. I arrived in the country about six weeks after voting had taken place, but before the parliament had formally selected the next prime minister. Since a military coup in 2014, General Prayuth Chan-o-cha had led the country. In the elections, his political party, the pro-military Palang Pracharath Party (PRP), won enough seats to enable Prayuth to become prime minister.[1] In the course of rubber-stamping Prayuth's victory, a wrinkle arose: the emergence of a new party, the Future Forward Party (FFP), fronted by telegenic billionaire Thanathorn Juangroongruangkit. FFP had captivated much of the country, particularly Thailand's youth. At only forty-two years old, Thanathorn is handsomely athletic, with short, spiked hair and a preference for open-shirt suits. His family made its wealth running Thailand's largest car parts manufacturer. Yet despite his pedigree, Thailand's political establishment viewed him as an outsider.[2] When Thanathorn launched FFP, he proclaimed that he might have been born "from the 1 per cent, but I represent the 99 per cent," prompting some local journalists to refer to him as the "billionaire peasant."[3]

Future Forward represented a very different political movement than the country had previously seen. For one, the party's primary method of organizing took place online. Unlike other opposition parties, such as former prime minister Thaksin Shinawatra's Pheu Thai Party, Future Forward eschewed traditional political organizing in favor of social media: it used Facebook groups to coordinate campaign rallies, Twitter hashtags to promote political messages, and Instagram posts to encourage peers to vote. Consequently, millions of young voters were mobilized as Future Forward cast itself as the party of liberal values and dissent.[4]

In the 2019 elections, FFP encountered unexpected success. Propelled by a surging youth vote, savvy online campaigning, and a clear message of change, Future Forward claimed eighty-one parliamentary seats, far exceeding its projected totals. Both during his campaign and following the election, Thanathorn came out swinging against Thailand's military-royalist establishment (see Figure 4.1).

The Rise of Digital Repression. Steven Feldstein, Oxford University Press (2021). © Oxford University Press.
DOI: 10.1093/oso/9780190057497.003.0004

Figure 4.1 Thanathorn Campaigning to an Adoring Crowd in Thailand

He called for ending junta rule, railed against the 2017 military-backed constitution, and argued for eliminating "the repercussions of the coup."[5] In a live, televised debate, Thanathorn aggressively challenged the Thai army chief, asking if he would dare to attack the Thai legislature: "Would you shoot us, all 500 of us?"[6]

The junta wasn't pleased. The government started to deploy tactics taken directly from the repression toolkit against Future Forward. It issued a barrage of lawsuits designed to thwart Thanathorn's candidacy and hamstring Future Forward. Citing Thailand's Computer Crime Act (CCA), the state charged him with criticizing the junta during a "Facebook Live broadcast."[7] It accused him of sedition, alleging that he "provided assistance" to 2014 protests against the military coup.[8] It tried to prosecute him for spreading fake news after he shared an item that slammed General Prawit Wongsuwan, then Thailand's minister of defense, for allegedly spending twelve thousand baht (approximately $380) on a cup of coffee.[9] There was little doubt that the government was prepared to use every instrument at its disposal to hamstring, discredit, and silence Thanathorn. Sure enough, in February 2020, Thailand's constitutional court formally dissolved FFP and prohibited its leadership from participating in politics for ten years (it also paved the way for future criminal charges against Thanathorn).[10]

While the court's decision may have truncated FFP's political future, the sentiments unleashed by FFP have only gained in momentum. By the summer of 2020, mass protests returned—organized largely along generational lines.[11]

Student activists are demanding constitutional reforms and new elections, and they are explicitly pushing back against royal power. They come from all corners of Thai society, including elite families that have formed the traditional base of support for the royalist-military establishment. As commentator James Row writes, "Current protesters hail from families that were staunchly pro-establishment and anti-Thaksin during the Bhumipol era. But rather than back royalist and military authority efforts to marginalize electoral authority like past generations, they are now flat-out rejecting the twin pillars of the Thai state."[12]

Just as Future Forward's political organizing relied on online methods, the current protests are also heavily reliant on the Internet to mobilize activists. Consequently, we can expect that as Thailand continues to experience political convulsions, the state's use of digital methods to constrain this new political movement will only intensify. Already Thai authorities have forced Facebook to block a private group with one million members—Royalist Marketplace—due to its criticisms of the monarchy.[13] What digital repression currently looks like in Thailand, how the government intends to carry out future repression, and the political implications of the escalating digital struggle are the focus of this chapter.

Thailand's situation offers insights into how an autocratic state with a tradition of censorship and political suppression has adapted to a new digital environment. The Thai government has adeptly paired new information controls with old repressive methods, giving the state potent capabilities to control dissent. Thailand also demonstrates how digital repression is born from and develops out of internal drivers; external actors have only limited influence in shaping the state's digital strategies.

I will investigate three sets of questions related to Thailand's digital repression.

First, why is the Thai government expanding its reliance on digital repression? What factors are responsible for the Thai state's increased use of digital tools? I argue that three conditions are critical in creating this situation: long-standing military-bureaucratic repression, established censorship practices, and political challenges due to heightened online communication and social media.

Second, how is the Thai state implementing its digital repression strategy? I contend that, first and foremost, Thailand's program of digital repression is characterized by an emphasis on strategies of control—taking actions particularly focused on censorship, surveillance, formal and informal pressure on relevant tech companies, and the targeted persecution of online users.

Third, to what extent is China influencing the enactment of digital repression in Thailand? I propose that while China's influence is significant in Thailand, the Thai government consciously balances Chinese interests with those of other countries—including the United States. Ultimately, the scope of digital repression in Thailand is more a product of internal dynamics and domestic drivers than the result of a concerted Chinese program to proliferate advanced authoritarian technology.

My research in Thailand led to some unexpected insights.

First, the government is both lenient and harsh in how it chooses to deploy digital repression. The vast majority of Thais have access to a wide variety of information—particularly juxtaposed with comparable regimes in the region. While the government blocks certain websites that contain prohibited content—largely related to the monarchy or to gambling/pornography—and monitors what people say (particularly Thai "influencers"), the Thai state generally leaves the bulk of its citizens alone. I repeatedly heard both civil society activists and government officials insist that "we are not China," and that they have no desire to go in China's direction. However, for a special category of people whom the regime views as a threat, it is adopting increasingly hardline tactics. In the past year, Thai pro-democracy activist Wanchalearm "Tar" Satsaksit, a fierce critic of the military and monarchy, was abducted by unidentified gunmen in Cambodia, three more activists "vanished" during a trip to Vietnam, and a prominent academic critic, Pavin Chachavalpongpun, was attacked with chemical spray at his home in Japan.[14] This troubling behavior is also occurring within Thailand. Another well-known activist, Anurak "Ford" Jeantawanicha, was assaulted by pipe-wielding pro-government thugs for publishing Facebook posts about planned protests.[15] Likewise, Sirawith "Ja New" Seritiwat was sent to the hospital after being beaten with baseball bats by four men the evening before a planned pro-democracy rally.[16] From time to time, the government also makes examples of ordinary citizens as a pointed reminder of the costs of defying the state.

The government complements its digital repression tools with an extensive set of repressive laws and directives that provide wide discretion to suppress dissent and tamp down challenges to the state. Since 2017, the government has enacted a range of new provisions (supplementing existing lèse-majesté and defamation laws) that criminalize actions that violate public morals or run afoul of national security or public order. These laws represent a transition from an informal system of "door knocking"—used by government agents to carry out surveillance or censorship goals—to more formalized legal repression.

Second, key partners in the government's program of repression are royalist and conservative civil society organizations. Groups such as Social Sanction and the Rubbish Collection Organization have created group pages on Facebook and other social media sites where they "share the personal profiles of alleged lèse majesté offenders" for public bullying. They also report suspected offenders to the police.[17] Among those who are targeted are political opponents (particularly Future Forward members), scholars, journalists, and human rights activists. Reports indicate that the government has trained over one hundred thousand students as part of a "cyber scouts" program intended not only to surveil fellow citizens for lèse-majesté infractions, but also to undertake cyber trolling and harassment of those deemed insufficiently loyal to the state. Regrettably, this behavior indicates that civil society is not always a force for liberalism; at least in Thailand, the state has successfully instrumentalized a portion of civil society to help carry out its repressive agenda.

Third, Thailand's complicated and opaque political system makes it difficult to disentangle exactly what represents official policy and which actors are driving particular agendas. The country's political system is beset by multiple poles of influence and power, many of which are undefined or based on custom or tradition. The evolving role of the monarchy, the start/stop nature of military rule, and the contestation between royalist, establishment, and upstart communities—urban inhabitants versus rural dwellers, young versus old—are all factors that have brought tremendous flux to the country.

Fourth, I had anticipated a higher level of partnership on advanced surveillance techniques (including the use of artificial intelligence) between Chinese companies and the Thai government. While experts have documented growing business links between Sino interests and Prayuth, I encountered scant evidence that Chinese firms are actively disseminating sophisticated surveillance in Thailand. In fact, I was surprised by how much the Thai government is "balancing" its procurement of ICT instruments from a variety of countries, including Israel.

Fifth, the digital repression model advanced by Thailand's government is not unique to the region. Similar efforts are taking place in neighboring countries. Singapore, Cambodia, Myanmar, and Vietnam have all enacted cybercrime legislation to provide legal authorization to suppress dissent. The latest trend has been for governments to enact anti-fake news statutes. These laws provide even greater discretion for state actors to take down content deemed politically threatening. Singapore's bill passed in May 2019; several other governments have drafted similar provisions—including Thailand.[18]

Context of Political Repression in Thailand

State repression, military heavy-handedness, and political interventions by the monarchy are regular features of Thailand's history. Its current political environment continues these troubling trends. Freedom House, for example, ranks Thailand as "partly free," noting that its government uses unchecked powers to constrain political rights, undertake widespread surveillance, and censor and intimidate those who speak out against the regime.[19] Likewise, the US State Department's annual human rights report lists a range of abuses by the Thai government: unlawful killings and torture by government security forces, arbitrary arrests and detentions, widespread censorship and site blocking, and restrictions on political participation.[20]

Globally, Thailand ranks 164th of 179 countries on V-Dem's 2019 electoral democracy index. This global ranking places Thailand near the bottom, classifying it as a closed autocracy. Its ranking on civil liberties (142nd of 179) and level of repression against civil society organizations (136th out of 179) exemplify the Thai state's disregard for political freedoms.[21] Figure 4.2 provides a statistical snapshot of Thailand's performance.

This graph shows that during the past decade Thailand's governance indicators have fluctuated—particularly government repression of civil society—reflecting the country's tumultuous politics. In 2001, Thaksin Shinawatra, who ran on a populist platform, was first elected prime minister. Subsequently, Thais became increasingly polarized into two camps: the "yellow shirts," an assemblage of royalists, ultranationalists, and members of Bangkok's middle class, and Thaksin's "red shirts," who are typically poorer and tend to come from rural areas. In 2006, the first of several military-initiated coups drove Thaksin from power. In subsequent elections, Thaksin's political bloc resoundingly defeated its opponents. Several times, the military stepped in to take back power and push Thaksin's coalition out of office (including cracking down on red shirt protests in 2010 that led to the deaths of over eighty citizens in Bangkok's central business district). Academic Duncan McCargo writes that this adds up to "eight prime ministers, two military coups, five general elections (two of them annulled by the courts), three full-scale constitution-drafting processes, five rounds of widespread and protracted street demonstrations (one culminating in mass violence), and two contentious national referendums."[22] In the most recent

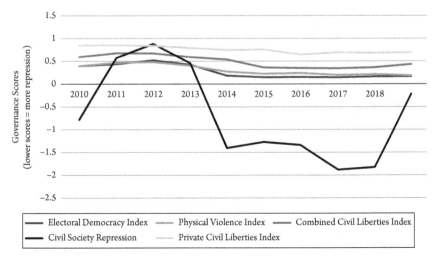

Figure 4.2 Thailand's Performance on Key Governance Indicators, 2010 to 2019

military coup in 2014, the junta forced Thaksin's sister, Yingluck Shinawatra, out of the prime minister's office. Led by Prayuth and operating under the auspices of the National Committee on Security and Order (NCPO), they have run the country ever since.

There is, of course, another wrinkle: the ascendance of a new king for the first time in over seventy years. The monarchy holds an exalted place in Thailand. Alongside religion and the nation, the monarchy is one of the three pillars of Thai society, functioning in close coordination with "traditional military, business and bureaucratic" stakeholders as part of an intricate system of political control.[23] To protect the sanctity of the monarchy, Thailand has one of the strictest lèse-majesté provisions in the world. Under Article 112 of Thailand's criminal code, anyone who "defames, insults or threatens the king, the queen, the heir-apparent or the regent" is subject to a prison sentence between three and fifteen years.[24] This has become an untouchable law: to even suggest that it is being used improperly would be to risk accusations of trying to weaken (or insult) the monarchy. Accordingly, state authorities use lèse-majesté expansively to check would-be challengers—all in the name of the king.

Thailand's new king is a wild card. His reputation is shoddy, including, as the New York Times reports, a taste for "airplanes, fast cars, women and the high life."[25] He lives an opulent and carefree lifestyle and spends a good portion of the year in the small Bavarian town of Feldafing, where he is free to visit pumpkin farms, go strawberry picking, tour the countryside on mountain bikes, and patronize high-end ski resorts.[26]

Many palace insiders expressed grave doubts about Vajiralongkorn's fitness to inherit the throne. Says journalist Andrew Marshall, "Decades of animosity between Vajiralongkorn and the traditional establishment had hardened into vicious mutual loathing."[27] Yet since Bhumibol's death in 2016, Vajiralongkorn has defied expectations. Vajiralongkorn insisted on a provision in the new 2017 constitution that stripped the privy council (specifically longtime royalist adviser Prem Tinsulanonda) of its power to act as regent when he leaves the country. He took personal control of the Crown Property Bureau so that its assets would now be registered under the king's name.[28] And he appointed a member of his personal guard, General Apirat Kongsompong, as the new army chief, cementing his hold on the military. Finally, he imposed a moratorium on the military's use of lèse-majesté to prosecute political opponents—effectively neutering one of the military's "main tools of repression" and allowing him to recapture political power from the junta (however, he subsequently lifted the moratorium in November of 2020 in response to escalating mass protests against the monarchy).[29]

Clearly, Vajiralongkorn is in a powerful position to shape Thailand's political future. His consolidation of authority and continued alliance with the military puts him directly at odds with Thailand's youthful protestors.[30] Vajiralongkorn also faces acute political vulnerabilities. His father, King Bhumibhol, was known as the "people's king" due to his public efforts to improve the livelihood of the rural poor. This image helped Bhumibhol sustain the monarchy's legitimacy.[31] In contrast, Vajiralongkorn's attempts to fortify his power may derive less from a position of strength than from his own concerns about the monarchy's waning influence.

In fact, as democracy protests have escalated in 2020, one of the protestors' key requests has been to curb the king's authority. Activists have laid out a manifesto incorporating ten demands, including scrapping the lèse-majesté laws and removing Vajiralongkorn's control of the $30 billion Crown Property Bureau.[32] Protestors have also publicly disparaged the king, including, as the *New York Times* reported, spray-painting "bus stops and pavement in the capital's central business district with graffiti describing his sexual activity."[33] These developments represent an unprecedented assault on the monarchy's stature and signify a looming struggle ahead.

Given Thailand's high levels of political repression, the regime's embrace of digital instruments to sustain its authority comes as no surprise. My index assigns Thailand a digital repression score of 0.582 for 2019, ranking it fifty-first out of 179 countries for its prevalence of digital repression.[34] Unexpectedly in Southeast Asia, Thailand places in the median, displaying lower rates of digital repression than Cambodia, Vietnam, Laos, and even the Philippines. Nonetheless, the 2020 Freedom on the Net report ranked Thailand "not free" for the seventh year in a row.[35]

Of the five digital repression components measured by the Digital Society Project, Thailand exhibits high levels of social media surveillance (twelfth highest out of 179 countries), social manipulation and disinformation (twenty-sixth highest globally), and online censorship (forty-seventh highest).[36] However, its Internet shutdown rates are low, ranking ninety-second globally. Figure 4.3 provides a breakdown of Thailand's 2019 scores.

If we break down Thailand's performance for each of the five digital repression components across a ten-year period, we can see that in 2014, the year of the military coup, digital repression indicators worsened across the board. In the ensuing years, several techniques have stayed at high levels, such as social media surveillance, censorship, and social manipulation, while others have subsequently declined, particularly arrests of online users (as Figure 4.4 illustrates).

Interestingly, despite a bump in 2014, Internet shutdown levels have otherwise remained low. This trend can be explained, in part, by the tacit bargain formed between military rulers and the country's middle class: citizens will tolerate military rule so long as the authorities refrain from disrupting the wheels of commerce.

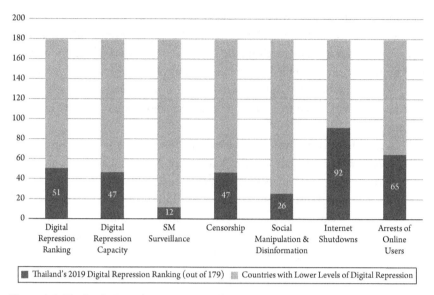

Figure 4.3 Thailand's Digital Repression Performance in 2019

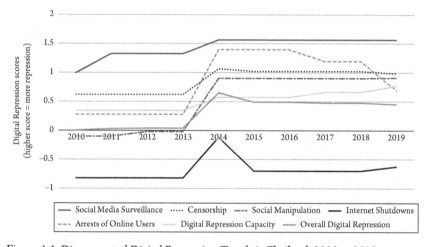

Figure 4.4 Disaggregated Digital Repression Trends in Thailand, 2010 to 2019

Thailand's Network of Digital Repression

Thailand's Internet penetration rate is 53 percent, placing the country in the middle of the pack for Southeast Asia, behind Malaysia and the Philippines, but ahead of Vietnam and Indonesia.[37] Thailand's Internet access places it ninetieth out of 173 countries—close to the median. Social media penetration is a robust 75 percent, ranking it sixteenth globally.[38] Ten Internet exchanges connect

Thailand to international networks; the largest is overseen by state-owned CAT Telecom.

Thailand's Internet and mobile service providers comprise a mixture of state-owned and private sector companies. The three fixed-line operators are True, TT&T, and TOT (state-owned). The main mobile service providers are AIS, DTAC, and True. Of these companies, only DTAC is operated by a foreign entity, Norway's Telenor Group. The other providers are managed by Thai families. From the outset, the Thai government has kept tight control over its Internet structure. Despite the appearance of a market-based system, the government maintains a close relationship with its telecoms—described by Privacy International as a "revolving door," whereby "former politicians or family members hold key positions."[39] This represents a key component of the Thai state's network of control.

Recently, key regulatory bodies have been formed in Thailand, including the Ministry of Digital Economy and Society (MDES) in 2016, and the National Broadcasting and Telecommunications Commission (NBTC) in 2010. Such agencies have overlapping mandates, making it difficult to discern which agency is specifically in charge of what functions.

As one tech company official complained, "So many groups in the Thai government . . . worry about this [tech regulations]. You have the police . . . ministry of ICT. You have the broadcasting telecom commission. There are so many players."[40] When I asked NBTC deputy secretary-general Korkit Danchaivichit which agency was responsible for setting national ICT guidelines, he responded with a sly smile, "Good question . . . MDES could answer that."[41] Figure 4.5 diagrams key stakeholders and methods of repression related to Thailand's digital ecosystem.

As the diagram illustrates, Thailand's network of digital repression is convoluted, but almost all decisions originate from the top. Until recently, the NCPO (under Prayuth's leadership) was responsible for all decisions with one caveat: given that Thailand is a constitutional monarchy, the king has the authority to overrule the junta. Vajiralongkorn's decision to temporarily put a moratorium on the military's enforcement of lèse-majesté offenses represents one such example.

When it comes to digital repression, the relationship between the military and Thai police is complex. Ordinarily, the Thai police would take the lead on monitoring violations (likely in coordination with MDES), investigating charges, and arresting offenders. The advent of the junta, however, thrust the military into a more prominent position. Military units from the Internal Security Operation Centre routinely conduct surveillance operations. Often, military officers accompany the police on "door knocking" missions.[42] And offenders are frequently tried in military courts. The restoration of civilian rule theoretically moves the military back to a secondary role.

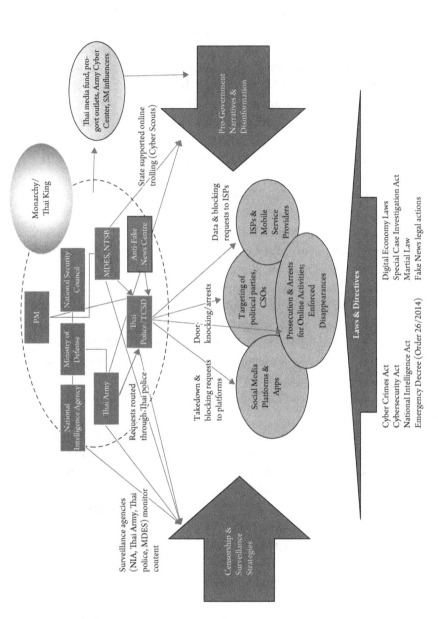

Figure 4.5 Network of Digital Repression in Thailand

Three Conditions for Digital Repression
in Thailand

What conditions are facilitating digital repression in Thailand? What factors help us understand why the Thai state has chosen to expand its use of and reliance upon digital tools to control the population? I contend that three conditions have facilitated the Thai state's increased reliance on digital repression: long-standing military-bureaucratic repression, established censorship practices, and political challenges due to heightened online communication and social media use.

Long-Standing Military-Bureaucratic Repression

Thailand's military and police have historically played an oversized role when it comes to running the country. While Thailand's political system has fluctuated dramatically over the decades—encompassing military regimes, personalist dictators, populist leaders, as well as a parliamentary democracy—one constant has remained: the "resilience of the military-bureaucratic elements" of the state.[43]

Thailand's political order defies easy categorization. Scholars such as McCargo describe Thailand's politics as a dense layer of political networks, with the most relevant one, "network monarchy," centered around the palace.[44] Others researchers, such as Eugénie Mérieau, focus on an "anti-democratic alliance composed of the broader security forces, including the military, police and the judiciary," and contend that examining Thailand's "deep state," driven by a resurgent judiciary, provides a more consistent understanding of motives that drive political governance in the country.[45] Another group, led by Paul Chambers and Napisa Waitoolkiat, proposes the concept of a "parallel state," or "monarchised military," that sustains a palace-centered order "from which the military obtains legitimacy."[46]

These theories offer important insights related to Thailand's political development, but for our purposes, two underlying factors are most relevant. First, regardless of how one describes Thailand's political trajectory, it has enabled the emergence of strong coercive institutions that play a central role in governing the country and carrying out political repression. Second, the most recent military junta, which assumed power in 2014, has accelerated authoritarian and repressive trends beyond the historical norm.

The military and police serve as both instruments of and partners to the monarchy and establishment elite. Their method of repression relies heavily on symbolic prosecutions of a small number of people. Digital activist Yingcheep Atchanont explained in an interview, "The numbers are around fifty, sixty, seventy who really express against the government and who are charged." The state, Yingcheep noted, which coordinates with conservative or royalist cyber trolls, will "just pick a victim . . . who doesn't have any support, don't have any reputation before. Just pick one."[47] Frequently, the police will hold a public press conference where they will lay out the particular offenses committed by this individual and invite the media to take pictures. As Yingcheep sees it, the purpose is to "spread out fear" so that "other people will stop posting [objectionable] things."[48]

Because the Thai public considers the military to be a legitimate political institution, this perception empowers military leaders to periodically step into power to act as a conservative corrective. During an interview with M. L. Nattakorn Devakul, a prominent commentator on Voice TV, he observed:

> In Thailand, the military is the equivalent to the Republican Party. . . . It steps into power once in a while to do a bunch of stuff, which includes taking up military spending. And then once in a while, when they become less popular, like right now, they gradually leave office, and then the politicians come back to run the country—until the politicians are less popular.[49]

Some Thais welcome the military's periodic involvement, particularly when they perceive politics to have gotten out of hand. A representative from the US-ASEAN Business Council advised: "If you talk to business people here, they will say the coup had to happen because Thailand could become a failed state because of these two factions who were about to clash. And there were demonstrations everywhere. . . . That was really bad. Somebody had to be the adult and come in and sort it out. And luckily we do have that."[50] More astute observers will recognize how closely this argument hews to propaganda talking points put out by the military to justify the coup.

Under General Prayuth, the junta implemented an ambitious agenda of digital repression. In the weeks after the 2014 coup, scholar Janjira Sombatpoonsiri writes, the regime "blocked access to hundreds of websites" and established special working groups to "monitor and analyze content, identify problematic sites, and combat online crimes, including the dissemination of illegal information."[51] The regime supplemented Internet controls with offline strategies, such as outlawing gatherings of five or more people. In a country that has ample experience with military governance, experts consider the junta's actions historically anomalous.[52] Such repression was especially prevalent on the digital front and has led to what many civil society activists and journalists deem the "new normal" in Thailand. As one civil society contact relayed to me, "People are terrified. There's a muzzle."[53]

The junta's leadership openly acknowledged its program of repression. During a recent research trip to Thailand, I obtained an audience with Panitan Wattanayagorn, chairman of the prime minister's security advisory committee. We met at Thailand's Government House, a stately complex spread over eleven acres that dates back to 1923. I asked him whether Thailand's security forces track individuals who pose threats to the government. With marked satisfaction, he responded, "You can see over the last few years the prosecution, the arrests, and the prosecuting of some of these people have been on the rise." He emphasized that the government keeps a close watch on Facebook and other online platforms. It heavily monitors "extreme activities," particularly speech that violates "defamation and also lèse-majesté" laws. Panitan explained that the state's goal is to "bring those people to the justice system to charge them."[54] In his words, suppressing online speech is a major part of Thailand's strategy for maintaining internal security.

Established Censorship Practices

The second driver of digital repression in Thailand—which complements Thailand's history of military-bureaucratic repression—is long-established censorship practices. Censorship has a lengthy history in Thailand, particularly when it comes to lèse-majesté laws, which prohibit defamation, insults, or threats against the royal family.[55] While other countries also have lèse-majesté laws, Thailand is one of the few places that actively enforces such provisions. Violators face from three to fifteen years in prison. One of the big loopholes with lèse-majesté laws is that they leave substantial discretion to the government to determine who will be charged and for what offense. Accordingly, human rights groups accuse the state of exploiting lèse-majesté—raising charges against political opponents when it suits the government's interests.[56]

Furthermore, the origin of specific lèse-majesté charges often remains unclear. As one contact from the tech industry observed, "Who is the one that really expands the scope [of lèse-majesté]—this is not clear. Whether it is a top-down approach from the very top of the government, or just the way that law enforcement does things for some reason, we don't know."[57]

Despite regular abuses of lèse-majesté provisions, Thais are extremely reluctant to condemn their use due to their strong reverence for the monarchy. I asked Paopoom Rojanasakul, a high-ranking member of the opposition Pheu Thai Party, whether he thought the government was using lèse-majesté for political purposes. He reiterated his belief that no law should be manipulated for politics, concluding, "That is all I can say." He didn't feel comfortable elaborating further.[58] Such is the power of censorship.

Notably, since 2018, the application of lèse-majesté laws has temporarily ceased, presumably on orders from the king (which has effectively allowed Vajiralongkorn to wrest control of political power away from the military). But while use of lèse-majesté laws may have momentarily ebbed, the government has simply replaced that approach with aggressive enforcement of cyber and defamation laws. Recently, the government even elevated charges for criticizing the constitutional court.[59]

Although such laws have been on the books for years, they are selectively prosecuted. Online media have brought a new twist: there is a huge discrepancy between criminal sentences for offline defamation convictions (one year in jail) and online defamation convictions (seven years in jail). The motivations behind the offline/online sentencing inconsistency are clear. As a technology representative explained during an interview, "I think it's a struggle, an ongoing competition. And the battle is in social media. It is clear that they [the Thai government] effectively can control conventional media. They have to self-censor. That's been ongoing for five years. So the support and the real feeling of the parties, of the people, are affected on social media. Now the question is, how do you handle that?"[60] The regime hasn't quite figured out how to deal with social media. The current strategy involves public crackdowns on certain prominent individuals, filing new charges against high-profile influencers (such as those brought against Thanathorn), and using civil society groups like the Rubbish Collectors to do their dirty work online.

Why does the Thai public tolerate such heavy-handed restrictions? Following the turmoil of the Thaksin era, the Thai state essentially made a bargain with the more conservative parts of society, traditionally comprised of Bangkok's middle class: the government would preserve "order and social harmony" and maintain a thriving economy in exchange for the middle class accepting constraints on their privacy rights and individual freedoms. This trade-off has allowed the state to cultivate a narrative that skillfully combats activists who oppose certain legislation—such as the new cybersecurity act—on human rights grounds. The state contends that such concerns are a political pretext for red shirt leaders to advance their agenda. This argument has allowed the junta to "divide and rule and prevent a broad alliance from emerging" against restrictive legislation.[61] But as Thailand moves further away from the Thaksin era, royalist-military leaders are losing their leverage in this dynamic.

Thaksin's legacy feels distant—particularly for younger generations. Former Future Forward spokesperson Pannika noted: "In the latest election we've seen 5.6 million first-time voters. And every year we've got nearly a million more new voters. These new voters they rarely understand the legacy of Thaksin. . . . They were too young at the time Thaksin was in exile."[62] This development helps explain why Future Forward's youthful followers were so threatening to Thailand's conservative establishment. They don't understand the history of Thailand's political bargain and they don't care. The red shirt / yellow shirt divide means much less to them. They are looking for change and are increasingly frustrated by the regime's vote rigging and electoral manipulation—and by the corrupt excesses of the monarchy.

Increased Online Communication and Social Media

The third explanation for the expansion of digital repression in Thailand is the result of political challenges that have arisen in connection with the population's all-consuming embrace of online communication and social media. Thailand's social media penetration level stands at 74 percent, the equivalent of fifty-one million users.[63] Its highest-ranking platforms are primarily from the United States: Facebook, YouTube, Line (Japan), Instagram, and Twitter. Thus far, Chinese platforms such as WeChat have had limited success penetrating Thailand's market.

Thais use different platforms for distinctive functions, often self-segregating by age. For example, the Japanese social media platform Line is especially popular with Thai baby boomers, although Thais of all ages consider it essential for business or workplace communication (email use is increasingly rare in Thailand). Likewise, Thais consider Facebook to be a "Generation X" platform, one that is increasingly monitored by the government. Twitter is the platform of choice for Thailand's youth. The edgiest political content occurs on Twitter, which has become a major vehicle for voicing dissent and organizing politically. While Twitter "doesn't hit critical mass at the moment," one tech observer noted, it is "very active among those who are currently [politically] active."[64]

In fact, several civil society activists expressed both admiration and concern regarding the youthful Thai Twitterati, commending their boldness, but worrying that the state may crack down on them in the near future. Reflecting on this development, Janjira noted, "These days you can find outrageous comments [on Twitter], not only about the junta but also the palace. Most tweets involve the use of coarse language, satires and puns and euphemisms. For me, this scale of public defiance is unprecedented, indicating changing popular mood regarding the establishment elites (at least among the youth)."[65]

It is no accident that a movement like Future Forward derived significant momentum and energy from social media; in effect, Twitter turned Thanathorn into a star. Social media have given Thai youth a voice and transformed them from content receivers into content producers.

If most public expressions of dissent in Thailand originate on social media, the logical response from Thai authorities is to increase online repression. A widely accepted political science theory—the "law of coercive responsiveness"—holds that when "challenges to the status quo take place, authorities generally employ some form of repressive action to counter or eliminate the behavioral threat."[66] In other words, dissent provokes repression. Because authorities derive a benefit from reducing domestic threats, and because "repression is cheap" relative to accommodation, it is in the Thai regime's interests to crack down hard on social media.[67] For the Thai state, effectively controlling online expression is essential to its claims on legitimacy.

I heard a similar message repeatedly during my visit to Thailand. Said one international technology representative: "Social media is one of the battles happening. It is the most important one. Aside from the constitutional court. Aside from the election commission."[68] But important constraints exist as to how far the state will go when it comes to exerting digital repression. While battles over censorship and surveillance will undoubtedly persist and grow, this struggle is bounded by economic calculations: Thai authorities are hesitant to take any actions that will lead to economic harm.

Thailand's economy is heavily reliant on technology. The ITU's development index ranks Thailand seventy-eighth in the world and tenth in the Asia Pacific region when it comes to its level of ICT advancement. High technology makes up 22 percent of its total manufacturing exports, and the World Economic Forum considers Thailand (along with China) a "top five" economy in the region in terms of its overall ICT readiness.[69] Tech is a source of strength for the country; the regime is reluctant to pursue policies like authorizing Internet shutdowns that might compromise its economic reputation and instigate the ire of Bangkok's middle class.

The last recorded instance of a full social media shutdown occurred on May 28, 2014, six days after the coup. For thirty minutes during the afternoon, the Thai military ordered Thailand's ISPs to take Facebook (and its twenty-eight million users) offline. Initially, the junta trumpeted its actions: "We have blocked Facebook temporarily and tomorrow we will call a meeting with other social media, like Twitter and Instagram, to ask for cooperation from them."[70] Quickly, the junta started to receive significant backlash, both domestically and internationally. It soon backtracked, denying any role in ordering the Facebook blockage and instead blamed "technical glitches" for the outage. Two weeks later, on June 9, DTAC, Thailand's second largest mobile Internet provider, publicly refuted the government's convoluted story, releasing the following statement:

> Telenor Group can confirm that on Wednesday 28 May DTAC received a notification at 15:00 local time from the National Broadcasting and Telecommunications Commission of Thailand to restrict access to Facebook temporarily. This restriction, which was implemented at 15:35, potentially had impact on DTAC's 10 million Facebook-using customers.[71]

The government immediately lashed out at DTAC for its momentary lapse into truth-telling and demanded an apology, which DTAC subsequently provided (although it pointedly did not refute the basic facts included in the June 9 statement).

What was the backstory for this situation? The government was likely "testing the waters" when it authorized the ban and got cold feet once it realized that middle-class anger was beginning to boil over.[72] Thailand's middle class and business communities will afford a lot of leeway to the government, but there are certain lines that the military knows not to cross. One private sector contact considering the situation noted, "All they [business] care about is stability, and rule of law, and predictability in terms of laws and regulations, which Thailand has plenty of. . . . They don't care about democracies as such."[73] Thus, the rules of the game are clear. The government can censor, selectively prosecute individuals, and block websites. It can violate human rights principles and suppress political dissent. Only when its actions threaten the country's commercial activity has it gone too far.

The government's ill-fated "single gateway" Internet initiative, which proposed decreasing the twelve existing Internet gateways into one gateway overseen by state-owned CAT Telecom to enhance content monitoring, is another instance where perceived economic harms forced the state to reconsider its proposal. As Janjira has written, "Although the middle class's values are oriented toward the preservation of order and social harmony, their livelihood and everyday convenience depends on Thailand's economic growth and global connections. The Internet has become a basic necessity for these citizens. They were not bothered much by the Single Gateway's threat to privacy rights and freedoms, but they did care about its potential to damage the economy."[74]

How Thailand Implements Its Digital Repression Strategy

Thailand's program of digital repression emphasizes strategies of control—particularly focused on censorship, surveillance, formal and informal pressure on relevant tech companies, and legal persecution of online users.

Door-Knocking and the Growth of Legal Repression

A leading characteristic of Thailand's system of repression is its door-knocking strategy. Rather than use formal procedures to solicit information from ISPs, the Thai government leverages informal relationships with ISPs, opting instead for a "friendly knock on the door of the telecommunications providers."[75]

This approach puts inordinate pressure on companies to consent to government requests for access. The door-knocking strategy is not limited to ISPs. It occurs elsewhere, such as in the media sector. TV commentator M. L. Nattakorn explained:

> They would invite you to come in and have a cup of coffee with them, which I've had. And in the Thai way, they're very nice about it. So, for example, I had this cup of coffee . . . with a general rank officer of the First Army Area Command. . . . He was telling me that we're trying to achieve reconciliation, trying to get people to stop protesting, maintain stability for the country, so it's good if you don't invite this guy, that guy to appear on the show.

As a result, Nattakorn doesn't invite particular politicians on the show who may be harshly critical of the government. "They ask for cooperation nicely, so you basically comply. You only comply to the point whereby you choose your words more nicely. Instead of calling someone stupid, you say that's not the best decision. . . . You become a diplomat on TV. And you don't invite particular guests who might be a bit on the extreme."[76] The Thai state thereby imposes a polite form of coercion that can appear almost friendly. But this method has a specific censorship purpose, and the consequences are severe for those who fail to conform.

While door-knocking has served the state well, the government has also decided to beef up its formal authority—providing even greater leverage. Thailand has passed a raft of new laws that authorize additional surveillance and content restrictions intended to compel further cooperation from ICT companies. First came a set of 2017 "digital economy" bills that included amendments to the CCA. Section 20 of the CCA grants legal authority to the government to require that service providers block websites that are deemed threats to national security or to have violated public morals or public order.[77] The Cybersecurity Act, newly minted in February 2019, includes additional provisions that authorize security services to seize data and equipment in cases of "national emergency."[78] But the law's full effect won't be known for some time. Chiranuch Premchaiporn, editor-in-chief of *Prachatai*, warned, "It's kind of like the storm is brewing. Because the Cybersecurity Act needs one more year to finish up the details. After that it will be in use."[79]

The National Intelligence Act complements the Cybersecurity Act, specifically authorizing Thailand's National Intelligence Agency (NIA) "to order any person or government agency to submit, within a specified period, data or document(s) which impact national security."[80] Undoubtedly, this law will have an impact. In a conversation with a group of Thai security officials, they noted: "Before the law, the NIA had to rely on the goodwill of ISPs in order to cooperate when there are threats. With the law we will now have a formalized process. . . . After you have the law, it makes them [ISPs] feel comfortable to cooperate."[81]

The passage of these laws brings two major implications.

First, they indicate a transition from informal door-knocking practices to a more codified set of regulations that give disproportionate leverage to the Thai state. Rather than needing to rely on unofficial pressure to persuade companies or media figures to do their bidding, security and intelligence agencies now have formal legislative backing.

Second, these laws demonstrate the power of Thailand's bureaucracy—particularly at the expense of a deliberative, democratic process. Somkiat Tangkitvanich, president of the Thailand Development Research Institute, claimed that the junta has issued "over four hundred laws recently—many related to cybersecurity."[82] Even though the junta has formally turned over power, its repressive legacy will remain in force.

Censorship and Surveillance Strategies

Thailand also maintains significant structural censorship impediments to Internet access. While Internet filtering capabilities have been present since 2002, following the 2006 coup the government began actively monitoring web content and filtering banned content. In order to get legal cover to implement an extensive monitoring and filtering regime, the government passed the 2006 CCA. As the scholar Pinkaew Laungaramsri relates, this represented the "first step to state legalization of information control on the Internet."[83] Very quickly, the government developed the ability to implement automatic filtering. Pirongrong Ramasoota describes this technique as based on "proxy-based filtering strategies," which funnels Internet traffic through a system that checks specific HTTP addresses against a blocked list of URLs or keywords in URLs. Users who try to access these sites are blocked, although instead of showing a government block page, "The new system has created a block page that looks like the browser's default error page, possibly to disguise the fact that the government is blocking these sites."[84] At various times during the past decade, particularly periods correlated with government crackdowns, censorship tactics have been expansively deployed. A 2010 investigation by the Thai Netizen Network revealed, for example, that the government had blocked more than ten thousand URLs.[85]

The government has authorized extensive blocking and filtering for a range of reasons: national security, antimonarchy content, gambling, intellectual property, or hosting VPN applications. For example, a report published by the Open

Observatory of Network Interference (OONI) in 2017 revealed that the Thai government had blocked thirteen websites across six ISPs between November 2016 and February 2017. Restricted sites included news outlets (e.g., *New York Post, Daily Mail*), sites providing anonymity or censorship circumvention tools, pornography, and Wikileaks.org.[86] Similarly, I ran an OONI measurement test for web connectivity from January 1, 2020, through January 31, 2020. The test yielded 117 "anomalies" (signs of potential network interference leading to website blocking) across five ISPs—CAT, True, AIS, Jasmine, and 3BB. Blocked sites appear to include Yale Press (responsible for publishing Paul Handley's *The King Never Smiles*, which is banned in Thailand), Wikipedia, Human Rights Watch, Amnesty International, the *New York Post*, as well as a string of gambling and pornography sites.[87]

Along with filtering, the government aggressively enforces content removal requests for users, publishers, web hosts, and tech platforms. Thai authorities will sometimes go to comical lengths to remove unwanted content. In June 2019, for instance, "A French satirist living in Bangkok was pressured to remove a music video mocking the NCPO's anthem from his social media accounts. Police officers visited his house and ordered him to sign a memorandum that such content was 'improper' and damaged Thailand and its people."[88] While content removal requests are hard to quantify numerically, we can get a general sense of trends by looking at tech companies' disclosure reports. In the following section, I will present data from Facebook, Google, and DTAC.

The result of Thailand's censorship regime is a profound chilling effect on what people will say and where they will say it. Part of their calculus is determining whether they are relevant enough to warrant the Thai state's scrutiny. Cofounder of the Thai Netizen Network Arthit Suriyawongkul explained, "You are actually free to say a lot. . . . As long as I'm a nobody, I'm safe. . . . The government will say I'm not going to be a troublemaker—I only have, like, twenty followers. I'm not going to destabilize the government."[89] Similarly, "I would say self-censorship takes place with guys like me . . . when we have some following, we have something to lose."[90]

People describe a pattern where the government keeps "slapping on charges." Again and again, potential defendants are forced to explain themselves—why they posted certain content, why it should not be interpreted as defamation. Over time, many people just stop commenting: "What happens after several years of doing this is you basically have less influencers in society willing to criticize the government," Nattakorn explained, "because the other famous names who have more to lose in their professional life or family life don't want the legal trouble, knowing full well this junta could stay on for another five years."[91]

When it comes to surveillance, Thai authorities possess sophisticated capabilities, including both passive and targeted monitoring. For example, technical investigations from the Citizen Lab concluded that the Royal Thai Police and Royal Thai Army were likely users of Hacking Team's Remote Control System malware (subsequently verified in leaked documents).[92] Thai authorities have also purchased advanced surveillance products from NSO Group and Cyberbit.[93] It is worth noting that surveillance costs have also dropped significantly in recent years, making state acquisition of these tools costly but hardly prohibitive.[94]

A contact involved in social media monitoring relayed a story that had been widely circulated: "There was a photographer who took a photo of General Prawit having a coffee in a hotel. . . . After ten minutes the photographer was arrested—in that hotel. What he did was he just posted [the photo] on his timeline. And kept it 'friends only' on Facebook." Within ten minutes, Thai authorities had identified that someone had posted a sensitive photo to a closed network, located that specific individual, and then made an arrest.[95] What kind of technology is needed to execute this type of operation? "Bots that scan through lots of timelines trolling for prohibited material," he replied.[96] Perhaps Thailand's AI capabilities are more advanced than many people think. But social surveillance does not require sophisticated algorithms to be effective—simpler solutions exist.

For example, Thai security relies heavily on informants who make friend requests to certain individuals and help the authorities penetrate closed chat groups.[97] Often, authorities will deploy "social engineering" techniques.[98] An informant might post a phone number to a closed group of human rights activists, claiming it belongs to CNN International. They'll urge group members to upload content to this number (e.g., videos of protests) that will in fact go straight to government authorities, enabling tracking and spying. Other times the police will arrest an individual, force that person to give up personal passwords, and then log in to that person's account and access private groups for monitoring.

Prior to the 2014 coup, the government had initiated a national "cyber scout" training program, which would eventually total more than one hundred thousand students, to monitor and report online behavior deemed a threat to public order and national security.[99] While it is unclear how functional the program still is, there are hundreds of government supporters online who closely watch posts by opposition and civil society actors in order to report users for "expressing the least criticism of the monarchy."[100]

Who does the Thai government monitor? Political opponents, democracy activists, journalists, academics, and civil society organizations. Thai Lawyers for Human Rights and iLaw have both been frequent targets of surveillance. Independent media outlets like *Prachatai* are also watched. Chiranuch admitted, "We're also concerned about [surveillance]. . . . We often joke that if they want to bug something in our office, it's easy."[101] Chiranuch was one of the first individuals prosecuted under the CCA. In 2010, she was arrested by the Thai police and faced up to eighty-two years in prison for "failing to remove antimonarchy comments from Prachatai's Web board."[102] Her trial was widely interpreted as an ominous signal of the government's intention to crack down on dissent. After two years of courtroom battles, she eventually received a one-year suspended prison sentence.[103]

But there are also constraints on government surveillance. While the re-gime rarely hesitates to go after specific individuals, it is reluctant to persecute en masse: "They would give you so many warnings, to a point where . . . next time we're going to come and arrest you," my social media monitoring contact explained. "But having them come in and do a dawn raid or something, I don't think so. They still care about international image and international reputa-tion."[104] In such situations, business considerations help mitigate the Thai state's drive toward greater repression. Authorities will push repression to a certain point, but remain keenly aware of their international reputation, rarely crossing lines that will scare away international investment.

How Tech Companies Respond to Content Requests

While the Thailand's digital repression program puts tech firms in a tricky po-sition, companies have developed a set of internal protocols to resist Thai state directives. A big part of the tech companies' strategy is to exclude local Thai offices from any decision-making authority when it comes to content requests or takedown orders. One tech company official put it simply: "I'm totally not in the loop. Totally out." Another emphasized, "In reality they have to understand that they can raid the office right now, they can take my PC, they can take our servers here. They just have to understand they're not going to get anything."[105]

Requests often get routed to regional centers in Singapore, or, in the case of Facebook, directly to lawyers in Menlo Park. This not only removes the onus from the Thai office, it also protects the physical safety of employees who oth-erwise might face retribution. Several companies I talked to conceded that per-sonnel security is a constant concern, but they "can't be too open about it." If the government knows that physical intimidation will help it advance its objectives, this could open the door to escalating attacks. "For us, to be honest, personnel security comes first. We're not sacrificing someone's life for our principles," ac-knowledged one telecom executive. "But we don't say that because then they will get the confirmation. Not just talking about Thailand, talking about throughout the market."[106]

Companies have also developed standardized processes for govern-ment requests. In an interview with NTBC deputy secretary-general Korkit Danchaivichit, he explained, "Right now the process works quite well after a learning period. The government knows how to prepare certain information, what are the documents that are required. . . . They know the channel in which to make a submission. They know the turnaround time."[107] In other words, tech companies are subtly using their own bureaucratic processes to thwart government content requests.

Unsurprisingly, this behavior has led to frustration among government officials. Korkit vented about US platforms: "They just say that 'we don't have it.' Even now in the United States, it is not as easy as that. You have some hard questions, but you have to answer." He continued, "There will be a time when all the ASEAN countries come together and say, all right, we're fed up with this. When it happens, it happens. Because as a government agency you cannot beg. You cannot beg, you have to order, you have to comply. This is our sovereign. It's our people. You have to abide by the laws that govern us."[108] In fact, there is a limit to how much social media companies are willing to push back. The last three years illustrate a trend toward increased restrictions.

Facebook discloses that in 2019 it blocked 1,461 pieces of content as a result of government requests based on lèse-majesté and CCA violations. These numbers represent a huge increase from 2018, when it blocked 869 pages, or from 2017, when it took down 365 pieces of content.[109] Most prominently, in August 2020, Thailand ordered Facebook to close a private chat group, Royalist Marketplace, featuring over one million users. Thai authorities claimed its antimonarchy content ran afoul of lèse-majesté laws. Facebook has subsequently filed an appeal in the Thai courts stating that such requestions "contravene international human rights law and have a chilling effect on people's ability to express themselves."[110]

Google content restrictions were even more severe. Since 2009 (through June 2020), Google has cumulatively removed 28,595 items (mostly from Google search and YouTube). The majority of takedown requests relate to "government criticism." In 2018, Google removed 11,652 items, while in 2019, the company removed 4,768 items.[111]

DTAC's disclosure of the Thai government's data requests is even more troubling. It has only updated its records through 2018, revealing that the Thai government made 18,611 requests for historical telecommunications data and 296 requests for content restrictions in 2018. DTAC did not disclose how many of these requests it agreed to pursue. Furthermore, DTAC did not provide any information about the number of "lawful interception" surveillance requests made by the Thai government or how many of these requests it accepted.[112] Finally, DTAC does not provide any historical data prior to 2018, making year-by-year comparisons impossible. Unsurprisingly, the Ranking Digital Rights report criticizes DTAC for being "particularly opaque" about how it handles government requests for user data or content blocking even though there are "no legal restrictions preventing the company from being more transparent in

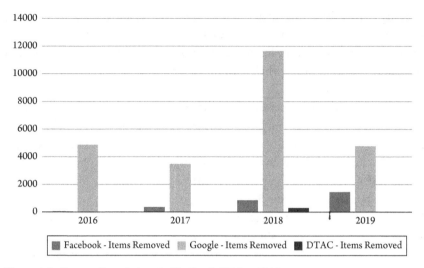

Figure 4.6 Content Restrictions in Thailand, 2016 to 2019

these areas."[113] Figure 4.6 shows content restriction comparisons for Google, Facebook, and DTAC between 2016 and 2019.

One tech official acknowledged the difficulties of fighting government requests and conceded that "tech companies basically follow the law in this country. Thailand has the Computer Crime Act, Cybersecurity Act. . . . They revamped the law to give them more power. That is the foundation, the way they exercise power and how far they go after people who are deemed to be threats to the country." Often, there are tough judgment calls, and companies seek a balance: "Yes, in one way, we work with the Thai government. We have to work with the junta. We have to follow what they say," the tech official conceded. "But we also value freedom of speech and other things that they benefit on the platform. So it's that balance."[114]

Social Manipulation and Disinformation

State-sponsored social manipulation and disinformation efforts are also prevalent and closely linked to the government's surveillance and censorship agenda. Social manipulation in Thailand incorporates two key elements used by autocratic regimes to ensure their stability: "countermobilizing" regime supporters to rally political support against the opposition, and "discourse-framing" to shape public perceptions in order to sustain the legitimacy of the regime.[115] Specifically, the Thai state carries out a four-part strategy.

First, the government deploys social surveillance. Agencies such as the Thai police's TCSD unit or the army cyber center deploy scores of officers who operate "around the clock, scanning online postings and following up complaints from the public on cybercrimes, including royal defamation."[116] These officers keep tabs on trending issues, target specific individuals for persecution, and collect information to compile false narratives.

Next, the state uses information from social surveillance to generate false narratives. Operatives from the newly formed army cyber center begin to generate "true facts" to counter information they believe is disparaging or critical of the Thai state. Their goal is to convey preferred regime narratives to its official news outlets.[117] Those who post dissenting viewpoints may be forcibly brought to army detention camps to deter future critiques.[118]

Subsequently, it supplements false narratives with cyber trolling from royalist netizens and other outside groups. Royalist netizens—comprised of well-intended citizens, aggressive vigilantes, and cyber trolls-for-hire—amplify the government's narratives and monitor online forums for additional posts critical of the state. They use vicious language to discredit regime critics, calling antiregime protestors "Thaksin lackeys," or "red shirt traitors." As Janjira noted, they often use "doctored images, sometimes containing obscene and sexist descriptions" to vilify dissidents. Politicians from Future Forward were "the latest targets of these vicious online attacks."[119] These groups now rarely comprise genuine "yellow shirt" supporters. Instead, the bulk of these attacks stem from royalist Facebook pages that "link to one another and circulate the same news reports and anti-red shirt 'memes.'"[120] Former Future Forward spokesperson Pannika Wanich confirmed this to me during our interview: "They have strings of pages. Facebook pages and Line groups. . . . But they are not actually news outlets. They are just proliferating fake news and hate speech. And they share information and pictures, fake ones, across platforms."[121] The result of this trend is the creation of a disinformation ecosystem that efficiently suppresses dissent and severely limits free speech in the online sphere.

Fourth, the government suppresses genuine free speech through liberally deploying the CCA to prosecute a "wide range of dissenting opinion." Pannika noted that the government had "seven or eight" CCA charges pending against Future Forward before the court shut the party down. These prosecutions, she contended, were systematic: "When they file charges against our leadership and our party, it's not just these cases but also information operations in social media to discredit us." The Thai state appears to be doubling down on this strategy. In August 2019, the government announced the establishment of an anti-fake news center under MDES, intended to teach digital literacy and combat false information.[122] Most activists, however, are convinced that the center will be yet another tool for the government to suppress information that contradicts its official version of the truth. The government has also announced its intent to

initiate legal actions to stop the spread of fake news, including bringing responsible individuals to trial.[123]

What about China's Role?

Chinese companies are exporting advanced digital capabilities—from smart
cities to facial recognition systems—through the Belt and Road Initiative, which
bolsters Chinese influence. I was curious to see how this dynamic would unfold
in Thailand.

Looking at the numbers, Thailand appears ripe for Chinese influence.
Thailand is a member of China's Belt and Road Initiative (BRI)—forming part
of the China-Indochina Peninsula corridor—and ranks eighteenth in the world
for Chinese overseas direct investment, representing a sharp increase from
prior years.[124] Imports from China comprise 8.4 percent of Thailand's GDP, and
China has made significant investments (estimated to be at least $1.4 billion)
under BRI's Digital Silk Road adjunct.[125] Thailand is also a member China's
newly established Asia Infrastructure Investment Bank. My research indicates
that Thailand is one of at least fifty-seven countries worldwide with access to
Chinese AI surveillance technology—linked to both Huawei and Megvii (see
Appendix 4 for a full list of countries with AI capabilities).

I asked Thai stakeholders from many different sectors—government, private
tech companies, civil society, academia—their perceptions of Chinese influence
in Thailand. Their answers were mixed.

On the one hand, most acknowledge Thailand's long and intertwined relationship with China. As Panitan observed, "Our link with China is over a thousand years old. Not only in terms of ethnic background but in terms of people to
people, top-level, and in general."[126] But this relationship has undergone many
ups and downs. For much of the Cold War, for example, Thailand stood as a reso-
lute US ally in opposition to communist encroachment from China. The United
States may view China as a newly ascendant strategic competitor, but Thailand
has been grappling with the China question for most of its history.

Thai leaders are natural foreign policy balancers. They have cultivated a slew
of alliances and are careful not to side too strongly with any one country: "Always
been that way. That's why we're still a kingdom," Deputy Secretary-General
Korkit observed. "We compromise, we negotiate, and we balance."[127] They
don't see the world in zero-sum terms and prefer not to choose sides between
partnering with China or aligning with the United States. They believe their best
bet is to seek coexistence with both countries—to acquire certain technology
from China and to procure other systems from the United States or Europe.[128]
When discussing new weapons systems, for example, Panitan stressed that the

Thais "attempt to stay away from one or two suppliers . . . we have Chinese, Russian, European, US systems." He emphasized that "Thailand will pick and choose as it can . . . our missile systems based on European system. Submarine systems based on Chinese. Heavy equipment first on US, then Chinese, then back to the US."[129]

In fact, Thailand has made a conscious effort to source from an array of countries; Israeli companies, for example, have formed key partnerships in Thailand. Several people I spoke to mentioned a recently signed deal between Israel's Verint Systems and the Thai government to develop its cyber capabilities. One contact suggested that the military relies heavily on "cyberwarfare software from Israel." He described a demo staged by an Israeli cybersecurity surveillance company ("The pitching quote is quite nice") where they demonstrated how they can "set up a lot of fake accounts, become your friend, then sweep through your timeline. . . . It's AI."[130] Researchers from the Citizen Lab have documented malware infections in Thailand linked to Israeli firms NSO Group and Cyberbit.[131] A 2015 investigation by *The Intercept* identified Israeli-based Nice Systems as a key partner that helped close spyware deals worldwide, including "winning [government] contracts in Azerbaijan and Thailand."[132]

I repeatedly pressed different contacts whether Chinese companies were peddling advanced AI and big-data surveillance equipment and encouraging Thai stakeholders to build up sophisticated monitoring systems. No one indicated that the Chinese were pushing a concerted agenda in this area. An official from Thailand's Ministry of Interior noted that while AI technology is "out there" and something the government is thinking more about, "China hasn't offered any AI. It doesn't give AI—Thais have to ask."[133] Another source remarked that "China is not openly marketing artificial intelligence. China's focus is on network infrastructure."[134]

I also made inquiries about new "smart cities" planned for Thailand, such as on the island of Phuket. Smart cities or safe cities (discussed at length in Chapter 7) were initially conceived by companies as a way to make cities more efficient and to enable better service delivery by integrating technology and data. But there is growing concern that smart cities are also facilitating a dramatic rise in public surveillance and intrusive security.

In Thailand, Huawei is working closely with local telecom companies and municipal authorities to push forward its safe city model in several locations in the country.[135] When I asked Somkiat whether he was concerned about the smart city concept in Thailand, he laughed, responding, "The idea of a smart city is a joke." He then relayed his recent conversation with Thailand's ICT minister: "He boasted about the smart city in Phuket. . . . He told me that we are thinking about giving wristbands to tourists so that we can track them, we can help them. Something like that. But it's not really implemented. Smart city in

Phuket turns out to be providing free Wi-Fi and Internet to tourists!"[136] While in other countries smart cities have been linked to police-state surveillance built on user data, in Thailand this concept has yet to take off.

Government security agencies do not claim to show a strong interest in implementing mass surveillance, which would require procuring advanced artificial intelligence technology. I shared pineapple smoothies with a senior Thai security official who lamented the government's inability to track sensitive threats. At the same time, he was clear that his agency was not interested in setting up a surveillance system like "social credit in China": "Our agenda is not like that. In Thailand, we don't do mass monitoring. It's a waste of our time. . . . We don't think about a mass monitoring system." He did acknowledge using "semilegal software like WebIntelligence" to monitor the public whereabouts of certain individuals. For him, there was a clear distinction between tracking individuals on national security grounds versus carrying out mass surveillance for broader political purposes.[137] Notably, while this official drew a hard line on mass surveillance, senior political leaders have been on the record pushing for the establishment of a single Internet gateway to control information flowing in and out of the country—which would dramatically enhance the state's mass surveillance capacity.[138]

One artificial intelligence technique that the Thai government has shown increasing interest in is the deployment of facial recognition systems. Such technology is being piloted in greater numbers by Thai police departments, although one local technology expert observed that officials are "mostly matching people in photo databases" and not feeding images into big-data algorithms in real time.[139] There is also a growing effort by the Thai government to build a national biometric database, which would incorporate facial recognition properties.[140] The most significant step toward mass adoption of facial recognition occurred in June 2019. The Thai government ordered all mobile phone users in its southern provinces—where there has been unrest due to conflict between the majority Buddhist Thai central government and the local Muslim population—to submit photos of themselves for facial recognition purposes. Unsurprisingly, this order caused an uproar, with activists accusing the government of heavy-handedness and suggesting that the new technology would augment the risks of "racial discrimination."[141] While some Chinese tech companies like Megvii are linked to Thailand's facial recognition programs, more consistent evidence of a concerted Chinese push in this area has yet to surface.[142]

Even if the case for Chinese proliferation of algorithmic repression is overstated in Thailand, recent years have witnessed a genuine warming of ties between China and Thailand—partially coming at the expense of frayed US-Thai relations. After the military deposed the democratically elected government, most US security assistance was automatically frozen. As a result, Thailand was forced to seek new partners, specifically the Chinese. Panitan observed that the downgrading of US cooperation was a "major problem," and that "the Chinese, they say, 'Well we're not going to attach political conditions.'" He chuckled, adding, "Of course they are not in a position to say anything much about democracy."

There have also been increasing reports of ties between Chinese state media outlets and Thai newspapers. The news outlet *Khao Sod*, known for its independent reporting, formed a partnership with China's state-run press agency, Xinhua. Kurlantzick notes, "Among the first Xinhua pieces Khao Sod ran . . . were articles on the Hong Kong protests that portrayed the protestors as tools of Western agitators."[143] Other Thai media organizations have reportedly followed suit.

Commentators like Nattakorn suggest that while Thailand's population remains wary of Chinese influence, the junta—and some members of the elite— are perceived to be exceptionally close to China: "It's a big problem [Chinese influence]. Because for some reason, it's largely due to particular personalities in this government, mainly General Prawit [deputy prime minister] and Dr. Somkid [another deputy prime minister]. For some reason these two guys are very pro-Chinese. And for some reason not in the US camp."[144]

Undoubtedly, significant Chinese influence exists in Thailand's tech sector. Chinese technology is deeply embedded in Thailand, and the country is growing more economically dependent on China. But many point out that Chinese engagement is not state-driven so much as propelled by Chinese companies becoming more aggressive in closing deals for economic reasons.

A good way to conceptualize the nature of Chinese influence in Thailand is that Chinese expansion is not an absolute condition. Some view Chinese products with suspicion, especially because of perceived security vulnerabilities; nonetheless, companies like Alibaba and Huawei are substantially growing their presence. While certain Thai elite have become captivated by the Chinese model, this is balanced by their desire to remain respected and connected to the West.

For some Thai officials, of course, Chinese technology is strictly about the money. Siriwat Deepor, deputy chief of the Thai police's Technology Crime Suppression Division, insisted that "Chinese tech doesn't matter. It depends on the company. Most equipment that is lower-priced is usually Chinese. Whomever offers the cheapest prices will get the bid. It's a matter of price."[145]

As my meeting with Panitan wrapped up, he raised a concern that stuck with me: "Why is the US so nervous? Is something wrong with the US or not? Right now, China shouldn't shake the US this bad. . . . We are concerned that the US is getting nervous. It is getting unsettled about the rise of China. And that an unsettled US is also shaking our confidence. You have the largest effective forces in the world. . . . If you're still that nervous, then it gives us nervousness too."[146]

It was hard to argue with him.

Conclusion

The Thai government seeks to balance two ICT priorities: exerting sufficient control over the political activities of its citizens while at the same time ensuring that these efforts don't jeopardize its economic growth agenda. To achieve its goals, the state deploys a variety of censorship tools: door-knocking and "coffee conversations," restrictive legislation that prohibits a wide range of online content, and targeted arrests, charges, and detentions against ICT users. The state also prioritizes surveillance and disinformation. While it does not appear to rely heavily on AI and big-data surveillance, it is aggressively carrying out less costly tactics, including forced password handovers, using informants to infiltrate closed groups, and social surveillance. The government is also increasingly emphasizing activist digital strategies such as social manipulation and disinformation, although this remains less of a priority than its censorship strategies.

The rise (and subsequent fall) of Future Forward introduced a key question: would the government increase its reliance on social manipulation and disinformation strategies to counteract Future Forward's influence? Or would it instead double down on censorship and persecution to constrain the party's impact? Initially, the state seemed to try a bit of both—relying on legal harassment to blunt Future Forward's path while also encouraging state-sponsored trolls to bash party leadership. The February 2020 decision by the constitutional court to ban Future Forward indicated that the Thai state had opted to pursue legal means to subdue the party.

Thailand's political and human rights environment may be just tolerable enough for the majority of its citizens—making the likelihood of real change remote. In some respects, this condition makes Thailand's situation more tragic. As Chiranuch pointedly said at the close of our conversation, "It's true that it is manageable and it's also sad that it is manageable. . . . You cannot call for change easily because people feel they have no choice. People are not thinking about change because this society hardly changes. . . . It's manageable, this is true. But manageable is also bad, because the public isn't aware of how serious the situation is that they live in."[147]

Her words were still echoing in my mind as I boarded my flight to the Philippines.

Notes

1. Thais commonly refer to individuals by their first name or by their full name; they rarely refer to persons by their last name only. This chapter will follow that convention and use first names or full names in the text.

2. Chayut Setboonsarng, "Interview—Top Thai Auto Parts Maker Looks Overseas as Home Market Slows," *Reuters*, October 27, 2017, https://www.reuters.com/article/thaisummit-business-idUKL4N1N22OI.

3. Jitsiree Thongnoi and Bhavan Jaipragas, "Everyone Loves 'Daddy': Meet the Thai Junta's New Billionaire Rival," *South China Morning Post*, February 24, 2019, https://www.scmp.com/week-asia/politics/article/2187362/everyone-loves-daddy-forget-thaksin-heres-thai-juntas-new.

4. Duncan McCargo, "We Are Grown-Up Now and Can Choose for Ourselves," *New York Times*, March 29, 2019, https://www.nytimes.com/2019/03/29/opinion/thailand-election-thanathorn-future-forward-youth-vote.html

5. Thongnoi and Jaipragas, "Everyone Loves Daddy."

6. McCargo, "We Are Grown-Up."

7. "NCPO Pressures Political Opposition; Summons Thanathorn on Sedition Charge," *Prachatai English*, April 3, 2019, https://prachatai.com/english/node/8007.

8. Patpicha Tanakasempipat, "Thailand's Rising Political Star Charged with Sedition," *Reuters*, April 6, 2019, https://www.reuters.com/article/us-thailand-election-thanathorn-idUSKCN1RI03X.

9. "FFP Deputy Leader Says He Unknowingly Shared Fake News," *Prachatai English*, March 5, 2019, https://prachatai.com/english/node/7957.

10. "FFP Dissolved, Executives Banned for 10 Years," *Bangkok Post*, February 21, 2020, https://www.bangkokpost.com/thailand/politics/1862769/ffp-dissolved-executives-banned-for-10-years.

11. Pavin Chachavalpongpun and Joshua Kurlantzick, "Why Thailand's Protestors Are Up in Arms against the Monarchy," *World Politics Review*, September 10, 2020, https://www.worldpoliticsreview.com/articles/29044/as-protests-rock-thailand-monarchy-comes-under-pressure.

12. James Row, "Behind Thailand's Protests, Cracks in the Establishment," *The Diplomat*, August 27, 2020, https://thediplomat.com/2020/08/behind-thailands-protests-cracks-in-the-establishment/.

13. Rebecca Ratcliffe, "Facebook Blocks Access to Group Criticising Thailand's Monarchy," *The Guardian*, August 25, 2020, https://www.theguardian.com/world/2020/aug/24/facebook-blocks-access-group-criticising-thailand-monarchy.

14. George Wright and Issariya Praithongyaem, "Wanchalearm Satsaksit: The Thai Satirist Abducted in Broad Daylight," *BBC News*, July 2, 2020, https://www.bbc.com/news/world-asia-53212932; Joshua Kurlantzick, "Pressure Increases on Thai Activists Abroad," Council on Foreign Relations, August 5, 2019, https://www.cfr.org/blog/pressure-increases-thai-activists-abroad.

15. Caleb Quinley, "'Can't Give Up': Rise in Attacks against Thai Democracy Activists," June 14, 2019, https://www.aljazeera.com/news/2019/06/give-rise-attacks-thai-democracy-activists-190612044146566.html.

16. "'Ja New' Assaulted Again, Sent to ICU," *Bangkok Post*, June 28, 2019, https://www.bangkokpost.com/thailand/politics/1703660/ja-new-assaulted-again-sent-to-icu.

17. Janjira Sombatpoonsiri, "'Fake News' and Thailand's Information Wars," *The Diplomat*, July 2019, https://thediplomat.com/2019/07/fake-news-and-thailands-information-wars/.

18. See Mong Palatino, "What Will It Take to Combat Digital Authoritarianism in Southeast Asia?," *Global Voices* (blog), June 27, 2019, https://globalvoices.org/2019/06/27/what-will-it-take-to-combat-digital-authoritarianism-in-southeast-asia/.

19. "Thailand," Freedom House in the World 2020, March 4, 2020, https://freedomhouse.org/country/thailand/freedom-world/2020.

20. "2019 Country Reports on Human Rights Practices: Thailand," US Department of State, March 11, 2020, https://www.state.gov/reports/2019-country-reports-on-human-rights-practices/thailand/.

21. Rankings are extracted from the 2020 V-Dem electoral democracy index. Coppedge et al., "V-Dem Dataset v10."

22. Duncan McCargo, "New Media, New Partisanship: Divided Virtual Politics in and beyond Thailand," *International Journal of Communication* 11 (2017): 4139.

23. Michael Peel, "Thailand's Monarchy: Where Does Love End and Dread Begin?," *Financial Times*, October 11, 2017, https://www.ft.com/content/149d82a4-ae17-11e7-beba-5521c713abf4.

24. "Lese-Majeste Explained: How Thailand Forbids Insult of Its Royalty," *BBC News*, October 6, 2017, https://www.bbc.com/news/world-asia-29628191.

25. Alison Smale and Thomas Fuller, "Thailand Looks to Likely Future King with Apprehension," *New York Times*, October 14, 2016, https://www.nytimes.com/2016/10/15/world/asia/thailand-looks-to-likely-future-king-with-apprehension.html.

26. Stories of Vajiralongkorn's extravagance abound. Once, after sampling a tasty lunch at the Thai Kingdom restaurant in Stratford-upon-Avon, England, Vajiralongkorn directed Thai embassy staff to pick up 350 boxes of food from the restaurant and to put them on a twelve-hour flight to his residence in Bangkok. Said the restaurant owner: "It may seem a long way to fly food, but I suppose that what the prince likes, he gets. If he's happy, everybody else is happy. It's a great honour, especially for the staff. They are gobsmacked." Tania Branigan, "Bangkok Prince Orders Takeaway—from Warwickshire," *The Guardian*, November 11, 2000, https://www.theguardian.com/uk/2000/nov/11/thailand.

27. Andrew MacGregor Marshall, *A Kingdom in Crisis: Thailand's Struggle for Democracy in the Twenty-First Century* (London: Zed Books, 2015), 151.

28. "Assets Registered to Thai Crown Property Bureau to Be Held under King's Name," *Reuters*, June 16, 2018, https://www.reuters.com/article/us-thailand-king-property-idUSKBN1JC0EK.

29. Eugénie Mérieau, "A Military Dictatorship Like No Other," *New York Times*, February 9, 2019, https://www.nytimes.com/2019/02/09/opinion/thailand-election-king-sister-junta.html; Feliz Solomon, "Thailand Uses Controversial Lèse-Majesté Law Against Pro-Democracy Protesters," *The Wall Street Journal*, November 30, 2020, https://www.wsj.com/articles/thailand-uses-controversial-lese-majeste-law-against-pro-democracy-protesters-11606761747.

30. I asked Pannika Wanich, former spokesperson for the Future Forward Party, how Thais perceive their new king. After a pause, she said, "He engages in politics in a very different way from his father in the past. Different network, different methods, and I think in another degree of intensity." She continued, "And one thing we know about the king is he's unpredictable. So no one really knows what he's doing next. So it's very interesting. But it's quite clear that he sees himself as one of the main bosses in Thai politics. It's quite clear." Pannika Wanich (spokesperson, Future Forward Party), interview with the author, June 23, 2019.

31. Kasian Tejapira, "The Irony of Democratization and the Decline of Royal Hegemony in Thailand," *Southeast Asian Studies* 5, no. 2 (2016): 219–37.

32. "Protesters Up Pressure for Monarchy Debate with 10-Point Manifesto," *Nation Thailand*, August 11, 2020, https://www.nationthailand.com/news/30392817.

33. Hannah Beech and Ryn Jirenuwat, "'Now, We Fight Face to Face': Thailand's Protests Shatter Taboos," *New York Times*, November 18, 2020, https://www.nytimes.com/2020/11/18/world/asia/thailands-protests-kings-taboo.html.

34. The 2019 digital repression measurements incorporate social media penetration interactions per the model described in Chapter 3. Digital repression time-series calculations (2010–19) do not incorporate this interaction due to data limitations.

35. "Thailand," Freedom on the Net 2020, 2020, https://freedomhouse.org/country/thailand/freedom-net/2020.

36. Mechkova et al., *Digital Society Project Dataset v2*.

37. The most recent ITU Internet access data is from 2017. "Statistics—ITU," International Telecommunications Union, 2020, https://www.itu.int/en/ITU-D/Statistics/Pages/stat/default.aspx.

38. Simon Kemp, "Digital 2020: Global Digital Yearbook," *DataReportal*, 2020, https://datareportal.com/reports/digital-2020-global-digital-yearbook.

39. For example, TRUE is owned by the Thai conglomerate Charoen Pokphand (CP), which is controlled by the Chearavanont family. CP runs some of the largest companies in Thailand. The Chearavanont family "is close to the military government that has been in power since the 2014 coup . . . the board of Charoen Pokphand contains people affiliated with the military establishment. Anti-Thaksin generals have been appointed as advisors." "Who's That Knocking," Privacy International.

40. Author interview with an international technology company representative, May 17, 2019.

41. Korkit Danchaivichit (deputy secretary-general of telecommunication of the Office of the National Broadcasting and Telecommunications Commission), interview with the author, May 17, 2019.
42. "Who's That Knocking," Privacy International.
43. Eugénie Mérieau, "Thailand's Deep State, Royal Power and the Constitutional Court (1997–2015)," *Journal of Contemporary Asia* 46, no. 3 (2016): 445–66.
44. Duncan McCargo, "Network Monarchy and Legitimacy Crises in Thailand," *Pacific Review* 18, no. 4 (2005): 499–519.
45. Mérieau, "Thailand's Deep State."
46. Paul Chambers and Napisa Waitoolkiat, "The Resilience of Monarchised Military in Thailand," *Journal of Contemporary Asia* 46, no. 3 (2016): 425–44.
47. Yingcheep Atchanont (program manager, iLaw), interview with the author, May 16, 2019.
48. Yingcheep Atchanont, interview with the author.
49. M. L. Nattakorn Devakul (commentator, Voice TV), interview with the author, May 13, 2019.
50. Author interview with a representative from the US-ASEAN Business Council, May 13, 2019.
51. Janjira Sombatpoonsiri, "Growing Cyber Activism in Thailand," Carnegie Endowment for International Peace, August 14, 2017, https://carnegieendowment.org/2017/08/14/growing-cyber-activism-in-thailand-pub-72804.
52. Academic Chris Baker observes: "In sum, the junta kept tight control, suppressed all opposition and outlawed all debate in order to push through a large-scale programme of change. This placed 2014 on the list of Thailand's major history-changing coups with 1932, 1957 and 1976." Chris Baker, "The 2014 Thai Coup and Some Roots of Authoritarianism," *Journal of Contemporary Asia* 46, no. 3 (2016): 388–404.
53. Author interview with an international civil society representative, May 15, 2019.
54. Panitan Wattanayakorn (security adviser to the deputy prime minister of Thailand), interview with the author, May 16, 2019.
55. See Section 112 of the legal code: "Criminal Code: Royal Family (Sections 107-112)," Thailand Law Library," 2019, http://library.siam-legal.com/thai-law/criminal-code-royal-family-sections-107-112/.
56. See for example Pavin Chachavalpongpun, "Thailand's Lèse-Majesté Laws: A Potent Weapon," East Asia Forum, December 26, 2011, https://www.eastasiaforum.org/2011/12/26/thailands-lese-majeste-laws-a-potent-weapon/.
57. Author interview with an international technology company representative, May 17, 2019.
58. Paopoom Rojanasakul (counselor to the secretary-general, Pheu Thai Party), interview with the author, May 17, 2019.
59. Teeranai Charuyastra, "Gov't Warns Public Not to Criticize Constitutional Court," *Khaosod English*, August 30, 2019, http://www.khaosodenglish.com/politics/2019/08/30/govt-warns-public-not-to-criticize-constitutional-court/.
60. Author interview with an international technology company representative, May 17, 2019.
61. Janjira Sombatpoonsiri, "Growing Cyber Activism."
62. Pannika Wanich, interview with the author.
63. "Digital 2019: Thailand," *DataReportal*, January 31, 2019, https://datareportal.com/reports/digital-2019-thailand.
64. Author interview with a Thai technology company representative, May 18, 2019.
65. Janjira Sombatpoonsiri, email message to author, September 30, 2019.
66. Davenport, "State Repression," 7.
67. Jacqueline DeMeritt, "The Strategic Use of State Repression and Political Violence," *Oxford Research Encyclopedia of Politics*, October 2016, https://oxfordre.com/politics/view/10.1093/acrefore/9780190228637.001.0001/acrefore-9780190228637-e-32.
68. Author interview with an international technology company representative, May 17, 2019.
69. "High-Technology Exports (% of Manufactured Exports)," World Bank, 2019, https://data.worldbank.org/indicator/TX.VAL.TECH.MF.ZS?locations=TH&view=chart; Silja Baller, Soumitra Dutta, and Bruno Lanvin, "The Global Information Technology Report 2016: Innovating in the Digital Economy," World Economic Forum, 2016, http://www3.weforum.org/docs/GITR2016/WEF_GITR_Full_Report.pdf.

70. "Thai Ministry Sparks Alarm with Brief Block of Facebook," *Reuters*, May 28, 2014, https://in.reuters.com/article/thailand-politics-facebook-idINKBN0E80U520140528.

71. Mia Vals, "Operator Says Thai Government Ordered Facebook Shutdown," *Next Web*, June 9, 2014, https://thenextweb.com/asia/2014/06/09/operator-dtac-says-thailands-government-forced-shut-access-facebook/.

72. Olivia Becker, "Thailand's Military Denies Briefly Banning Facebook," *Vice* (blog), May 28, 2014, https://www.vice.com/en_us/article/wjybny/thailands-military-denies-briefly-banning-facebook.

73. Author interview with a representative from the US-ASEAN Business Council, May 13, 2019.

74. Janjira Sombatpoonsiri, "Growing Cyber Activism."

75. "Who's That Knocking," Privacy International.

76. M. L. Nattakorn Devakul, interview with the author.

77. "Thailand," Freedom on the Net 2018.

78. "Thailand Passes Controversial Cybersecurity Law That Could Enable Government Surveillance," *TechCrunch* (blog), February 18, 2019, http://social.techcrunch.com/2019/02/28/thailand-passes-controversial-cybersecurity-law/.

79. Chiranuch Premchaiporn (editor-in-chief, Prachatai), interview with the author, May 13, 2019.

80. "New Thai National Intelligence Act Issued: Government Authorized to Access Private Sector Data and Devices," *Baker McKenzie*, April 2019, https://www.bakermckenzie.com/en/insight/publications/2019/04/new-thai-national-intelligence.

81. Author interview with senior officials from a Thai government security agency, May 16, 2019.

82. Somkiat Tangkitvanich (president, Thailand Development Research Institute), interview with the author, May 14, 2019.

83. Pinkaew Laungaramsri, "Mass Surveillance and the Militarization of Cyberspace in Post-coup Thailand," *Austrian Journal of South-East Asian Studies* 9, no. 2 (2016): 197.

84. Pirongrong Ramasoota, "Internet Politics in Thailand after the 2006 Coup: Regulation by Code and a Contested Ideological Terrain," in Ronald Deibert, John Palfrey, Rafal Rohozinski, and Jonathan Zittrain, eds., *Access Contested: Security, Identity, and Resistance in Asian Cyberspace* (Cambridge, MA: MIT Press, 2011), 98.

85. "The State of Internet Censorship in Thailand," Open Observatory of Network Interference, March 20, 2017, https://ooni.org/post/thailand-Internet-censorship/.

86. "Internet Censorship in Thailand," OONI.

87. I used OONI's explorer tool to assess website blocking in Thailand for specified dates in January. The tool can be accessed here: https://explorer.ooni.org/search?until=2020-01-25.

88. "Thailand," Freedom on the Net 2019.

89. Arthit Suriyawongkul, interview with the author.

90. Although in rebuttal, many will point that all sorts of ordinary Thais are reported to the authorities for prosecution, such as a hotel worker and tour operator who were convicted of lèse-majesté offenses in 2015 and sentenced to multiple years in prison. "Thai Courts Give Record Jail Terms for Insulting King," *BBC News*, August 7, 2015, https://www.bbc.com/news/world-asia-33819814.

91. M. L. Nattakorn Devakul, interview with the author. Experts describe this process as the "weaponization of cyber law." Janjira Sombatpoonsiri, "Weaponizing Cyber Law," Project Syndicate, May 13, 2019, https://www.project-syndicate.org/commentary/cyber-law-autocratic-regimes-southeast-asia-by-janjira-sombatpoonsiri-2019-05.

92. Bill Marczak et al., "Mapping Hacking Team's 'Untraceable' Spyware," Citizen Lab, February 17, 2014, https://citizenlab.ca/2014/02/mapping-hacking-teams-untraceable-spyware/.

93. Bill Marczak et al., "Hide and Seek: Tracking NSO Group's Pegasus Spyware to Operations in 45 Countries," Citizen Lab, September 18, 2018, https://citizenlab.ca/2018/09/hide-and-seek-tracking-nso-groups-pegasus-spyware-to-operations-in-45-countries/; Bill Marczak et al., "Champing at the Cyberbit: Ethiopian Dissidents Targeted with New Commercial Spyware," Citizen Lab, December 6, 2017, https://citizenlab.ca/2017/12/champing-cyberbit-ethiopian-dissidents-targeted-commercial-spyware/.

94. "Who's That Knocking," Privacy International.

95. Author interview with a representative from a Thai social media monitoring company.

96. Author interview with a representative from a Thai social media monitoring company.

97. Privacy International released a comprehensive report on social surveillance in Thailand in 2016 that describes how the government "has empowered networks of citizens whom it encourages to denounce those who post online content considered contrary to government policies. With increased tension between supporters and opponents of the military government, some individuals have also created citizen-led initiatives to spy and inform on other citizens, thereby fostering a network of social surveillance." Eva Blum-Dumontet, "Friends, Followers, Police Officers, and Enemies: Social Surveillance in Thailand," *Medium.com*, September 20, 2016, https://medium.com/privacy-international/friends-followers-police-officers-and-enemies-social-surveillance-in-thailand-bd46a13a6b71.

98. "How Journalists and Human Rights Defenders Are Targeted Online," Access Now, June 2019, https://www.accessnow.org/cms/assets/uploads/2019/06/MENA-report.pdf. See also "Submission on the Right to Privacy in Thailand, Human Rights Committee, 119th Session," Privacy International, February 2017, https://tbInternet.ohchr.org/Treaties/CCPR/Shared%20Documents/THA/INT_CCPR_CSS_THA_26657_E.pdf; Mong Palatino, "The Truth about Thailand's Social Media Surveillance," *The Diplomat*, October 3, 2016, https://thediplomat.com/2016/10/the-truth-about-thailands-social-media-surveillance/.

99. "Vietnam's 'Cyber-Troop' Announcement Fuels Concern about Troll Armies," RSF, January 12, 2018, https://rsf.org/en/news/vietnams-cyber-troop-announcement-fuels-concern-about-troll-armies.

100. "Vietnam's Cyber-Troop Announcement," RSF.

101. Chiranuch Premchaiporn, interview with the author.

102. Aim Sinpeng, "State Repression in Cyberspace: The Case of Thailand," *Asian Politics and Policy* 5, no. 3 (July 2013): 421–40.

103. Thomas Fuller and Kevin Drew, "Thai Message Board Manager Is Given Suspended Prison Sentence," *New York Times*, May 30, 2012, https://www.nytimes.com/2012/05/31/world/asia/google-and-rights-groups-condemn-thai-courts-conviction-of-a-webmaster.html.

104. Author interview with an international technology company representative, May 14, 2019.

105. Author interview with an international technology company representative, May 17, 2019.

106. Author interview with an international technology company representative, May 15, 2019.

107. Korkit Danchaivichit, interview with the author.

108. Korkit Danchaivichit, interview with the author.

109. "Content Restrictions—Thailand," Facebook, accessed December 11, 2020, https://transparency.facebook.com/content-restrictions/country/TH.

110. Hannah Beech, "Facebook Plans Legal Action after Thailand Tells It to Mute Critics," *New York Times*, August 25, 2020, https://www.nytimes.com/2020/08/25/world/asia/thailand-facebook-monarchy.html.

111. "Government Requests to Remove Content—Google Transparency Report," Google, accessed December 11, 2020, https://transparencyreport.google.com/government-removals/by-country/TH.

112. "Authority Requests Disclosure Report," Telenor Group, 2018, https://www.telenor.com/wp-content/uploads/2019/03/Telenor-Authority-request-report-2018.pdf.

113. "2019 Ranking Digital Rights Corporate Accountability Index—Telenor ASA," Ranking Digital Rights, 2019, https://rankingdigitalrights.org/index2019/companies/telenor/index/.

114. Author interview with an international technology company representative, May 17, 2019.

115. Seva Gunitsky, "Corrupting the Cyber-Commons: Social Media as a Tool of Autocratic Stability," *Perspectives on Politics* 13, no. 1 (2015): 42–54.

116. "Friends, Followers," Privacy International.

117. Janjira Sombatpoonsiri, "Fake News."

118. "[Update] Peaceful and Normal Actions Forbidden under the Junta Regime after 6 Months," *Prachatai English*," December 10, 2014, https://prachatai.com/english/node/4578.

119. Janjira Sombatpoonsiri, "Fake News."

120. Janjira Sombatpoonsiri, "Fake News."

121. Pannika Wanich, interview with the author.

122. Pitcha Dangprasith, "Thailand to Set Up Center to Combat 'Fake News,'" *AP*, August 21, 2019, https://apnews.com/fcd766532ab44f248222c89d550b3574.

123. "Prawit Wants 'Fake News' Crackdown," *Bangkok Post*, June 27, 2019, https://www.bangkokpost.com/thailand/politics/1702408/prawit-wants-fake-news-crackdown.

124. "China Going Global Investment Index 2017," Economist Intelligence Unit, 2017, http://pages.eiu.com/rs/753-RIQ-438/images/ODI_in_China_2017_English.pdf.

125. Prasso, "China's Digital Silk Road."

126. Panitan Wattanayakorn, interview with the author.

127. Korkit Danchaivichit, interview with the author.

128. David Shambaugh classifies Thailand as an "aligned accommodationist," in that its leaders maintain "extremely close and extensive relationships with China, are quite comfortable with these ties, seek to enhance them, and do not chafe under dependency to Beijing—precisely because they simultaneously maintain considerable ties with the United States (particularly in the defense realm)." David Shambaugh, "US-China Rivalry in Southeast Asia: Power Shift or Competitive Coexistence?," *International Security* 42, no. 4 (2018): 100–101.

129. Panitan Wattanayakorn, interview with the author.

130. Author interview with a representative from the US-ASEAN Business Council, May 13, 2019.

131. Marczak et al., "Hide and Seek." A separate Citizen Lab investigation uncovered logfiles placing Cyberbit employees, a wholly owned subsidiary of Israeli-based Elbit Systems, at IP addresses linked to the Royal Thai Army. Marczak et al., "Champing at the Cyberbit."

132. Ryan Gallagher, "Hacking Team Emails Expose Proposed Death Squad Deal, Secret U.K. Sales Push and Much More," *The Intercept*, July 8, 2015, https://theintercept.com/2015/07/08/hacking-team-emails-exposed-death-squad-uk-spying/.

133. Author interview with a representative from a Thai social media monitoring company, May 18, 2019.

134. Thai technology consultant, interview with the author, May 16, 2019.

135. "Thailand PEA's Digital Transformation Starts from the IP-Based Evolution of Its Transmission and Transformation Network," Huawei, 2019, https://e.huawei.com/topic/leading-new-ict-en/thailand-pea-case.html.

136. Somkiat failed to mention the thirteen hundred CCTV cameras already in use in Phuket—with plans to deploy an additional three thousand cameras to cover public areas. While they may not be linked to AI algorithms, they still present an intrusive security presence. See Medha Basu, "Exclusive: Phuket's Smart City Vision," *GovInsider*, December 7, 2017, https://govinsider.asia/smart-gov/phuket-smart-city-digital-economy-pracha-asawathira/

137. Author interview with senior officials from a Thai government security agency, May 16, 2019.

138. Wassana Nanuam, "Prawit: Single Gateway Is a Must," *Bangkok Post*, December 14, 2016, https://www.bangkokpost.com/tech/1159396/prawit-single-gateway-is-a-must.

139. Thai technology consultant, interview with the author.

140. "Thailand to Introduce Facial and Fingerprint Scans for SIM Cards Nationwide," *DW*, June 11, 2017, https://www.dw.com/en/thailand-to-introduce-facial-and-fingerprint-scans-for-sim-cards-nationwide/a-41252427.

141. "Thailand's Army Demands Photos from Phone Users for Facial Recognition," *South China Morning Post*, June 26, 2019, https://www.scmp.com/news/asia/southeast-asia/article/3016165/thailand-causes-uproar-muslim-majority-south-ordering.

142. Chris Burt, "Megvii Expanding Facial Recognition Technology Market Reach into Southeast Asia," *Biometric Update*, June 26, 2018, https://www.biometricupdate.com/201806/megvii-expanding-facial-recognition-technology-market-reach-into-southeast-asia.

143. Joshua Kurlantzick, "Thailand's Press Warms to Chinese State Media," Council on Foreign Relations, January 8, 2020, https://www.cfr.org/blog/thailands-press-warms-chinese-state-media.

144. Prajak Kongkirati and Veerayooth Kanchoochat argue that the military junta has formed a partnership with Sino-Thai conglomerates to "create a new mode of economic participation" in Thailand to serve as a counterweight to Thaksin's economic populism. Prajak Kongkirati

and Veerayooth Kanchoochat, "The Prayuth Regime: Embedded Military and Hierarchical Capitalism in Thailand," *TRaNS: Trans-Regional and-National Studies of Southeast Asia* 6, no. 2 (2018): 279–305.

145. Siriwat Deepor (spokesman and deputy commander of the Royal Thai Police's Technology Crime Suppression Division), interview with the author, May 15, 2019.

146. Panitan Wattanayakorn, interview with the author.

147. Chiranuch Premchaiporn, interview with the author.

5

Social Manipulation and Disinformation in the Philippines

I arrived in the Philippines in May 2019, a week after the country held midterm congressional elections. Opposition candidates had endured a historic beating. For the first time, not a single senate candidate from an opposition party won any of a dozen seats up for grabs. Only three opposition senators remained in the legislature. Opponents of the Philippines' autocratic president, Rodrigo Duterte, were reeling. Families with traditionally strong political followings, such as the Aquinos and Roxas, failed to gain a foothold. Even more jarring, many of the winning candidates Duterte had supported were not particularly impressive. For example, Duterte's personal aide, Christopher "Bong" Go, known as the "selfie photobomb king," and ex-police chief Bato dela Rosa, architect of Duterte's murderous drug war, both secured senate seats.[1] (Figure 5.1 depicts one of Bong Go's notorious selfies.)

While speaking with a prominent Duterte supporter, I asked him how the president had managed to pull off such a resounding victory. Why had people voted in droves for political newcomers like Bong Go? He responded, "I voted for Bong Go. You know what? Simply was a spite vote." He continued, "I'm a lawyer with a master's degree in public administration. I had all this experience in government. I voted for Bong Go. Ask me why? Because he was endorsed by the president. That's it! I didn't even look at his credentials anymore." He got more heated. "I knew it would piss off my yellowtard friends or people I know or people who were angry at this. I know that they won't be happy with this. And this is my way of saying, 'Fuck you.' You can quote me on that. I voted for Bong Go. I said, 'Fuck you.' It's a message to you guys."[2]

Duterte's triumph in the midterms not only confirmed the strong levels of support he enjoys in the country—his approval ratings consistently hover around 80 percent—it also solidified his control over the three branches of government in the Philippines: executive, legislative, and judicial.

The Rise of Digital Repression. Steven Feldstein, Oxford University Press (2021). © Oxford University Press.
DOI: 10.1093/oso/9780190057497.003.0005

Figure 5.1 Bong Go Photo Selfie with US president Donald Trump in the background

But Duterte's electoral success is not a straightforward story about personal charisma translating into massive political victories. There is another troubling aspect to Duterte's political rise—his embrace and use of dubious digital tactics, particularly social manipulation and disinformation strategies, to maintain popularity and win elections. For example, when I arrived in Manila, a strange digital conspiracy known as the "ouster matrix" had just made the rounds.

On April 22, 2019, the *Manila Times*, a pro-government newspaper, published an article that alleged the existence of a conspiracy to oust Duterte from office. Not written by the newspaper's regular reporting staff, the article was instead penned by chairman emeritus Dante Ang, who currently serves as Duterte's "special envoy for international public relations," the administration's top PR position.[3] The article included a detailed matrix linking a broad array of media outlets and civil society organizations to an anti-Duterte conspiracy.[4] The matrix identified Maria Ressa (head of *Rappler*), Ellen Tordesillas (president of Vera Files), and leaders of the Philippine Center for Investigative Journalism (PCIJ) and the Philippines National Union of People's Lawyers as conspirators. Also included on the list was Karol Ilagan, a reporter for PCIJ, who personally helped set up research interviews during my visit (see Figure 5.2).

Association Matrix Between BIKOY and ELLEN TORDESILLAS

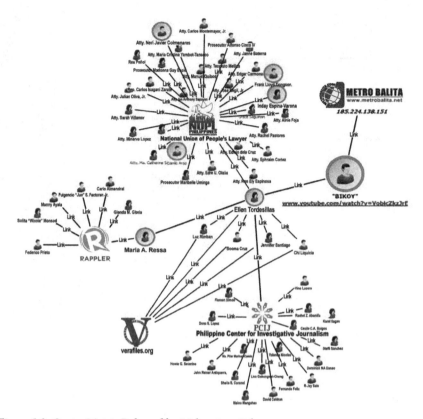

Figure 5.2 Ouster Matrix Released by Malacañang Palace

The same day that the *Manila Times* released the matrix, Duterte's spokesperson, Salvador Panelo, held a press conference at the presidential residence (Malacañang Palace). Panelo confirmed the authenticity of the ouster matrix and claimed it was based on foreign intelligence reports provided directly to Duterte.[5]

The disclosure of the matrix ignited a firestorm. Initially, the government vowed to prosecute the alleged coup plotters.[6] As doubts emerged about the veracity of the matrix (the Department of Justice [DOJ] and Philippines National Police [PNP] soon stated there was no basis to pursue an investigation), Malacañang was put on the defensive. On May 1, Panelo declared that it was "totally unnecessary" to provide evidence to prove the ouster matrix.[7] A day later, amid further criticism, Panelo admitted that he had mixed up the source of the matrix; in fact, he explained, he had not received it from Duterte, but from an unnamed person "via a text message."[8]

With credibility running low, Malacañang changed its tune once again. On May 8, Panelo released a revised matrix, accusing political parties, opposition candidates, a television host, and even an Olympic silver medalist of plotting to overthrow the president.[9] Filipinos took the new accusations far less seriously. Pierre Gallo, cofounder of Democracy.net, observed that "people started pointing out, 'Hey hold on. That's a Philippine Olympian right there. That's a Philippine anchor right there.' You're saying that they were involved? So that took away from the impact."[10]

So what exactly was going on? Why had the Philippines government chosen to squander precious political capital on an easily debunked conspiracy theory? As Peter Pomerantsev succinctly explains: "Conspiracy is a way to maintain control."[11] With censorship becoming increasingly difficult to enforce in most countries, the next best alternative is to flood citizens with excessive cynicism—"to persuade them that behind every seemingly benign motivation is a nefarious, if impossible-to-prove plot."[12] The goal of this tactic is to get people to lose faith in politics and tune out political life. The presidential spokesperson's deliberate intent to spread demonstrably false information, to do so within days of congressional midterm elections, and then to stubbornly stick with his story even as the facts came out, speaks volumes about the Duterte administration's strategy to obfuscate, misinform, and manipulate the truth.

This chapter examines how under President Rodrigo Duterte's leadership the Philippines government has implemented a unique method of digital repression to advance its political objectives. I will focus on four questions. First, what set of political factors and governance trends enabled an illiberal populist like Duterte to get elected in the first place? Second, what are the key drivers of digital repression in the Philippines? Third, how does digital repression work in the Philippines—what mixture of strategies does Duterte employ to advance his political objectives? And fourth, to what extent are outside actors—such as Facebook or the Chinese government—responsible for spreading digital repression in the Philippines?

I argue that three factors drive digital repression trends in the Philippines: (1) hyperconnectivity and extensive social media use, (2) democratic weakness, and (3) specific leadership attributes related to Duterte. I show that when it comes to implementing digital repression, the Duterte regime's preferred tactics are social manipulation and harassment paired with targeted persecution. While the government also employs surveillance techniques, these methods are sporadic and inconsist. I also discuss the influence of outside actors in the Philippines—particularly Facebook's role in enabling social media manipulation, and China's role in providing advanced technology to facilitate digital repression—but contend that their overall influence is limited.

Democratic Backsliding in the Philippines

As discussed in Chapter 1, there is a growing consensus that the world is experiencing a "third wave of autocratization."[13] Prominent countries that demonstrate backsliding include liberal democracies like the United States, flawed democracies and hybrid regimes such as Brazil, India, and Turkey, and autocratic states like Thailand and Venezuela.[14] Notably absent from the list is the Philippines, which until Duterte's 2016 election, had actually shown encouraging signs of democratic consolidation. But Duterte has reversed those gains, leading to a precipitous decline in the quality of democracy in the Philippines. V-Dem researchers identified the Philippines as the country most at risk in 2019–2020 of undergoing an "adverse regime transition" that will lead to an autocratic shift in its politics.[15]

In 2019, the Philippines democracy ranking was ninety-eighth of 179.[16] This puts it near the global median. However, Duterte's increased flouting of democratic norms and violations of human rights has worsened its trend line. Freedom House categorizes the Philippines as "partly free," describing "haphazard" application of the rule of law, a culture of impunity for those committing crimes against activists and journalists, and a devastating war on drugs that has led to "thousands of extrajudicial killings."[17] Similarly, the US State Department's annual human rights report documents a litany of concerns: arbitrary killings by state security forces, forced disappearances, torture, arbitrary detention, criminal libel, threats against journalists, and official corruption.[18] Figure 5.3 provides a statistical snapshot of the Philippines' governance performance from 2010 to

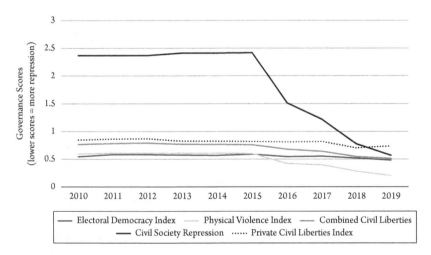

Figure 5.3 The Philippines' Performance on Key Governance Indicators, 2010 to 2019

2019, measured against five indicators: electoral democracy, physical violence committed by the state, overall protection of civil liberties, protection of private civil liberties, and civil society repression.

The indicators demonstrate cumulative governance decline. In particular, civil society repression and state physical violence have dramatically worsened, beginning in 2016—when Duterte came to power.

The people I spoke to during my visit acknowledged the Philippines' deteriorating democratic climate. Liza Garcia, for example, executive director of the Foundation for Media Alternatives, lamented that "we are a very young democracy compared to other countries" and "there's still a lot for us to learn." She observed, "Maybe we could have learned our lessons from the dictatorship. . . . There was a lot of opportunity for us after 1986, after the People Power Revolution. I think we should have done more maybe. People were so euphoric during the time that they forgot." Decades later, as corruption and sclerosis have captured Filipino politics, Garcia believes that people have become tired of the way things are done and want change: "That's why . . . you have somebody like Duterte who will say, 'No, I'm going to change things.' He was . . . saying things that they couldn't say. He was articulating those things that they wanted to say. Maybe that's why he became popular."

Until the 2016 election, the Philippines appeared headed in a positive direction. Under the leadership of Duterte's predecessor, Benigno "Noynoy" Aquino III, the country experienced impressive economic growth, averaging 6 to 7 percent per year. While fighting crime and the scourge of drugs constituted one of the main pillars of Duterte's campaign, crime rates actually declined under Aquino.[19] But Aquino's administration—and other liberal politicians in the Philippines—may have suffered from a gap between expectations and delivery. Aquino promised to implement "straight path" reforms to stamp out corruption and provide honest governance.[20] Yet many commentators criticized him for failing to fix the country's crumbling infrastructure or shielding his own officials from anticorruption investigations.[21]

Exit polls from the 2016 election confirmed that Duterte won a plurality of wealthy, educated voters, reflecting middle-class anxieties about crime, ineffectiveness, and corruption. In essence, Duterte's victory represented "the angry protest of the wealthy, newly rich, well off, and the modestly successful new middle class (including call centre workers, Uber drivers, and overseas Filipino workers abroad)."[22] Rather than believe their lives had improved from consecutive years of economic growth, middle-class voters revolted against poor public services, worsening traffic congestion, the perceived breakdown of law and order, and unending graft by public officials.

But Aquino's failure to deliver on promised reforms tells only half the story. Duterte's victory was as much about his charismatic appeal, muscular storytelling ability, and crafty social media strategy as it was a repudiation of Aquino.

The Meaning of Duterte

It is almost impossible to separate Duterte from broader questions about politics and the impact of digital repression in the Philippines.[23] Duterte has perfected running as an underdog and positioning himself as a small-time mayor who has much more in common with ordinary Filipinos than the country's elite (in fact, Duterte is a "scion of one of the Philippines' oldest political clans").[24] His reconstitution as a man of the people is a key part of Duterte's myth-making.

When I asked Filipinos to describe Duterte's appeal, several themes emerged. One supporter acknowledged, "This guy's not perfect. No rational person would say that he [Duterte] is perfect. No one would actually even agree all those jokes, all those rape jokes, are okay. They're not." Nonetheless, he countered that Duterte's crudeness and ability to relate to common citizens is part of his appeal, observing, "It's not as if a regular person would not also be saying those things. You do that, I do that. Just don't be so hypocritical. . . . That is not how the president should speak? Why? How should the president speak? It goes deeper to the issue of who set up the standards anyway."[25] Duterte's "crass politics" and use of rough language to establish emotional ties with Filipinos is crucial to his popularity. Sociologist Nicole Curato observes: "Duterte may be offending the norms of respectful communication when he prefaces his remarks with 'mother fucker,' but he brings to the surface the collective frustration many feel."[26]

Others point to Duterte's hands-on style—acting like he's the mayor of the Philippines—as a key part of his charm: "The president here is a mayor. . . . We are used to see presidents as being very cool, very professional, and all of that. This is a new kind of leadership, very local and a man of action. And people like that. What the president says—if he curses—they laugh."[27] Figure 5.4 shows a photo released by Malacañang in 2019 of Duterte relaxing casually with Bong Go.

Reflecting on the same question about Duterte's appeal, John Nery, a longtime reporter with the *Philippine Daily Inquirer*, told me, "Duterte is a very charismatic person. I've seen him work a room of fifty. And a rally of five hundred thousand. Very charismatic." Nery imparted that Duterte's political strategy relies on the concept of *sampol*—to make an example of someone. "He did that when he was mayor. And he does it now. He doesn't go after everyone. So that everyone else in the journalism profession gets the message." Nery concluded, "He's really a fascist. The whole populist thing is, it's just a cloak that he wears every now and then. In fact he has said things that have been directed at his home

Figure 5.4 Duterte and Bong Go Relaxing in Mindanao

base, saying, 'You're poor. Why should I worry about you?' He can be very rough when he speaks, even to his perceived base."[28]

Populism, Not Fascism

Nery isn't the first person to deride Duterte as a fascist. After Duterte recounted an order he had given as mayor of Davao City—"Tell the soldiers. There's a new order coming from mayor. We won't kill you. We will just shoot your vagina"—a prominent Filipino women's coalition publicly called Duterte "the most dangerous macho-fascist in government."[29] Scholar Walden Bello argues that "fascism came to the Philippines in the form of Rodrigo Duterte." He maintains that Duterte's bias toward authoritarian rule, support of systematic violations of human rights, and intent to dramatically change the existing political system in a way that fundamentally contravenes basic values of liberal democracy makes Duterte a "fascist personality that is an original."[30]

There is little doubt that Duterte embodies quintessential elements of a populist. As Larry Diamond explains, populism incorporate four qualities: anti-elitism (condemning the arrogance of the powerful), anti-institutionalism (against institutions perceived as hostile to the interests of the people), plebiscitary (mobilizing citizens through direct emotional appeal from a charismatic leader), and ultra-majoritarianism (opposed to any checks on power that constrain their ability to act).[31]

To that end, Duterte effortlessly fits the populist label. His crude statements are calculated to extract maximum emotional appeal and present a contrast to effete elites, who are offended by "real" talk. There's a paternal quality to Duterte's outbursts: As one prominent Duterte supporter explained, "A lot of people see him [Duterte] as a father figure. This is exactly how my father talks. . . . That's how he would curse, that's how he would address situations."[32]

But does this behavior make Duterte a fascist?

Historian Sheri Berman offers a clear distinction between populists and fascists. She posits that while both sets of actors intensely critique the existing order—denouncing incumbents as "inefficient, unresponsive, and weak"— fascists seek to bury and replace the old system. In contrast, populists are more interested in improving how the current structure operates. Populists "critique the functioning of contemporary democracy but offer no alternative to it, just vague promises to make government stronger, more efficient, and more responsive. . . . In other words, they are certainly antiliberal, but they are not antidemocratic. This distinction is not trivial."[33]

Over halfway through Duterte's term, there is little indication that he intends to drastically overhaul the country's political order. Many of the political allies he has cultivated—such as the Marcos, Arroyos, and Ayalas— are longtime establishment players who are looking to stay relevant or make comebacks.[34] They are not revolutionaries seeking to remake a system that has generously rewarded them over the years. Duterte's policy platform, in fact, is fairly conventional: combat drugs and crime, invest in infrastructure, sustain economic growth, stabilize Mindanao, and "reorient" the Philippines' foreign policy.[35]

Duterte's critics maintain that his most notable attribute isn't his sweeping vision for changing the Philippines. Rather, it's his knack for attracting the worst kind of operatives and followers, "those without scruples who are opportunistic and Machiavellian," observed Senator Leila de Lima, a prominent opponent of Duterte who is currently imprisoned on dubious charges. She told me that his regime is "basically the first kakistocracy in the Philippines" and that "Marcos at least had achievers among his cronies, while Duterte's men come from his local fiefdom in Mindanao. But they are mostly thieves and corrupt nonetheless."[36]

Regime Violence and Persecution

In keeping with his populist persona, Duterte has not hesitated to embrace punitive tactics to carry out his agenda, particularly sanctioning heavy violence, often extrajudicial, in his war on drugs, and aggressively persecuting political opponents.

Duterte honed his drug war strategy when serving as mayor of Davao City. He established a brutal police unit known as the "Davao Death Squad" that shot hundreds of alleged criminals, including street children, on sight. In a BBC interview, Duterte himself admitted that he shot and killed three people while serving as mayor.[37] Rather than hide from this brutality, Duterte has flaunted it, and continued these practices on a national scale as president. Soon after he was elected, he warned: "If you are still into drugs, I am going to kill you. Don't take this as a joke. I'm not trying to make you laugh. Sons of bitches, I'll really kill you."[38] Duterte wasn't kidding. While the official tally of drug war-related killings stands at approximate fifty-five hundred (the government has taken to using the hashtag #TheRealNumbersPH to publicize its statistics), advocacy groups estimate that the death toll is as high as twenty-seven thousand.[39] In December 2020, the International Criminal Court's chief prosecutor, Fatou Bensouda, indicated for the first time that there is a "reasonable basis to believe" that the drug war was responsible for crimes against humanity.[40]

Duterte has also been aggressive in persecuting select political opponents and government critics, often female, and making effective use of *sampol*. For over two years, the government has held Senator de Lima in detention. She has emerged as one of the staunchest critics of Duterte's drug war. As early as 2009, as chair of the Commission on Human Rights, she launched an investigation of the Davao Death Squad. More recently, de Lima led a 2016 senate committee investigation into the drug war and held a series of well-publicized hearings about extrajudicial killings.[41] In response, Duterte's administration initially smeared her with allegations of a sex tape involving her driver. Then the government used coerced testimony from convicted drug offenders to charge and arrest de Lima in February of 2017. She's been sitting in jail awaiting trial ever since (while still conducting senate business and casting votes from her prison cell). Resignedly, she said, "Definitely Duterte wants a conviction and to see me in jail for the rest of my life. There is no longer any doubt about that. I just hope I do not suffer the fate he wants me to."[42]

Duterte's persecution of journalist Ressa is also widely known. Ressa's long career as a journalist includes nearly two decades as CNN's lead investigative reporter for Southeast Asia. In 2012, she cofounded the online news site *Rappler*. "When we started *Rappler*," she explained in an interview, "we thought that we could help use this technology to build institutions bottom up."[43] She came in at the right time. Online use in the Philippine was skyrocketing, and her site garnered significant traffic and publicity. In the lead-up to the 2016 elections, Ressa organized an online town hall and invited all the presidential candidates to appear. Only Duterte showed up. For two hours, she used crowdsourced questions from Facebook to interview him. The impact was significant: "It was broadcast on two hundred television and radio stations, and viewing parties on more than forty college campuses across the Philippines tuned in as the event was livestreamed."[44] Figure 5.5 shows an outtake from the online town hall.

But their relationship soon soured. After Duterte was elected president, Ressa published a three-part piece about the government's weaponization of the Internet.[45] Ressa became the target of vicious online trolls. Then the government started pursuing legal means to persecute her. As she explained this evolution, "I was a journalist. Now I'm a criminal. And I watch that transformation start online, be repeated, and then be helpless. And then I hear it come from the president's mouth."[46] She has faced multiple charges and arrests on the basis of cyber libel and tax evasion. Death threats are a common occurrence. Most recently, she was convicted in June 2020 by a Manila count on cyber libel charges and faces up to six years in prison.[47] In response to Ressa's verdict, Sheila Coronel, a fellow journalist teaching at Columbia University, wrote the following:

> This is how democracy dies in the 21st century: in a musty courtroom, with a judge invoking Mandela. There are no power grabs in the dead of night, no tanks rolling down the streets, no uniformed officers taking over TV stations. Just the steady drip, drip, drip of the erosion of democratic norms, the corruption of institutions, and the cowardly compromises of decision makers in courts and congresses.[48]

Figure 5.5 Ressa Interviewing Duterte in 2016

While Duterte's violent tactics and persecutions have raised notice, he is even more exceptional for the manner in which his team has perfected the deployment of digital repression tools, particularly social manipulation and harassment, to uphold his popularity and vilify his opponents.

The Philippines' Digital Repression Context

The Philippines demonstrates increasingly high levels of digital repression. My data assigns the Philippines a digital repression score of 0.627 for 2019, ranking it fiftieth of 179 countries for prevalence of digital repression.[49] In Southeast Asia, only Cambodia, Vietnam, and Laos display higher levels of digital repression. Yet, as Figure 5.6 shows, its global ranking across the five categories of digital repression is uneven. The Philippines ranks twelfth globally for the prevalence of social manipulation and disinformation; it registers the fifteenth-highest level of social media surveillance in the world. In contrast, it has lower levels of censorship and arrests of online users.[50] My research also indicates that the Philippines is one of at least seventy-seven countries worldwide that have acquired AI and big-data public surveillance capabilities (see Appendix 4 for a full list of countries with AI capabilities).

Since Duterte's election, the Philippines' digital environment has deteriorated across the board. In 2018, the Freedom on the Net report downgraded the Philippines from a ranking of "free" to "partly free," due to concerns about constraints on Internet freedom, growing numbers of journalists being charged with libel, increased instances of state surveillance, and even technical attacks

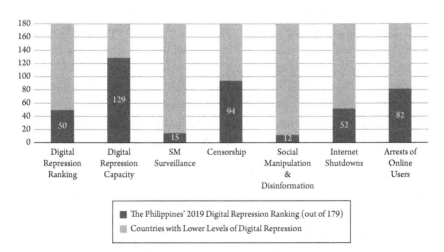

Figure 5.6 The Philippines' Digital Repression Performance in 2019

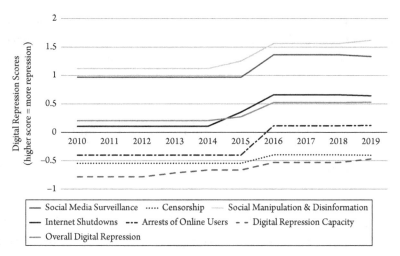

Figure 5.7 Disaggregated Digital Repression Trends in the Philippines, 2010 to 2019

against independent media groups.[51] Figure 5.7 shows a troubling increase in all measures of digital repression beginning in 2016.

The sizable gap between the government's digital repression capacity and its actual deployment of digital techniques is worth noting. The implication of this disparity is that the government is finding ways to make up the gap, most likely through extensive external sourcing of equipment and technology from China, Israel, the United States, and others.[52]

When it comes to the country's deteriorating digital environment, some activists, like Human Rights Watch's Carlos Conde, believe the government's sensitivity to criticism of the drug war is fueling restrictions: "I think the estimation of the government is to shut down potential critics, just as it is shutting down journalists who are critical of the drug war."[53] Concern about the government's growing intolerance of disagreement was echoed by Marc Siapno, spokesperson for the Philippines' Commission on Human Rights: "As you can see, any form of dissent is being targeted as a means to destabilize the government."[54] Their apprehensions may be bearing out. In May 2020, the government refused to renew the license of its largest media broadcaster, ABS-CBN. The network has long had a combative relationship with Duterte, but denying it the ability to continue operating came as a shock. The National Union of Journalists of the Philippines released a blunt statement, saying, "It sends a clear message: What Duterte wants, Duterte gets. And it is clear, with this brazen move to shut down ABS-CBN, that he intends to silence the critical media and intimidate everyone else into submission."[55]

Other commentators are less discouraged and contend that the government has a vested interest in maintaining free expression—particularly because Duterte has derived so much benefit from a no-holds-barred speech environment. Winthrop Yu, chair of the Philippines Internet Society, pointedly observed, "Let me put it this way. Do you think that the Duterte administration would suppress quote-unquote 'online freedoms' given that they benefited so obviously from it in 2016? And even now in the midterm elections in 2019? Was it actually a burden on them even with the Facebook crackdown? No."[56]

Likewise, the public provides a mixed reaction about the perceived ability to speak freely. An August 2019 survey shows that nearly 60 percent of respondents maintain that they can say anything they want, even if it is against the administration (18 percent disagreed). But in the same poll, 51 percent agreed that it is risky to broadcast an opinion about the government even if it represents the truth (20 percent disagreed).[57] This inconsistency may reflect Filipinos' inner conflict when it comes to balancing their free speech rights with the realities of an increasingly restrictive online environment.

Drivers of Digital Repression in the Philippines

What are the primary drivers of digital repression in the Philippines? What explains why the Duterte regime has so aggressively relied on a specific set of digital tools to advance its political objectives? I contend that three domestic factors are primarily responsible for the expansion of digital repression in the Philippines.

First, more than most other countries globally, the Philippines' population is *hyperconnected to social media*. By most estimates, 97 percent of Filipinos who are connected to the Internet are on Facebook. This means that digital strategies have an outsized impact in the country.

Second, the *weakness of democracy* in the Philippines makes it particularly suited to certain types of digital repression strategies, namely social manipulation and harassment.

Third, *Duterte has proven exceptionally adept* at weaponizing the Internet and deploying social manipulation strategies like disinformation to reinforce his political agenda. Without the rise of Duterte's particular brand of explosive populism, the Philippines would be far less likely to be awash in disinformation-led repression.

Hyperconnectivity and Social Media Use in the Philippines

Filipinos are exceptionally ardent users of social media. Before Facebook, YouTube, or WhatsApp even existed, Filipinos were champion texters and social media devotees. From early on, the Philippines became known as "the texting capital of the world," and continues to maintain one of the highest rates of texting globally.[58] Likewise, pre-Facebook, Filipinos used the social media site Friendster to connect with strangers, strike up conversations, and facilitate dating. Even as the site began to flounder in the United States, it remained strong in the Philippines. As late as 2008, it was the most visited website in the country, maintaining an active user base of twelve million people.[59]

Notwithstanding Filipinos' affection for Friendster, in time they migrated en masse to Facebook. Currently, 97 percent of all Internet users in the Philippines access the web through Facebook. (Ressa famously relayed this figure to Mark Zuckerberg to emphasize Facebook's impact in the country; he apparently frowned and responded, "Oh well. What are the other three percent doing, Maria?")[60]

This data reinforces just how dominant social media are to the Philippines. An estimated 76 million people there (of the total population of 107 million) actively use social media. However, two statistics are particularly eye-popping. First, the Philippines leads the world when it comes to the amount of time per day that its citizens spend on social media sites: four hours and twelve minutes. Second, the percentage of the Philippines' eligible population—adults thirteen years and older—who access social media is 99 percent, also the highest in the world.[61] The top five sites in the Philippines, according to percentage of total Internet users, include Facebook (97 percent), YouTube (96 percent), Instagram (64 percent), Twitter (54 percent), and Skype (44 percent).

Why have Filipinos embraced social media to such an extent?

One reason is economic. While the Philippines economy has made strides in recent years, it is still a poor country; over 20 percent of its population falls below the poverty line.[62] As a result, many citizens lack the means to pay for mobile data plans to access the Internet. To fill this gap, SMS promotions frequently bundle "free Facebook" in their packages, allowing users to access Facebook via the Free Basics app with no deduction from their data plans. For many Filipinos, Facebook has thereby become synonymous with the Internet, giving the platform tremendous market power.[63]

A second reason for social media's prevalence is geographic fragmentation. The population of the Philippines is spread out across 7,641 islands. Communication can be challenging, particularly with antiquated telecom infrastructure, variable weather, and unreliable transport. Social media fill this void, providing an instant means for different communities to stay in touch. The Philippines also has one of the highest migrant working populations in the world. The last recorded numbers from 2013 show that over ten million "overseas Filipino workers" (OFW) were working abroad in various capacities, comprising almost 10 percent of the country's population.[64] As Conde noted, social media are in such high demand for "the same reason why text messaging exploded in the Philippines in the 1990s. Because wherever we are in the world, we need to get in touch."[65]

Not only is social media use prevalent, but surveys show that it has significant influence in shaping Filipino voting patterns and political views. The polling firm Pulse Asia Research ran several surveys in 2018 and 2019 to assess social media's political impact. One of the questions in a 2018 survey asked Filipinos whether they had ever changed their views about politics or government based on something they had seen on social media. Fifty-one percent replied affirmatively.[66] The same survey also found that 88 percent of Filipinos had encountered fake news on social media. In a follow-up 2019 survey conducted prior to the midterm elections, respondents were asked how much candidates' social media postings would affect their vote. Seventy-five percent responded that these posts were "very influential" or "somewhat influential" in determining whom they would vote for.

What these survey results indicate is that high social media usage, combined with strong reliance on social media as a political news source, renders these platforms exceptionally vulnerable to political manipulation in the Philippines. It is logical that political candidates would seek to influence social media messaging to benefit their objectives. Duterte's targeting of the OFW population is a good case in point.

Duterte's team perceived that OFWs were preoccupied by a few key issues. Conde related: "Ask them, what are the things that you really care about? They say that 'I earn enough money abroad so that I can send them back to my family in the Philippines, so I'm putting food on the table. Second, I hope that they [children] use the money that we send them for school. . . . And the third is, I am hoping that they don't go into drugs or into a life of crime.'" Duterte's antidrug messaging was perfectly tailored to this group's primary fears. He pushed a narrative that said, "Vote for me and your family back home will be OK. I'm going to be the father. I'm going to be the father that you're not right now. I'm going to be a parent that you're not right now."[67] His campaign preyed on the central OFW insecurity that crime was overtaking the country and belief that only a superempowered leader could turn the tide. Predictably, OFWs made up a huge bloc of Duterte's support. An estimated 1.3 million OFWs voted in 2016, the majority of whom sided with Duterte.[68]

One additional cultural aspect that's worth noting is the country's low level of digital literacy. While the Philippines has a long track record of engaging with social media, its rural-based population in particular struggles with basic literacy and educational attainment.[69] This limitation may make the general population more susceptible to social media manipulation. De Lima said it bluntly: "Our literacy achievement is barely basic and does not closely approach functional levels. When you combine a well-oiled social media operation with this kind of audience, you come up with ignorant and unenlightened people who cannot determine fact from fake news, and who end up echoing and sharing the latter."[70]

Democratic Weakness in the Philippines

A second driver of digital repression is democratic weakness. While the Philippines has been an electoral democracy for many years, its system is also plagued by serious governance shortcomings. Its "democratic deficit" is marked by elite control, institutional fragility, extensive abuse of public office, and patronage politics.[71] Democratic fragility is further exacerbated by a constitution that reserves extraordinary powers for the president. While its constitution was modeled after the American version, and includes three independent branches with associated checks and balances, the president was also given enhanced powers: control over decisions to suspend habeas corpus, discretion to assume emergency powers, and control over "national finance and budgetary appropriations" as well as amendments to the constitution.[72] This enhancement has supported the rise of a "strong presidency," a condition easily exploited for repressive purposes by a forceful leader. Unsurprisingly, political parties are historically weak in the country. They tend to be vehicles for charismatic politicians and carry low institutional weight.

Despite these structural constraints, scholars Paul D. Hutchcroft and Joel Rocamora observe, "No country in Asia has more experience with democratic institutions than the Philippines."[73] In the decades since the 1986 People Power uprising, weakened, liberal norms have persisted in the Philippines.[74] This suggests that the public may have a lower tolerance for overt repression (blanket censorship, extensive surveillance, and mass persecution of critics), but is susceptible to more subtle forms of repression, particularly social manipulation and harassment.

Social manipulation and disinformation are well suited to illiberal political environments. These tactics are just repressive enough to have significant political impact and cement Duterte's illiberal governance. But they are not so repressive as to generate a popular backlash. Disinformation allows the state to stay consistent with the Philippines' political culture while aggressively pushing a political agenda to demonize opponents and maintain power. As Seva Gunitsky notes, social media not only allow incumbents to spread propaganda more efficiently, but "Propaganda via message framing goes beyond brute-force censoring to choreograph and channel the bounds of acceptable deliberation."[75]

Similarly, when it comes to censorship, the government knows that if it started banning websites and directly restricting speech, such aggressive measures would risk a sharp popular reaction. Instead, the government selectively prosecutes a small number of cases against government critics like Ressa, Senator Antonio Trillanes IV, and de Lima. This approach not only keeps Ressa, Trillanes, and de Lima off balance and preoccupied with upcoming trials, but serves as a warning to the broader community about the consequences of speaking out against Duterte. Ressa cautions, "This case of cyber libel stretches the rule of law until it breaks. Ludicrous doesn't begin to describe how the law has been weaponized today against perceived critics."[76] In an ominous turn, Duterte signed antiterrorism legislation in July 2020 that provides even greater prosecutorial discretion for the government to arrest its critics. The law includes a purposefully vague provision that criminalize speeches, writings, banners, or other representations that incite terrorism, even if the action itself lacks a direct connection to the commission of a terrorist act.[77]

Democratic weakness has enabled Duterte to take advantage of systemic flaws of the "once dominant liberal reformist order," and to erect elements of an illiberal democracy in its place.[78] The government has reduced media freedoms, enacted a campaign to punish critics and opponents, committed serious human rights violations against alleged drug war culprits, and justified these actions through inflammatory statements, false information, and the deliberate dissemination of misleading content.

The Duterte Effect

A third driver of digital repression relates to Duterte himself. Digital repression would be a much lower concern in the Philippines if not for the presence of a leader willing to activate these strategies. Had one of the liberal presidential candidates such as Senator Grace Poe or Interior Secretary Mar Roxas won the 2016 election, it is unlikely that the Philippines would face such problems. Unlike in Thailand, where digital repression is a function of deeply rooted censorship and autocratic norms, the Philippines lacks the same tradition of authoritarian control.

Duterte brings two important qualities relevant to digital repression. First, his fiery populist rhetoric aligns well with specific digital tactics. He successfully manufactured a crime and drug war crisis, and then employed bellicose rhetoric to describe how he would handle it. By calling out critics as "sons of bitches" and telling soldiers that if they commit rape, "that's on me," he is signaling resolve to his supporters and painting a sharp contrast with his opponents. This strategic positioning allows him to reset standards of appropriate conduct and empower a wider army of "Dutertards" to threaten similar vile acts against his opponents.[79]

Second, Duterte assembled a crack social manipulation team that has proved incredibly adept at disseminating false information, inflaming segments of the population against his critics, and reinforcing his macho narrative. Partly, these actions were taken out of necessity. For much of his presidential campaign, Duterte faced long odds. He lacked the resources and exposure to get sufficient airtime on TV or radio. So he turned to social media.

As his former social media manager, Nic Gabunada, explains: "When we realized we didn't have money for TV, radio, print, billboards, etc., we made the decision to tap up the social media groups."[80] They reached out to the OFW community and tailored specific messages of the week to chapters known as "Duterte warriors."[81] Gabunada's P10 million budget (approximately $200,000) helped him leverage a volunteer network of four hundred to five hundred persons, each of whom were connected to thousands more members. But the campaign didn't just rely on accounts connected to real people. They also created fake accounts, known as "sock puppets," that were followed by millions of people. A *Rappler* investigation revealed that one particular fake account had 2.9 million followers; another "was linked to over 990,000 members of groups supporting President Rodrigo Duterte," and a third "connected to an estimated 3.8 million members of various overseas Filipino organizations and buy-and-sell groups."[82] All told, *Rappler* identified twenty-six fake accounts connected to the Duterte campaign in mid-2016; these accounts ultimately reached an audience of over three million Facebook users.

The campaign also enlisted the help of high-profile social media influencers to magnify specific narratives. Controversial personalities like singer Mocha Uson, who has more than four million Facebook followers, publicly backed Duterte. His team used clever hashtags, such as #Du30 (which plays off the president's name). They harnessed their efforts around the clock, twenty-four hours a day: "Late at night the people from abroad, the [workers] in a different time zone took over, people from Europe, people from down under, or the Middle East."[83] They created a never-ending stream of provocations and incitements that dominated the political conversation. A month before the election, Duterte dominated "64 percent of all election-related conversations on the Facebook pages in the Philippines."[84]

Following Duterte's victory, his team did not scatter. Instead, they shifted focus and applied the same strategies to advance his political objectives. Their efforts gained potency. They are no longer a band of upstarts trying to disrupt politics as usual. They now oversee all the organs of state. They control the airwaves, dominate social media, and direct key institutions—including the DOJ, PNP, and the bully pulpit of Malacañang Palace—to execute Duterte's agenda. In three short years, Duterte's team has effectively mainstreamed digital repression tactics into his governance.

How Digital Repression Works in the Philippines

This section will begin by explaining how the network of digital repression operates in the Philippines, then describe how the government implements its social manipulation strategy, how legal persecutions complement this strategy, and the role and impact of surveillance.

The Philippines' Network of Digital Repression

A complex web of political actors work together to coordinate digital repression in the Philippines. They comprise three main nodes. The first node includes Duterte and close aides in the executive branch. This group undertakes three primary activities: directing information operations, coordinating financing for such activities, and overseeing legal enforcement and persecution. Panelo and his team in the Presidential Communications Operations Office (PCOO) oversee messaging and coordinate with outside influencers and editorialists, such as RJ Nieto, Sass Sassot, and Rigoberto Tiglao from the *Manila Times*.

Conde observed that "the PCOO is the nerve center of a lot of this [disinformation], supposedly with the help of the Chinese, probably even the Russians."[85] Often Panelo will set a top-line message that influencers and pro-government media will amplify. But it can go the other way as well. Tiglao in particular generates stories that Malacañang later picks up. As Nery, Tiglao's former colleague observed, "What Tiglao is, he tries out different themes, talking points, so to speak. And then the others try to spread that and see which ones stick."[86]

On the financial side, many experts identify Carlos Dominguez, the secretary of finance, as the key person working with outside funders to keep the Philippines disinformation machine running.[87] Dominguez has longtime political and business ties, including serving as the chief executive of Philippine Airlines.

When it comes to legal enforcement, Menardo Guevarra, the secretary of justice, conducts operations on Duterte's behalf—in conjunction with security-intelligence agencies like the PNP, National Bureau of Investigation, National Security Council, and National Intelligence Coordinating Agency. Activities range from prosecuting the war on drugs to developing cases against political critics like de Lima, Trillanes, and Ressa. Duterte keeps a close watch on all of these activities and seems to have a direct hand in their implementation: as Conde explained, "They get all of those things, all of these directives, from the president himself. It's not even clear [the role] of the executive secretary or his closest confidants, because they rarely speak in public. It's always him. It appears top down."[88]

The second node coordinating digital repression is represented by Duterte's major political allies. One such important cluster has been deemed the "three Marias": Sara Duterte (the president's daughter and mayor of Davao City), Gloria Macapagal Arroyo (the former president), and María "Imee" Marcos (the regional governor and daughter of longtime ruler Ferdinand Marcos).[89] Not only does each of these figures hold influential political offices, but they are part of powerful family dynasties that wield significant sway in Philippines politics.[90] They regularly talk to each other and coordinate different parts of Duterte's agenda. This node also includes two new senators—Bong Go and Ronald "Bato" dela Rosa—each of whom is personally close to Duterte and ran important parts of his executive branch agenda prior to attaining elected office in 2019. Finally, Diosdado Peralta, chief justice of the Philippines Supreme Court (installed after Duterte engineered the ouster of the prior chief justice, Maria Lourdes Sereno) and senate president Tito Sotto are critical allies helping Duterte move legislation and obtain favorable court rulings.

The third node comprises outside actors who play important roles in amplifying disinformation narratives or financing those operations. This group includes prominent social media influencers (Uson, Sassot, Nieto) as well as anonymous page owners who "occupy the middle ground in the networks of disinformation.... They have a massive online real estate with organic followers ranging from 50,000 to 2 million."[91] Also included are TV media personalities who anchor government broadcasts (Tulfo brothers), and wealthy financiers with links to Duterte (Dennis Uy, Antonio "Tonyboy" Floirendo Jr., and the Alcantaras).[92] With midterm elections concluded and a lull until the next presidential campaign heats up, Conde explained that at the moment the major influencers were relatively quiet: "They've done their thing. They've done their purpose.... Sort of like saying it's quieter now because your noisy neighbor is not noisy. But they're still there. There's still noise.... They're going to come out of the woodwork you know in 2020."[93] Figure 5.8 shows how these three nodes work together to mutually reinforce digital repression strategies.

As the diagram illustrates, the Philippine state focuses its digital repression efforts in two main areas: social manipulation and disinformation, and targeted persecution of government opponents. The government also periodically uses surveillance technology, albeit less frequently. What follows is a more detailed exploration of each of these tactics.

Social Manipulation and Disinformation

While social manipulation may appear to be a messy, chaotic effort only loosely overseen by the state, this is far from the case. Social manipulation in

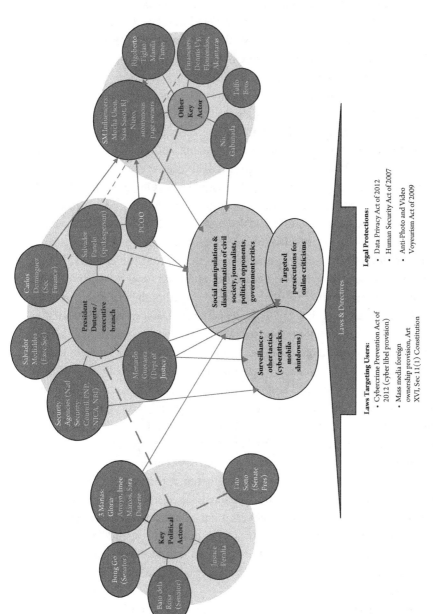

Figure 5.8 Network of Digital Repression in the Philippines

the Philippines is a systematic, state-sponsored strategy to deliberately spread a combination of true and false information to shape beliefs and manipulate political narratives. This is not unusual. Researchers from the Institute for the Future observe that "the approach is uniquely designed to take advantage of the current digital ecosystem, leveraging the virality and familiarity of social media to amplify state messaging, and deploying bots, hashtags, and memes to disguise industrial campaigns as organic groundswells."[94]

The government's social manipulation strategy rests on an intertwined set of messages and tactics. Its messaging hews to one of four themes: (1) spreading pro-government propaganda, (2) attacking and smearing opposition politicians and government critics, (3) driving distrust and polarization, and (4) deploying personal attacks and harassment to suppress disfavored speech.[95]

Pro-government propaganda can take many forms. On September 2, 2016, months after Duterte became president, a bomb killed fourteen people in a night market in Davao, where Duterte had formerly served as mayor.[96] This attack represented a major security crisis for Duterte. Almost immediately, he declared a "state of lawlessness" (akin to martial law) throughout the country.[97] Soon Facebook posts started appearing, sharing an unrelated news story from March 2016, about how police had arrested a man carrying a bomb in Davao. This older story rapidly became conflated with the newer crisis. Dates were manipulated so that it appeared that Duterte's "state of lawlessness" announcement had directly prevented a new bomb attack. This false news story was "picked up and shared by Facebook political advocacy pages for President Rodrigo Duterte. Other websites took the entire dated story and reposted it on their sites."[98] Additional Facebook pages picked up the thread, including pro-government sites like Digong Duterte and Duterte Warrior. And just like that, Duterte's regime leveraged a real emergency into a beneficial disinformation campaign.

In another notorious stunt orchestrated by Duterte's camp, Duterte campaign spokesman Peter Tiu Laviña posted a picture on Facebook of a nine-year-old girl who allegedly had been raped and murdered by drug criminals—the very targets of the government's war on drugs (see Figure 5.9). Laviña lambasted human rights activists, religious figures, and "presstitutes" for their silence on this incident. But it was soon uncovered that this was a manufactured event; Laviña had used a widely available photo from an unrelated crime in Brazil.[99]

From the outset, Duterte's team made it a top priority for Duterte to receive plenty of positive coverage—whether real or fake. For example, four days after he declared his candidacy for president, from midnight to 2: 00 a.m. "More than 30,000 tweets mentioning Rodrigo Duterte were posted, at times reaching more than 700 tweets per minute." This represented more tweets than any presidential candidate received over the previous twenty-nine days.[100]

Peter Tiu Lavina
August 27 at 5:02am · ❸

🔊 Follow

Truly revolting - Nine year-old raped and murdered and we haven't heard
condemning this brutal act from human rightists, bishops and "presstitutes"
who are derailing the government's war against drugs and crime. Among
others, they are more concerned with the human rights of criminals and
worried about our country's so-called "image" abroad. They clearly exhibit
elitist mindsets in trying to keep up with the Joneses to be good in
appearances but rotten to the core. Ngek! Our righteous battles against
drugs and crime are fierce and relentless because we face the Devil himself.
We cannot be soft or let our guards down lest we ourselves will be devoured
and be defeated!

👍 Like   💬 Comment   ↪ Share

Figure 5.9 Debunked Photo Used by Duterte Supporters to Justify the Government's
War on Drugs

The second messaging theme is to deliberately smear opposition figures and
government critics. A favorite tactic is to mimic choice insults from Duterte
and direct them toward specific politicians or journalists. The use of the phrase
"sons of bitches" is a good illustration. This has become a catchphrase of the
president, who employs it liberally to disparage investigative journalists, thorny
activists, or political opponents. His supporters have taken notice. Mocha Uson,
who briefly served in Duterte's government, publicly lambasted vice president
Leni Robredo: "Leni, you are stupid. You and your whole staff are stupid. You're
all sons of bitches." Similarly, Bruce Rivera, a prominent Duterte supporter,
posted the following tirade against the National Union of Journalists of the

Philippines: "You sons of bitches, you are not above the President because he has the support of the people." RJ Nieto, who runs the well-known Facebook page "Thinking Pinoy," employs similar language: "You Malacañang Press Corps, you act like you're for the Filipino people, but you're sons of bitches!"[101]

These sorts of attacks, particularly accusations that government opponents are committing treason or betraying the country, are a common strategy that predates social media. What is new is how much social media rapidly amplify provocative charges, bringing a cascade effect. For example, Leila de Lima has emerged as the foremost public critic of Duterte's drug war. As a result, she has attracted tremendous online vitriol; Facebook posts routinely disparage her as the "patron saint of drug lords." Then a social media campaign with the hashtag #ArrestLeilaDeLima went viral. In February 2017, the government arrested her on dubious drug charges; she has languished in prison ever since.[102] In email correspondence, she told me that "Duterte's mainstream media verbal assaults against me were complemented by orchestrated, organized, and government-funded social media attacks launched by Duterte fanatics like Mocha Uson, RJ Nieto, and Sass Rogando Sasot. Adding to all this is the chorus of vilification and slut-shaming launched by Duterte henchmen."[103]

Online users have tried to replicate the success of that campaign by initiating a similar offensive against Ressa—#ArrestMariaRessa. While Ressa has avoided imprisonment thus far, she faces an upcoming trial for violating foreign ownership laws.

Third, the state deploys messages to drive distrust and foment polarization in the Philippines. The state's primary target has been liberal and leftwing activists, especially those who have been critical of Duterte's drug war tactics. The government has taken to labeling these individuals as communists in a manner known as "red tagging." In February 2018, the DOJ issued a formal petition listing over six hundred people, including the UN special rapporteur on the rights of indigenous people, as members of the Communist Party of the Philippines and its armed wing. Not only did this step stir up hatred and distrust toward those individuals, but it also put them "at risk of extrajudicial execution."[104] Eventually, the DOJ admitted that it had not personally verified names included on the list and reduced the names from 649 to only 8.[105]

Similarly, Duterte's regime targets journalists. *Rappler* documents four words that the government uses repeatedly to delegitimize Philippines media: "bias," *bayaran* (meaning corrupt), "oligarchs" (referring to journalists who work for paid interests), and "clickbait" (journalists only interested in using clickbait headlines for cash).[106] To get a sense of the scale of this usage, in the period of time *Rappler* monitored the deployment of these words (2016–2018), close to fifty thousand posts and over 1.8 million comments used the term *bayaran*, most of them in reference to the media.[107]

Fourth, state-sponsored actors use personal attacks and harassment against individuals to suppress speech and intimidate targets. These actions can include both online and complementary offline actions. A chilling example relates to a Facebook Live broadcast that took place at *Rappler* headquarters in early 2019. On the afternoon of February 21, two bloggers, Mark Lopez and Jovybev Aquino, trespassed into *Rappler* headquarters and started livestreaming to thousands of viewers. As Gemma Bagayaua-Mendoza, head of research for *Rappler*, described it, "They actually went to our office and did a live stream there, in front of our office. And what was very disturbing to us—within the live stream, in the comments section, people were saying, 'We'd like to go there also.'" She continued, "They were commenting, saying . . . threats. When someone asked that person where the office is, . . . he gave the address. It's like you have a whole stream here where people are commenting, provoking others to bomb our place, bomb our office, set fire to it, stuff like that. And then you give that [address] . . . that was live-streamed."[108] During the incident, the bloggers exhorted *Rappler* to pay taxes owed to the government instead of embarrassing the country in front of an international audience. One comment declared that "the people should attack, then drag that whore out of their office since they are destroying the Philippines!" Another declared, "Just bomb the *Rappler* office so the problem is solved."[109] The deliberate targeting of government critics through abuse and harassment in order to create silence is a classic social manipulation tactic used by governments, comments Camille Francois, from "Venezuela to Turkey, Ecuador to India" (some experts term these actions "patriotic trolling").[110]

To carry out this messaging, Duterte's team relies on four social manipulation tools: (1) disinformation, (2) trolling and harassment, (3) flooding, and (4) bots and automation.[111]

Disinformation is a favored tactic employed by Duterte's network. For example, photos that purported to show Senator de Lima in a compromising sexual situation went viral in 2016, helping delegitimize her efforts to check Duterte's drug war. Subsequent sleuthing revealed that the photos were doctored and taken from a porn site, but the damage to de Lima's reputation had already accrued.[112]

Trolling and harassment are also widely used. The frequent use of the term "presstitutes" by pro-Duterte supporters is a good illustration of trolling and was first invoked by Mocha Uson (*Rappler* traces first usage of "presstitute" to 4:45 a.m. on August 27, 2016). Seventeen minutes later, Duterte's campaign spokesperson, Peter Tiu Laviña, used "presstitute" to attack critics of the government's drug war. At its peak, *Rappler* documented 194 pro-government Facebook groups using "presstitute" in posts reaching 6.57 million members.[113]

Flooding acts as a "tax" on good information by requiring more time to separate out legitimate sources from false ones. This tactic is especially relied upon by state-sponsored trolls to drown out abuse allegations related to Duterte's drug war.

Bots and automation are the fourth set of tools used by Duterte's team. The surge in mentions of Duterte's candidacy after he announced his intent to run for president (thirty thousand tweets posted in two hours) is a prime example of how bots can manipulate discourse and prop up a candidate. Figure 5.10 shows the interplay between messaging narratives and social manipulation tools in the Philippines.

How Culpable Is Facebook?

The amount of disinformation permeating Philippines social media has reached such astronomic proportions that employees at Facebook refer to the country as "patient zero."[114] Some experts argue that Facebook is directly responsible for making this situation possible. In his book *Antisocial Media*, Siva Vaidhyanathan contends that Facebook formed a mutually beneficial partnership with Duterte and is riding his coattails to ever greater market influence: "With the rise of Duterte, Facebook solidified itself as the only media service that matters in the Philippines."[115] Moreover, Vaidhyanathan charges that Facebook has allowed itself to serve "as the chief propaganda and harassment platform for the Duterte regime." He contends that if Facebook wants to continue raking in profits, it has little choice but to "continue to support Duterte as he expands his campaigns of terror."[116] Other experts echo Vaidhyanathan's criticisms about Facebook's role

Figure 5.10 Social Manipulation Messaging and Tactics in the Philippines

in the Philippines. Ressa has famously decried that "Facebook broke democracy."[117] Facebook, she told me, served as the "perfect weapon for somebody like him [Duterte]."[118]

But blaming Facebook for the Philippines' polarized politics and vitriolic online environment doesn't convey the whole story. Facebook is a conduit and reflection of deeper societal ills. While social media can enhance and accelerate distrust and division, platforms don't operate in a vacuum. Social media require an underlying set of conditions that they exacerbate. If Facebook were to cease its operations in the Philippines, causing the population to migrate to alternative platforms, it is inconceivable that cyber trolling, online harassment, and other associated problems would disappear from the country's politics.

This is why individuals like Maria Ressa, who are so deeply entrenched in the Philippines' media landscape, find themselves torn about how to treat Facebook. She cautioned, "You can't throw the baby out with the bathwater. . . . It's so easy to paint Facebook as the devil." She admitted, "I'm so conflicted. I don't know. I don't think it's enough. But I know that they're good people and they're trying. And so, you know, you tell me if you see a solution."

Facebook officials readily admit in public and private that they made many missteps along the way in the Philippines. But they argue that they are learning from their mistakes and insist their recent actions demonstrate a new awareness. One contact noted, "It's not just about money. . . . There was a collective decision to go from, 'OK, this is going to be something that these guys [trollers] have been earning,' to, 'Oh my God, they're earning from the platform and earning because of disinformation. You have to take them down.' "[119] Officials at Facebook seem to be coming around to the idea that in the long run such alarming behavior is bad for business and bad for the future growth of the platform. They are more willing to kick the worst offenders off the platform—even those with high-level ties to Duterte. For example, in March 2019, Facebook took down two hundred pages and accounts linked to Omnicom, which is overseen by Nic Gabunada, Duterte's former social media campaign chief.[120] Earlier in the year, Facebook also banned 220 pages and accounts linked to Twinmark Media for "coordinated inauthentic behavior."[121]

Unsurprisingly, Facebook's recent actions haven't endeared it to the Duterte government. Government officials aren't shy about pushing back against the company and accusing it of bias against Duterte. When new members of Facebook's Philippines public policy team are hired, the government scrutinizes their backgrounds for political leanings. The government is not averse to publicly trolling new hires—creating online posters, memes, and hashtags alleging political unfairness. One tech official related, "They [government] make a general statement and then that's done. And then the trolls pick it up. And then they start an attack. But normally it just lasts for a few days." Pushback also occurs in closed-door meetings, where the government frequently charges that "someone high up is biased against them in Facebook" (paralleling a tactic used with increasing frequency by Republican operatives in the United States alleging anti-conservative bias).[122]

While Facebook has started to grudgingly receive the message that it must change its way of doing business, there is a limit to how much reform Facebook is prepared to undertake. Often the company appears to be a willing participant in a slow-moving game of whack-a-mole: ban just enough bad actors to appease its critics but refrain from undertaking serious changes that would jeopardize Facebook's moneymaking machine.

Legal Repression Complementing Online Harassment

Duterte doesn't just rely upon social manipulation to suppress critics and advance his agenda. The government supplements disinformation campaigns with legal prosecutions (frequently charging individuals under the Cybercrime Prevention Act of 2012 or for violations of the mass media foreign ownership provision in the constitution).[123] The Philippines' new national security law will further amplify the government's ability to prosecute individuals at will. Opposition politicians are major targets. That list includes de Lima, who continues to languish in jail, former chief justice Sereno (ousted from office ostensibly for tax misconduct), and Trillanes (on trial for old sedition charges pardoned under Benigno Aquino).[124]

Independent media outlets are also under increasing legal pressure. The Committee for the Protection of Journalists (CPJ) notes that "the government is using a tri-pronged approach to intimidate the press via verbal assaults, social media attacks, and threats to withdraw media groups' licenses or hit their commercial interests."[125] Authorities have suspended the license of TV network ABS-CBN. *Rappler* faces a litany of charges. Before Ressa was convicted on cyber libel charges, she told me that she was fighting "eleven cases that were filed by the government in about fourteen months," adding up to almost one case per month. "That's had an impact on everything in my world. It's prevented us from innovating, obtaining resources."[126]

But it is not just high-profile figures that face the Philippines state's persecution. The human rights group Karapatan documents 1,831 activists whom the Duterte government has arrested and detained since July 2016 "as a consequence of doing human rights work in the Philippines."[127] Many of these activists are first identified and attacked online by state-sponsored trolls, and later detained on spurious grounds by the PNP. A significant number are killed under suspicious circumstances. CPJ's 2018 Global Impunity Index ranks the Philippines fifth worldwide for the number of unsolved journalist deaths as a percentage of a country's population. Duterte must be pleased. After all, he has warned that "just because you're a journalist you are not exempted from assassination if you're a son of a bitch."[128]

I met with Kris Ablan, a senior official in PCOO who oversees the government's freedom-of-information program (an odd position given the government's relentless campaign to discredit and harass journalists). From the outset, he emphasized that "press freedom is very much alive" and that other countries were implementing much more oppressive restrictions: "You have the anti-fake news laws of Germany. You have Singapore recently passed one a few years ago, Malaysia, and also in Singapore the new one that just got passed a couple weeks ago." When I asked him how the government could claim it was a defender of press freedoms while simultaneously allowing criminal libel statutes to be weaponized against government critics, he clarified that these cases were filed by individuals "for one thing or another," and that people were using the statute "whether or not there is a collaborative [government] effort to maximize the use of libel or cyber libel." He concluded, "I think this should be left to you to study. But for me they are there and they're being used."[129] That wasn't a particularly satisfying answer, but Ablan didn't seem to have anything better to offer. A few months after this meeting, Duterte's allies in the senate introduced an anti-false content bill. The legislation authorizes the government to take down content deemed false or misleading. Human Rights Watch blasts the law as opening the door for the government to "wantonly clamp down on critical opinions or information not only in the Philippines, but around the globe."[130]

State of Surveillance

The government has shown increased interest in adopting advanced surveillance techniques, particularly for law enforcement and crime prevention purposes. While these tactics carry far less weight in the Philippines than social manipulation or legal repression, the potential exists for surveillance to take on a greater role in the future. One sign of the government's interest in surveillance relates to the controversial "Safe Philippines" program. In 2018, Duterte signed a series of partnerships with China during Xi Jinping's state visit to Manila. Among these alliances was a $400 million agreement to establish a twelve-thousand-camera surveillance system to be implemented by China International Telecommunication and Construction Corporation and Huawei.[131] The deal would establish eighteen command centers scattered around metro Manila and Davao City, linking facial recognition cameras with intelligent operations posts. The project is financed by a Chinese state loan that requires the Philippines government to pay 20 percent of costs,[132] and has caused enough consternation that the Philippines senate has provisionally blocked its funding.[133]

But this would not be the first time that advanced surveillance found its way into the Philippines. In 2004, for example, the "Hello Garci" scandal involving former president Gloria Arroyo stunned the nation: A recorded confidential phone conversation concerning electoral fraud between Arroyo and an election commissioner was leaked by unknown individuals. The source of the tape has never been verified, but there is strong reason to believe that a military intelligence group used signals interception technology to carry out the wiretapping and then disclosed it for unclear reasons. The resulting furor led to mass demonstrations in the streets and nearly took down Arroyo's government.[134]

In 2012, the Davao City government—under Sara Duterte's leadership (her father was temporarily serving as vice mayor due to term limits)—partnered with IBM to install an intelligent operations center to "monitor residents in real time with cutting-edge video analytics, multichannel communications technology, and GPS-enabled patrol vehicles."[135] While this technology was coming to Davao, the city's police forces were facing increasing scrutiny for extrajudicial killings related to Davao's drug war and for fostering a "climate of impunity."[136] Whether local police forces relied upon this technology to assist in counterdrug operations is unclear. But at least one law enforcement expert claims that the program assisted the police in "gathering intelligence on the activities of the political opposition in Davao," and admitted that he could not "rule out" that the data feed was implicated in extrajudicial killings.[137]

There are also reports that the government is expanding its use of social media surveillance. Freedom House notes that Philippine officials traveled to the United States in 2018 to support the development of a social media monitoring unit—presumably to combat disinformation from terrorist groups.[138] Similarly, the Department of Information and Communications Technology (DICT) recently contracted with the Israeli tech firm Verint Systems to set up a new cybersecurity management system that will include social media monitoring capabilities.[139]

Philippine officials defend the adoption of surveillance technology as a necessary step to keep the public safe. In a conversation with Secretary Eliseo Rio, who was running DICT at the time, he acknowledged, "We know all of this facial recognition is not perfect. . . . But our police and law enforcement say that it's better than nothing. In other words it gives you something to start with. It may lead to false arrest . . . but you have to undergo these birth pains."[140] Given the poor record and alarming impunity of the Philippines police, arming them with sophisticated surveillance equipment is troubling. Even if the government currently has no intent to implement a mass surveillance program, as Conde noted,

"The danger is that the Chinese are giving this guy [Duterte] ideas, ideas that he may never have thought of."[141]

Yet many activists I talked to were skeptical that the police had the capacity to take advantage of advanced surveillance capabilities. Frances Acero, who serves on the National Privacy Commission, observed: "I don't think it's on the radar yet [mass surveillance]. There is generally the assumption that these guys don't have the funds to operate it anyway. So a lot of the intelligence is just gathered by people outside and people on the ground. It's a lot less reliant on tech."[142]

Several people I spoke to made the point that widespread surveillance wasn't necessary because the government already knows what people are saying. Duterte had demonstrated that he can set the agenda for what people talk about and manipulate what they believe. So why bother with surveillance? Acero believes much of the chatter about surveillance resembles security theater: "Do it for the press. Do it for the photo op. Does it get used? No." He pointed to guards across the street brandishing security wands: "Even here, you see that preference for security theater. In the mall, there is someone who waves the metal detector at you, goes through your bag. Like that's going to stop anything."[143]

What about China's Role?

Many experts cite the Philippines as a crucial illustration of how Chinese influence and its deliberate spreading of repressive technologies is empowering anti-democratic forces and shifting a traditional US ally. My research indicates a more complicated picture in the Philippines. While Chinese efforts to influence the Philippines are very real, and Duterte has responded favorably to its outreach, there are few indications that China is driving the spread of digital repression in the country.

China has a complex relationship with the Philippines. Militarily and politically, the Philippines has long allied itself with the United States. Tensions between China and the Philippines have periodically turned hostile. In recent years, China has built military outposts on disputed islands in the South China Sea that multiple countries, including the Philippines, claim as their sovereign territory. In 2013, the Philippines filed a claim against the Chinese government in an international tribunal, alleging that China had violated international law by falsely claiming sovereignty over vast swaths of the South China Sea. The panel ruled decisively in favor of the Philippines in 2016—a legally binding decision that China has ignored.[144] China continues to engage in aggressive behavior against Philippine vessels. For example, in June 2019, a Chinese fishing boat sank a Filipino vessel, leaving twenty-two sailors stranded at sea until they were rescued by a Vietnamese trawler.[145]

But Duterte has gone to great lengths to reset the relationship with China. In 2018, Philippines armed forces joined a regional military exercise organized by the Chinese for the first time.[146] Duterte has pointedly called for the two countries to ratchet down tensions, describing territorial conflicts as a "flashpoint for trouble."[147] His military officers have echoed the same conciliatory messages; one of the first statements from Duterte's new head of armed forces was to emphasize that "war is not a primary instrument in resolving international conflict" in terms of dealing with maritime disputes with China.[148] Perhaps the most potent symbol of Duterte's embrace of China was an elaborate two-day state visit by Xi Jinping to the Philippines in 2018.[149] Not only was the visit a public display of the increasing closeness of the two nations, but it led to the signing of twenty-nine separate agreements on issues ranging from oil and gas exploration to increased investment through the Belt and Road Initiative. One of the agreements established an investment partnership for the Safe Philippines surveillance project.[150]

The data reinforces the Philippines' growing ties with China. The Philippines is a member of the Belt and Road Initiative and part of the Chinese-established Asia Infrastructure Investment Bank. The country ranks twenty-eighth in the world when it comes to the level of Chinese overseas direct investment; China exports comprise over 10 percent of the Philippines' GDP.[151] The Philippines is also the beneficiary of an estimated $2.6 billion worth of investment from China's Digital Silk Road" initiative, a connectivity spin-off of BRI.[152] Headline projects include the awarding of a third telecom license to a new consortium (called Dito Telecommunity)—a joint venture between China Mobile and longtime Duterte ally Dennis Uy.

The linkages between the two countries extend beyond tech infrastructure. The Chinese government is also funding study exchanges and sponsoring delegation trips to encourage Philippine officials to promote positive narratives about China. Ablan informed me, "Our department has had good relations with our counterpart in China, which is the State Council Information Office. We have since, including myself, sent officers and officials to China to learn about their communications systems." He stated that "they have sent some equipment . . . the latest communication equipment to, for example, some of our radio stations." When pressed about whether the Chinese maintain certain expectations in return for providing this equipment, he insisted, "I have not seen any condition or any sort of influence from them on what to publish here in the Philippines. So they have not influenced us on content at all." But he acknowledged that the Chinese encourage visiting delegations to write positive stories about China when they return to the Philippines: "They don't tell us, 'Oh, we've been bashed. Can you tone it down a bit?' I have never heard them say that. But they focus on number two—kindly please also report the good things that China does."[153]

In a study of China's relations with countries in Southeast Asia, scholar David Shambaugh classifies the Philippines and Brunei as "tilters." They lean toward China, but less so than states like Malaysia and Thailand. In each case, "Elements of the regime and society remain wary of Beijing" even as US influence declines and they edge toward a closer embrace of China.[154] Despite Duterte's efforts to "tilt" toward China, the public continues to hold uniformly negative views of China. A July 2019 poll taken by the Social Weather Stations, for example, found that public trust in China stood at just 24 percent (in comparison, 73 percent of the population held favorable view of the United States).[155] Moreover, Duterte himself may be rethinking aspects of the Philippines' embrace of China. In February 2020, Duterte announced his intent to terminate the Visiting Forces Agreement with the United States, a long-standing defense agreement that gives US troops a legal basis to be in the country. But in June, the Philippines foreign secretary, Teodoro Locsin, reversed course and announced that the government would not withdraw from the agreement "in light of political and other developments in the region."[156]

An alternative way to think about the Philippines' increased adoption of Chinese products is to focus less on geopolitics and more on affordability. Moya told me bluntly, "China makes it cheap. And in a developing country, price is king. So whether there is a strong push, I think it is not so much the hand of Mao, but the invisible hand of the market that's really pushing the presence of Chinese products."[157] I heard a similar story from Secretary Rio. He informed me that Huawei has been present in the Philippines since 2010 and estimated that 80 percent of telecom equipment is provided by Huawei. He warned, "If we pull out all Huawei equipment, our telecommunication industry will fall apart."[158] In some respects, Chinese geopolitical interests and Filipino financial motivations have fostered a symbiotic relationship that shows few signs of ebbing. China gets a toehold with a traditional US ally undergoing a serious populist turn. Likewise, Duterte gets a partner that asks few questions, keeps the financial spigot flowing, and offers useful capabilities to help him remain in power. Ressa observed, "On China's end, it's geopolitical. On the Philippines' end, and the government officials that are approving these deals, that is financial. You know you can see that they need to maintain growth. Growth has already declined significantly."[159]

This returns us to the original question: by effectively providing economic subsidies to the Philippines and offering cutting-edge technology at cut-rate prices, is China bankrolling the spread of digital repression in the Philippines?

The answer is generally no.

The area of greatest Chinese involvement is surveillance. But surveillance is not a major instrument of digital repression in the Philippines, at least not today. China's impact is therefore peripheral, at best. While China is using its economic power to exert greater influence in the Philippines—from offering sweetheart oil and gas exploration deals to providing sizable financial inducements for stakes in the Philippines' telecom sector—this relationship does not mean China is actually driving digital repression.

As this chapter has laid out, the primary method of digital repression Duterte uses is social manipulation combined with legal persecution—with Facebook being the platform of choice. Not only has Duterte and his army of supporters perfected their ability to manipulate Facebook to spread harmful narratives, but Facebook first chose to work with Duterte's campaign to help him realize his online political potential. It wasn't a coincidence that after Duterte won the election, he banned the mainstream press from covering his inauguration and instead streamed the inaugural events live on Facebook.[160]

Just as it isn't accurate to hold China chiefly responsible for the rise of digital repression in the Philippines, it is equally mistaken to assign primary fault to Facebook. Duterte and his cohorts are ultimately accountable for running the country and deciding whether to wield powerful digital tools in an irresponsible and reckless manner. It is not inevitable that social media will serve as a fount of disinformation and harassment—at least not to the extent seen in the Philippines. Duterte's team has made deliberate choices to poison the well of online information in the country, and to manipulate discourse in ways never before seen.

Conclusion

Will digital repression in the Philippines outlast Duterte's rule? While Duterte didn't introduce disinformation and cyber trolling to the Philippines, his team perfected methods of exploiting social media for political gain. He is the country's first leader to carry out hostile manipulation techniques at scale. It is fair to ask whether politics in the Philippines will transcend this current period of information exploitation or whether these tactics are here to stay. Historically, Philippine politics have gone through cycles of "repudiation" and "preemption."[161] Past leaders, such as Corazon Aquino and Joseph Estrada—and now Duterte—defined themselves in opposition to their predecessors. Accordingly, it is conceivable that Duterte's successor may steer the country back onto a more liberal path (although it is equally plausible that Duterte could be replaced by a similarly minded populist). If the next president restored a more balanced political tone, would it be possible to reverse course in the Philippines?

Some argue that it is already too late. De Lima, for example, fears that "under Duterte, the crazies in Philippine society have come out of the woodwork, seemingly drawn by this wave of idiocy, opportunism, and corruption that Duterte ushered in." She argued that knowing what will happen once he finishes his term is difficult, but "it is doubtful if it will disappear with him."[162]

Others, like Maria Ressa, offer more hope. "Why have I not given up? Aside from the fact that I can't give up. You know I think this battle matters. I think that the future of journalism is at stake, because journalists in general are still in denial." She continued, "I've never felt as vulnerable as I do today. And it's existential. I've never been asked to sacrifice as much as I'm sacrificing today. We jumped off the cliff because I don't think we have a choice."[163]

There aren't easy solutions to getting the Philippines out of the disinformation quagmire in which it is stuck. Improved responsiveness from social media platforms in the short term, combined with longer-term strategies to increase digital literacy, may represent optimal approaches. But another way to think about the Philippines' situation is to consider how built-up historical grievances against an insulated class of elites may have finally come home to roost (even if Duterte's regime merely substitutes enriching one set of elites for another). As de Lima observed: "The poor have age-old grievances on social injustice, economic inequality, and disproportional opportunities. The minute they are born, the odds are already weighed against them. . . . This corruption and thievery are all causes for widespread unrest or even revolution, and it is a wonder why Filipinos up to this time have not gathered that sort of courage and determination to turn the tables against these corrupt politicians and officials."[164] In a sense, social manipulation and disinformation in the country may be less a new phenomenon than the manifestation of existing injustices and disparities that Philippines politics has been wholly unable—or unwilling—to rectify.

Notes

1. Bato has since had his US visa revoked on account of human rights violations he authorized while overseeing the government's murderous drug war. Aika Rey, "Dela Rosa Confirms U.S. Visa Canceled," *Rappler*, January 22, 2019, https://www.rappler.com/nation/249936-bato-dela-rosa-confirms-us-visa-canceled-january-2020.
2. In the Philippines, the term "yellowtard" refers to followers of the Liberal Party, who are often pilloried as elitist and out of touch with ordinary Filipinos. It can be used as a term of derision by Duterte supporters (or "Dutertards"). Author interview with a senior supporter of president Rodrigo Duterte, May 23, 2019.
3. Camille Elemia, "Manila Times' Big Boss Is Duterte's PR Guy," *Rappler*, May 17, 2017, https://www.rappler.com/nation/170038-manila-times-dante-ang-appointed-envoy-public-relations.
4. Dante A. Ang, "Oust-Duterte Plot Bared," *Manila Times*, April 22, 2019, https://issuu.com/manilatimes/docs/22manilatimes_61e94d51e2be03.
5. Vernise L. Tantuco and Gemma Bagayaua-Mendoza, "False: 'Ouster Plot' against President Duterte 'Bared,'" *Rappler*, April 24, 2019, https://www.rappler.com/newsbreak/fact-check/228877-ouster-plot-against-duterte-bared.

6. Catherine S. Valente, "Malacañang Confirms 'Matrix,' Warns Plotters," *Manila Times*, April 23, 2019, https://www.manilatimes.net/2019/04/23/news/headlines/malacanang-confirms-matrix-warns-plotters/544036/544036/.

7. Pia Ranada, "'Totally Unnecessary' for Duterte to Prove 'Ouster Matrix'—Malacañang," *Rappler*, May 1, 2019, https://www.rappler.com/nation/229398-malacanang-says-totally-unnecessary-duterte-prove-ouster-plot-matrix.

8. Arianne Merez, "Panelo Backtracks, Says Copy of 'Oust Duterte' Matrix from Unknown Source," *ABS-CBN News*, May 2, 2019, https://news.abs-cbn.com/news/05/02/19/panelo-backtracks-says-copy-of-oust-duterte-matrix-from-unknown-source.

9. Arianne Merez, "In New 'Matrix,' Palace Claims Liberal Party, Magdalo in Cahoots to Oust Duterte," *ABS-CBN News*, May 8, 2019, https://news.abs-cbn.com/news/05/08/19/palace-claims-liberal-party-magdalo-in-cahoots-to-oust-duterte.

10. Pierre Tito Gallo (cofounder, Democracy.net), interview with the author, May 20, 2019.

11. Pomerantsev, *This Is Not Propaganda*, 49.

12. Pomerantsev, *This Is Not Propaganda*, 49.

13. Lührmann and Lindberg, "Third Wave of Autocratization."

14. Lührmann et al., "Autocratization Surges," 12.

15. Anna Lührmann and Staffan I. Lindberg, "Democracy Facing Global Challenges: V-Dem Annual Democracy Report 2019," 2019, 27–28.

16. Rankings are extracted from the 2020 V-Dem electoral democracy index, Coppedge et al., "V-Dem Dataset v10."

17. "Philippines," *Freedom in the World* , March 4, 2020, https://freedomhouse.org/country/philippines/freedom-world/2020.

18. "2019 Country Reports on Human Rights Practices: Philippines," US Department of State, March 11, 2020, https://www.state.gov/reports/2019-country-reports-on-human-rights-practices/philippines/.

19. Louis Bacani, "Palace: Crime Rate Down under PNoy," *PhilStar Global*, June 18, 2014, https://www.philstar.com/headlines/2014/06/18/1336251/palace-crime-rate-down-under-pnoy.

20. Mark R. Thompson, "Southeast Asia's Troubling Elections: Is There a Silver Lining?," *Journal of Democracy* 30, no. 4 (2019): 149–57, https://doi.org/10.1353/jod.2019.0058.

21. Mark R. Thompson, "Why Duterte Remains So Popular: The Failure of the Philippines' Liberal Reformism," *Foreign Affairs*, October 9, 2018, https://www.foreignaffairs.com/articles/philippines/2018-10-09/why-duterte-remains-so-popular.

22. Julio C. Teehankee, "Duterte's Resurgent Nationalism in the Philippines: A Discursive Institutionalist Analysis," *Journal of Current Southeast Asian Affairs* 35, no. 3 (December 2016): 72.

23. A growing literature analyzes the rise, impact, and consequences of Duterte's reign in power. See Nicole Curato, "Politics of Anxiety, Politics of Hope: Penal Populism and Duterte's Rise to Power," *Journal of Current Southeast Asian Affairs* 35, no. 3 (January 30, 2017): 91–109; Nicole Curato, ed., *A Duterte Reader: Critical Essays on Rodrigo Duterte's Early Presidency* (Ithaca, NY: Cornell University Press, 2017); Pia Ranada, "Rody Duterte: The Man, the Mayor, the President," *Rappler*, June 29, 2016, http://www.rappler.com/newsbreak/in-depth/137583-rodrigo-duterte-philippine-president-profile; Thompson, "Why Duterte Remains So Popular"; Teehankee, "Duterte's Resurgent Nationalism"; Björn Dressel and Cristina Regina Bonoan, "Southeast Asia's Troubling Elections: Duterte versus the Rule of Law," *Journal of Democracy* 30, no. 4 (2019): 134–48, https://doi.org/10.1353/jod.2019.0057; Davey Alba, "How Duterte Used Facebook to Fuel the Philippine Drug War," *Buzzfeed News*, September 4, 2018, https://www.buzzfeednews.com/article/daveyalba/facebook-philippines-dutertes-drug-war; Lian Buan and Jodesz Gavilan, "Duterte's War on Dissent," *Rappler*, June 29, 2019, http://www.rappler.com/newsbreak/in-depth/234183-duterte-halfway-mark-war-on-dissent-human-rights-defenders; Sheila S. Coronel, "The Vigilante President," *Foreign Affairs*, August 15, 2019, https://www.foreignaffairs.com/articles/philippines/2019-08-12/vigilante-president; David G. Timberman, "Philippine Politics under Duterte: A Midterm Assessment," Carnegie Endowment, 2019, https://carnegieendowment.org/2019/01/10/philippine-politics-under-duterte-midterm-assessment-pub-78091; Matthew David

Ordoñez and Anthony Lawrence Borja, "Philippine Liberal Democracy under Siege: The Ideological Underpinnings of Duterte's Populist Challenge," *Philippine Political Science Journal* 39, no. 2 (2018): 139–53; R. J. Heydarian, *The Rise of Duterte: A Populist Revolt against Elite Democracy* (Singapore: Palgrave Macmillan, 2018).

24. Heydarian, *The Rise of Duterte*, 33.
25. Author interview with a senior supporter of president Rodrigo Duterte, May 23, 2019.
26. Nicole Curato, "We Need to Talk about Rody," in Curato, *A Duterte Reader*, 30.
27. Author interview with a Philippines public relations professional, May 23, 2019.
28. John Nery (reporter, *Philippine Daily Inquirer*), interview with the author, May 23, 2019.
29. Martin Perry, "Don't Take the President Literally, Aide Says, after Women Deride 'Macho-Fascist' Duterte," *Reuters*, February 13, 2019, https://www.reuters.com/article/us-philippines-duterte/dont-take-the-president-literally-aide-says-after-women-deride-macho-fascist-duterte-idUSKBN1FX1FQ.
30. Walden Bello, "Rodrigo Duterte: A Fascist Original," in Curato, *A Duterte Reader*, 77–78.
31. Larry Diamond, *Ill Winds: Saving Democracy from Russian Rage, Chinese Ambition, and American Complacency* (New York: Penguin, 2019), 62–63.
32. Author interview with a senior supporter of president Rodrigo Duterte, May 23, 2019.
33. Sheri Berman, "Populism Is Not Fascism. But It Could Be a Barbunger," *Foreign Affairs*, November–December, 2016, https://www.foreignaffairs.com/articles/united-states/2016-10-17/populism-not-fascism.
34. Lisandro E. Claudio and Patricio N. Abinales, "Dutertismo, Maoismo, Nasyonalismo," in Curato, *A Duterte Reader*, 93–110.
35. Timberman, "Philippine Politics under Duterte."
36. Leila M. de Lima, email message to author, November 14, 2019. The *Oxford English Dictionary* defines kakistocracy as "the government of a state by the worst citizens." "Kakistocracy," *Oxford English Dictionary*, December 17, 2020, https://www.oed.com.
37. "Philippines: Duterte Confirms He Personally Killed Three Men," *BBC News*, December 16, 2016, https://www.bbc.com/news/world-asia-38337746.
38. "License to Kill: Philippine Police Killing in Duterte's War on Drugs," Human Rights Watch, March 2, 2017, https://www.hrw.org/report/2017/03/02/license-kill/philippine-police-killings-dutertes-war-drugs.
39. Matthew Tostevin and Neil Jerome Morales, "War on Numbers: Philippines Targets Drug Killing Data," *Reuters*, July 18, 2019, https://www.reuters.com/article/us-philippines-drugs/war-on-numbers-philippines-targets-drug-killing-data-idUSKCN1UD1CJ.
40. Alan Robles, "Duterte's war on drugs: ICC sees 'reasonable basis' for crime against humanity probe in Philippines," *SCMP*, December 15, 2020, https://www.scmp.com/week-asia/politics/article/3114056/dutertes-war-drugs-icc-sees-reasonable-basis-crime-against.
41. "Philippines: Outspoken Senator Arbitrarily Detained Two Years," Human Rights Watch, February 22, 2019, https://www.hrw.org/news/2019/02/22/philippines-outspoken-senator-arbitrarily-detained-two-years.
42. Walden Bello, "De Lima on the Wreckage of the Duterte Years and How to Emerge from It," *Rappler*, September 16, 2019, https://www.rappler.com/thought-leaders/240209-de-lima-wreckage-duterte-years-how-emerge-from-it-part-2.
43. Maria Ressa (cofounder, *Rappler*), interview with the author, August 27, 2019.
44. Lauren Etter, "What Happens When the Government Uses Facebook as a Weapon?," *Bloomberg News*, December 7, 2017, https://www.bloomberg.com/news/features/2017-12-07/how-rodrigo-duterte-turned-facebook-into-a-weapon-with-a-little-help-from-facebook.
45. Maria Ressa, "Propaganda War: Weaponizing the Internet," *Rappler*, February 7, 2019, https://www.rappler.com/nation/148007-propaganda-war-weaponizing-Internet.
46. Ressa, interview with the author.
47. Jason Gutierrez and Alexandra Stevenson, "Maria Ressa, Crusading Journalist, Is Convicted in Philippines Libel Case," *New York Times*, June 14, 2020, https://www.nytimes.com/2020/06/14/business/maria-ressa-verdict-philippines-rappler.html.
48. Sheila Coronel, "This Is How Democracy Dies," *The Atlantic*, June 16, 2020, https://www.theatlantic.com/international/archive/2020/06/maria-ressa-rappler-philippines-democracy/613102/.

49. The 2019 digital repression measurements incorporate social media penetration interactions per the model described in Chapter 3. Digital repression time-series calculations (2010–19) do not incorporate this interaction due to data limitations.

50. Mechkova et al., *Digital Society Project Dataset v2.*

51. "Philippines: Country Profile," Freedom on the Net 2017, Freedom House, 2017, https://freedomhouse.org/report/freedom-net/2017/philippines.

52. For a comprehensive analysis of the Philippines' ICT infrastructure and Internet governance framework, see Al Alegre et al., "An Overview of Internet Infrastructure and Governance in the Philippines," Cyber Stewards Network—Research Brief, March 2017, https://citizenlab.ca/wp-content/uploads/2017/04/An-Overview-of-Internet-Infrastructure-and-Governance-in-the-Phillippines.pdf.

53. Carlos Conde (Philippines researcher, Human Rights Watch), interview with the author, May 21, 2019.

54. Marc Louis O. Siapno (Commission on Human Rights), interview with the author, May 24, 2019.

55. "[Statement] #NoDeadAir: Resist All Assaults on Freedom of the Press and Expression," National Union of Journalists of the Philippines, May 5, 2020, https://nujp.org/statement/statement-nodeadair-resist-all-assaults-on-freedom-of-the-press-and-expression/.

56. Winthrop Yu (chair, Internet Society Philippines), interview with the author, May 24, 2019.

57. "Second Quarter 2019 Social Weather Survey," *Social Weather Stations,* August 3, 2019, https://www.sws.org.ph/downloads/media_release/pr20190803%20-%20SWR2019-II%20Freedom%20of%20Speeach%20and%20of%20the%20Press%20(special%20report).pdf.

58. Mirca Madianou and Daniel Miller, *Migration and New Media: Transnational Families and Polymedia* (New York: Routledge, 2012), 26. See also Eric Bellman, "Talk? In the Philippines, They're Too Busy Texting," *Wall Street Journal,* March 3, 2000, https://www.wsj.com/articles/SB952029995796469188.

59. Ling Woo Liu, "Friendster Moves to Asia," *Time,* January 29, 2008, http://content.time.com/time/business/article/0,8599,1707760,00.html.

60. Eric Johnson, "Memo from a 'Facebook Nation' to Mark Zuckerberg: You Moved Too Fast and Broke Our Country," *Vox,* December 11, 2018, https://www.vox.com/2018/11/26/18111859/maria-ressa-rappler-facebook-mark-zuckerberg-philippines-kara-swisher-recode-decode-podcast.

61. Simon Kemp, "Digital 2019: Global Digital Overview," *DataReportal,* January 31, 2019, https://datareportal.com/reports/digital-2019-global-digital-overview.

62. "The World Bank in the Philippines," World Bank, April 4, 2019, https://www.worldbank.org/en/country/philippines/overview#1.

63. Cheryll Ruth Soriano, Ruepert Jiel Cao, and Marianne Sison, "Experiences of ICT Use in Shared, Public Access Settings in Philippine Slums," *Development in Practice* 28, no. 3 (2018): 358–73.

64. "Stock Estimate of Overseas Filipinos as of Dec. 2013," Commission on Filipinos Overseas, December 2013, https://www.cfo.gov.ph/images/statistics/stock_estimate/2013-Stock-Estimate.xlsx.

65. Conde, interview with the author.

66. "September 2018 Nationwide Survey on Social Media Use," *PulseAsia Research,* September 2018, http://www.pulseasia.ph/september-2018-nationwide-survey-on-social-media-use/.

67. Conde, interview with the author.

68. Pia Ranada, "Over 600,000 OFWs Mobilizing for Duterte Campaign," *Rappler,* January 30, 2016, https://www.rappler.com/nation/politics/elections/2016/120572-overseas-filipino-workers-support-rodrigo-duterte.

69. Madianou and Miller, *Migration and New Media,* 26–27.

70. De Lima, email correspondence to author.

71. Dressel, Björn, "The Philippines: How Much Real Democracy?," *International Political Science Review* 32, no. 5 (2011): 529–45.

72. Julio C. Teehankee, "Weak State, Strong Presidents: Situating the Duterte Presidency in Philippine Political Time," *Journal of Developing Societies* 32, no. 3 (2016): 295.

73. Paul D. Hutchcroft and Joel Rocamora, "Strong Demands and Weak Institutions: The Origins and Evolution of the Democratic Deficit in the Philippines," *Journal of East Asian Studies* 3 (2003): 259–92.

74. Timberman, "Philippine Politics under Duterte."

75. Seva Gunitsky, "Corrupting the Cyber-Commons: Social Media as a Tool of Autocratic Stability," *Perspectives on Politics* 13, no. 1 (2015): 45.

76. "Cyber Libel Trial Opens against Philippine Journalist Maria Ressa," Committee to Protect Journalists, July 25, 2019, https://cpj.org/2019/07/cyber-libel-trial-opens-against-philippine-journal.php.

77. Karen Lema and Martin Petty, "Opponents Dismayed as Philippines' Duterte Approves 'Monstrous' Anti-terror Bill," *Reuters*, July 3, 2020, https://www.reuters.com/article/us-philippines-security/opponents-dismayed-as-philippines-duterte-approves-monstrous-anti-terror-bill-idUSKBN24419T; Aaron Sobel, "The Philippines' Antiterror Bill Will Stifle Dissent," Carnegie Endowment for International Peace, June 30, 2020, https://carnegieendowment.org/2020/06/30/philippines-antiterror-bill-will-stifle-dissent-pub-82215.

78. Mark Thompson, "Duterte's Illiberal Democracy," *East Asia Forum*, August 7, 2017, https://www.eastasiaforum.org/2017/08/07/80706/.

79. Pia Randa, "The Duterte Insult List," *Rappler*, June 28, 2019, https://www.rappler.com/newsbreak/in-depth/list-duterte-insults-second-year.

80. Kate Lamble and Megha Mohan, "Trolls and Triumph: A Digital Battle in the Philippines," *BBC*, December 7, 2016, https://www.bbc.com/news/blogs-trending-38173842.

81. Chay F. Hofileña, "Fake Accounts, Manufactured Reality on Social Media," *Rappler*, February 6, 2019, https://www.rappler.com/newsbreak/investigative/148347-fake-accounts-manufactured-reality-social-media.

82. Hofileña, "Fake Accounts."

83. Lamble and Mohan, "Trolls and Triumph."

84. Vaidhyanathan, *Antisocial Media*, 192.

85. Conde, interview with the author.

86. Nery, interview with the author.

87. Yu, interview with the author.

88. Conde, interview with the author.

89. Martin Petty and Manuel, Mogato, "As Philippines' Duterte Starts to Flag, His Daughter Reaches Out to a Marcos," *Reuters*, August 18, 2018, https://www.reuters.com/article/us-philippines-politics/as-philippines-duterte-starts-to-flag-his-daughter-reaches-out-to-a-marcos-idUSKBN1L400Q.

90. See Michael Bueza and Glenda Marie Castro, "Major Political Families in PH after the 2019 Elections," *Rappler*, August 31, 2019, https://www.rappler.com/newsbreak/in-depth/238673-map-major-political-families-philippines-after-elections-2019.

91. Pamela Combinido, "When Illiberal Social Media Takes Over Democratic Philippines," *New Mandela*, February 6, 2019, https://www.newmandala.org/when-illiberal-social-media-takes-over-democratic-philippines/.

92. Michael Bueza, "Who's Who in Duterte's Poll Contributors List," *Rappler*, December 9, 2016, https://www.rappler.com/newsbreak/iq/155060-duterte-contributors-list-2016-presidential-elections.

93. Conde, interview with the author.

94. Carly Nyst and Nick Monaco, "State-Sponsored Trolling: How Governments Are Deploying Disinformation as Part of Broader Digital Harassment Campaigns," Institute for the Future, 2018, http://www.iftf.org/fileadmin/user_upload/images/DigIntel/IFTF_State_sponsored_trolling_report.pdf.

95. In a global index on social media manipulation, researchers confirm the widespread presence of four online messaging narratives deployed by government trolls in the Philippines: pro-government support, attacks against the opposition, drivers of division, and suppression of individual speech. Samantha Bradshaw and Philip N. Howard, "The Global Disinformation Disorder: 2019 Global Inventory of Organised Social Media Manipulation," working paper, Oxford: Project on Computational Propaganda, 2019, https://comprop.oii.ox.ac.uk/research/cybertroops2019/.

96. "Philippines: Bomb Attack on Davao Market Kills 14," *BBC*, September 3, 2016, https://www.bbc.com/news/world-asia-37262499.

97. "Duterte Declares State of Lawlessness in PH," *Rappler*, September 3, 2016, https://www.rappler.com/nation/145043-duterte-declares-state-of-lawlessness-ph.

98. "Duterte Declares State."

99. Camille Elemia, "Fact Check: Photo Used by Duterte Camp to Hit Critics Taken in Brazil, not PH," *Rappler*, August 29, 2016, https://www.rappler.com/nation/144551-duterte-camp-brazil-photo-rape-victim-critics.

100. Ressa, "Propaganda War."

101. Natashya Gutierrez, "State-Sponsored Hate: The Rise of the Pro-Duterte Bloggers," *Rappler*, June 2, 2018, https://www.rappler.com/newsbreak/in-depth/178709-duterte-die-hard-supporters-bloggers-propaganda-pcoo.

102. Etter, "What Happens."

103. De Lima, email correspondence to author.

104. "Philippines, Events of 2018," Human Rights Watch, 2018, https://www.hrw.org/world-report/2019/country-chapters/philippines.

105. Mara Cepeda, "DOJ Didn't Verify before Seeking Terrorist Tag for 649 People," *Rappler*, August 6, 2018, https://www.rappler.com/nation/208923-doj-did-not-verify-names-people-before-seeking-terrorist-tag.

106. Ressa, "Propaganda War."

107. "Philippine Media under Attack: Press Freedom after 2 Years of Duterte," *Rappler*, June 29, 2018, https://www.rappler.com/newsbreak/investigative/206017-attacks-against-philippine-press-duterte-second-year.

108. Gemma Bagayaua-Mendoza (head of research and strategy, *Rappler*), interview with the author, May 22, 2019.

109. "Duterte Supporters Call for Attacks on Rappler Newsroom, Journalists," *Rappler*, February 23, 2019, https://www.rappler.com/nation/224115-duterte-supporters-call-for-attacks-newsroom-journalists-february-2019.

110. Camille Francois, "Camille Francois Explains Patriotic Trolling," *Disinfo Portal*, April 3, 2019, https://disinfoportal.org/camille-francois-explains-patriotic-trolling/; Carly Nyst, "Patriotic Trolling: How Governments Endorse Hate Campaigns against Critics," *The Guardian*, July 12, 2017, https://www.theguardian.com/commentisfree/2017/jul/13/patriotic-trolling-how-governments-endorse-hate-campaigns-against-critics.

111. When it comes to how disinformation networks are managed, organized, incentivized, and funded in the Philippines, there is an emerging literature that provides ethnographically informed analyses of the key operators involved in the production of fake news and content. See Jonathan Corpus Ong and Jason Cabanes, "Architects of Networked Disinformation: Behind the Scenes of Troll Accounts and Fake News Production in the Philippines," *Newton Tech4Dev Network*, 2018, https://newtontechfordev.com/wp-content/uploads/2018/02/ARCHITECTS-OF-NETWORKED-DISINFORMATION-FULL-REPORT.pdf.

112. Alba, "How Duterte Used Facebook."

113. "Philippine Media under Attack," *Rappler*.

114. Katie Harbath, "360/OS: Facebook's Katie Harbath on Protecting Election Integrity," YouTube video, 2018, https://www.youtube.com/watch?v=dJ1wcpsOtS4.

115. Vaidhyanathan, *Antisocial Media*, 192.

116. Vaidhyanathan, *Antisocial Media*, 193.

117. Alexandra Stevenson, "Soldiers in Facebook's War on Fake News Are Feeling Overrun," *New York Times*, October 9, 2019, https://www.nytimes.com/2018/10/09/business/facebook-philippines-rappler-fake-news.html.

118. Ressa, interview with the author.

119. Author interview with an international tech company official, July 17, 2019.

120. Gaurika Juneja and Karen Lema, "Facebook Removes Online Network in Philippines over 'Inauthentic Behavior,'" *Reuters*, March 28, 2019, https://www.reuters.com/article/us-facebook-fake-accounts/facebook-removes-online-network-in-philippines-over-inauthentic-behavior-idUSKCN1RA0CO.

121. Gaurika Juneja, "Facebook Bans Philippines' Twinmark Media Enterprises," *Reuters*, January 10, 2019, https://www.reuters.com/article/us-philippines-facebook-twinmark/facebook-bans-philippines-twinmark-media-enterprises-idUSKCN1P50D7.

122. Author interview with an international tech company official.

123. Article XVI, Section 11(1) of the Constitution states: "The ownership and management of mass media shall be limited to citizens of the Philippines, or to corporations, cooperatives or associations, wholly-owned and managed by such citizens." Oscar Franklin Tan, "Of PDRs and 'Foreign Ownership' of PH Media," *Rappler*, January 28, 2018, https://www.rappler.com/thought-leaders/176774-pdrs-media-ownership.

124. Buan and Gavilan, "Duterte's War on Dissent."

125. Shawn W. Crispin, "Mission Journal: Duterte Leads Tri-pronged Attack on Press amid Condemnation of Controversial Policies," Committee to Protect Journalists, July 5, 2018, https://cpj.org/blog/2018/07/mission-journal-duterte-leads-tri-pronged-attack-o.php.

126. Ressa, interview with the author.

127. Buan and Gavilan, "Duterte's War on Dissent"; "The Duterte Government's Mid-life Crisis," *Karapatan Monitor*, January–March 2019, https://www.karapatan.org/print/1631.

128. Crispin, "Mission Journal."

129. Kristian Ablan (assistant secretary, Presidential Communications Operations Office), interview with the author, May 20, 2019.

130. "Philippines: Reject Sweeping 'Fake News' Bill," Human Rights Watch, July 25, 2019, https://www.hrw.org/news/2019/07/25/philippines-reject-sweeping-fake-news-bill#.

131. Camille Elemia, "Senators Sound Alarm over China-Funded DILG Surveillance Project," *Rappler*, December 14, 2018, https://www.rappler.com/nation/218831-dilg-china-telecom-affiliate-partnership-video-surveillance-system-philippines.

132. "Huawei Jitters Spread to Philippines Security Project," *China Economic Review*, February 21, 2019, https://chinaeconomicreview.com/huawei-jitters-spread-to-philippines-security-project/.

133. Niharika Mandhana, "Huawei's Video Surveillance Business Hits Snag in Philippines," *Wall Street Journal*, February 20, 2019, https://www.wsj.com/articles/huaweis-video-surveillance-business-hits-snag-in-philippines-11550683135.

134. Alecks P. Pabico, "Wiretap Central: The Tale of the Tangled 'Hello, Garci' Tapes," *PCIJ*, August 25, 2007, https://www.gmanetwork.com/news/news/specialreports/57661/pcij-wiretap-central-the-tale-of-the-tangled-hello-garci-tapes/story/; Alegre et al., "Overview of Internet Infrastructure," 28.

135. George Joseph, "Inside the Video Surveillance Program IBM Built for Philippine Strongman Rodrigo Duterte," *The Intercept*, March 20, 2019, https://theintercept.com/2019/03/20/rodrigo-duterte-ibm-surveillance/.

136. "Philippines: Prosecute Officials for 'Death Squad' Killings," Human Rights Watch, August 16, 2012, https://www.hrw.org/news/2012/08/16/philippines-prosecute-officials-death-squad-killings.

137. Joseph, "Video Surveillance Program."

138. Shahbaz and Funk, "Social Media Surveillance."

139. Allan Cabanlong, the self-proclaimed "father of Philippine cybersecurity," who oversaw the cybersecurity project implemented by Verint, emphasized to me that the system would provide "open-source intelligence that can help law enforcement and other areas of the government to be educated and aware of current threats that are coming into the government and the Philippines." Allan Cabanlong (assistant secretary, Department of Information and Communications Technology), interview with the author, May 22, 2019.

140. Eliseo Rio (acting secretary, Department of Information and Communications Technology), interview with the author, May 21, 2019.

141. Conde, interview with the author.

142. Francis Acero (division chief, National Privacy Commission), interview with the author, May 23, 2019.

143. Acero, interview with the author.

144. Jane Perlez, "Tribunal Rejects Beijing's Claims in South China Sea," *New York Times*, July 12, 2016, https://www.nytimes.com/2016/07/13/world/asia/south-china-

sea-hague-ruling-philippines.html?module=inline. In September 2019, Duterte claimed that Xi Jinping offered the Philippines a major stake in a joint energy project in the South China Sea if the Philippine government agreed to set aside the arbitral ruling. Martin Petty, "Philippines' Duterte Says Xi Offering Gas Deal If Arbitration Case Ignored," *Reuters*, September 10, 2019, https://www.reuters.com/article/us-philippines-china-southchinasea/philippines-duterte-says-xi-offering-gas-deal-if-arbitration-case-ignored-idUSKCN1VW07O.

145. Jason Gutierrez and Hannah Beech, "Sinking of Philippine Boat Puts South China Sea Back at Issue," *New York Times*, June 13, 2019, https://www.nytimes.com/2019/06/13/world/asia/south-china-sea-philippines.html.

146. Kristin Huang, "Philippines Joining Beijing's South China Sea Drill 'Shows Nations Are Hedging Bets' in Sino-US Tussle," *South China Morning Post*, October 9, 2018, https://www.scmp.com/news/china/military/article/2167694/philippines-joining-beijings-south-china-sea-drill-shows-nations.

147. Kelley Olsen, "Philippines' Duterte Calls for Action to Reduce the Risk of Military Conflict in the South China Sea," *CNBC*, June 1, 2019, https://www.cnbc.com/2019/06/01/philippines-duterte-need-to-reduce-risk-of-south-china-sea-conflict.html.

148. "New Philippine Military Chief Expects No 'Shooting War' over South China Sea," *Radio Free Asia*, October 10, 2019, https://www.rfa.org/english/news/china/philippines-southchinasea-10102019195805.html.

149. "Xi Jinping's State Visit to the Philippines," *Rappler*, November 21, 2018, https://www.rappler.com/nation/217087-watch-state-visit-china-president-xi-jinping-philippines-november-2018.

150. Pia Ranada, "PH-China Deal Signed during Xi Jinping Visit," *Rappler*, November 27, 2018, https://www.rappler.com/nation/217615-documents-philippines-china-deals-signed-xi-jinping-visit-november-2018.

151. Ben Steil and Benjamin Della Rocca, "Belt and Road Tracker," Council on Foreign Relations, May 8, 2019, https://www.cfr.org/article/belt-and-road-tracker; "China Going Global Investment Index 2017," *Economist Intelligence Unit*, 2017, https://www.eiu.com/public/topical_report.aspx?campaignid=ChinaODI2017.

152. Prasso, "China's Digital Silk Road."

153. Ablan, interview with the author.

154. Shambaugh, "US-China Rivalry," 102.

155. "Second Quarter 2019 Social Weather Survey," *Social Weather Stations*, July 19, 2019, https://www.sws.org.ph/swsmain/artcldisppage/?artcsyscode=ART-20190719100415.

156. Jason Gutierrez, "Philippines Backs Off Threat to Terminate Military Pact with U.S.," *New York Times*, June 2, 2020, https://www.nytimes.com/2020/06/02/world/asia/philippines-military-pact-us-duterte.html.

157. Moya, interview with the author.

158. Rio, interview with the author.

159. Ressa, interview with the author.

160. Some argue that Chinese (and by extension Russian influence) may have played a big role in facilitating disinformation narratives in the Philippines, but this appears more speculative than based on fact. As researchers note, "Despite media coverage about 'foreign interference' on social media, our research found minimal evidence that foreign companies were involved in the Philippines midterms, and no evidence that foreign countries (e.g., Russia or China) were involved in executing digital campaigns." Ong, Tapsell, and Curato, "Tracking Digital Disinformation in the 2019 Philippine Midterm Election."

161. Teehankee, "Weak States, Strong Presidents," 301.

162. De Lima, email correspondence to author.

163. Ressa, interview with the author.

164. De Lima, email correspondence to author.

6

Transformation and Setbacks in Ethiopia

I traveled to Ethiopia in the winter of 2020, nearly two years after Prime Minister Abiy Ahmed ascended to power. Signs of change abounded in the country.[1] Political opposition figures exiled or jailed by the previous regime had now established formally recognized political parties. Individuals who had advocated for the violent overthrow of the Ethiopian government were now freely campaigning for upcoming parliamentary elections. Many of the journalists and human rights activists whom the old government had imprisoned had begun writing public commentary and organizing open meetings. In most parts of the country—particularly the booming capital of Addis Ababa—a sense of hope was blossoming.

Of course, such changes in Ethiopia had not put everyone in an ebullient mood. During my trip, I traveled north to the regional capital of Mekele (close to the Eritrean border), which is also the seat of the Tigrayan ethnic group. Until 2018, members of the Tigray People's Liberation Front (TPLF) resided in a political governing coalition known as the Ethiopian People's Revolutionary Democratic Front (EPRDF).[2] As a result of heavy Tigrayan influence, this coalition had ruled the country since 1991. The EPRDF controlled all levers of state power—dominating the security forces and reaping disproportionate economic benefits.

But its reign proved unsustainable. Members of Ethiopia's other ethnic groups—particularly the majority Amhara and Oromo populations—began to protest in large numbers for a greater voice in the government. By the fall of 2017, dramatic political change was clearly needed in order to confront Ethiopia's escalating political crisis. In February 2018, the previous prime minister, Hailemariam Dessalegn, submitted his resignation. This decision paved the way for the EPRDF's reformist wing to promote its favored candidate, Abiy Ahmed, as a replacement. Not only does Abiy come from a younger generation

The Rise of Digital Repression. Steven Feldstein, Oxford University Press (2021). © Oxford University Press.
DOI: 10.1093/oso/9780190057497.003.0006

(he was forty-one years old when he was sworn in as prime minister in April 2018), but he is also not Tigrayan. Abiy emerged from the Oromo Democratic Party as one of the four main coalition partners of EPRDF. As Freedom House's Jon Temin and Yoseph Badwaza write, he was chosen "more out of the EPRDF's urge to preserve itself" and to mollify the demonstrators "than out of any desire to embrace liberalization."[3]

In one sense, the gambit worked. Protests ebbed as Ethiopians swore in their new leader. But the Tigrayan ruling clique failed to consider just how sweeping and ambitious Abiy's reforms would be. Before they knew what had hit them, Abiy had purged large numbers of senior TPLF officials from the government ministries and the military. Some were jailed. A few went into exile. Many hightailed it back to Mekele, stunned by the rapid pace of change. Two years later, they were still trying to make sense of their swift fall from power and to figure out what would come next.

In the months following my February 2020 visit to Ethiopia, political circumstances once again shifted in quite dramatic ways. First, the coronavirus pandemic disrupted Ethiopia's election timetable. National elections scheduled for August were postponed indefinitely. As of September, Abiy indicated that he "personally believed" there would be elections next year, but more concrete assurances were hard to come by.[4] More concerning, on June 29, a popular Oromo artist and activist, Hachalu Hundessa, was shot and killed in Ethiopia's capital. The motives behind his death remain unclear. However, his assassination precipitated a wave of unrest resulting in hundreds of deaths, including mourners, protestors, and law enforcement. The government responded forcefully. As of August 2020, authorities had arrested at least nine thousand individuals, many without being formally charged.[5] Among those taken into custody and facing trial were Jawar Mohammed and Bekele Gerba, leaders of the Oromo Federalist Congress and prominent critics of Abiy; Lidetu Ayalew, a founder of the Ethiopian Democratic Party; former officials from the TPLF; as well as Lammi Begna of the Oromo Liberation Front (interviews with Jawar and Lammi feature prominently in this chapter).[6]

While the government crackdown was partially in response to escalating violence, many accused Abiy and the state bureaucracy of using the threat of civil unrest as a means to purge rivals and consolidate power. Indeed, Human Rights Watch reported that authorities have detained "dozens of opposition members and journalists for prolonged periods and often without charge since late June 2020, raising serious rights concerns."[7]

Then in November 2020, war came to Tigray. In response to an alleged armed attack by the TPLF militia against the army's northern command headquarters (coming on the heels of months of tension), Abiy sent in the military to reassert control over the region.[8] He billed the operation as a quick and decisive "law enforcement campaign" that would apprehend a criminal "clique" of senior TPLF generals and leaders.[9] Indeed, after a month of heavy fighting, the Ethiopian military captured Mekele and sent TPLF forces streaming into the hinterlands. But Abiy's actions came with a high cost. For one, the humanitarian impact and casualty count has been significant. As of December 2020, the UN reported that approximately 50,000 refugees had fled to Sudan.[10] The International Crisis Group estimated "thousands" of casualties due to the conflict.[11] Because the government had cut off Internet communications and denied humanitarian access to outside organizations, accurate figures were hard to come by. In another worrisome trend, there were growing reports that ethnic Tigrayans were being targeted around the country—harassed, rounded up, and imprisoned—prompting the UN's special advisor on the prevention of genocide to issue a special plea for persecutions to cease.[12]

These developments raise crucial questions regarding Abiy's political intentions—a leader celebrated in the West who was awarded the Nobel Peace Prize in 2019. Does the military intervention in Tigray and government crackdown against opposition figures represent an end to Abiy's democratization agenda? Will repression return in full force to Ethiopia? Or does this spate of violence represent a serious detour to Abiy's democracy project, but perhaps not a complete derailment? It is impossible to predict how events will unfold in the country, but one aspect is clear: the contradictions inherent in Abiy's tenure— his desire for outreach to the West and to institute democratic reforms balanced against his need to maintain credibility with the military and show a strong political hand to prevent ethnic fissures from splitting the country—continue to persist. This duality demonstrates the paradox of Abiy's tenure and Ethiopia's tentative liberalization. On the one hand, real political change started to take hold in the country, including the broadening of political freedoms. On the other hand, old habits die hard. Even as Abiy has preached about *medemer*, a political philosophy to promote synergy and unity within the country, the Ethiopian military continued to rely upon heavy-handed tactics to subdue dissent, including the use of instruments directly from the digital repression playbook.

This chapter focuses on the immense political changes occurring in Ethiopia and their implications for digital technology. Since the early 2000s, Ethiopia has displayed a dismal track record when it comes to digital freedom. The most recent Freedom on the Net ranking (2019) labeled Ethiopia as "not free," assessing the country a marginal score of 28 out of a possible 100. Internet shutdowns, rising disinformation, and traditions of online censorship and surveillance characterize Ethiopia's digital environment. And yet, such concerning information only tells half the story. Abiy's leadership has ushered in major reforms, many of which are still in the beginning phases of implementation. In this chapter, I will discuss political change in Ethiopia and the impact of Abiy's reform agenda.

I will describe the landscape of digital repression in the country, focusing on Internet shutdowns, rising levels of social disinformation and disinformation, as well as ongoing surveillance and censorship concerns. I will then explain relevant factors that have shaped Ethiopia's digital repression environment before turning to examine China's influence in the country.

My research in Ethiopia led to several crucial insights.

First, Abiy is both a transcendent and polarizing figure who has personally altered the country's political dynamics. His reform agenda has profoundly affected Ethiopia's digital repression calculus. The state's reliance on surveillance, restrictive information controls, and the persecution of online users is diminished from just a few years before (at least until the advent of unrest in the summer of 2020). Political activists, online bloggers, and journalists who languished in jail or resided in exile have much more discretion to say what they'd like and associate with whom they choose with decreased state interference. The onset of new political freedoms is startling to many people. On the flip side, ethnic tensions and societal polarization are on the rise. As the country inches towards national elections, there is growing concern about political instability, ethnic fissures, and the prospect of future violence.

Second, the diminishment of certain forms of surveillance and censorship does not mean that the Ethiopian state has abandoned its reliance on digital repression instruments. The government continues to use Internet shutdowns—in conjunction with security force operations—as a tool to pacify restive regions, from western Oromia to Tigray. Social manipulation, online hate speech, and social media-fueled offline violence are also on the rise. Many people I spoke to identified polarized online rhetoric and communications, which often instigate offline violence, as the biggest obstacle to political progress. While surveillance activities have decreased and information controls are less central to the government's agenda, such behavior has not disappeared from view. The authorities regularly restrict access to certain websites and periodically block social media messaging applications (WhatsApp, Facebook Messenger, Telegram).

Third, two events are especially relevant for shaping the development of Ethiopia's digital repression apparatus. The first was the fallout from disputed elections in 2005 that led to mass unrest and a violent government crackdown. The state jailed thousands of citizens and drove many more into exile. At the same time, security officials acquired an array of digital tools to keep the population in check. The second shock to Ethiopia's political order was the onset of Arab Spring demonstrations. Events in the Middle East and North Africa reaffirmed that authoritarian control in those regions was illusory. This recognition caused the EPRDF to seek even harsher means of controlling the population through surveillance, censorship, and online persecution strategies. Despite possessing a powerful assortment of digital instruments, the government was outwitted by innovative adversaries who sidestepped Internet shutdowns and mass detentions through the adoption of emergent learning strategies. These grassroots tactics offer larger lessons for civil society groups that are struggling to push back against the seemingly insurmountable odds of digital repression.

Fourth, over several decades, China has formed a close economic partnership with Ethiopia. China's financial sway is visible throughout Ethiopia, from glass-clad skyscrapers and six-lane highways running through Addis, to massive hydroelectric dams powering the country's national grid. A key question is whether China's influence has fueled digital repression in Ethiopia. I contend that China's role in this regard is limited. Although China has been a willing supplier of advanced technology, when requested, Chinese behavior doesn't vary significantly from that of liberal democracies. Rather, several other factors—fallout from the 2005 elections, government nervousness related to Arab Spring protests, and long-standing practices of state repression—are more relevant explanations for digital repression practices in Ethiopia.

Political Change in Ethiopia

The changes Abiy has wrought in Ethiopia are significant. He freed thousands of political prisoners, including accelerating the release of 60,000 political prisoners. He overturned oppressive legal restrictions on freedom of association and knocked back the country's notorious antiterrorist proclamation. Abiy personally brokered peace negotiations with Eritrea and encouraged prominent political exiles to return home. He closed the infamous Maekelawi detention center (transforming it into an art gallery).[13] Abiy publicly acknowledged government culpability for past abuses, and in response to escalating protests, hastened the release of nearly forty-six thousand people who had been detained between 2015 to 2018.[14]

When I asked a longtime Ethiopian blogger whom I have known for many years how she would describe the new environment, she replied, "Oh my God, it's so big. It's completely different. Absolutely. It's something else."[15] I was also able to speak with numerous contacts who, only a few years ago, had been languishing in exile or locked away in prison. Daniel Bekele, for example, was held in Ethiopia for three years as a "prisoner of conscience" following the country's 2005 election crackdown.[16] He then spent many years working as a senior adviser for Human Rights Watch and Amnesty International in New York. He now serves as the new chief of Ethiopia's human rights commission, a government body mandated to investigate violations within the country. Or consider Berhanu Nega: in 2015, he gave up a tenured position at Bucknell University to move to Eritrea and assume leadership of an armed group, Ginbot

7, which was fighting to overthrow the Ethiopian government. For years, one the government's top requests was for the United States to designate Ginbot 7 a terrorist organization and put Berhanu on a terrorist watchlist. Fast-forward to 2020, Berhanu now leads a prominent opposition political party, Ethiopian Citizens for Social Justice, which is headquartered in Meskel Square, in the center of Addis.

In 2019, Ethiopia ranked 128th of 179 global countries when assessing its level of democracy.[17] While this marks as an improvement from prior years (in 2018 it ranked 140th globally), this ranking still places Ethiopia in the company of low-performing states such as Pakistan, the Democratic Republic of the Congo, and Kuwait.

Figure 6.1 provides a statistical snapshot of Ethiopia's governance performance from 2010 to 2019 measured across five indicators: electoral democracy, physical violence committed by the state, protection of private civil liberties, overall protection of civil liberties (combined private and political), and civil society repression. For each indicator, higher scores equal greater levels of democracy and heightened protections of civil liberties.

The indicators show dramatic governance improvements beginning in 2018, paralleling Abiy's rise to power. The loosening of restraints on civil society is particularly noteworthy. Ethiopia went from being one of the foremost repressors of civil society to scoring above the global median by 2019. One laggard is the protection of private civil liberties, which has registered declines since 2013. This may be more a reflection of frayed government capacity—such as the state's inability to control religious or ethnic violence—than an indication of affirmative state actions intended to deprive citizens of these rights.

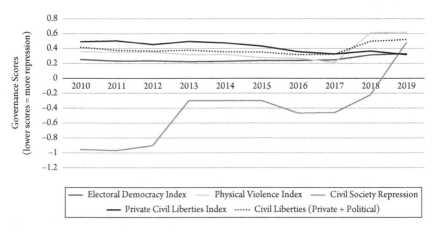

Figure 6.1 Ethiopia's Performance on Key Governance Indicators, 2010 to 2019

Ethiopia's Freedom House score also reflects the government's progress. While Freedom House's 2020 report continues to categorize Ethiopia as "not free," its aggregate score (combined measurement of political rights and civil liberties) has dramatically improved—doubling between 2018 and 2020.[18] The US State Department's 2019 human rights report similarly highlights progress under Abiy: "The government decriminalized political movements that past administrations had accused of treason, invited opposition leaders to return to the country and resume political activities . . . continued steps to release thousands of political prisoners, and undertook revisions of repressive laws."[19] However, the same report cautions that significant human rights issues remain, including unlawful killings by security forces, violence and killings based on ethnicity, arbitrary arrests and detentions by security forces, and persistent censorship.[20]

Perspectives on Abiy

Much like in the Philippines, political changes in Ethiopia are almost impossible to separate out from a discussion of Abiy himself. Almost singlehandedly, Abiy has shifted the country's political environment. Yet there is considerable disagreement about whether these changes are sustainable, what Abiy's true motivations are for enacting these reforms, and what their effect will be on Ethiopia's ethnic social fabric and federalist governance structure. Undoubtedly, events in the latter part of 2020, including the post-Hachalu crackdown and the conflict in Tigray, have taken much of the shine off of Abiy.

Abiy's path to becoming PM was swift. In the early phases of his career, he served in the military and departed with the rank of lieutenant colonel. He then assumed a series of increasingly senior government positions, including serving as deputy director of Ethiopia's Information Network Security Agency (INSA), which is responsible for the bulk of Ethiopia's digital repression activities. In 2010, Abiy won election to Ethiopia's parliament as an Oromo Democratic Party candidate, but didn't build a significant public profile. As Temin and Yoseph Badwaza note, until he became prime minister in 2018, he was "little known outside Oromia."[21]

Abiy has generated optimism in many corners. Bekele, for example, noted that "people are buying into that new vision articulated by the prime minister in trying to bring the country back to the notion of common Ethiopian identity."[22] Berhanu acknowledged that "there is commitment on the part of Abiy and his group that the only way forward is some kind of meaningful democratization."[23]

But Abiy has also prompted a backlash, particularly from those who feel sidelined by his reform agenda. During my visit to Mekele, I heard an array of critiques.[24] I spoke to Getachew Reda, whom I first met when he served as the EPRDF's minister of communications. Getachew maintains a high profile in Tigray and is one of the region's most popular politicians. I asked him about Abiy's agenda and he bluntly responded: "Abiy is pretending to be 'I have a vision for my country.' What vision? Doesn't pass. This is small-time crook who found himself in charge because we didn't do our job. That's it." He went on, "Abiy has hardly been in politics. Personally, he's a friend of mine, and I know he lies left and right."[25]

Jawar Mohammed, a prominent organizer of the 2016 Ethiopian protests, one of the founders of the Oromo Media Network (OMN), and a former ally of Abiy, also had negative things to say. "So what Abiy is actually doing will doom the country because, one, the state is actually too weak to exert [authority]. . . . You have a very fragile and confused state." He continued, "I think he's going to lose so much not because of the strength of the opposition but because of his own stupidity."[26]

Others offer more nuanced viewpoints. Befeqadu Hailu, one of the founders of the online blogging network "Zone 9" (and previously jailed as an activist), observed that "Abiy is interested in doing a lot of reforms. But that interest is only until he consolidates his power." He warns that "once he does [consolidate power], there will be no single interest for his power, because the privileges of being in power are unlimited. Literally they're unlimited."[27] Likewise, when I asked longtime journalist and political commentator Will Davison about Abiy's political motivations, Davison reflected, "I don't think that Abiy is a natural liberal. For example, I don't think he really appreciates the importance of freedom of expression." Davison stressed that Abiy seems to lack appreciation for the importance of political dissent, and that "the conditions are there" for a repressive turn in the future.[28]

One of the bigger questions is to what extent Abiy's personal vision drives his reforms, or whether they represent more fundamental change. The contacts I spoke to offered decidedly mixed responses on this issue. "I think it looks like it is primarily driven by the reform leaders and obviously the PM is at the center," said Bekele. "But I get the impression that it is also embraced by the other actors and other institutions, other government offices and so on."[29] Berhanu observed, "It would be erroneous in my view to think of this change as something that is triggered by Abiy only, or the reform forces within the ruling party. You must understand that the pressure on the regime has been coming from different directions, from army groups, from local groups." Berhanu noted that internal contradictions in Ethiopia's system had come to a head by the time Abiy assumed power and that whether or not Abiy had decided to pursue a reform agenda, the lid had already blown off in Ethiopia and was threatening to envelop the entire country in civil unrest.

No one expected Abiy to act as aggressively as he did in his first two years in office. While many hoped that he would find a way to reconcile the country's warring political factions, not even the most idealistic activist would have predicted that Abiy would authorize the release thousands of political prisoners, throw open the headquarters of the national intelligence agency for citizens to tour, and successfully seek a rapprochement with Eritrea. In this regard, Abiy's initial accomplishments cannot be downplayed: major change occurred precisely because of his resolve.

Nonetheless, Abiy faces monumental challenges in keeping the country together and navigating treacherous terrain when it comes to sticky issues of ethnic identity and federalism. He needs to find a pathway to reconciliation with the Tigrayans, who seem poised to execute a protracted insurgency barring major shifts. He must manage nationalist expectations from Amhara and Oromo factions, whose populations are largely uninterested in sharing power after years of marginalization. Abiy must also convince the plurality of citizens to buy into a pan-Ethiopian identity, represented by his newly formed Prosperity Party (a reconstituted amalgam of the EPRDF coalition minus the TPLF), while assuring nervous political groups that he intends to preserve Ethiopia's federalist structure and not impose centralized authority on autonomous regions. As Abiy's crackdown in the wake of Hachalu's assassination shows (as does the war in Tigray), it is increasingly likely that Abiy will revert to standard coercive tactics wielded by past Ethiopian regimes in order to maintain power.

The Evolving Nature of Digital Repression in Ethiopia

Despite Abiy's reforms, digital repression persists in Ethiopia. The onset of political liberalization has shifted the emphasis and focus of the state's digital strategies. But security services and law enforcement agencies continue to rely on an array of digital tools to subdue opponents and suppress dissent. Discerning exactly what has changed under Abiy's tenure is difficult. Several contacts emphasized that security force capabilities had not diminished, but had shifted the focus of their activities. A senior intelligence official told me, "The only difference between before and now is we used to work on civil issues . . . , something that was not in our mandate. Now we only focus on intelligence production and security operations."[30] When I pressed him, he underscored his assertion that "previously the focus was on journalists and others, but now the focus is on those who make violence. . . . We only focus on those who want to create violence here in Addis or somewhere else."[31]

To some extent, his perspectives aligns with the overall political climate. Journalists, politicians, and activists are generally free to express their opinions, often in very provocative and edgy ways. Undoubtedly, the government's focus has shifted away from tracking, monitoring, or harassing such individuals. At the same time, the Ethiopian state has not fully given up surveilling civilians of interest. Particularly in areas with ongoing military operations, such as western Oromia and Tigray, it is highly likely that security services are using sophisticated tools to track a wide range of individuals.[32]

Ethiopia's Internet and social media penetration rates remain low despite encouraging progress during the last few years. While 41 percent of its population of 105 million has access to mobile phones, Internet penetration stands at only 19 percent.[33] Social media use is even lower, with an estimated penetration level of 5.5 percent.[34] Ethiopia's Internet access level places it in the median for sub-Saharan Africa, ranking it twenty-sixth out of fifty countries. Globally, Ethiopia fares poorly, ranking 144th out of 179 countries. At present, Ethiopia only has one telecom provider, state-owned Ethio Telecom, although plans are in the works to partially privatize Ethio Telecom as well as to approve two additional private mobile service providers in the future.

Digital repression in Ethiopia reveals a bleak picture. My data assigns Ethiopia a digital repression score of 1.07 for 2019, ranking it thirty-third of 179 countries for prevalence of digital repression.[35] As Figure 6.2 shows, its global ranking among the five DSP categories of digital repression consistently places Ethiopia among the world's lowest performers.[36] Ethiopia scores particularly poorly when it comes to online censorship, social manipulation and disinformation, and

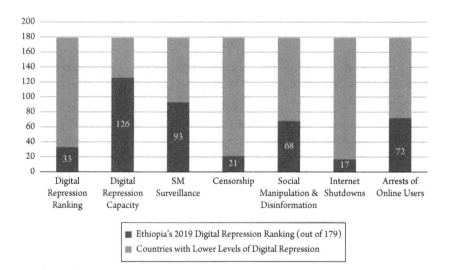

Figure 6.2 Ethiopia's Digital Repression Performance in 2019

Internet shutdowns. The country's ranking is much improved when it comes to arrests of online users, a distinct break from the practice of Abiy's predecessors.

When we break down Ethiopia's performance for each of the five digital repression components over a ten-year period, we can see general improvements starting in 2016 (as Figure 6.3 illustrates).

That being said, some components, particularly social manipulation and disinformation, seem to have risen sharply during the past year. This reversal matches expert concerns that a growing tide of disinformation threatens to upend political stability in the country.

Notably, the recent plunge in Ethiopia's digital repression capabilities parallels decreasing levels of enactment. It is possible that this startling drop in capacity reflects a mismatch between what Ethiopian intelligence operatives claim they are capable of doing, and the extent to which the country's political leaders— and the public at large—recognize those abilities. The same intelligence official noted that "the government doesn't recognize its capacity. The government doesn't understand how much capacity they have." He relayed a story to me where thirty operatives were sent to Israel for four months of instruction. At the end of that period, they had so impressed their Israeli trainers that "Israeli intelligence was trying to hire them, four of them, for private companies. Private companies were insisting to hire them because of their capabilities."[37] Despite this seeming capacity, the bulk of Ethiopia's digital repression—both in the past and currently—involves shutting down the Internet. Such a rudimentary tactic doesn't require any special expertise.

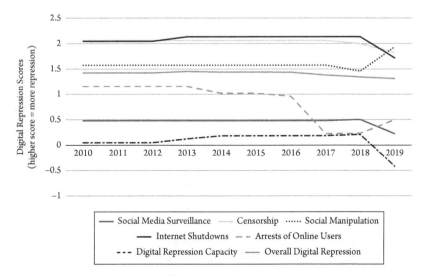

Figure 6.3 Digital Repression Trends in Ethiopia, 2010 to 2019

Ethiopia's Internet Shutdown Strategy

Ethiopia's government relies heavily on Internet shutdowns; however, almost everyone I spoke with—security officials, politicians, civil society activists— agreed that this was an inferior method for accomplishing the state's objectives. Tekleberhan Woldearegay, the director of INSA under the previous government, curtly said, "From my personal point of view, Internet shutdowns are stupidity. If you aren't capable to manage, if you are not intelligent, if you are not smart, you choose the hard force, hard power." He proceeded to emphasize that the strategy was outdated and ineffective: "We didn't learn. We did this for twenty-seven years. We were using this since 1999, even 1997. So there is no improvement. There is no learning."[38] Likewise, an expert from the government's advisory unit remarked, "That's a lazy way of ensuring security, right? Unplugging the cable is not the smartest way. You don't need an institution for that. You just need a guy who unplugs the cable. If you have a security agency, their activities should be more nuanced. . . . So that, that reflects the weakness of the intelligence agencies."[39]

Despite widespread skepticism about the effectiveness of shutdowns, their prevalence has not decreased under Abiy. In 2018, Access Now recorded three shutdowns in Ethiopia that were graded as level 2, meaning that they affected "more than one city in the same state, province, or region." In 2019, Access Now documented three level 1 shutdowns that entailed nationwide disruptions.[40] Most recently, in connection with the Hachalu crackdown and the conflict in Tigray, Ethiopian authorities shut down the Internet yet again in 2020.[41] This trend appears wholly incompatible with Abiy's efforts to modernize the economy and build up its digital infrastructure. I asked Addis Alemayehou, a prominent tech entrepreneur and CEO, about how Ethiopia's Internet shutdowns affect its nascent digital sector. He gestured to the floor above and said, "The guys upstairs [Nigerian e-payments company Paga] are supporting twenty-five million people in Nigeria with transactions on a daily basis. You shut down the Internet, then you shut these guys down. It doesn't make sense."[42]

Even in regions that lack significant Internet penetration, shutting down on-line access brings major spillover costs. When the state cuts off the Internet, students in regional universities can't look for jobs. Banks can't provide loans or offer financial services. People can't talk to relatives in other parts of the country and lose access to news and information. In 2019, Ethiopia experienced an estimated 346 hours of Internet shutdowns that affected 19.5 million users. The economic cost of shutting down the Internet was approximately $56.8 million.[43]

Ethiopia's command structure for authorizing shutdowns is somewhat ambiguous. My intelligence contact mentioned that "there is a one group, one division, in INSA. They monitor online traffic 24/7. And whenever they come up with something dangerous at the country level, they tell the telecom and they shut it down." Mostly this situation relates to technical issues such as cyberattacks against the Bank of Ethiopia that required temporarily cutting off Internet access. However, he clarified that "when there is a political problem—that means violence, disturbance all over the country—then INSA doesn't have any say." Instead, the prime minister's office or the minister of defense makes the call.

Recently, the government established a new entity, the Ethiopian Telecommunications Authority, headed by Balcha Reba. This organization is ostensibly leading government efforts to privatize Ethio Telecom as well as establish regulatory ground rules for how commercial service providers will function. Some observers believe Balcha carries considerable sway when it comes to determining whether to proceed with an Internet shutdown. Endalkachew Chala, a professor at Hamline University, described Reda as the "righthand man of Abiy," commenting that "he has broad authority in deciding Internet shut downs. They are the ones who decide when to shut down, why to shut down, everything. So that is a very important government organization."[44] Whether the PM's national security adviser or Balcha has greater influence in authorizing shutdowns, what is clear is that Ethio Telecom does not enjoy independent authority to push back against these decisions. The intelligence official pointedly told me, "They decide whatever the government says. They are service providers." He stressed that Ethio Telecom is "one of the government agencies. The board member is the prime minister. So whatever the PM decides, comes directly to the telecom."[45]

So if Internet shutdowns are poor tools to accomplish the state's political objectives, and if they subject the country to inordinate economic burdens, why do they remain a favored tool of the government? Part of the answer relates to capacity. Despite claims that INSA and other intelligence agencies have an abundance of digital instruments, the truth is that these organizations are limited in what they can accomplish (whether tracking insurgent communications during a military operation or preventing unrest from escalating into violent protests). Thus, Internet shutdowns continue to be a primary tool in the government's arsenal. "It must be partly a knee-jerk reaction but also perhaps because they just see it as just an indispensable tool of security management when there is perceived to be the risk of spreading instability," suggested Davison.[46] Another explanation, at least in the context of western Oromia, is that Internet shutdowns match the limited capabilities of the government's adversaries. As Yoseph Badwaza explained, the deputy chief of staff of the armed forces told state media reporters that one of the reasons the government is shutting down all forms of electronic communications was that the insurgents largely rely on text messaging to communicate with each other—they don't even have radio communications capabilities.[47]

Given Ethiopia's low Internet penetration rate, it is also valid to ask whether shutting down the Internet really matters at all. If the majority of the population isn't online, how impactful can this strategy be? Ahmed Mohammed, a senior governance adviser for the UK's Department of International Development, offered an insight: "I think because it's the elite that can make difference.... The most important [question] is who can make a difference in politics. It is those elites who use the Internet, who can, you know, disseminate this information to others."[48] In other words, Internet shutdowns are an important strategy to preempt elite challenges, whether from Tigray operatives in the north or from Oromo separatists in Wellega. In the absence of more finely tuned instruments, Ethiopia's government will likely continue deploying its shutdown strategy.

Social Manipulation and Disinformation

Social manipulation and disinformation comprise a second set of techniques that are becoming increasingly prevalent in Ethiopia. Unlike Internet shutdowns, which the state alone wields, these tactics are deployed by a range of actors, including government officials and state-sponsored influencers, political parties, and social media personalities. Social media's influence in Ethiopia may have a short history, but it has already brought outsized political reverberations. In 2015, social media-fueled protests in Oromo and Amhara spread throughout the country. Despite enforcing extensive Internet shutdowns—followed by violence and killings—the government was unable to contain the unrest. Events moved so quickly that they caught many political activists off guard. Jawar admitted, "We underestimated how fast the interaction of social movement in social media work." He had planned for protests to escalate in 2020, but he relayed that by 2016, the government looked like it might topple: "Much of the problem you see today is succeeding more than you expect."[49] Accordingly, he says that the movement wasn't able to build the right structures, like a strong party organization, that could help it take advantage of the political moment.

By 2017, the government was reeling—and before long, Abiy came into power. If social media helped propel Abiy into office, his subsequent actions to open up political space in the country have allowed social media to flourish. This development has led to positive and negative outcomes. On the positive side, citizens are far more engaged in politics. For many people, this is the first time they have been able to participate in genuinely competitive elections (as a point of comparison, the EPRDF won 100 percent of all parliamentary seats in 2015 national elections). As a result, Ethiopia is experiencing a burst of public dialogue and commentary, uncircumscribed by the government. More negatively, reduced information controls have also enabled the proliferation of hate speech, disinformation, and trolling. Getachew Reda noted that Abiy was "very much keen on using social media, to ratchet up support for his goals. But unfortunately, the forces that gave rise to the disgruntled are still at play. And the use of social media, if anything, has become even more polarizing."[50]

Data from the Digital Society Project for 2017 and 2018, showed that overall levels of societal polarization, instances of hate speech, and social media instigation of offline violence had fallen precipitously (coinciding with the political transition that ushered in Abiy). I looked at three specific new variables—use of social media to organize offline violence, polarization of society, and political parties hate speech—over a ten-year period and compared them to the two disinformation variables (government dissemination of false information, party dissemination of false information).[51] As Figure 6.4 shows, by 2019, most of the gains from 2017 and 2018 had reversed. Social media-fueled offline violence and government disinformation have, in fact, exceeded median levels under the previous government.

These trend lines show us that the fallout from the 2015–2017 nationwide protests has not yet ebbed. Instead, the protests seem to have embedded new disruptive dynamics, presenting ominous signs for the country.

How do social media, hate speech, and incitement to offline violence intersect in Ethiopia? Violent confrontations in October 2019 offer some insights. On October 23, Jawar wrote an urgent Facebook post to his 1.8 million followers. He claimed that Ethiopian authorities had withdrawn his security detail and surrounded his house. Rather than arrest him, he believed they planned to kill

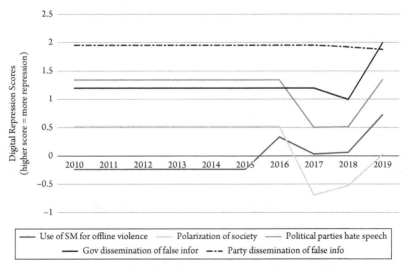

Figure 6.4 Disinformation, Hate Speech, and Polarization Trends in Ethiopia, 2010 to 2019

him and pin the blame on civilian intruders.[52] Abiy's plan, he told me, was to "re-move my security. Send some civilians. Do me. Then blame the security. Easy!" But, he said, "Shit didn't work that way. So it failed, because movies are movies. Whether they're good with Hollywood, they're movies. Real life doesn't work that way." Soon after Jawar's Facebook post, a group of his followers rushed to his residence in force. In the ensuing days, his Oromo supporters filled the streets, clashing with members of other ethnic groups. At least eighty-six people died during the subsequent violence. Not until the second day of confrontations did Jawar hold a news conference calling for an end to the violence: "Open the blocked roads, clean the towns of barricades, treat those who have been injured during the protests and reconcile with those you have quarreled with."[53] At that point, the killing stopped.

Was Jawar responsible for inciting this violence? The details of these October events remain in dispute. Jawar contends that the government was primarily at fault: "I believe on the second day they realized they had been beaten. So they wanted to turn things from Jawar against the government, to people to people." He maintains that the "violence was created by them. They turned it into this communal violence between their own communities. . . . They can't blame me because they have been on the record saying they were wrong."[54] Others are hes-itant to absolve Jawar of instigating the violence. When I asked Bekele about Jawar's role, he paused for a moment before voicing his concerns:

> I could say that Jawar could've acted much more responsibly than he did knowing the kind of influence he has on his followers. . . . He has a lot of active followers who will seem to listen to what he has to say, which means it should create more responsibility. For example, he could start by clearly denouncing all forms of violence and urging all his followers to only use peaceful means to advance their cause.[55]

Whether or not Jawar is to blame for the October violence, several facts are rel-evant. Social media facilitated the swift spread of Jawar's message and instantly mobilized scores of agitated followers, who rushed en masse to his residence. Moreover, the rapidity with which Jawar's supporters and the counterprotestors resorted to violence indicates the heightened, polarized atmosphere gripping the country.

In Ethiopia's current environment, social media have become a major fault line and battleground. Particularly as ethnically based parties seek to mobilize their base of supporters, misinformation and historical revisionism have proliferated. For example, Facebook pages with large followings like "EthiopianDJ" are major disseminators of false or misleading information. In one incident, EthiopianDJ posted photos that ostensibly showed security forces confiscating green, yellow, and red flags from followers of the Ethiopian Orthodox Church while permitting Oromo Liberation Front flags ("the green, yellow and red flag is associated with Ethiopia's past emperors while the OLF flag represents Oromo resistance").[56] While the images are real, they are presented in a manner that is deeply misleading. The photos actually came from two separate celebrations held some days apart. During each event, security personnel confiscated flags deemed unlawful by the government—they did not single out flags from one group or another.

The accumulation of these events, amplified by social media, has led to a "contagion effect," which Endalkachew describes as "galvanizing sympathizers by employing misinformation, inflammatory stories, memes and videos on social media."[57] Just how much of a threat disinformation and a polarized information environment pose to Ethiopia is a subject of debate. Some experts caution that the destabilizing impact of disinformation can be devastating. Ahmed advises: "It is probably the biggest risk, the biggest issue with this country because of the polarizing politics in this country. Now you have very polarized groups, and these polarized groups are resorting to kind of violence, including news, disinformation."[58] Similarly, Berhanu warned that "the damage has been extremely significant. A good [amount] of the bloodshed that we saw in the last eighteen months or so is fueled by social media more than anything else."[59]

Others, however, are less troubled by social media's impact. "I know a lot of my fellow brothers and sisters in Ethiopia are very concerned," said Daniel Bekele. "I share some of the concerns. . . . The way some of the activists or politicians have used social media, it's quite irresponsible." But he also noted that "there are lots of other places where social media is totally being abused, more than we have seen in Ethiopia. So I wouldn't be overly concerned about it. You know, it's a new thing. It's a new political space and there's a lot of venting."[60]

The government is taking the threat posed by unfettered speech on social media seriously. During my visit, Ethiopia's parliament approved a new hate speech and false information law that many find problematic. The new law prohibits the dissemination of speech that "promotes hatred, discrimination or attack against a person or an identifiable group based on ethnicity, religion, race, gender, and disability" (although dissemination apparently does not include liking or tagging such content on social media).[61] Experts are concerned that the definition of promotion is overly vague and doesn't "require a direct link between the speech and the consequences."[62]

For many, the disinformation provision is even more worrisome, muddling definitions of what constitutes "speech based on false information" and lacking clarity about what specific types of dissemination could incur liability.

Daniel acknowledged concerns with the disinformation component of the law: "Disinformation laws have historically been a tool to attack media and freedom of expression as well as to restrict access to information. So that part continues to worry me." But he was willing to reserve judgment, observing, "We'll have to see how it [the law] is implemented because at least this time around, I know that the drafters of this law and the government are not necessarily coming with an evil intention."[63] While this change provides some measure of reassurance in the short term, it does not auger well for longer-term political freedom in Ethiopia given the government's long-standing reliance on suppression tactics.

In April 2020, Yayesew Shimelis became the first person charged under the law. Shimelis, who hosts a weekly political show on a regional government broadcaster, Tigray TV, posted a message on Facebook falsely asserting that Ethiopian authorities were preparing two hundred thousand burial places in anticipation of the coronavirus. Facebook immediately suspended his account. He was detained by government authorities the next day.[64] Several groups have expressed concern about the charges. The Committee to Protect Journalists released a statement cautioning that "imprisoning a journalist at this time, when the public needs information rather than censorship, is likely to discourage critical reporting and dissenting opinions."[65]

Ethiopia's Surveillance Capacity

While the full extent of Ethiopia's surveillance capacity remains largely unknown, several groups have carried out investigations that shed light on instruments deployed by the government's intelligence and security forces to suppress opposition voices both inside and outside the country. Between 2013 and 2017, the Citizen Lab published a series of reports on the abuse of spyware that were linked to Ethiopia's government.[66] The reports found that the Ethiopian government had purchased intrusion and surveillance software from a range of firms— including Germany's FinFisher, Italy's Hacking Team, and Israel's Cyberbit. The government used this spyware to target Ethiopian dissidents living abroad, opposition media outlets, and political opponents. The software was designed to "steal files and passwords, and intercept Skype calls and instant messages."[67] Ethiopian authorities' consistent abuse of these tactics vividly illustrates how far the country's security agencies were willing to go—not only to keep tabs on and disrupt perceived opponents, but also to extend the country's surveillance reach far beyond its borders.

Another important accounting of Ethiopia's information technology capabilities can be found in Human Rights Watch's 2014 report, "They Know Everything We Do." This report details how "Ethiopia has acquired some of the world's most advanced surveillance technologies," including network interception capabilities, deep packet inspection, and sophisticated customer management databases. One of the products it highlighted, "ZSmart," was developed by the Chinese firm ZTE, and provides Ethiopian authorities with the ability to access SMS text messages and full recordings of phone conversations occurring on the country's sole telecom network, Ethio Telecom. The report identified specific Chinese and European companies—such as Huawei, ZTE, Orange, Hacking Team, and Gamma International—which "provided the products, services, and expertise to modernize the sector," and laid the groundwork for the country's surveillance infrastructure. But the report also acknowledges that Ethiopia's telecom surveillance "is limited by human capacity issues and a lack of trust among key government departments." This tracked with what several contacts reported to me. Befeqadu, a prominent target of the previous government, remarked, "I don't think they were advanced, by the way." "I mean, for example, other than my public posts, when they were surveilling me . . . they didn't have a single email conversation that I had, not a single private conversation that I had. They did not have the capacity to actually do sophisticated things."[68]

Thus, Ethiopians' fears about what the state might be able to surveil may not match its actual competencies. In many respects, this disparity was immaterial. As long as sufficient numbers of citizens chose to self-limit their communication because they believed the government could monitor their conversations, the authorities would achieve their desired outcome: silencing independent voices and limiting dissent.

I asked Felix Horne, the author of the Human Rights Watch report, what he made of Ethiopia's digital surveillance capacity. "My sense is that the capabilities, at the time for sub-Saharan Africa, were pretty complete. As you saw with ZSmart, it is pretty simple. If they had a target, then they recorded all of that target's phone calls, acquired all of that metadata with little in the way of any sort of due process or legal protections."[69] Yet Horne also recounted an interview that made him question the importance of digital capabilities to the Ethiopian state:

> One of the interviews that really kind of stuck in my mind was a former federal police officer in one of the larger regional towns. He was a good contact and he was fairly high up. He was very open to speaking. He didn't have any protection concerns outside of Ethiopia at the time. So I interviewed him a number of times. I kept pressing about issues around digital surveillance. And after a while he got annoyed with me and he said, "Look, you're asking the wrong question, you know. Because of our grassroots systems of surveillance, our one-to-five system, we know everything that is going on in there. . . . Our security forces are all reporting information to us. We know everything that's

going on. We don't need to use this digital surveillance. We have them available, but we don't really need to use them."[70]

Under Abiy, the country's surveillance strategy is undergoing a major shift. One of the most visible changes has been the decline of Ethiopia's "one-to-five" physical surveillance network, a system affecting millions of people where volunteers would typically be assigned five people to monitor and oversee. As the country entered a tumultuous period beginning in 2015, this system started to fray. Now many experts like Endalkachew maintain that "the offline surveillance system is dismantled once and for all."[71]

At this point, a larger question we might consider is whether digital surveillance will emerge to take the place of the one-to-five network. Endalkachew posits that when the authorities wish to use their digital surveillance capabilities, "they will activate it." He mentions periodic instances when the government has revealed political opponents' embarrassing online activity because they represent direct challenges to the Abiy administration.[72] Indeed, while the mandate of its intelligence services has narrowed, they still rely on a full range of surveillance tools to maintain political stability and preempt challenges to the government (such as in western Oromia and now Tigray).

Similarly, the government does not seem particularly interested in pursuing mass surveillance or procuring AI-powered surveillance tools such as facial recognition or safe city systems. "Mass surveillance is not something the government is interested in," remarked the government advisory unit expert. He did note that in Unity Park, where the prime minister's office is located, the government is installing facial recognition cameras. But he was quick to clarify that "we're talking about a couple of hundred cameras. It's not a big system connected with an AI or we'd invest heavily on it. It's just a [basic] security system."[73] That being said, the government recently announced the establishment of a new artificial intelligence research and development center intended to safeguard Ethiopia's national interests.[74] The center will be headed by former deputy director of INSA Worku Gachena.

Censorship and Information Controls

Censorship in Ethiopia presents a more complicated story. While there are undoubtedly fewer information controls under Abiy, recent events are cause for concern. Coming hand in hand with their Internet shutdowns, Ethiopian authorities continue to block numerous websites and restrict access to social media and messaging applications (like WhatsApp, Telegram, and Facebook Messenger). Midway through 2019, the Open Observatory of Network Interference (OONI) released a report that warned of tightening controls and a reversion back to old censorship practices: "Ethiopia seems to be sliding back to old ways when Internet censorship was a pervasive practice." The report notes that recent Internet blackouts, social media restrictions, and blocking of WhatsApp and Facebook indicate a "dangerous path for freedom of expression, access to information, and associated human rights in the country."[75]

I used OONI's explorer probe to test for website blocking in Ethiopia from January 1, 2020, through March 1, 2020.[76] The test yield twenty-three anomalies (signs of potential network interference leading to website blocking) across one ISP—Ethio Telecom. Sites blocked by Ethiopian authorities appear to include the University of Minnesota's Human Rights Resource Center, an Islamic State propaganda outlet (www.khilafahcom), as well as an array of pornographic and gambling web pages. While this censorship does not indicate extensive blocking—compared, for example, to Thailand—it does show a pattern of restrictions and reveals how such controls could ramp up in parallel with Internet shutdowns at key political moments.

Another set of data that I examined were transparency reports released by Google, Facebook, and Twitter. For each platform, I looked at a range of dates between January 2013 and June 2019. None of the platforms recorded any requests by the Ethiopian government to restrict user content. In contrast with Thailand or even the Philippines, none of the three platforms had any record that Ethiopian authorities had approached the companies with content restriction requests.[77] This doesn't mean that the Ethiopian state isn't interested in limiting content posted on Facebook, Google, or Twitter. Rather, it indicates that Ethiopian authorities either lack a reliable channel by which to communicate their demands to these companies, or do not have the requisite bureaucratic capacity to generate official content requests. Instead, when Ethiopian authorities have chosen to censor content, they've relied on Internet shutdowns and selective social media or app blocking, or they have directly applied filtering technology to block unwanted websites.

My conversations in Ethiopia reflected this mixed picture. Befeqadu, for example, noted that while he was currently free to write what he'd like, he worried that he "can be jailed anytime in the future." Because the "right institutions are not yet in place," even if Abiy is committed to political reform, the laws currently on the books offer blanket discretion to authorities to crack down on free speech.[78] Jawar was even blunter: "It [repression] is coming back. It's coming back now. They're going back to where they were in 2016 or 2017. They are returning to the old one, and we're returning ourselves."[79] Given that Jawar now languishes in jail awaiting trial, and that the media outlet he founded, OMN, has once again been forced to broadcast from the United States (authorities have repeatedly raided OMN's Addis offices), his concerns are warranted.

Consequently, "There's a lot of uncertainty," said an Ethiopian think-tank analyst. "It depends on the maturity and responsibility of the different political actors. It can go either way." He observed, however, that "we have two options: democratize or perish. If you democratize, the possibility of sustaining a repressive regime for long, it's not possible."[80] Ethiopia's democratization process is in its infancy; the extent to which the state will cease relying upon information controls as a core political strategy is an open question.

Which Factors Have Shaped Digital Repression in Ethiopia?

Ethiopia has a long tradition of repression—and a more recent tradition of digital repression. The natural fallback, particularly when faced with political instability, is to revert back to those tools. Such a pattern explains the government's repeated reliance on Internet shutdowns to maintain order. Yet, despite recent setbacks, Abiy has taken many real steps to open up the political system. How do we make sense of how digital repression has evolved in Ethiopia since the early 2000s—from EPRDF rule through Abiy's administration? Two events are significant in this regard.

First, the 2005 national elections represented a signal moment for Ethiopian politics. The regime had long relied on policies of control to maintain dominance over the population (lending itself very well to strategies of digital repression). Meles Zenawi's leadership proved to be no exception to the rule. Yet as Gérard Prunier describes it, in 2005, for the first time, the EPRDF decided to allow for competitive elections, "no matter what the consequences might be."[81] The consequence were disastrous. Opposition groups formed coalitions, held public rallies, and put together a genuine challenge to the ruling party. Early election returns showed opposition candidates performing well. Sensing potential defeat, the ruling party preemptively declared victory and initiated a post-election period marred by contentious disputes, court challenges, mass protests, and violence. Simegnish Mengesha writes, "The months after the elections saw the killing of 193 civilians by the Ethiopian police, the injury of 763 more, the arrest of roughly 20,000 protesters, and the arrest and trial for treason and attempted genocide of up to 150 opposition leaders, aid workers, and reporters."[82] Very quickly, Meles pivoted from holding relatively free and fair elections to instigating a brutal crackdown and a campaign of repression that would endure for the next ten years. The government changed electoral laws to hamstring future opposition challenges; it adopted constricting media regulations to suppress political speech; it restricted the ability of civil society organizations to obtain outside funding; and it enacted the Anti-Terrorism Proclamation in 2009 that provided the state further powers to lock up political challengers, arrest journalists, and break up advocacy organizations.

The crackdown devastated the opposition. As Lammi Begna, a spokesperson for the OLF, recounted, "We were finally weakened by the regime. Most of us were arrested. Other had to flee the country. Many of our fellow youths were killed. Very, very difficult."[83] Lammi himself was arrested and thrown in prison, serving a five-year sentence.

Alongside physical repression measures, the Ethiopian government adopted digital techniques as well. The timing of the crackdown coincided with the arrival of the Internet as a new means of communication in the country. Opposition actors used a variety of digital methods to organize. Initially, Lammi explained, email was the only electronic tool available to activists: "There was no Facebook. There was no digital media available to us. . . . We were the first people to get Internet access because we were university students. Using the Internet that the university provided for us, we organized assemblies, we organized groups."[84]

As the government intensified its crackdown and drove greater numbers of political dissidents out of the country, exiled political and media elites began to organize via social media and use those platforms to communicate with those back in Ethiopia. In fact, many experts credit social media with uniting diaspora and national politics into a single forum. "Before the Internet and emergence of social media, there was a clear divide between diaspora politics and local politics," observed an Ethiopian think-tank expert. "When social media came, it became seamless. It became a single platform where, you know, people in Addis or in Gondar or in Jimma could debate and discuss ideas with political dissidents based in Washington, DC or Minnesota."[85]

Thus, jailing political opponents or exiling them out of the country proved insufficient for the government to achieve its repression objectives. Activists' ability to use digital communications to transcend physical boundaries and sustain resistance caused the state to seek new tools to beat back those challenges. This challenge became a driving impetus for the Ethiopian state to adopt passive and targeted surveillance techniques and restrictive information controls.

The second shock to Ethiopia's political order occurred in 2011, with the onset of Arab Spring demonstrations. At that point, even if the Ethiopian government had started to feel more secure after having thoroughly subdued its political opponents (including rigged elections in 2010 where the EPRDF won 99.6 percent of the seats in parliament), events in Egypt, Tunisia, and Syria proved their control was illusory.[86] "Those uprisings demonstrated the power of technology, the Internet in toppling down repressive regimes. It created a lot of nervousness in the Ethiopian regime," observed the same think-tank analyst.[87] And the authorities were right to be nervous. The protest served as an inspiration for the opposition. Lammi observed, "The impact of the Arab Spring on our youth was so huge." They watched as Egyptian activists staged multiday sit-ins in Tahrir Square. "Our youth started considering that if you organize and use digital media, it is possible to nail down any repressive forces."[88]

Jawar echoed Lammi's perspective about the influence of Arab Spring protests on his thinking. "The Arab Spring was something. It was like watching and testing the theories, if you will. . . . Arab Spring significantly influenced me. I think without Arab Spring, probably I would've gone for the complete collapse of the regime here. The Arab Spring kind of shocked me."[89] The protests opened activists' eyes to new possibilities. It provided a real-time model for how to successfully leverage digital communications to network citizens, mobilize political action, and undermine violently repressive regimes. And it presented a viable alternative to armed struggle for those, like Jawar, who were searching for ways to topple Ethiopia's authoritarian system.

It took a few years, but the unrest sparked by the Arab Spring eventually spread to Ethiopia. By the fall of 2015, Ethiopian authorities were frantically trying to contain escalating protests. Like their Egyptian counterparts, they shut down the Internet, persecuted online bloggers, blocked websites and social media applications, and jailed political opponents. None of these tactics proved effective.

Prime Minister Hailemariam's resignation and Abiy's ascension to power marked a natural bookend to an era of digital repression characterized by a heavy reliance on surveillance instruments, information controls, and persecutions of online activists. Abiy's arrival has ushered in a new digital period—one that is still being defined. The country's tentative embrace of political and economic liberalization is colliding against a dominant political order that has prioritized repression and centralized state control for decades. This history helps explain the state's fluctuation, and the fears people have that recent political freedoms may reverse course.

Protest Strategies and Adaptive Tactics

One major question regarding Ethiopia's transition was how protestors were able to circumvent Ethiopia's information controls and digital repression operation to sustain their movement. Given the low Internet penetration rate in the country—particularly outside of cities—and the massive resources that Ethiopian authorities had invested in controlling online dissent, how was it possible that undermanned activists managed to beat the state? The answer lies with their use of emergent learning strategies that rely heavily on trial and error, enabling them to outwit the government's clunky repression approach.

Jawar, whose movement bore considerable responsibility for sustaining mass protests, gave an interesting response. First, he explained, they needed to "define the enemy." They built their movement with the assumption that Meles would still be in power. When he passed away in 2012, "We were completely unsure what to do. . . . The dictatorship became faceless. We couldn't really turn people against Hailemariam, because people were like, *He's not a very charismatic figure.*" So they had to invent and personify a new enemy to rally against. They created a damaging portrait of Ethiopian leadership—"Corrupt. Tigrayan. TPLF. So we can rally people on him. . . . We were able to personify the enemy. If you don't define the enemy, you can't destroy it. You have to personify it. You have to say, look at this guy."[90]

One of the big hurdles the protestors faced was how to get around information controls and Internet shutdowns. As Jawar related, the authorities made a big mistake. "They were shutting down for four days. Five days. We realized we were too dependent on the Internet." So they asked themselves how to circumvent such restrictions. They realized that the authorities were only shutting down the Internet in Oromia, the heart of the protests, but were leaving online access intact in the capital. "So every district would finance one person to come here [to Addis]. I post whatever we hear from them, back there. They send information through SMS or sometimes they send it through papers. I put it back online." Unless the government was willing to shut down the Internet nationwide for week or months, then the activists had an easy way to get around those restrictions. Jawar admits that their tactics weren't part of a grand strategy. "It would be a lie for me to think that I knew [what to do] about that. . . . People started dropping ideas. I said, okay, that's good. You have to be creative about it. So we started to modify."[91] The activists' ability to iterate new ideas, adapt to changing circumstances, and come up with innovative strategies to counter new government restrictions made all the difference.[92]

They were even able to turn mass detention camps to their advantage. As Jawar explained, "Remember, we didn't have much opportunity to network people because we didn't have money and we didn't have the freedom of movement. Now we had a government that would take twenty thousand people from one part of Oromia and put them in one military camp." They were able to take advantage of this situation to use it for networking. "I created this training manual where they train, where they share experiences," Jawar recalled. "They spent two months [in prison] and they get out well networked! And after that they don't even need Internet. They can just call each other."[93] The social media networking turned into physical networking. So even when the government shut down the Internet, people knew how to contact each other and how to funnel information to outside sources who could broadcast them worldwide.

The adaptive innovations described by Jawar align closely with the "emergent strategy" school of thought in international relations. Ionut Popescu describes this perspective as a "process of navigating through an unpredictable world by improvisation and continuous learning."[94] Rather than fully forming plans in advance, organizations can learn over time and shift goals based on new inputs and adaptations. Researchers Aliaksandr Herasimenka, Tetyana Lokot, Olga Onuch, and Mariëlle Wijermars offer similar observations regarding Internet shutdowns in Belarus: "When the Internet was down, protesters used what was available. They plastered the walls of apartment blocks with printed leaflets sharing news of police violence and planned strikes."[95] In other words, the ability of online information blackouts to break the backs of resistance movements is highly suspect. Instead, activists identify alternate means and offline networks to carry key messages.

Jawar's experience is a perfect illustration of emergent strategy in action. As he admitted, "I really didn't know anything." Instead, he innovated through experimentation. "I just post on Facebook. I said, what is going to happen to us? They shut down Internet, we started writing stuff."[96] He makes a move, the authorities react. He tries something else and sees what sticks. Such techniques form the core of emergent strategy and offer larger lessons for civil society groups that are struggling to push back against powerful digital capabilities.

What about China's Role?

The final question this chapter explores is the extent to which China is a driver of digital repression in Ethiopia.[97] While China has readily provided sophisticated technology at the Ethiopian government's request, I contend that this relationship is distinct from actively driving digital repression in the country.

Indisputably, China exercises significant influence in Ethiopia. China's economic impact largely exceeds that of the United States or Europe. I have periodically visited Addis over the course of my career. Each time I return, I see more skyscrapers, wider highways, modernized train lines, and expanded airports. The bulk of this work has been undertaken by Chinese companies supported by massive Chinese state loans. The data shows that the cumulative Chinese loan total to the Ethiopian government from 2000 to 2017 equaled $13.8 billion.[98] This figure ranks Ethiopia second on the continent, behind only Angola, when it comes aggregate levels of Chinese investment.

Ethiopians recognize China's immense economic influence. Addis observed, "You can't ignore it, whether it's tech or anything else in the country. I've been back twenty years now. I don't think we would be anywhere near where we are if it wasn't for the Chinese influence in investment."[99] Hailemelekot Asfaw, the

Center for International Private Enterprise's Ethiopia representative, noted that the Chinese came "not only with the technology, but they came with money." He describes how the relationship works: "They do a simple negotiation with the government. We come with money, give us a contract. The government has the money, so it's easy. They built the telecom system, even the expansion of Ethiopian Airlines, significantly using the Chinese. Many airports in this country—there's a big expansion of the airport again, using Chinese money." Hailemelekot emphasized that when it comes to B2B transactions, "all those types of products we have in this country are imported from China. All of our business people—I would say more than 90 or 95 percent—are traveling to China."[100]

But there is scant evidence that China's economic sway has directly instigated digital repression in the country. I inquired with Tekleberhan about the level of Chinese influence he experienced running INSA. He smiled and said, "Always the Americans think we're working behind the door with the Chinese. Never. That's a completely false perception." He continued, "So we, for example, bought technology from Israel, from Italy, even from Germany, including from America, also from China, always to protect our country to create a secure environment. We were searching the best technologies from every part of the world."[101] In fact, he emphasized, "China was not our model. . . . My model was Israel because we focus on the technological capabilities, rather than repressing people. We were not worried about public disobedience. We were worried about terrorist acts, specific threats. So China couldn't be our model. Never."[102]

I posed the same question to my national intelligence contact. He acknowledged that Chinese infrastructure is "cheap" and "also available," and that as a result, Ethiopia and China maintain a strong relationship. I asked him whether the Chinese were pushing specific capabilities or advanced systems. He responded, "In most cases, we go to them, and ask for help and that does seem different than the Israelis. They always come in, they want to sell stuff. They're marketers, and always they tell us, we have this product, we have that product, something like that. Well, the Chinese, we go to them." Part of the reason that he felt that the Chinese could afford to be less aggressive was that "they know that you will come to them. They know that demand. There is a demand all over Africa for the technology. They are not so desperate to push their products for us. Because we are not producing it, but we do need the product." He noted that because of export controls, many European or US companies refuse to sell to them. Instead, his agency reaches out through Chinese government officials (rather than directly approach Chinese suppliers). The Ethiopians identify their requirements, "And ta-da! they [the Chinese] would send their experts." However, like Tekleberhan, he also stressed that his organization works closely with US intelligence counterparts—"There is a constant discussion between the CIA, NSA, and us. There is a constant partnership."[103]

Documenting China's contribution to Ethiopia's digital repression capacity is difficult. The aforementioned Human Rights Watch report on telecom surveillance remains one of the most comprehensive accounts of China's digital involvement in Ethiopia. And yet much of what the report describes, insofar as it relates to Chinese companies, appears less troubling than other capabilities, such as advanced cyber hacking tools and middlebox equipment acquired from Western companies. As Horne notes, "I think China has lots of questions to answer continent-wide and around the world. . . . But what we know they provided to Ethiopia, no, I don't think that's particularly problematic, to be honest, at least compared to the spyware, the DPI [deep packet inspection], and stuff that clearly was to be used for repression."[104]

Iginio Gagliardone explores this issue in his book *China, Africa and the Future of the Internet.* Gagliardone argues that the US global antiterrorism agenda helped bring about "policies leading to greater surveillance and censorship."[105] He describes how an "unholy alliance" between East and West led to a paradox where the Chinese government quietly took care of the "material implementation of a highly centralized and securitized information space," while the United States offered "the discursive terrain for Ethiopian authorities to justify the creation of such a space" through its counterterrorism efforts.[106] He contends that no one has clean hands when it comes to external support for Ethiopia's digital repression apparatus.

That being said, the normative impact of Chinese technology should not be overlooked. As researcher Emeka Umejei writes, the demonstration effect of China's model causes many leaders to ask, "If China could become a world power without a free Internet, why do African countries need a free Internet?"[107] At a minimum, digital infrastructure supplied by the Chinese government may help facilitate the illiberal ambitions of certain African leaders. Likewise, Christopher Walker, Shanthi Kalathil, and Jessica Ludwig observe that "even if the authoritarian behemoths do not explicitly seek to remold the world in their own image, the dangers to civil liberties are growing as authoritarian styles of social management are being baked into the world's technological architecture."[108] The surveillance capabilities that ZTE integrated into Ethiopia's ICT network illustrate this point. Even if China is not directly urging governments to promulgate oppressive policies, its inclusion of surveillance and censorship instruments in its digital infrastructure offerings promotes coercive outcomes.

Some commentators maintain that China's influence in Ethiopia is on the wane. Abiy has made a push to restore greater balance to Ethiopia's bilateral relations. In 2019, he received a multi-billion-dollar loan package from the IMF and World Bank—perceived by many as a direct repudiation of China. Abiy described IMF and World Bank support as "like borrowing from one's mother," and contrasted it to assistance from the Chinese, which he criticized for forcing debt repayment even before projects were completed.[109] The upcoming telecom privatization provides a good illustration of the shifting dynamic. Despite China's extensive history developing the current network, the consensus is that Chinese companies will not receive any preferences in the bidding process, and that the government is interested in seeing a Western company win the contract. The government advisory unit expert I interviewed noted that privatization is a "big sign that the government also wants to let in other players, not just the Chinese. It doesn't mean that we're skeptical of the Chinese or we want them out. It just means that it's more open now to Western organizations or companies or technologies to compete."[110]

How, then, can we conceive of China's shifting role in Ethiopia? Similar to Thailand or the Philippines, the issue of a country's "agency" becomes an essential analytic point. The Chinese have ample digital capabilities that they are more than willing to subsidize, but the acquisition of these tools is dependent on the needs, motivations, and requirements of the country in question. As Gagliardone writes, "African states, rather than being passive recipients of blueprints developed elsewhere, have demonstrated remarkable skills in making use of Beijing's openings in the ICT sector to bolster their own development projects."[111]

Indeed, when I asked different contacts to describe the supply-and-demand dynamic of Ethiopia's digital relationship with China—whether China was pushing its technologies on the Ethiopian state, or whether Ethiopian demand was more salient (e.g., the Ethiopian government proactively requesting certain digital capabilities)—most people emphasized the latter. "Of course, there are pull and push factors. But it is mostly the Ethiopian government that wants them [the Chinese] to come, because they come without the pressure, that democratic reform pressure," commented Befeqadu.[112] Ultimately, the biggest selling points of Chinese technology may be its hands-off model that furnishes advanced capabilities to governments while demanding few policy conditions in return, and the generous accompanying subsidies that make Chinese equipment a relative bargain for resource-constrained governments.

Over several decades, China developed an exceptionally close relationship with Ethiopia's government. While the West hesitated to provide significant economic assistance or investment, China stepped in—in a big way. This partnership allowed the Ethiopian state to acquire low-priced equipment that helped lay its digital repression foundation. Notwithstanding Abiy's interest in improving relations with the West, the Sino-Ethiopian relationship remains strong, with the two countries partnering on everything from joint satellites to AI research. Yet their shared interests do not mean that China is responsible for driving digital repression in Ethiopia. On the contrary, a variety of other factors—fallout from 2005 elections, government nervousness related to Arab Spring protests, and long-standing practices of state repression—are more relevant in explaining patterns of digital repression in Ethiopia.

Conclusion

This concludes the book's third case study. Ethiopia's digital repression trajectory presents similarities and contrasts to Thailand and the Philippines. Perhaps the sharpest difference is that both Thailand and the Philippines are undergoing steady deteriorations in their governance and major upticks in the use of digital tools to control or manipulate their populations. Conversely, until the middle of 2020, Ethiopia had been in the midst of a political opening leading to significant changes in its digital strategies. While Ethiopia's democratization prospects are presently uncertain, the diminishment of surveillance, censorship, and online persecution is noticeable. At the same time, worrisome trends related to social manipulation, disinformation, and online incitement to offline violence parallel similar patterns in Thailand and the Philippines. Whether Ethiopia will be able to withstand these disruptive forces remains unclear. The country's complicated ethnic makeup, its history of state repression, and Abiy's wavering leadership raise a host of unanswered questions.

Notes

1. In Ethiopia, individuals are commonly referred to by their first name. There are no surnames in Ethiopia; second names derive from the father's personal name. Therefore, Ethiopian contacts in this chapter will be referred to either by their full name (first and last name) or just their first name.
2. The EPRDF was made up of four political parties conforming to Ethiopia's major ethnic communities: the TPLF, the Amhara Democratic Party (ADP), the Oromo Democratic Party, and the Southern Ethiopian People's Democratic Movement (SEPDM). Each was supposed to be equally represented in the ranks of EPRDF leadership, although in practice, the TPLF dominated the coalition.
3. Jon Temin and Yoseph Badwaza, "Aspirations and Realities in Africa: Ethiopia's Quiet Revolution." *Journal of Democracy* 30, no. 3 (2019): 143.
4. Samuel Gebre and Simon Marks, "Ethiopia Expects to Hold Delayed Elections within Next Year," *Bloomberg*, September 10, 2020, https://www.bloomberg.com/news/articles/2020-09-10/ethiopia-expects-to-hold-general-elections-in-next-12-months?sref=QmOxnLFz.
5. Dawit Endeshaw, "Mass Arrests in Ethiopia Raise Spectre of Repressive Past," *Reuters*, August 13, 2020, https://www.reuters.com/article/us-ethiopia-arrests/mass-arrests-in-ethiopia-raise-spectre-of-repressive-past-idUSKCN2591KH.
6. "Ethiopia: Opposition Figures Held without Charge," Human Rights Watch, August 15, 2020, https://www.hrw.org/news/2020/08/15/ethiopia-opposition-figures-held-without-charge.
7. "Ethiopia: Opposition Figures Held without Charge," Human Rights Watch.

8. Steven Feldstein, "Ethiopia's Conflict in Tigray Presents Hard Decisions," Carnegie Endowment for International Peace, December 1, 2020, https://carnegieendowment.org/2020/12/01/ethiopia-s-conflict-in-tigray-presents-hard-decisions-pub-83369.

9. "Ethiopia to launch 'final phase' of offensive in Tigray region, says PM," *Reuters*, November 26, 2020, https://www.reuters.com/article/us-ethiopia-conflict/ethiopia-to-launch-final-phase-of-offensive-in-tigray-region-says-pm-idUSKBN2860H1.

10. "Ethiopia—Tigray Region Humanitarian Update," UN OCHA, December 11, 2020, https://reports.unocha.org/en/country/ethiopia.

11. "CrisisWatch Ethiopia," International Crisis Group, November 2020, https://www.crisisgroup.org/crisiswatch#ethiopia.

12. "Note to Correspondents: UN High-level Officials Express Deep Concern Over Escalating Ethnic Tensions in Ethiopia," UN Secretary General, November 12, 2020, https://www.un.org/sg/en/content/sg/note-correspondents/2020-11-12/note-correspondents-un-high-level-officials-express-deep-concern-over-escalating-ethnic-tensions-ethiopia.

13. Laetitia Bader, "Gates Open on Ethiopia's Infamous Maekelawi Jail," Human Rights Watch, September 6, 2019, https://www.hrw.org/news/2019/09/06/gates-open-ethiopias-infamous-maekelawi-jail#.

14. Maggie Fick, "Ethiopia Offers Amnesty to Recently Freed Political Prisoners," *Reuters*, July 20, 2018, https://www.reuters.com/article/us-ethiopia-prisoners/ethiopia-offers-amnesty-to-recently-freed-political-prisoners-idUSKBN1KA1U0.

15. Author interview with an Ethiopian blogger, February 20, 2020.

16. "Ethiopia: Two Prisoners of Conscience Freed," Amnesty International, March 2008, https://www.amnesty.org/en/press-releases/2008/03/ethiopia-two-prisoners-conscience-freed-20080328/.

17. Ranking is extracted from the 2020 V-Dem electoral democracy index, Coppedge et al., "V-Dem Dataset v10."

18. "Ethiopia," Freedom House, 2020, https://freedomhouse.org/country/ethiopia/freedom-world/2020.

19. "2019 Country Reports on Human Rights Practices: Ethiopia," US Department of State, 2020, https://www.state.gov/reports/2019-country-reports-on-human-rights-practices/ethiopia/.

20. "2019 Country Reports on Human Rights Practices: Ethiopia," US Department of State.

21. Temin and Badwaza, "Aspirations and Realities," 143.

22. Daniel Bekele (chief commissioner, Ethiopian Human Rights Commission), interview with the author, February 21, 2020.

23. Berhanu Nega (Ethiopian politician), interview with the author, February 21, 2020.

24. During my trip to Mekele, several contacts raised the circumstances behind Abiy's departure from INSA. There are competing viewpoints on the matter. Tekleberhan Woldearegay, the former director of INSA who was responsible for pushing Abiy out of the agency, claims that Abiy was leveraging his office for political gain: "Every minister, every department head, was invited to visit INSA's work. . . . He exploited, he manipulated the naivete of the people, the ignorance of the people. . . . When I came back, it took me around six months to recover the organization, to bring the organization back on track. . . . I told him [Abiy], 'Choose. It's a conflict of interest, regarding INSA procedures and protocols. If you're a technocrat, if you are part of the security apparatus, you don't have to participate in the political power process, you know? So if you want to participate in the political parties, just go out.' I told him, 'You can't keep [politically] organizing because of this conflict of interest. . . . It's better to leave INSA and participate with your full energies as a full political activist.' So I told him at that time. He was out." Tekleberhan Woldearegay (former director of INSA), interview with the author, February 19, 2020. An alternative narrative is that while Abiy was leading INSA, he became increasingly upset about oppression carried out by the agency. He started "supporting the opposition and giving information" to outside organizations that were being targeted. When Tekleberhan came back and learned about Abiy's actions, he fired him. Author interview with an Ethiopian blogger, February 20, 2020.

25. Getachew Reda (Ethiopian politician), interview with the author, February 19, 2020.

26. Jawar Mohammed (Ethiopian politician), interview with the author, February 21, 2020.

27. Befeqadu Hailu (executive director of the Center for the Advancement of Rights and Democracy), interview with the author, February 18, 2020.

28. Will Davison (independent journalist), interview with the author, February 18, 2020.

29. Daniel Bekele, interview with the author.

30. Author interview with a senior intelligence official, February 16, 2020.

31. Author interview with a senior intelligence official.

32. Abiy's government has carried out a counterinsurgency campaign for most of 2020 centered in the western Oromia region against the Oromo Liberation Army, an armed group that had formerly been part of the Oromo Liberation Front (the OLF had signed a peace deal with the Ethiopian government in 2018, ending forty-five years of violent conflict). Tactics include months of blocked social media services and disconnected mobile phone networks along with a "pattern of mass detentions and government abuses." "Ethiopia: Communications Shutdown Takes Heavy Toll," Human Rights Watch, March 9, 2020, https://www.hrw.org/news/2020/03/09/ethiopia-communications-shutdown-takes-heavy-toll#.

33. The most recent ITU Internet access data is from 2017. "Statistics—ITU," International Telecommunications Union, 2020, https://www.itu.int/en/ITU-D/Statistics/Pages/stat/default.aspx.

34. Simon Kemp, "Digital 2020: Ethiopia," *DataReportal*, February 17, 2020, https://datareportal.com/reports/digital-2020-ethiopia.

35. The 2019 digital repression measurements incorporate social media penetration interactions per the model described in Chapter 3. Digital repression time series calculations (2010–19) do not incorporate this interaction due to data limitations.

36. See Mechkova et al., *Digital Society Project Dataset v2*, 2020.

37. Mechkova et al., *Digital Society Project Dataset v2*.

38. Tekleberhan, interview with the author.

39. Author interview with an expert from the government's advisory unit, February 17, 2020.

40. Taye, "Targeted, Cut Off."

41. "Back in the Dark: Ethiopia Shuts Down Internet Once Again," Access Now, July 16, 2020, https://www.accessnow.org/back-in-the-dark-ethiopia-shuts-down-internet-once-again/#:~:text=UPDATE%3A%20July%2016%2C%202020%2C,of%20Oromo%20musician%2C%20Haacaaluu%20Hundeessaa; Michael Oduor, "Ethio Telecom restores services to parts of Tigray—official," *Africanews*, December 2, 2020, https://www.africanews.com/2020/12/02/ethio-telecom-restores-services-to-parts-of-tigray-official//.

42. Addis Alemayehou (CEO, 251 Communications), interview with the author, February 18, 12020.

43. Woodhams and Migliano, "Global Cost of Internet Shutdowns."

44. Endalkachew Chala (professor, Hamline University), interview with the author, January 15, 2020.

45. Author interview with a senior intelligence official.

46. Davison, interview with the author.

47. Yoseph Badwaza, email message to author, April 20, 2020.

48. Ahmed Mohammed (senior governance advisor, DFID Ethiopia), interview with the author, February 17, 2020.

49. Jawar, interview with the author.

50. Getachew, interview with the author.

51. Mechkova et al., *Digital Society Project Dataset v2*.

52. "Ethiopia: Youth Gather at Jawar Mohammed's House to Show Support," *Al Jazeera*, October 24, 2019, https://www.aljazeera.com/news/2019/10/ethiopia-youth-gather-jawar-mohammed-house-show-support-191023135139619.html.

53. Simon Marks, "After a Massacre, Ethiopia's Leader Faces Anger, and a Challenger," *New York Times*, November 18, 2019, https://www.nytimes.com/2019/11/18/world/africa/ethiopia-jawar-mohammed-abiy-ahmed.html.

54. Jawar, interview with the author.

55. Daniel Bekele, interview with the author.

56. Endalkachew, "How Ethiopia's Ruling Coalition Created a Playbook for Disinformation," Global Voices, October 18, 2019, https://globalvoices.org/2019/10/18/how-ethiopias-ruling-coalition-created-a-playbook-for-disinformation/.

57. Endalkachew, "Ethiopia's Ruling Coalition."

58. Ahmed, interview with the author.

59. Berhanu, interview with the author.

60. Daniel Bekele, interview with the author.

61. "Ethiopia Passes Controversial Law Curbing 'Hate Speech,'" AlJazeera, February 13, 2020, https://www.aljazeera.com/news/2020/02/ethiopia-passes-controversial-law-curbing-hate-speech-200213132808083.html.

62. Girmachew Alemu, "Narrow Hate Speech Law Will Not Broaden Minds," *Ethiopia Insight*, January 24, 2020, https://www.ethiopia-insight.com/2020/01/24/narrow-hate-speech-law-will-not-broaden-minds/.

63. Daniel Bekele, interview with the author.

64. Yohannes Eneyew Ayalew, "Is Ethiopia's First Fake News Case in Line with Human Rights Norms?," *Ethiopia Insight*, May 1, 2020, https://www.ethiopia-insight.com/2020/05/01/is-ethiopias-first-fake-news-case-in-line-with-human-rights-norms/.

65. "Ethiopian Journalist Yayesew Shimelis Detained Following COVID-19 Report," Committee to Project Journalists, April 1, 2020, https://cpj.org/2020/04/ethiopian-journalist-yayesew-shimelis-detained-fol.php.

66. See Bill Marczak et al., "Champing at the Cyberbit: Ethiopian Dissidents Targeted with New Commercial Spyware," Citizen Lab, December 6, 2017, https://citizenlab.ca/2017/12/champing-cyberbit-ethiopian-dissidents-targeted-commercial-spyware/; Bill Marczak, John Scott-Railton, and Sarah McKune, "Hacking Team Reloaded? US-Based Ethiopian Journalists Again Targeted with Spyware," Citizen Lab, March 9, 2015, https://citizenlab.ca/2015/03/hacking-team-reloaded-us-based-ethiopian-journalists-targeted-spyware/; Bill Marczak et al., "Hacking Team and the Targeting of Ethiopian Journalists," Citizen Lab, February 12, 2014, https://citizenlab.ca/2014/02/hacking-team-targeting-ethiopian-journalists/; and Morgan Marquis-Boire et al., "You Only Click Twice: FinFisher's Global Proliferation," Citizen Lab, March 13, 2013, https://citizenlab.ca/2013/03/you-only-click-twice-finfishers-global-proliferation-2/.

67. Marczak et al., "Hacking Team and the Targeting."

68. Befeqadu, interview with the author.

69. Felix Horne (former Ethiopia lead researcher, Human Rights Watch), interview with the author, March 18, 2020.

70. Horne, interview with the author.

71. Endalkachew, interview with the author.

72. Endalkachew, interview with the author.

73. Author interview with an expert from the government's advisory unit.

74. "Ethiopia to Establish AI Research Center," *Xinhua*, January 25, 2020, http://www.xinhuanet.com/english/2020-01/25/c_138733639.htm.

75. Maria Xynou, Moses Karanja, Berhan Taye, and Arturo Filastò, "Resurgence of Internet Censorship in Ethiopia: Blocking of WhatsApp, Facebook, and African Arguments," OONI, August 14, 2019, https://ooni.org/post/resurgence-Internet-censorship-ethiopia-2019/.

76. See OONI Explorer, https://explorer.ooni.org.

77. I carried out a thorough search for references to Ethiopia in Facebook's transparency website (https://transparency.facebook.com/content-restrictions/country/ET/jan-jun-2019), Google's transparency website (https://transparencyreport.google.com/government-removals/overview?hl=en&authority_search=country:ethiopia&lu=authority_search), and Twitter's transparency website (https://transparency.twitter.com/en/removal-requests.html#removal-requests-jan-jun-2019) without generating any hits.

78. Befeqadu, interview with the author.

79. Jawar, interview with the author.

80. Author interview with a think-tank analyst.

81. Gérard Prunier, "The Meles Zenawi Era," in Gérard Prunier and Éloi Facquet, eds., *Understanding Contemporary Ethiopia* (London: Hurst, 2015), 428.

82. Simegnish Yekoye Mengesha, "Ethiopia: Silencing Dissent," *Journal of Democracy* 27, no. 1 (2016): 90.

83. Lammi Begna (spokesperson for the OLF), interview with the author, February 20, 2020.

84. Lammi Begna, interview with the author.

85. Author interview with a think-tank analyst.

86. Xan Rice, "Unease over Extent of Ruling Party's Landslide in Ethiopia," *The Guardian*, May 26, 2010, https://www.theguardian.com/world/2010/may/26/ethiopia-election-result-meles-zenawi.

87. Author interview with a think-tank analyst.

88. Lammi, interview with the author.

89. Jawar, interview with the author.

90. Jawar, interview with the author.

91. Jawar, interview with the author.

92. It is important to note that social media-fueled protests weren't the sole instigators of change in Ethiopia. My think-tank contact observed: "Most people miss the fact the protests started with the Muslim community. And technology wasn't the biggest factor with the Muslims. Protests were very peaceful. It was very persistent. It was very articulate. And they used the mosques as the infrastructure, you know, the Friday prayers, the Jummah prayers as an infrastructure to express dissent and protest. So that the Oromo protests, Amhara protest, that came afterwards, they used the same methodology." Author interview with a think-tank analyst.

93. Jawar, interview with the author.

94. Ionut C. Popescu, "Grand Strategy vs. Emergent Strategy in the Conduct of Foreign Policy," *Journal of Strategic Studies* 41, no. 3 (2018): 446.

95. Aliaksandr Herasimenka, Tetyana Lokot, Olga Onuch, and Mariëlle Wijermars, "There's More to Belarus's 'Telegram Revolution' Than a Cellphone App," *Washington Post—Monkey Cage* (blog), September 11, 2020, https://www.washingtonpost.com/politics/2020/09/11/theres-more-belaruss-telegram-revolution-than-cellphone-app/.

96. Jawar, interview with the author.

97. Parts of this section are taken from previously published material by the author, including Steven Feldstein, "Testimony—Hearing on China's Strategic Aims in Africa," US-China Economic and Security Review Commission, May 8, 2020, https://www.uscc.gov/sites/default/files/Feldstein_Testimony.pdf.

98. "Loan Database," China Africa Research Initiative—School of Advanced International Studies, 2020, http://www.sais-cari.org/data.

99. Addis, interview with the author.

100. Hailemelekot Asfaw (Ethiopian representative, Center for International Private Enterprise), interview with the author, February 17, 2020.

101. Tekleberhan, interview with the author. Tekleberhan's reference to the purchase of Germany, Italian, and Israeli surveillance technology aligns with independent reporting from the Citizen Lab documenting extensive spyware contracts between Ethiopian intelligence and those same firms. See Marczak et al., "Champing at the Cyberbit"; Marczak, Scott-Railton, and McKune, "Hacking Team Reloaded"; Marczak et al., "Hacking Team and the Targeting"; and Marquis-Boire et al., "You Only Click Twice."

102. Tekleberhan, interview with the author.

103. Author interview with a senior intelligence official.

104. Horne, interview with the author.

105. Iginio Gagliardone, *China, Africa, and the Future of the Internet* (London: Zed Books, 2019), 10.

106. Gagliardone, *China, Africa*, 10.

107. Emeka Umejei, "The Imitation Game: Will China's Investments Reshape Africa's Internet?," National Endowment for Democracy Power 3.0 (blog), December 6, 2018, https://www.power3point0.org/2018/12/06/the-imitation-game-will-chinas-investments-reshape-africas-Internet/.

108. Christopher Walker, Shanthi Kalathil, and Jessica Ludwig, "The Cutting Edge of Sharp Power." *Journal of Democracy* 31, no. 1 (2020): 131.

109. Simon Marks, "How an African State Learned to Play the West Off China for Billions," *Politico*, February 7, 2020, https://www.politico.com/news/2020/02/07/ethiopia-china-west-power-competition-110766.
110. Author interview with an expert from the government's advisory unit.
111. Gagliardone, *China, Africa*, 7.
112. Befeqadu, interview with the author.

7

How Artificial Intelligence and Big Data Are Transforming Repression

Back in 2005, the Chinese government launched the "Skynet" national security network. Skynet was intended to provide continuous public surveillance of roads, districts, schools, universities, and commercial establishments across the country. By 2017, this network had grown to include 170 million cameras, with another 400 million devices planned by 2020.[1] The system incorporates advanced capabilities, including, as Berkeley scholar Xiao Qiang writes in a 2019 article in the *Journal of Democracy*, AI technology that allows authorities to "monitor the gender, clothing, and height of passers-by, transforming the information captured on screen into data."[2]

But Skynet only represents the tip of the iceberg for China's surveillance aspirations. The Chinese Communist Party (CCP) also established a safe cities program, funded with over RMB 1 trillion ($139.9 billion) in government investment.[3] The program's goal is to collect new forms of citizen data through cutting-edge information technologies—Internet of Things (IoT) devices, cloud computing, high-speed mobile networks, big-data systems—thereby enhancing social control. The initiative began in 2003—Beijing, Suzhou, Hangzhou, and Jinan served as its initial pilots. By 2005, the program had expanded to include twenty-two provinces; it now incorporates most urban centers in the country.[4]

In 2015, the CCP introduced its newest initiative, the Sharp Eyes program. Sharp Eyes builds upon Skynet and safe cities by combining existing public security video surveillance networks to private networks that guard homes, private businesses, and related structures. As the *Washington Post* has reported, the system "will use facial recognition and artificial intelligence to analyze and understand the mountain of incoming video evidence; to track suspects, spot suspicious behaviors and even predict crime; to coordinate the work of emergency services; and to monitor the comings and goings of the country's 1.4 billion people."[5] Moreover, this information will merge with a police cloud

The Rise of Digital Repression. Steven Feldstein, Oxford University Press (2021). © Oxford University Press.
DOI: 10.1093/oso/9780190057497.003.0007

database that will collect citizens' medical records, social media postings, travel reservations, criminal histories, online purchases, and possibly genomic information, and connect it to every citizen's identity card and face.

Like Skynet, the Sharp Eyes network incorporates advanced capabilities—high-definition cameras, vehicle and license plate recognition devices, and facial recognition technology. The scale of the system is enormous. In 2018 alone, the government funded 786 Sharp Eyes surveillance projects at a cost exceeding $5 billion.[6] To augment these efforts, the CCP is also deploying a genomic surveillance program, documented in extensive detail in a 2020 report from the Australian Strategic Policy Institute. The authors describe a mass DNA data collection initiative that "likely contains more than 100 million profiles and possibly as many as 140 million, making it the world's largest DNA database." Samples are drawn from minority communities as well as ordinary citizens without proper informed consent. Numerous biotechnology companies are assisting this effort, including US firms like Thermo Fisher Scientific.[7]

What does the rapid onset of public AI and big-data surveillance systems mean for China's people? This development is fundamentally transforming the population's expectations of privacy and altering the relationship between citizen and state.[8] In growing numbers of Chinese cities, individuals who commit minor infractions—such as jaywalking or failing to pay debts—may see their faces and ID numbers superimposed on huge, public digital billboards. Many train stations now deploy facial recognition cameras that actively scan incoming and outgoing passengers, matching them to most-wanted-criminal lists. As Qiang writes, after researchers "made a breakthrough in the deep-learning algorithm used for speech and image recognition" in 2010, authorities began employing facial recognition at scale, allowing them to "assess in real time the number and density of people in the frame, individuals' gender, and the characteristics of clothing and vehicles."[9] In Zhengzhou, police officers have used facial recognition glasses to identify a drug dealer at a train station. In Quingdao, AI-powered cameras helped officers nab multiple criminal suspects during an annual beer festival.[10] The onset of the coronavirus pandemic has precipitated the rollout of a mass QR code system that assigns citizens one of three colors based on infection risk. But as the *New York Times* reports, this public health data is also being shared with police forces, automatically providing an individual's location, city name, and identifying code number.[11]

Of course, these examples don't even include coercive actions undertaken by Chinese security services in regions like Xinjiang, which integrate cutting-edge AI and big-data surveillance technology with massive human policing, creating what researcher Adrian Zenz describes as a "frontline laboratory for surveillance" (which I will discuss later in this chapter).[12]

The deployment of AI and big-data surveillance in China demonstrates the dominant effect this technology can have in solidifying state control. Nonetheless, protestors in other contexts continue to find creative ways to push back against these advanced techniques—as the 2019 Hong Kong protests showed.

Demonstrators who thronged the streets of Hong Kong in 2019 faced an intimidating array of digital instruments. The Hong Kong police were rumored to be in possession of facial recognition body cameras supplied by the Australian firm iOmniscient. Such technology relies on high-definition cameras to live-scan crowds so police can pick out suspects and haul them into custody.[13] Many public areas where protestors congregated were ringed by "smart lampposts" that further augmented the city's surveillance net. But the authorities' digital tools were not limited to cameras embedded in the city's brick-and-mortar infrastructure.[14] The police used malware and phishing techniques to flush out anonymous activists and deployed advanced social medial surveillance tools to intercept private communications.[15] In many instances, the police would grab protestors off the street and shove their heads in front of their phones in order to use facial recognition ID to gain access to their devices. Sometimes police found a trove of personal information and incriminating messages. Other times, protestors were prepared for such confrontations, disabling their phones' facial recognition in advance.[16]

Hong Kong protestors fought back in creative ways and regularly neutralized the state's technological superiority. Activists consciously strove to minimize their digital footprint. Many relied on encrypted messaging applications like Telegram to communicate with fellow protestors. Another favored tactic was to use high-powered lasers to offset facial recognition cameras. If this failed, protestors would resort to more rudimentary methods—spray painting or smashing video cameras, or physically pulling down smart lampposts armed with advanced surveillance software. Protestors also began wearing ubiquitous black masks and brandishing large umbrellas to obscure their identities, making it difficult for facial recognition algorithms to function (as seen in Figure 7.1).

Protestors in Honk Kong also watched the watchers.[17] As more and more police started wearing unbadged uniforms, citizens began snapping pictures of officers and posting their images online. They would then match images to names and post detailed personal information about the officers and their friends and family—an act known as "doxxing." Protestors formed online groups, such as "Dadfindboy" (fifty thousand followers), that served as police doxxing forums, where they would include the home addresses and intimate social media photos of individual law enforcement officers. In one notorious incident, doxxers posted the details of a police officer's upcoming wedding, resulting in service disruptions and mass guest cancellations.[18]

Figure 7.1 Protestors in Hong Kong Brandishing Ubiquitous Umbrellas to Counteract State Surveillance

Finally, in mid-2020, the authorities deployed a new tactic taken from the traditional repression playbook—passing a national security law that criminalized dissent. The law, which came into effect on June 30, 2020, prohibits "secessionist, subversive and terrorist activities" in Hong Kong, including inciting hatred against the local government.[19] It also authorizes sweeping surveillance and censorship measures and essentially puts an end to the one-country, two-systems governing arrangement that had guaranteed Hong Kongers expanded rights of free expression beyond those held by citizens of mainland China.[20]

Authorities have moved swiftly to implement the law's provisions. Among the first casualties was Hong Kong media tycoon Jimmy Lai, owner of the pro-democracy newspaper *Apple Daily*. The police charged him with collusion and inciting secession (in response, Lai deemed his arrest a "symbolic exercise" by Chinese authorities meant to demonstrate that the new law has "teeth").[21] Subsequently, the courts sentenced pro-democracy activists Joshua Wong, Agnes Chow, and Ivan Lam to lengthy imprisonments for their roles in the 2019 protests.[22]

The law has also bolstered harsher tactics for Hong Kong's security forces. As Paul Mozur from the *New York Times* describes, authorities are closing a "digital dragnet" on pro-democracy activists and politicians, including "installing a camera outside the home of a prominent politician and breaking into the Facebook account of another."[23] Thus, where advanced technology failed to impede mass demonstrations, old-fashioned legal repression combined with hi-tech policing techniques has so far met with much greater success in Hong Kong.

Artificial intelligence technology is rapidly proliferating around the world.[24] Startling developments keep emerging, from the onset of deepfake videos that blur the line between truth and falsehood, to advanced algorithms that can defeat the best chess players in the world. Businesses harness AI and big-data capabilities to improve analytic processing; city officials tap the technology to monitor traffic congestion and oversee smart energy metering. In addition, a growing number of states are deploying advanced AI and big-data surveillance tools to monitor and track citizens to accomplish a range of policy objectives. Some of these actions may be legitimate; in other cases, these activities squarely align with repressive objectives.

To understand the political uses of this technology, it is important to assess what capabilities these tools provide, which states are deploying them, and how they are being used. This chapter proceeds as follows: I will provide a definitional understanding of AI and big-data technology, explaining why they are a boon for autocratic leaders. I explore two in-depth scenarios that describe how states may deploy AI and big-data techniques to accomplish repressive objectives. Next, I present a global index of AI and big-data surveillance that measures the deployment of these tools in 179 countries. I then present a detailed explanation for specific types of AI and big-data surveillance: safe cities, facial recognition systems, smart policing, and social media surveillance. Subsequently, I examine China's role in proliferating AI and big-data surveillance technology, and I review pressing questions for democracies regarding use these technologies.

This chapter offers several insights related to the global spread of AI and big-data surveillance.

First, this technology offers key advantages to autocratic leaders. It not allows regimes to automate many tracking and monitoring functions that were formerly delegated to human operators, but it permits authorities to discover new patterns and insights that were formerly not accessible. In comparison to human operatives with limited reserves of time and energy, these systems never tire or fatigue. Their omnipresence induces changes in behavior and creates a considerable chilling effect.

Second, global adoption of AI and big-data surveillance is rapidly increasing. However, countries are only beginning to dabble with possible use of these techniques; for many states, this technology is still more aspirational than practical. But as capacity grows and costs decrease, more and more countries will adopt these techniques.

Third, China has emerged as a major player in this space. China is heavily invested in the development of domestic "AI champion" companies, with firms that are proliferating the spread of safe cities, public facial recognition systems, and advanced tools for law enforcement worldwide. Domestically, China is showcasing a new model of total surveillance that no other government has replicated.

Fourth, democracies are active adopters of AI and big-data surveillance technology. As my index shows, unlike other digital tools, this technology does not conform to regime type. A better predictor for whether a government will procure this technology is the size of a country's military expenditures: forty of the fifty highest-spending militaries are located in countries that also possess AI and big-data surveillance capabilities.

Finally, the regulatory framework guiding the responsible use of AI remains nascent. There is a large gap (and a concurrent opportunity) in this area to shape norms of responsible use and incorporate essential protections. The downside risk is that repressive states will further exploit AI and big-data technology for political gain.

What Is AI?

While the concept of AI has proven resistant to exact definition, according to computer scientist Nils Nilsson, its general goal is to "make machines intelligent" by automating or replicating behavior that "enables an entity to function appropriately and with foresight in its environment."[25] Some experts question the usefulness of such analogies. Jerry Kaplan argues that while a formal definition may be elusive, "the essence of AI—indeed, the essence of intelligence—is the ability to make appropriate generalizations in a timely fashion based on limited data."[26]

The current momentum behind AI stems from three major innovations: the increased availability of big data from public and private sources, enhanced machine learning and algorithmic approaches, and correspondingly advanced (and much cheaper) computer processing, especially related to cloud computing.

In particular, machine learning represents an important AI subfield that uses an iterative statistical process to analyze a large amount of information in order to discern patterns that explain current data and predict future uses.[27] Several breakthroughs have made new achievements in this field possible: the maturation of machine learning and the onset of deep learning and neural networks, cloud computing and online data gathering, a new generation of advanced microchips and computer hardware, the improved performance of complex algorithms, and market-driven incentives for new uses of AI technology.[28]

Unsurprisingly, AI's impact extends well beyond individual consumer choices. It can potentially transform basic governance patterns, not only by providing states with unprecedented capabilities to monitor their citizens and shape their choices, but also by giving governments new capacities to disrupt elections, elevate false information, and delegitimize democratic discourse across borders.

This chapter primarily examines government use of AI and big data for surveillance purposes. I focus specifically on surveillance functions (as opposed to other uses, such as disinformation or content manipulation) because surveillance represents a rapidly growing and visibly changing area of use.

Popular usage of the term "artificial intelligence" does not always equate to functional definitions used by technical experts. At the broadest level, people often describe artificial intelligence as comprising automated operations that were previously carried out by humans. One basic example relates to video surveillance: older technology required human operators to sift, frame by frame, through images in order to identify a particular individual who had been implicated in a crime. Automated technology can replace such laborious analysis with simple algorithms that can match images or search for specific incidents. While this change represents a technical advancement, most experts would not classify this technology as AI.

The next level of advancement would be to incorporate machine-learning techniques, such as deep learning, to autonomously classify information and predict resultant patterns. Rather than deploy an algorithm after the commission of a crime to search for culpable individuals ex post facto, a deep learning algorithm can monitor video footage in real time, alert human authorities when perceived anomalies occur, and improve the algorithm's learning while it operates. The longer it is deployed, the greater its ability to predict and recognize specific patterns of behavior—for example, whether a person entering a store wielding a suspicious object is likely to engage in violent activity.

A third distinction when assessing AI is the volume of data accessed. Deep learning algorithms that analyze data sets numbering in the millions rather than the thousands bring sharper insights based on the increased volume of information. This large-scale analysis requires substantially higher computing power and is not replicable by human analysis.

There is considerable empirical inconsistency when it comes to descriptions of AI surveillance technology, with articles and reports routinely conflating basic algorithms (automation) with more sophisticated methods (deep learning). For that reason, throughout this book, I refer to "AI and big data" surveillance rather than "AI" surveillance. In the book *Big Data: A Revolution That Will Transform How We Live, Work, and Think*, authors Viktor Mayer-Schönberger and Kenneth Cukier define big data as "things one can do at a large scale that cannot be done at a smaller one, to extract new insights or create new forms of value, in ways that change markets, organizations, the relationship between citizens and governments, and more."[29] Because AI-enabled surveillance deployed by governments blurs the line between strictly incorporating artificial intelligence and integrating related technologies, I use both terms to describe these methods.

Why AI and Big-Data Repression Are a Boon to Autocrats

AI offers significant benefits as a tool for governments everywhere. It can improve municipal service delivery, enable meaningful cost-efficiencies, and provide an additional check to offset human error. But these same qualities also yield specific benefits to authoritarian and illiberal regimes that rely on repression to sustain their rule.

A leader who opts to repress must rely on state security forces to apply necessary coercive measures. This situation brings two attendant problems. First, such repression is labor intensive and expensive; over time, it requires increasing resources to sustain. Second, it creates a principal-agent problem: "The very resources that enable the regime's repressive agents to suppress its opposition also empower them to act against the regime itself."[30] In other words, as a regime increasingly relies on police or soldiers to do its dirty work, it also grows more vulnerable to pressure or even insurrection from those same quarters. Leaders face a fraught decision as to whether the benefits of deploying security forces to crush challenges from without outweigh the potential threat that these forces themselves pose from within.

In such situations, the advantages of AI and big-data technology become apparent. First, such surveillance allows regimes to automate many tracking and monitoring functions that were formerly delegated to human operators. This change brings cost efficiencies, decreases reliance on security forces, and addresses principal-agent problems. A good point of comparison is the network of surveillance established in East Germany under the Stasi. In 1989, right before the fall of the Berlin Wall, the Stasi had 90,257 regular employees on its rolls, as well as 173,081 informants—comprising 1.57 percent of East Germany's population.[31] Not only did this network represent a stunning investment in human capital, but, as researchers Andreas Lichter, Max Löffler, and Sebastian Siegloch have documented, it had profound economic effects: "Our estimates imply that abolishing state surveillance would, on average, have reduced the long-term unemployment rate by 1.8 percentage points, which is equivalent to a ten percent drop given the average unemployment level in East Germany."[32] Thirty years later, countries can use AI and big-data technology to accomplish similar surveillance objectives at a fraction of the human investment or economic cost.

Second, in contrast to human operatives with limited reserves of time and attention, AI and big-data systems never tire or fatigue. Because of their omnipresence, AI and big-data systems can induce changes in behavior and create a significant "chilling effect" even in the absence of sustained physical violence. If citizens know that AI bots are monitoring their text messages, reading their social media posts, or geo-tracking their movements around town, the public has a powerful motivation to conform.[33] Such is the elegant simplicity of AI and bigdata repression: it requires considerably fewer human actors than conventional repression, entails less violence, and comes at a lower cost. Yet it may well have more wide-ranging and systematic impact.

As discussed in Chapter 1, the gravest threats to authoritarian survival today may be coming not from insider-led rebellions, but from discontented publics on the streets or at the ballot box. To that end, AI and big-data technology provide crucial advantages for incumbent leaders. Rather than rely on security forces to repress their citizenry—with all the resource costs and political risks that this method entails—autocratic leaders are increasingly resorting to this technology to monitor, surveil, and harass civil society movements and distort elections. A look at two scenarios helps to clarify this technology's relevance to some of the most pressing challenges facing contemporary authoritarian leaders.

Scenario 1: Keep Tabs on Popular Discontent and Control Mass Protest

In the first scenario, a government faces rising discontent over economic stagnation and political suppression. Intermittently throughout the past year, spontaneous protests have taken place, worrying the political leadership. The regime wants to take assertive steps to forestall mass political mobilization, but with limited resources, it cannot afford to rely on mass arrests and imprisonment. It also fears that such overt repression could trigger a popular backlash. Therefore, it has settled on a two-part strategy: (1) identify, monitor, and selectively detain opposition leaders and potential key followers, and (2) closely monitor crowd formations that could turn into mass rallies, keeping security forces on standby to break up protests before they reach scale.

To carry out this strategy, the regime must first identify dissident leaders and key followers who are most likely to mobilize. It begins reaching out to firms that provide social media surveillance capabilities. Companies such as Sandvine (Canada), Palantir (United States), Thales (France), Webintpro and Verint

(Israel), and Knowlesys and Semptian (China) offer information extraction services that enable mass monitoring of citizens' online behavior.[34] Kazakhstan, for example, has acquired an automated monitoring tool, supplied by a firm linked to Russia's Federal Security Service, that relies on deep learning to detect communications that disparage the state.[35] Similarly, Pakistan has contracted with Sandvine to install an $18.5 million "web monitoring system" that gives authorities the ability to maintain constant surveillance of citizens' digital communications.[36]

Because certain platforms rely on privacy settings or encryption to prevent government snooping, authorities may reach out to international malware firms, such as FinFisher or NSO Group, that peddle active surveillance software designed to penetrate closed groups. Alternatively, the regime may choose a cheaper option and procure the services of an international "hacker for hire" or a second-string malware vendor to undertake this task.[37] These tactics can help the regime discern threatening patterns, identify individuals of interest, and target relevant conversations. Countries such as Saudi Arabia and the UAE have purchased advanced intrusion software, enabling their intelligence services to hack into encrypted devices and spy on opposition leaders, human rights activists, and journalists.[38]

As the surveillance operation builds profiles of political activists and maps civic and opposition networks, it feeds this information into an AI algorithm; sifting through multiple data sets, this algorithm then uses pattern-recognition software to identify individuals with tendencies toward political dissent. The algorithm also helps the regime monitor issues that are provoking popular dissatisfaction, and scans for communications indicating imminent protest. Armed with this information, the regime carries out targeted detentions and makes preventive arrests in order to forestall mass disruptions.

If protests start despite these efforts, AI and big-data technology can help the regime contain them. One technique already made available by Chinese communications platform WeChat produces "heat maps" that show crowd density and measure foot traffic in specific locations.[39] The regime could embed tracking technology in similar chat platforms, enabling it to know instantly when crowds begin to form. Alternatively, the regime could install facial recognition systems in urban public spaces (akin to "smart" lampposts found in Singapore and Hong Kong). Intelligence operations centers manned by security personnel can use such cameras to monitor crowd density, search for individuals carrying political signage, and keep tabs on the whereabouts of persons of interest. When needed, they can rapidly deploy to hot spots and make immediate arrests, preempting further unrest.

Scenario 2: Keep a Restive Province in Check

In this example, an authoritarian regime grapples with potential instability in an outlying province where an ethnic minority makes up the bulk of the population. The regime's legitimacy in this province is historically tenuous, and the region periodically experiences bouts of unrest. Recently, the central government has decided to curb political turbulence through heavy-handed repression that combines traditional tactics with new technology.

This scenario closely hews to the current state of affairs in Xinjiang Province. The PRC's ongoing efforts to quell dissent in the region vividly illuminate the vast repressive potential of AI and big data when used in conjunction with older coercive tactics.

In 2016, reports began trickling out about Chinese authorities deploying ominous new techniques in the far-off province of Xinjiang. Historically, the region's 10 million Muslim Uighurs have had a fraught relationship with the Chinese central government. Tensions have periodically erupted in bouts of violence, including knife attacks, bombings, and plane hijackings.[40] Recently leaked documents indicate that after a particularly bad spate of incidents in 2014 (including a mass stabbing by Uighur militants that killed thirty-one persons at the Kunming train station), President Xi Jinping called for using the "organs of dictatorship" to take "decisive measures" against terrorism.[41] By 2016, Beijing had installed Chen Quanguo, a security-minded governor who would accelerate its crackdown in Xinjiang. Quanguo had previously served in Tibet, where he gained a reputation for applying novel repressive measures—such as blanketing the province with small-sized "convenience police stations"—as a means to control dissent.[42]

In Xinjiang, Quanguo quickly went to work. He initiated "Physicals For All," a program that collected mandatory DNA samples—along with fingerprints, blood types, and iris scans—from all residents between the ages of twelve and sixty-five.[43] (Sophie Richardson, Human Rights Watch's China researcher, has warned that the government was "moving its Orwellian system to the genetic level.")[44] Quanguo also established a grid policing system, which divided communities into "geometric zones so that security staff can systematically observe all activities with the aid of new technologies."[45] In targeted districts, the state established police stations every few hundred feet staffed by tens of thousands of security agents. Each station was equipped with advanced surveillance capabilities, including facial recognition cameras, Wi-Fi sniffers (to collect identifying information from laptops and smartphones), license plate spotters, and Internet infiltration technology. The stations were connected to a central policing platform, known as the Integrated Joint Operations Platform (IJOP), that collects mass quantities of personal data to identify potential detainees and provide predictive-policing capabilities.[46]

While the degree of integration between IJOP and other PRC data-collection efforts is unknown, it is noteworthy that Chinese authorities are increasingly deploying handheld scanning devices to break into smartphones and extract contacts, social media communications, emails, photos, and videos.[47] Once the relevant information is fed into IJOP computers, algorithms sift through reams of data looking for patterns that could signify threatening behavior. As Human Rights Watch reports, authorities "have enlisted artificial intelligence technologies, provided by private companies ... to help them automatically identify people from public surveillance footage streams and telephone calls; they are also using big data systems to identify individuals posing political threats."[48] What confidence thresholds Chinese authorities are using to run these tests remains unclear, but the algorithms are likely generating significant numbers of false matches due to system errors. Once the machine flags an individual, security forces pick up that person and detains them for an indefinite period.

Chinese authorities have supplemented Xinjiang's technological dystopia with mass arrests and imprisonment. The US State Department estimates that "possibly more than two million Uighurs, ethnic Kazakhs, and other Muslims" are being held in internment camps for indefinite periods of time.[49] This number represents a sizable portion of Xinjiang's roughly twenty-one million people. Detainees are reportedly subjected to torture and beatings, or even killed. This situation represents the most extensive mass imprisonment of an ethnic-religious minority since World War II.[50] During June 2017, in one seven-day period alone, security officials apprehended 15,683 residents who had been flagged by IJOP and were subsequently placed in internment camps.[51]

Developing this system has not been cheap. Xinjiang's public security budget almost doubled from 2016 to 2017, increasing to $9.16 billion, according to local government data obtained by the *Financial Times*. This growth rate is eight times higher than increases allocated for China's total public security budget.[52] Yet this is not an exorbitant figure relative to the amount the state would have to spend to build a comparable system of surveillance and repression without using AI technology.

Democracies Also Rely on AI and Big-Data Surveillance

Of course, reliance on AI and big-data technology for law enforcement and surveillance purposes is not limited to authoritarian states. Democratic governments are actively using these tools to police borders, apprehend potential criminals, monitor citizens for bad behavior, and extract suspected terrorists from crowds. This doesn't mean that democracies are using this technology illegitimately. A critical factor determining whether governments will exploit this technology for repressive purposes is the quality of their governance: Is there an existing pattern of human rights violations? Are there strong rule-of-law traditions and independent institutions of accountability? This correlation should provide a measure of reassurance for citizens residing in liberal democratic states where there is a presumption that governments largely reject systems designed to infringe upon political freedoms and civil liberties.

Nonetheless, democracies have long wrestled with balancing security concerns with civil liberties protections. AI surveillance technology adds a new dimension to this struggle. In some instances, it may tip the scales in favor of expanded intrusion over privacy considerations.

In the United States (as described in Chapter 3), increasing numbers of cities have adopted advanced surveillance approaches.[53] A 2016 investigation by Axios's Kim Hart revealed, for example, that the Baltimore police had secretly deployed aerial drones to carry out daily surveillance over the city's residents: "From a plane flying overhead, powerful cameras capture aerial images of the entire city. Photos are snapped every second, and the plane can be circling the city for up to 10 hours a day."[54] The information is then uploaded to servers where "efforts are under way" to use machine learning to analyze the data.[55] Baltimore's police also deployed facial recognition cameras to monitor and arrest protesters, particularly during the 2018 riots that occurred in the city.[56] The ACLU condemned these techniques as the "technological equivalent of putting an ankle GPS [Global Positioning System] monitor on every person in Baltimore."[57]

On the US-Mexico border, an array of hi-tech companies also operate advanced surveillance equipment. Israeli defense contractor Elbit Systems has built "dozens of towers in Arizona to spot people as far as 7.5 miles away," writes the *Guardian*'s Olivia Solon.[58] Its technology was first perfected in Israel from a contract to build a "smart fence" to separate Jerusalem from the West Bank. Another company, Anduril Industries, has created guard towers that incorporate laser-enhanced cameras and radar communications to scan a two-mile radius to detect motion. Captured images "are analysed using artificial intelligence to pick out humans from wildlife and other moving objects."[59] The extent to which these surveillance deployments are permissible under US law is unclear, as is the question of whether these actions meet the necessity and proportionality standard.

The United States is not the only democracy embracing AI and big-data surveillance. In France, the port city of Marseille initiated a partnership with ZTE in 2016 to establish the "Big Data of Public Tranquility" project.[60] The program's goal is to reduce crime by establishing a vast public surveillance network featuring an intelligence operations center and nearly one thousand intelligent closed-circuit television (CCTV) cameras (the number will double by 2020). Marseilles's town hall confirmed to *Coda Story*, that it is "already using 'predictive policing' technology that allows authorities to use big data to 'anticipate' crimes likely to take place in the future."[61] In early 2020, the city went to court to defend its use of intelligent video surveillance that relies on AI to "search through surveillance footage, automatically spot crimes and alert police officers to suspicious behavior."[62] Similarly, in 2017, Huawei "gifted" a showcase surveillance system to the northern French town of Valenciennes to demonstrate its safe city model. The package included upgraded high-definition CCTV surveillance and an intelligent command center powered by algorithms to detect unusual movements and crowd formations.[63]

The fact that so many democracies—as well as autocracies—are adopting this technology means that regime type is a poor predictor for which countries will use these techniques.

A better predictor relates to military expenditures. A breakdown of military spending in 2018 shows that forty of the top fifty military-spending countries also have AI and big-data surveillance capabilities.[64] These countries range from full democracies to dictatorial regimes (and everything in between). They comprise leading economies like France, Germany, Japan, and South Korea and poorer states like Pakistan and Oman. This finding is not altogether unexpected; countries with substantial investments in their militaries tend to have higher economic and technological capacities as well as more specific security concerns. If a country takes its security seriously and is willing to invest considerable resources in maintaining robust military-security capabilities, then it should come as little surprise that it will also seek the latest AI tools. European democracies' motivations for deploying AI and big-data surveillance (migration control, tracking terrorist threats) may differ from Egypt's or Kazakhstan's interests (keep a lid on internal dissent, crack down on activist movements before they reach critical mass), but the instruments are remarkably similar.

AI and Big-Data Global Surveillance Index

As we have seen, governments of all types find AI surveillance technology useful. To obtain a more detailed worldwide understanding of which states are deploying these instruments and how they are being used, I developed an AI and big-data global surveillance index—representing one of the first research efforts of its kind. This index was originally published in a Carnegie Endowment working paper in 2019.[65] The version below builds on the original index, but includes several refinements, including a new index category: social media surveillance.

This index compiles empirical data on AI and big-data surveillance use for 179 countries around the world between 2012 and 2020—although the bulk of the sources stem from between 2017 and 2020. *The index does not distinguish between legitimate and illegitimate uses of AI and big-data surveillance. Rather, the purpose of the research is to show how new surveillance capabilities are transforming governments' ability to monitor and track individuals or groups.*

This index addresses three primary questions: Which countries have documented AI and big-data public surveillance capabilities? What types of AI and big-data public surveillance technologies are governments deploying? And which companies are involved in supplying this technology?

The index measures AI and big-data public surveillance systems deployed by state authorities, such as safe cities, social media monitoring, or facial recognition cameras. It does not assess the use of surveillance in private spaces (such as privately owned businesses in malls or hospitals), nor does it evaluate private uses of this technology (e.g., facial recognition integrated on personal devices). It also does not include AI and big-data surveillance used in automated border control (ABC) systems that are commonly found in airport entry and exit terminals. Finally, the index includes a list of frequently mentioned companies—by country—which source material indicates provide AI and big-data surveillance tools and services. Originally, this list was presented as a "key companies" category; here, this aspect has been modified. This index does not purport to list all key AI and big-data surveillance companies by country. Rather, it intends to provide an illustrative list of firms that frequently appear in source material.

A big challenge for gathering accurate data is that companies have incentives to both under-represent and over-represent their capabilities in this domain. Some companies purposely seek to maintain a low profile and downplay their integration of advanced AI and big-data techniques for surveillance. In many instances, this situation is applicable to firms based in liberal democracies that seek to avoid government scrutiny of their practices. Conversely, for companies based in authoritarian countries like China and Russia, which are establishing themselves as cost-effective alternatives to Western suppliers, they have a strong incentive to trumpet their products' AI surveillance capabilities (whether true or not).

This index is presented in full in Appendix 4. It can also be accessed online at http://dx.doi.org/10.17632/gjhf5y4xjp.1.[66]

All reference source material used to build the index has been compiled into an open Zotero library, available at https://www.zotero.org/groups/2347403/global_ai_surveillance/items. The index includes detailed information for seventy-seven countries where open-source analysis indicates that governments have acquired AI and big-data public surveillance capabilities.[67] The index breaks down AI and big-data public surveillance tools into the following categories: smart city / safe city, public facial recognition systems, smart policing, and social media surveillance.[68]

The findings indicate that at least 77 out of 179 countries are actively using AI and big-data technology for public surveillance purposes:

- Smart city / safe city platforms: 55 countries
- Public facial recognition systems: 68 countries
- Smart policing: 61 countries
- Social media surveillance: 36 countries

Three key insights emerge from this index's findings.

First, global adoption of AI and big-data public surveillance is increasing at a fast pace around the world. Seventy-seven countries, representing 44 percent of total countries assessed, employ AI-powered public surveillance for both legitimate and illegitimate purposes. The pool of countries is heterogeneous—they come from all regions, and their political systems range from closed autocracies to advanced democracies. The 2018 Freedom on the Net report raised eyebrows when it noted that eighteen out of sixty-five assessed countries were using AI and big-data surveillance technology procured from Chinese companies.[69] That report's assessment period ran from June 1, 2017, to May 31, 2018. By early 2020, the index shows that figure had increased to at least thirty-six countries out of the same group.

Unsurprisingly, countries with authoritarian systems and few political rights are investing heavily in AI and big-data public surveillance techniques. China's use of this technology remains cutting-edge. No other government—autocratic or democratic—comes close to matching the scale, investment, or sophistication of China's rapidly expanding surveillance system. Many governments in the Gulf, East Asia, and South and Central Asia are procuring advanced analytic systems, facial recognition cameras, and sophisticated monitoring capabilities. But liberal democracies are also racing ahead to install predictive policing, safe cities, facial recognition systems, social media surveillance, and automated border controls.

Regionally, there are clear disparities. The East Asia and Pacific and the Middle East and North Africa regions are robust adopters of these tools. South and Central Asia and the Western Hemisphere also demonstrate sizable adoption of AI and big-data surveillance instruments. Sub-Saharan Africa is a laggard—less than one-quarter of its countries are invested in this technology. Most likely this is due to technological underdevelopment (African countries are struggling to extend broadband access to their populations; the region contains eighteen of twenty countries with the lowest levels of Internet penetration).[70] However,

Chinese firms are aggressively moving into African markets, meaning that this situation will likely shift.[71]

Second, China is a major supplier of AI and big-data surveillance. Public surveillance technology linked to Chinese companies—such as Huawei, ZTE, Hikvision, Dahua, SenseTime, Megvii, Face++, iFlytek, Meiya Pico, Yitu, CEIEC, and Yixin—is found in at least fifty-seven countries worldwide, thirty-three of which are members of China's Belt and Road Initiative (BRI). The true number is likely higher, as public documentation of Chinese exports is limited. My research also indicates that in at least twenty-four countries, Chinese firms appear to be the primary suppliers of AI and big-data surveillance technology to those respective governments.[72]

However, Chinese companies are far from the only suppliers of advanced surveillance technology. US companies—such as Palantir, Anduril, Avigilon, PredPol, Qognify, Genetec, Honeywell, Amazon, and others—are relevant players. Israeli companies are also well positioned in the market (AnyVision, BriefCam, Elbit Systems, Verint). Major suppliers are headquartered in Japan, Australia, South Korea, and Western Europe (NEC, Panasonic, Hanwha Techwin, BAE, Herta, Idemia, Cognitec, Secunet, iOmniscient). Finally, Russian firms cannot be overlooked (AxxonSoft, Analytical Business Solutions, Speech Technology Center, NTechLab, Ladakom-Service).

Third, liberal democracies are major users of AI and big-data surveillance. Equivalent numbers of democracies and autocracies deploy this technology. The index shows that 44 percent of democracies use AI and big-data public surveillance systems, while 41 percent of autocracies rely upon these capabilities (see Figure 7.2). Again, it is important to underscore that the presence of this technology does not imply that a government is using AI and big-data techniques in a repressive manner.

The next sections provide more specific detail about different types of AI and big-data surveillance technology.

Types of AI and Big-Data Surveillance

Governments use AI and big-data technology to accomplish a broad range of surveillance goals. This section details four primary public surveillance tools evaluated in the index: smart city / safe city platforms, public facial recognition systems, smart policing, and social media surveillance. Table 7.1 summarizes each technique.

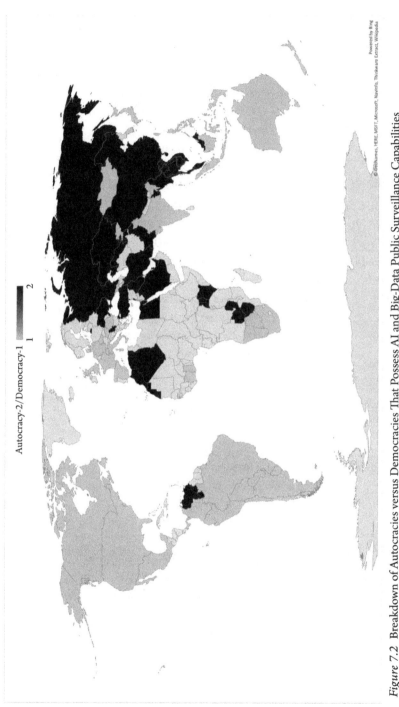

Figure 7.2 Breakdown of Autocracies versus Democracies That Possess AI and Big-Data Public Surveillance Capabilities

Table 7.1 **Summary of AI and Big-Data Surveillance Techniques**

Technique	Description	Estimated global proliferation
Smart cities / safe cities	Cities with sensors that transmit real-time data to facilitate service delivery, city management, and public safety. Often referred to as "safe cities," they incorporate sensors, facial recognition cameras, and police body cameras connected to intelligent command centers to prevent crime, ensure public safety, and respond to emergencies. Only platforms with a clear public safety focus are incorporated in the index. *Tagged as "safe city" in the Zotero library.*	55 countries
Public facial recognition systems	Biometric technology that uses cameras (still images or video) to match stored or live footage of individuals with images from databases. Not all systems focus on database matching; some systems assess aggregate demographic trends or conduct broader sentiment analysis via facial recognition crowd scanning. This category refers to public systems managed by national or subnational government entities for purposes of surveillance. *Tagged as "facial recognition" in the Zotero library.*	68 countries
Smart policing	Data-driven analytic technology used to facilitate investigations and police response; some systems incorporate algorithmic analysis to make predictions about future crimes. *Tagged as "smart policing" in the Zotero library.*	61 countries
Social media surveillance	Automated collection and processing of personal data obtained from digital communications platforms permitting real-time accumulation, aggregation, and analysis of bulk amounts of metadata and content. *Tagged as "SM Monitoring" in the Zotero library.*	36 countries

Smart Cities / Safe Cities

The World Bank describes smart cities as "technology-intensive" urban centers featuring an array of sensors that gather information in real time from "thousands of interconnected devices" in order to facilitate improved service delivery and city management.[73] Such technology helps municipal authorities manage traffic congestion, direct emergency vehicles to needed locations, foster sustainable energy use, and streamline administrative processes. But there is growing concern that smart cities are also enabling a dramatic increase in public surveillance and intrusive security capabilities. IBM, one of the original coiners of the term, designed a brain-like municipal model where information relevant to city operations could be centrally processed and analyzed.[74] A key component to the smart city model is public safety, which incorporates an array of sensors, tracking devices, and surveillance technology to increase police and security force capabilities.

Huawei has been up front about trumpeting public safety technologies for smart cities. The company popularized the term "safe cities" as a marketing tool for law enforcement communities that would help "predict, prevent, and reduce crime," as well as "address new and emerging threats."[75] In a 2016 white paper, Huawei describes a "suite of technology that includes video surveillance, emergent video communication, integrated incident command and control, big data, mobile, and secured public safety cloud" to support local law enforcement and policing as well as the justice and corrections system.[76] Huawei explicitly links its safe city technology to confronting regional security challenges, noting that in the Middle East, its platforms can prevent terrorism; in Latin America, safe cities enable governments to reduce crime; and in North America, its technology will help the United States advance "counterextremism" programs.[77]

How do these platforms work to advance surveillance goals in practice? The IT firm Gartner, which partners with Microsoft on smart cities, provides an example:

> Saudi Arabia's Makkah Region Development Authority (MRDA) created a crowd-control system to increase safety and security of Hajj pilgrims. Data is collected via a wristband embedding identity information, special healthcare requirements and a GPS. In addition, surveillance cameras are installed to collect and analyze real-time video along the Al Mashaaer Al Mugaddassah Metro Southern Line (MMMSL), as well as in the holy sites, such as Great Mosque of Mecca, Mount Arafat, Jamarat and Mina.[78]

Unsurprisingly, such systems lend themselves to improper use. In 2019, Huawei's safe city project in Serbia, which is installing one thousand high-definition cameras with facial recognition and license plate recognition capabilities in eight hundred locations across Belgrade, sparked national outrage.[79] Huawei posted a case study (since removed) about the benefits of safe cities, describing how similar surveillance technology had facilitated the apprehension of a Serbian hit-and-run perpetrator who had fled the country to a city in China: "Based on images provided by Serbian police, the . . . [Chinese] Public Security Bureau made an arrest within three days using new technologies."[80] Rather than applaud the efficiency of the system, Serbian commentators observed that in a country plagued by endemic corruption and encroaching authoritarianism, such technology offers a powerful tool for Serbian authorities to curb dissent and perpetrate abuses.

Public Facial Recognition Systems

Facial recognition is a biometric technology that uses cameras—both video or still images—to match stored or live footage of individuals with images from a database. Not all facial recognition systems focus on individual identification via database matching. Some systems are designed to assess aggregate demographic trends or to conduct broader sentiment analysis via facial recognition crowd scanning.

Facial recognition systems tend to fall into one of three categories: one to one, one to many, and many to many. *One-to-one* identification is a standard process used, for example, in ABC systems in international airports. A person's passport photo is compared to a facial image captured by a camera. If the computer establishes a sufficient match, then the person is allowed to proceed. *One-to-many* identification involves comparing a single person's photo to a database of images (for example, matching a specific individual against an image set of terrorist suspects). This technique may be used at checkpoints to determine whether a stopped person belongs to a prohibited group. *Many-to-many* facial recognition systems represent the most complex process. This method entails continuously scanning crowds, for example, to match individuals against an image watchlist of known security risks. Authorities might use this technique to surveil mass demonstrations for political organizers who those authorities intend to arrest. What makes many-to-many facial recognition challenging is that image quality is often poor and frequently comes from "low resolution images available from standard surveillance cameras," where individuals "may be presented at a variety of angles."[81]

Unlike ordinary CCTV, which has been a mainstay of police forces for twenty-five years, facial recognition cameras are much more intrusive. They can scan distinctive facial features in order to create detailed biometric maps of individuals without obtaining consent. Often, facial recognition surveillance cameras are both mobile and concealable. They are routinely linked to operations centers where increasingly automated processes continuously monitor public areas for specific individuals or mass actions of concern.

Facial recognition technology is becoming increasingly ubiquitous; most high-end smartphones incorporate this capability, meaning that the number of personal devices with facial recognition runs into the millions (and is growing exponentially). However, the index measures something different. This index specifically focuses on public surveillance systems, overseen by state authorities, which incorporate a surveillance purpose. Facial recognition body cameras worn by a municipality's police department and linked to a central analytic database would qualify (e.g., security personnel in Malaysia who are equipped with facial recognition body cameras provided by Yitu that allows officials to "rapidly compare images caught by live body cameras with images from a central database").[82]

Experts detail several concerns associated with facial recognition.

First, few rules govern the use of and access to image databases (repositories that store captured images from facial recognition cameras). How governments use this information, how long images are stored, and where authorities obtain such images in the first place are opaque and vary by jurisdiction. Recent disclosures that US law enforcement agencies (the Federal Bureau of Investigation and Immigration and Customs Enforcement) scanned through millions of photos in state driver's license databases without prior knowledge or consent come as little surprise. The vacuum of legal checks and balances has led to a "surveillance-first, ask-permission-later system," reporter Drew Harrell wrote in the *Washington Post*.[83]

Second, the accuracy of facial recognition technology varies significantly. Certain tests have disclosed unacceptably high false-match rates. A recent independent report of the UK's Metropolitan Police found that its facial recognition technology had an extraordinarily high error rate of 81 percent.[84] Similarly, Axon, a leading supplier of police body cameras in the United States, announced that it would cease offering facial recognition on its devices. Axon's independent ethics board stated, "Face recognition technology is not currently reliable enough to ethically justify its use."[85]

But other assessments demonstrate more favorable results. The US National Institute for Standards and Technology Evaluations conducted between 2014 and 2018 of 127 algorithms from thirty-nine developers showed that "facial recognition software got 20 times better at searching a database to find a matching photograph." The failure rate during the same period dropped from 4.0 percent to 0.2 percent.[86]

One reason for the discrepancy is that under ideal conditions, facial recognition can perform very well. But when unexpected variables are thrown in—poor weather or fuzzy database images (let alone personal face masks)—failure rates begin to shoot up. My personal experience with an ABC gate in London Heathrow airport demonstrated that simply wearing eyeglasses was enough to prevent three different machines from properly matching my face to my passport. Only when I removed my glasses—on my fourth try—was a new device able to verify my face and authorized me to pass through. Facial recognition technology also has been unable to shake persistent gender and racial biases, which lead to elevated false positives for minorities and women: "The darker the skin, the more errors arise—up to nearly 35 percent for images of darker skinned women," noted Steve Lohr in the *New York Times*.[87]

Public facial recognition systems are rapidly spreading around the world. The index identifies at least sixty-eight countries that are actively incorporating facial recognition systems in their public surveillance programs (this does not include ABC systems in airports or other border control facilities).

Smart Policing

The idea behind smart policing is to feed immense quantities of data into an algorithm—geographic location, historic arrest levels, types of committed crimes, biometric data, social media feeds—in order to prevent crime, respond to criminal acts, or even make predictions about future criminal activity. As Privacy International notes: "With the proliferation of surveillance cameras, facial recognition, open source and social media intelligence, biometrics, and data emerging from smart cities, the police now have unprecedented access to massive amounts of data." Therefore, one major component to smart policing is to create automated platforms that can disaggregate immense amounts of material, facilitate data arriving from multiple sources, and permit fine-tuned collection of individual information.

An area that has received considerable recent attention is predictive policing. This technique accelerated in the United States after the National Institute of Justice started issuing grants for pilot predictive policing projects in 2009. At its core, these programs claim to predict with remarkable accuracy—based on massive data aggregation—where future crimes will be committed and which individuals are likely to commit those crimes. Predictive policing has exploded in popularity. The PredPol predictive analytics program, for example, is deployed "by more than 60 police departments around the country."[88] Almost every state in the United States now uses "pretrial risk assessment" algorithms to determine future behavior and prospective prison sentencing for defendants and incarcerated inmates.[89]

But there are growing concerns about algorithmic bias and prejudice, as well as the effectiveness of these predictions. Recent reporting by Caroline Haskins for *Vice* describes how PredPol's predictive crime forecasting algorithm operates. PredPol's software generates crime forecasts for police officers "on a scale as small as 500 by 500 square feet," which can pinpoint specific houses. The algorithm assumes that "certain crimes committed at a particular time are more likely to occur in the same place in the future."[90] PredPol reveals that "historical event datasets are used to train the algorithm for each new city (ideally using two to five years of data). PredPol then updates the algorithm each day with new events as they are received from the department." New predictions are highlighted in special red boxes superimposed on Google Maps, representing high-risk areas that warrant special attention from police patrols.[91] A key shortcoming in PredPol's methodology is that it generates future predictions based on data from past criminal activity and arrests. Certain minority neighborhoods that have suffered from "over-policing" and biased police conduct show up with higher frequency in PredPol's dashboard. Therefore, this technology may not represent fine-tuned algorithmic crime prediction so much as the perpetuation of structurally biased policing. Machine algorithms rarely consider that police bias may be the reason for disproportionate arrests of minority populations. Instead, the default algorithmic assumption is that certain minority groups are more prone to commit crimes. This dubious conclusion forms the basis for the subsequent predictions produced by these algorithms, underscoring a vital principle: AI machines are only as good as the data with which they are trained.

This situation also points to another flaw with algorithms: their conflation of correlation with causation. Put simply, algorithms don't comprehend causation: "They see that some events are associated with other events, but they don't ascertain which things directly make other things happen. It's as if you knew that the presence of clouds made rain likelier, but you didn't know clouds caused rain."[92] This is why algorithms can so easily get tripped up by racially biased data. Without being able to differentiate between correlation (more African Americans are incarcerated as a percentage of their population) and causation (police officers inordinately target African Americans for arrests), AI progress will stall.

Social Media Surveillance

Government use of social media surveillance has grown significantly in recent years, paralleling the increase in online-based protest movements. Social

media surveillance in the AI and big-data context refers to the automated collection and processing of personal data obtained from digital communications
platforms, permitting real-time accumulation, aggregation, and analysis of bulk
amounts of metadata and content. This technique incorporates machine-driven
programs designed to automatically monitor millions of communications for
specific keywords, or to detect more generalized patterns. As the 2019 Freedom
on the Net report warns, "Sophisticated monitoring systems can quickly map
users' relationships through link analysis; assign a meaning or attitude to their
social media posts using natural-language processing and sentiment analysis;
and infer their past, present, or future locations." Further, machine learning
"enables these systems to find patterns that may be invisible to humans, while
deep neural networks can identify and suggest whole new categories of patterns
for further investigation."[93]

The Chinese are world leaders when it comes to deploying social media
surveillance techniques. Companies such as Semptian, Knowlesys, and
Meiya Pico offer vast capabilities used by Chinese authorities to monitor the
communications of millions of individuals. The scope of China's communications surveillance enterprise is only beginning to come to light. In 2019, for
example, a security researcher "discovered an unsecured database consisting
of the social media profiles, messages, and shared files of some 364 million
Chinese users, updated daily" for law enforcement tracking.[94] Similarly,
Chinese authorities are developing big-data "police clouds"—linked to its
Sharp Eyes program—to aggregate information related to a user's web activity, social media accounts, phone records, biometric data, and captured
video surveillance footage. The system's goal, as reported in the *Washington
Post*, is to "track where people are, what they are up to, what they believe and
who they associate with—and ultimately even to assign them a single 'social
credit' score based on whether the government and their fellow citizens consider them trustworthy."[95]

Russia is another country with an extensive pattern of social media surveillance. Freedom House reported that in 2019, for instance, the government issued
a procurement tender for technology that could "collect, analyze, and conduct
sentiment analysis on social media content relating to President Vladimir Putin
and other topics of interest."[96]

Like the other techniques, social media surveillance is not solely deployed
by autocracies; liberal democracies are also avid users of these techniques. In
the United States, agencies such as Immigration and Customs Enforcement
have signed contracts with Palantir to develop custom-built database management tools that "enables agents to analyze trends and establish links between
individuals based on information gathered during border searches, purchased

from private data brokers, and obtained from other intelligence collection exercises."[97] Even in Canada, a project run by the Royal Canadian Mounted Police (RCMP) that was dubbed "Project Wide Awake" was found to have contracted with Salesforce to acquire its Social Studio social media monitoring application. The RCMP's goal?—carry out widespread surveillance of citizens' social media in order to predict the commission of future crimes and head off potential criminal incidents.[98]

The Role of China

The United States and China lead the world in AI technology, but they offer vastly different visions for its use. Unlike China, the United States is not pursuing an explicit industrial policy designed to elevate US firms over its rivals. Instead, the US approach, summarized in its 2019 executive order on AI, focuses on advancing research and development, promoting trustworthy development and responsible use frameworks, building an AI-ready workforce, and shaping AI technical standards.[99]

For China, AI is an essential component of the broader system of control that underpins Communist Party rule. Moreover, supplying new AI and big-data capabilities to bolster fellow authoritarians contributes to the regime's larger aims, described by scholar Minxin Pei as "undermining the Western liberal order while reaching for PRC hegemony in Asia and the expansion of Chinese influence worldwide."[100] China is actively developing new AI capabilities and peddling its products abroad. Under the flagship initiative Made in China 2025, the PRC is seeking to transform its manufacturing capacity in order to dominate a core set of hi-tech industries.[101]

The rapid advance of the AI startup Yitu is emblematic of China's push. Yitu was founded by two Chinese AI experts in 2012 and has passed several remarkable milestones in only a few years. Its "Dragonfly Eye" image platform already contains over 1.8 billion photographs, and Yitu claims that the system requires only three seconds to identify an individual within its database. This data set includes images from the PRC's national database, as well as an estimated 320 million entry and exit photos taken at the country's borders. Yitu's value reached an estimated $2.4 billion in 2018, and the company now employs more than five hundred persons spread across Shanghai, Singapore, and Silicon Valley. Most importantly, its algorithms work: Yitu's facial-recognition technologies have won top awards from the US National Institute of Standards and Technology and the US intelligence community's Intelligence Advanced Research Projects Activity program.

Empirically, the index shows that Chinese companies—with Huawei at the helm—are leading suppliers of AI and big-data public surveillance systems around the world. Figure 7.3 depicts the global spread of Chinese-supplied technology.

A growing consensus singles out China as a global driver of authoritarian technology, maintaining that as China develops a robust AI sector, it is using the BRI or Digital Silk Road program to spread sophisticated technology to governments worldwide.[102] But AI and big-data surveillance is not solely going from one authoritarian country (China) to other authoritarian states. Rather, transfers are happening in a much more heterogeneous fashion. China is exporting surveillance tech to liberal democracies as much as it is targeting authoritarian markets. Likewise, companies based in liberal democracies are actively selling sophisticated equipment to unsavory regimes.

Nevertheless, experts have specific reasons for applying greater scrutiny to Chinese companies. Huawei is a leading vendor of public safety systems powered by AI and big data. Its technology is linked to multiple countries in the index. It is aggressively seeking new markets in regions like sub-Saharan Africa. Huawei is not only providing advanced equipment, but also offering ongoing technological support to set up, operate, and manage these systems.

A 2019 investigative report by the *Wall Street Journal* provides an eye-opening example. Reporters found that Huawei technicians in both Uganda and Zambia helped government officials spy on political opponents. This included "intercepting their encrypted communications and social media, and using cell data to track their whereabouts." Not only did Huawei employees play a "direct role in government efforts to intercept the private communications of opponents," but they also encouraged Ugandan security officials to travel to Algeria so they could study Huawei's "intelligent video surveillance system" operation in Algiers.[103] Uganda subsequently agreed to purchase a similar facial recognition surveillance system from Huawei costing $126 million—subsidized by Chinese state loans.[104]

The Australian Strategic Policy Institute's project "Mapping China's Tech Giants" indicates that Huawei is responsible for seventy-five "smart city-public security projects," and has seen a colossal increase in its business line: "In 2017, Huawei listed 40 countries where its smart-city technologies had been introduced; by 2018, that reach had reportedly more than doubled to ninety countries (including 230 cities)."[105] Huawei is directly pitching the safe city model to national security agencies, and China's Exim Bank appears to be sweetening the deal with subsidized loans. As a result, a country like Mauritius can obtain long-term financing from the Chinese government, which mandates contracting with Chinese firms.[106] The Mauritian government then turns to

Presence of Chinese AI & Big Data Surveillance Technology

1

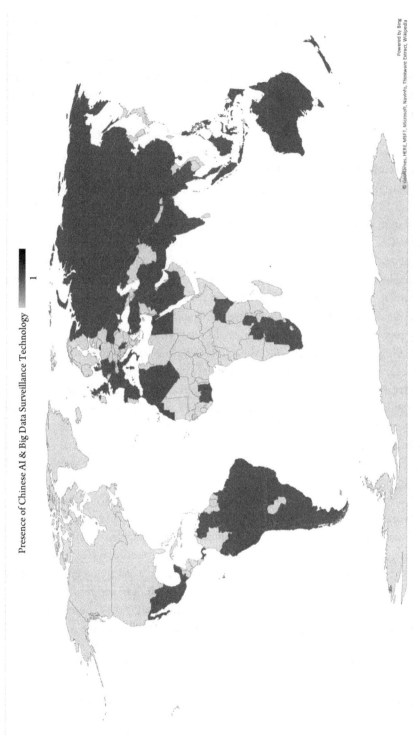

Figure 7.3 AI and Big-Data Public Surveillance Systems Supplied by Chinese Firms

Huawei as the prime contractor or sub-awardee to set up the safe city and implement advanced surveillance controls.[107]

It is also increasingly clear that firms like Huawei operate with far less independence from the Chinese government than they claim. Huawei was founded in 1987 by Ren Zhengfei, a former officer in the People's Liberation Army who served in its "military technology division," Anna Fifield at the *Washington Post* has noted.[108] There are consistent reports that Huawei receives significant subsidies from the Chinese government.[109] There also appear to be strong connections between Huawei's leadership and China's security and intelligence apparatus. Sun Yafang, for example, chairwoman of Huawei's board from 1999 to 2018, once worked in China's Ministry of State Security.[110] Max Chafkin and Joshua Brustein reported in *Bloomberg* that there are allegations that Ren may have been a "high-ranking Chinese spymaster and indeed may still be."[111] Experts maintain that the Chinese Communist Party increasingly is establishing "party cells" in private companies to enable enhanced access and control.[112] Huawei has publicly averred that it would "definitely say no" to any demands by the Chinese government to hand over user data,[113] but this claim contravenes a 2015 Chinese national security law that mandates companies to allow third-party access to their networks and to turn over source code or encryption keys upon request.[114] Huawei's declared ownership structure is remarkably opaque. A 2019 study by Christopher Balding and Donald C. Clarke concluded that 99 percent of Huawei shares are controlled by a "trade union committee"—which, in all likelihood, is a proxy for Chinese state control of the company.[115]

To get a better sense of the prevalence of Chinese AI and big-data surveillance technology, I used data from the index to identify specific countries that rely primarily or exclusively on capabilities provided by Chinese firms.[116] Overall, the list totaled twenty-four countries. Many of these states exhibit governance deficiencies—most are classified as hybrid regimes. They tend to share close geopolitical ties with China. Fourteen are members of the BRI. Regionally, countries in sub-Saharan Africa are overrepresented, with eight countries on the list. Finally, the group's economic influence is small. Iran and South Africa lead the pack, ranking twenty-seventh and thirty-third out of 180 countries on 2017 global GDP.[117] Kyrgyzstan and Tajikistan cluster at the bottom—ranked 147th and 151st, respectively.[118]

Indisputably, a considerable number of these countries would not be able to access advanced surveillance technology without China's help. For these governments, China provides crucial equipment that enables security agencies to monitor citizens and disrupt political challenges as needed. In exchange, China gains political influence, increases its economic leverage, and potentially receives intelligence advantages (e.g., the African Union headquarters, built by China, were implanted with bugs that siphoned confidential data to Chinese authorities nightly from 2012 to 2017).[119] Membership in this group will increase in the coming years, representing an worrisome sign about future trends of digital repression.

At the same time, countries considered to be client states of Chinese repressive technology—such as Saudi Arabia, the United Arab Emirates, or Kazakhstan—source from multiple suppliers in a variety of countries. Saudi Arabia is a good case in point. Huawei is helping the Saudi government to build safe cities, Google and Microsoft operate its cloud-computing servers, UK arms manufacturer BAE has sold it mass surveillance systems, NEC sells it facial recognition cameras, and Amazon and Alibaba may partner with it on a major smart city project in the kingdom.[120] Most governments, especially those with resources, purposely refrain from relying on one supplier of technology.

China's policies warrant continued scrutiny and attention from policymakers in democratic states. Recent actions, such as the 2019 US government designation of eight Chinese AI firms—Hikvision, iFlyTek, SenseTime, Megvii, Meiya Pico, Dahua, Hikvision, Yitu, and Yixin—to a restricted exports "Entity List" for human rights violations against Uighurs in Xinjiang, are significant steps.[121] But we should be mindful that China is not the only country engaged in spreading such technologies and techniques.

Questions for Democracies

The proliferation of AI and big-data technology and the rise of digital repression pose serious policy challenges to liberal democracies. A key question is whether these powerful tools will cause democracies themselves to become more repressive. Will the temptation to take advantage of AI's surveillance potential ultimately corrode democratic safeguards? Traditionally, liberal democracies and authoritarian states have approached the use and protection of data in very different ways. As Jon Bateman writes, democracies have focused on "protecting computer networks from being hacked" and emphasized safeguarding network infrastructure on the basis of three principles known as the "CIA triad": confidentiality (only authorized users can access or modify data), integrity (data should be kept in a correct state and no one should be able to modify it accidentally or intentionally), and availability (data is available to authorized users whenever necessary).[122] In contrast, authoritarians employ a broader concept—"information security"—underpinning the idea that the state should not only protect against unauthorized intrusions, but it should also guard against the "unrestrained spread of information and ideas" that threaten the existing political and social order.[123] These distinctions help explain the development of dual-value systems related to cybersecurity and Internet governance.

But in recent years, the United States and other democracies have become increasingly concerned about controlling the flow of information online from bad actors—whether confronting the Islamic State's "virtual caliphate" or combating electoral disinformation from Russian sources. As a result, democracies have experienced their own shifts when it comes to determining the proper role of the state in relation to online privacy and data governance.

In 2020, it is not difficult to imagine liberal democratic governments employing AI and big-data technology in ways that infringe on citizens' rights. Fortunately, citizens in advanced democracies have successfully combated government surveillance abuses in the past, and robust checks and balances exist that can push back against state overreach. While there is no guarantee that AI will not weaken democratic political systems, the risk there is less acute. In fact, there are growing indications that strong democracies intend to take serious steps to shape the normative framework for AI and big-data use. In early 2020, the EU released a set of digital strategies, including a detailed white paper on a European approach to AI.[124] Simultaneously, the US Defense Department released a set of ethical principles to guide the responsible use of AI in warfighting.[125] Leading experts are doing serious thinking about how to create a global framework to ensure, as Eileen Donahoe and Megan MacDuffee put it, that "AI is developed and applied in ways that respect human dignity, democratic accountability, and the bedrock principles of free societies."[126]

The coronavirus pandemic has brought new complications to this equation.[127] AI technology offers specific advantages to help bolster public health objectives, such as identifying contagion hot spots, assisting with contact tracing, and predicting the spread of the virus. According to the *LA Times*, for example, Singapore has "mobilized a system of state control" that relies on advanced surveillance technologies to ensure obedience to Covid-19 protocols. This system includes posting daily public updates with specific details about new cases, "down to the person's age, sex, nationality and the street where they live."[128] China and Russia have also deployed facial recognition systems, social media monitoring, and location-tracking data to maintain adherence to coronavirus quarantines.[129]

The risk posed by advanced surveillance technology is even greater in fragile democracies or countries with authoritarian tendencies. In backsliding regimes such as Poland, Hungary, or the Philippines, the repressive potential of AI and big-data techniques may lead to steeper deterioration. Illiberal governments that face prospective popular challenges have a natural interest in technology that could help them weather mass discontent. Even in political systems with democratic traditions, governments have a high incentive to arm security forces with intrusive technology, monitor the activities of political opponents and civil society, and take preemptive action against potential challenges to their authority.

India, for example, is moving forward with plans to create a national facial recognition system and has already issued a tender for bids.[130] States also closely
track one another's actions. As AI proves its repressive value for the autocracies
now pioneering new technologies, copycat behavior from other governments is
likely to follow.[131]

Finally, it is also worth noting that the cost of deploying surveillance technology is rapidly decreasing. Automated license plate readers are a good example. Conventional devices that police started buying in the 2000s cost
$15,000 to $20,000. As the technology improved and integrated AI software, the
price point plummeted. It is now possible to acquire AI-powered license plate
recognition technology for "as little as $50 a month."[132] What this means is that
countries with limited resources still have the capacity to deploy ever more powerful technology to advance their objectives.

Does AI Represent the Future of Repression?

It is certainly possible to envision a world, increasingly organized online, where
powerful machine-learning algorithms harvest individual data not only to keep
tabs on specific choices that are being made in real time, but also to predict future behavior where choices conform to anticipated preferences. In a mutually
beneficial manner, the interests of the surveillance state may find natural synergy
with corporate profit motives to anticipate and manipulate consumer behavior
(just as scholars like Shoshana Zuboff warn us).[133]

Yet, at present, this scenario remains remote—and would require a continuous level of technological advancement to materialize. Most parts of the
world are struggling to provide basic services like reliable Internet access or de-
pendable electricity. Their ability to establish, maintain, and effectively operate
state-of-the-art surveillance systems is dubious. The most comprehensive surveillance system in the world is overseen by Chinese authorities in Xinjiang. It
is not easily replicable in most other countries. The resources needed to recreate
this arrangement are massive. The human capacity requirements to maximize
the efficiency of the system are demanding. The reputational risks involved in
emulating China's mass surveillance model, even for authoritarian countries, are
prohibitive. In time, other countries with the right resources and a comparable
commitment to repression may mount similar efforts. But the barriers to entry
to establish such systems are considerable even as the cost of procuring such
technology decreases.

Artificial intelligence works best when it can access a large data sets to measure
and assess human behavior (which explains why social media are so beneficial
for machine-learning algorithms). But in many countries, such data either does

not yet exist or is at odds with how certain societies operate. Ethiopia is a good case in point. Despite a political system that has prioritized tracking its citizens, it continues to rely primarily on physical surveillance. This choice reflects long-standing practices embedded in its system of governance. As numerous contacts emphasized, the Ethiopian government has little interest in installing standard digital surveillance tools like facial recognition technology to replace ongoing networks based on human surveillance. Such systems would generate suspicion, cost significant sums of money, and might not provide much of an upgrade—at least in the short term.

Instead, we are likely to see a continued patchwork establishment of AI surveillance systems. It is unlikely that they will substitute lower-cost, traditional tools, but governments may selectively adopt these instruments to reinforce existing approaches. In certain countries or regions with abundant resources, pressing security needs, and consistent patterns of repression—such as the Gulf States—the use of AI and big-data surveillance will become more common.

The good news is that there is ample time to initiate a much-needed public debate about the proper balance between AI technology, government surveillance, private sector exploitation of user data, and citizens' privacy rights. But as these technologies become more embedded in governance, politics, and business, the window for change will disappear.

Notes

1. Stephen Chen, "How Tensions with the West Are Putting the Future of China's Skynet Mass Surveillance System at Stake," *South China Morning Post*, September 23, 2018, https://www.scmp.com/news/china/science/article/2165372/how-tensions-west-are-putting-future-chinas-skynet-mass.
2. Xiao Qiang, "The Road to Digital Unfreedom: President Xi's Surveillance State," *Journal of Democracy* 30, no. 1 (2019): 57.
3. Katherine Atha et al. "China's Smart Cities Development," U.S.-China Economic and Security Review Commission, January 2020, https://www.uscc.gov/sites/default/files/China_Smart_Cities_Development.pdf, 25.
4. As an example, Chinese AI company Megvii states in its IPO filing that it provides "City IoT Solutions" to 112 cities throughout China. City IoT solutions are designed "to make cities and communities safer and more efficient by digitizing the urban space. Our City IoT solutions encompass algorithms, software as well as AI-empowered sensors. Our smart city management solutions allow government agencies to enhance public safety, optimize traffic management and improve urban resource planning. Our smart community management solutions enable businesses to enhance the security of their properties and improve the experience of occupants and visitors." "Application Proof of Megvii Technology Limited," The Stock Exchange of Hong Kong Limited, 2019, https://ipvm-uploads.s3.amazonaws.com/uploads/f19d/2a89/megvii-ipo-doc.pdf. See also Charles Rollet, "Megvii Financials and Growth Examined," IVPM, August 30, 2019, https://ipvm.com/reports/megvii-ipo.
5. Simon Denyer, "Beijing Bets on Facial Recognition in a Big Drive for Total Surveillance," *Washington Post*, January 7, 2018, https://www.washingtonpost.com/news/world/

wp/2018/01/07/feature/in-china-facial-recognition-is-sharp-end-of-a-drive-for-total-surveillance/?noredirect=on.

6. Rudolph, "Sharper Eyes: Surveilling the Surveillers (Part 1)."

7. Emile Dirks and James Leibold, "Genomic Surveillance: Inside China," Policy Brief—Report No. 34/2020, Australian Strategic Policy Institute, 2020, https://s3-ap-southeast-2.amazonaws.com/ad-aspi/2020-06/Genomic%20surveillance_1.pdf?QhPFyrNVaSjvblm FT24HRXSuHyRfhpml.

8. Related to these developments is the emergence of China's "social credit system," a broad policy that employs a mix of coercive penalties and financial incentives tied to individual behavior to encourage adherence to state priorities. The degree of its cohesiveness and repression impact is the matter of some debate. Scholars such as Shazeda Ahmed and Jeremy Daum argue that commentators have "distorted the social credit system into a technological dystopia far removed from what is actually happening in China." Shazeda Ahmed, "The Messy Truth about Social Credit," *Logic*, May 1, 2019, https://logicmag.io/china/the-messy-truth-about-social-credit/. Other experts, such as Samantha Hoffman and Rachel Botsman, describe social credit as a "futuristic vision of Big Brother out of control." Rachel Botsman, "Big Data Meets Big Brother as China Moves to Rate Its Citizens," *Wired*, October 21, 2017, https://www.wired.co.uk/article/chinese-government-social-credit-score-privacy-invasion; see also Samantha Hoffman, "Social Credit," Australian Strategic Policy Institute, June 28, 2018, https://www.aspi.org.au/report/social-credit.

9. Qiang, "The Road to Digital Unfreedom: President Xi's Surveillance State," 56.

10. Paul Mozur, "Inside China's Dystopian Dreams: A.I., Shame and Lots of Cameras," *New York Times*, July 8, 2018, https://www.nytimes.com/2018/07/08/business/china-surveillance-technology.html.

11. Paul Mozur, Raymond Zhong and Aaron Krolik, "In Coronavirus Fight, China Gives Citizens a Color Code, With Red Flags," *New York Times*, August 7, 2020, https://www.nytimes.com/2020/03/01/business/china-coronavirus-surveillance.html.

12. Megha Rajagopalan, "This Is What a 21st-Century Police State Really Looks Like," *Buzzfeed News*, October 17, 2017, https://www.buzzfeednews.com/article/meghara/the-police-state-of-the-future-is-already-here.

13. Blake Schmidt, "Hong Kong Police Already Have AI Tech That Can Recognize Faces," *Bloomberg*, October 22, 2019, https://www.bloomberg.com/news/articles/2019-10-22/hong-kong-police-already-have-ai-tech-that-can-recognize-faces.

14. Paul Mozur, "Protesters in Hong Kong Are Targets of Scrutiny through Their Phones," *New York Times*, October 1, 2014, https://www.nytimes.com/2014/10/02/business/protesters-are-targets-of-scrutiny-through-their-phones.html.

15. Even individuals who merely posted online words of encouragement were in danger of possible arrest: one twenty-three year old user who wrote, "Tonight, if you're a man, let's revive Mong Kok" (an area of Hong Kong that was a center of protest activity), was arrested on charges of inciting fellow citizens to join an unlawful assembly. Michael Forsythe and Alan Wong, "Protesters in Hong Kong on Edge as Police Track Their Online Footprints," *New York Times*, October 28, 2014, https://www.nytimes.com/2014/10/29/world/asia/in-hong-kong-fears-of-a-police-crackdown-online.html.

16. Paul Mozur, "In Hong Kong Protests, Faces Become Weapons," *New York Times*, July 26, 2019, https://www.nytimes.com/2019/07/26/technology/hong-kong-protests-facial-recognition-surveillance.html.

17. These tactics relate to Steve Mann's theory of "sousveillance," which he coined in the early 2000s to describe the hierarchy reversal of "citizens photographing police, shoppers photographing shopkeepers, and taxicab passengers photographing cab drivers." Steve Mann, Jason Nolan, and Barry Wellman, "Sousveillance: Inventing and Using Wearable Computing Devices for Data Collection in Surveillance Environments," *Surveillance & Society* 1, no. 3 (2003): 334.

18. D. Lin and Sai Kung, "How Hong Kong Protests Turned Dream Wedding into a Nightmare for Policeman's Bride," *South China Morning Post*, 23 November 2019, https://www.scmp.com/comment/letters/article/3038809/how-hong-kong-protests-turned-dream-wedding-nightmare-policemans.

19. Chun Han Wong and Wenxin Fan, "Hong Kong Security Law Gives Beijing Broad New Powers," *Wall Street Journal*, June 30, 2020, https://www.wsj.com/articles/china-passes-hong-kong-security-law-aimed-at-crushing-protests-11593488146.

20. See Steven Feldstein, "China's Latest Crackdown in Hong Kong Will Have Global Consequences," Carnegie Endowment for International Peace, July 9, 2020, https://carnegieendowment.org/2020/07/09/china-s-latest-crackdown-in-hong-kong-will-have-global-consequences-pub-82264.

21. Will Ripley and Jenni Marsh, "Hong Kong Media Tycoon Says 'The Fight Has to Go On' after 'Symbolic' Arrest under New Law," *CNN Business*, August 14, 2020, https://www.cnn.com/2020/08/14/media/jimmy-lai-interview-hnk-intl/index.html.

22. Austin Ramzy and Tiffany May, "Joshua Wong and Agnes Chow Are Sentenced to Prison Over Hong Kong Protest," *New York Times*, December 16, 2020, https://www.nytimes.com/2020/12/02/world/asia/joshua-wong-agnes-chow-hong-kong.html.

23. Paul Mozur, "With Hacks and Cameras, Beijing's Electronic Dragnet Closes on Hong Kong," *New York Times*, August 25, 2020, https://www.nytimes.com/2020/08/25/technology/hong-kong-national-security-law.html.

24. Portions of this chapter derive from previously published material by the author, including Steven Feldstein, "How Artificial Intelligence Is Reshaping Repression," *Journal of Democracy* 30, no. 1 (2019): 40–52; Steven Feldstein, "The Global Expansion of AI Surveillance," *Carnegie Endowment for International Peace—Working Paper*, September 17, 2019, https://carnegieendowment.org/2019/09/17/global-expansion-of-ai-surveillance-pub-79847; Steven Feldstein, "When It Comes to Digital Authoritarianism, China Is a Challenge—but Not the Only Challenger," *War on the Rocks*, February 12, 2020, https://warontherocks.com/2020/02/when-it-comes-to-digital-authoritarianism-china-is-a-challenge-but-not-the-only-challenge/; and Steven Feldstein, "Beware the Implications of Coronavirus Surveillance," Carnegie Endowment for International Peace, March 31, 2020, https://carnegieendowment.org/2020/03/31/beware-implications-of-coronavirus-surveillance-pub-81411.

25. Nils J. Nilsson, *The Quest for Artificial Intelligence* (New York: Cambridge University Press, 2009), 4.

26. Jerry Kaplan, *Artificial Intelligence: What Everyone Needs to Know* (New York: Oxford University Press, 2016), 5.

27. "Preparing for the Future of Artificial Intelligence," whitehouse.gov, October 2016, https://obamawhitehouse.archives.gov/sites/default/files/whitehouse_files/microsites/ostp/NSTC/preparing_for_the_future_of_ai.pdf.

28. "Preparing for the Future of Artificial Intelligence," whitehouse.gov.

29. Viktor Mayer-Schönberger and Kenneth Cukier, *Big Data: A Revolution That Will Transform How We Live, Work, and Think* (New York: Houghton Mifflin Harcourt, 2013), 6.

30. Milan W. Svolik, *The Politics of Authoritarian Rule* (Cambridge: Cambridge University Press, 2012), 124.

31. Andreas Lichter, Max Loeffler, and Sebastian Siegloch, "The Economic Costs of Mass Surveillance: Insights from Stasi Spying in East Germany," IZA Discussion Papers no. 9245, 2015.

32. Lichter, Loeffler, and Siegloch, "Economic Costs," 4.

33. Nicholas Wright writes: "People will know that the omnipresent monitoring of their physical and digital activities will be used to predict undesired behavior, even actions they are merely contemplating. . . . In order to prevent the system from making negative predictions, many people will begin to mimic the behaviors of a "responsible" member of society. These may be as subtle as how long one's eyes look at different elements on a phone screen. This will improve social control not only by forcing people to act in certain ways, but also by changing the way they think." Nicholas Wright, "How Artificial Intelligence Will Reshape the Global Order," *Foreign Affairs*, July 10, 2018, https://www.foreignaffairs.com/articles/world/2018-07-10/how-artificial-intelligence-will-reshape-global-order.

34. See Shahbaz and Funk, "Social Media Surveillance"; Umer Ali and Ramsha Jahangir, "Pakistan Moves to Install Nationwide 'Web Monitoring System,'" *Coda Story*, October 24, 2019, https://codastory.com/authoritarian-tech/surveillance/pakistan-nationwide-web-monitoring/; Freedom House, "Additional Data FOTN 2019," 2019, https://www.freedomonthenet.org/sites/default/files/2019-11/ADDITIONAL_DATA_FOTN_2019_social-media-surveillance-election-intereference_Data_Nov_4.xlsx.

35. Shahbaz and Funk, "Social Media Surveillance."
36. Ali and Jahangir, "Pakistan Moves."
37. Collin Anderson, "The Hollowing Middle of the Surveillance Malware Market," *Motherboard*, December 14, 2017, https://motherboard.vice.com/en_us/article/595dkd/the-hollowing-middle-of-the-surveillance-malware-market.
38. Joel Schectman and Christopher Bing, "UAE Used Super-weapon to Spy on iPhones of Foes," *Reuters*, January 30, 2019, https://www.reuters.com/investigates/special-report/usa-spying-karma/; David D. Kirkpatrick, "Israeli Software Helped Saudis Spy on Khashoggi, Lawsuit Says," *New York Times*, December 2, 2018, https://www.nytimes.com/2018/12/02/world/middleeast/saudi-khashoggi-spyware-israel.html.
39. Josh Horwitz, "WeChat's New Heat Map Feature Lets Users—and Chinese Authorities—See Where Crowds Are Forming," *Quartz*, October 7, 2015, https://qz.com/518908/wechats-new-heat-map-feature-lets-users-and-chinese-authorities-see-where-crowds-are-forming.
40. "Why Is There Tension between China and the Uighurs?," *BBC*, September 26, 2014, https://www.bbc.com/news/world-asia-china-26414014.
41. Austin Ramzy and Chris Buckley, "'Absolutely No Mercy': Leaked Files Expose How China Organized Mass Detentions of Muslims," *New York Times*, November 16, 2019, https://www.nytimes.com/interactive/2019/11/16/world/asia/china-xinjiang-documents.html.
42. Chun Han Wong, "China's Hard Edge: The Leader of Beijing's Muslim Crackdown Gains Influence," *Wall Street Journal*, April 7, 2019, https://www.wsj.com/articles/chinas-hard-edge-the-leader-of-beijings-muslim-crackdown-gains-influence-11554655886.
43. Steven Feldstein, "Hybrid Repression Online and Offline in China: Foretelling the Human Rights Struggle to Come?," National Endowment for Democracy Power 3.0 (blog), January 25, 2018, https://www.power3point0.org/2018/01/25/hybrid-repression-online-and-offline-in-china-foretelling-the-human-rights-struggle-to-come/.
44. "China: Police DNA Database Threatens Privacy," Human Rights Watch, May 15, 2017, https://www.hrw.org/news/2017/05/15/china-police-dna-database-threatens-privacy.
45. Adrian Zenz and James Leibold, "Chen Quanguo: The Strongman behind Beijing's Securitization Strategy in Tibet and Xinjiang," Jamestown Foundation, *China Brief*, September 21, 2017.
46. Maya Wang, "China's Algorithms of Repression," Human Rights Watch, May 1, 2019, https://www.hrw.org/report/2019/05/01/chinas-algorithms-repression/reverse-engineering-xinjiang-police-mass-surveillance.
47. Cate Cadell, "From Laboratory in Far West, China's Surveillance State Spreads Quietly," *Reuters*, August 14, 2018; Human Rights Watch, "China: Minority Region Collects DNA from Millions," December 13, 2017, www.hrw.org/news/2017/12/13/china-minority-region-collects-dna-millions.
48. Wang, "China's Algorithms of Repression."
49. "2018 Country Reports on Human Rights Practices: China," US Department of State, March 13, 2019, https://www.state.gov/reports/2018-country-reports-on-human-rights-practices/china-includes-tibet-hong-kong-and-macau-china/.
50. Bethany Allen-Ebrahimian, "Exposed: China's Operating Manuals for Mass Interment and Arrest by Algorithm," International Consortium of Investigative Journalists, November 24, 2019, https://www.icij.org/investigations/china-cables/exposed-chinas-operating-manuals-for-mass-internment-and-arrest-by-algorithm/.
51. Allen-Ebrahimian, "Exposed."
52. Emily Feng, "Crackdown in Xinjiang: Where Have All the People Gone?," *Financial Times*, August 4, 2018, https://www.ft.com/content/ac0ffb2e-8b36-11e8-b18d-0181731a0340.
53. See Feldstein, "New Technologies, New Problems."
54. Kim Hart, "Baltimore Wrestles with Aerial Surveillance," *Axios*, July 31, 2019, https://www.axios.com/baltimore-wrestles-with-aerial-surveillance-to-reduce-crime-2d973591-0b33-4e25-94a7-c3f553dc2934.html.
55. Conor Friedersdorf, "Mass Surveillance Is Coming to a City Near You," *The Atlantic*, June 21, 2019, https://www.theatlantic.com/ideas/archive/2019/06/mass-surveillance-tech/592117/.
56. Kevin Rector and Alison Knezevich, "Maryland's Use of Facial Recognition Software Questioned by Researchers, Civil Liberties Advocates," *Baltimore Sun*, October 18, 2016,

https://www.baltimoresun.com/news/crime/bs-md-facial-recognition-20161017-story.html.

57. "Persistent Surveillance's Cynical Attempt to Profit Off Baltimore's Trauma," ACLU of Maryland, June 8, 2018, https://www.aclu-md.org/en/press-releases/persistent-surveillances-cynical-attempt-profit-baltimores-trauma.

58. Olivia Solon, "'Surveillance Society': Has Technology at the US-Mexico Border Gone Too Far?" *The Guardian*, June 13, 2018, https://www.theguardian.com/technology/2018/jun/13/mexico-us-border-wall-surveillance-artificial-intelligence-technology.

59. Solon, "Surveillance Society."

60. Alvaro Artigas, "Surveillance, Smart Technologies and the Development of Safe City Solutions: The Case of Chinese ICT Firms and Their International Expansion to Emerging Markets," IBEI Working Paper, 2017, https://www.ibei.org/surveillance-smart-technologies-and-the-development-of-safe-city-solutions-the-case-of-chinese-ict-firms-and-their-international-expansion-to-emerging-markets_112561.pdf.

61. Morgan Meaker, "Marseille's Fight against AI Surveillance," *Coda Story*, March 26, 2020, https://www.codastory.com/authoritarian-tech/ai-surveillance-france-crime/. See also Artigas, "Surveillance, Smart Technologies."

62. Meaker, "Marseille's Fight."

63. Theodore Terschlusen, "Valencienne: Demain les caméras de vidéosurveillance seront intelligentes et . . . chinoises," September 2, 2017, https://webcache.googleusercontent.com/search?q=cache:FS-IyIma564J:www.lavoixdunord.fr/116566/article/2017-02-09/demain-les-cameras-de-videosurveillance-seront-intelligentes-et-chinoises+&cd=1&hl=en&ct=clnk&gl=us.

64. SIPRI Military Expenditure Database, 2019.

65. Feldstein, "Global Expansion."

66. Steven Feldstein, "AI & Big Data Global Surveillance Index," Mendeley Data, V1, 2020, doi: 10.17632/gjhf5y4xjp.1.

67. The majority of sources referenced by the index occur between 2017 and 2020. A small number of sources date as far back as 2012. The index uses the same list of countries found in the V-Dem project, which includes all independent polities worldwide but excludes microstates with populations below 250,000. The research collection effort combed through open-source material, country by country, in English and other languages, including news articles, websites, corporate documents, academic articles, NGO reports, expert submissions, and other public sources. It relied on systematic content analysis for each country incorporating multiple sources to determine the presence of relevant AI surveillance technology and corresponding companies. Sources were categorized into tiered levels of reliability and accuracy. First-tier sources include major print and news magazine outlets (such as the *New York Times*, *Economist*, *Financial Times*, and *Wall Street Journal*). Second-tier sources include major national media outlets. Third-tier sources include web articles, blog posts, and other less substantiated sourcing; these were only included after multiple corroboration. Given limited resources and staffing constraints, the index is only able to offer a snapshot of AI surveillance levels in a given country. It does not provide a comprehensive assessment of all relevant technology, government surveillance uses, and applicable companies. Because research relied primarily on content analysis and literature reviews to derive its findings, there are certain built-in limitations. Some companies, such as Huawei, may have an incentive to highlight new capabilities in this field. Other companies may wish to downplay links to surveillance technology and purposely keep documents out of the public domain. Field-based research involving on-the-ground information collection and verification would be useful to undertake. A number of countries—such as Angola, Azerbaijan, Belarus, Sri Lanka, Tunisia, and Turkmenistan—provided circumstantial or anecdotal evidence of AI surveillance, but not enough verifiable data to warrant inclusion in the index.

68. A major challenge was determining which AI technologies should be included in the index. AI technologies that directly support surveillance objectives—smart city / safe city platforms, facial recognition systems, smart policing systems, automated Internet and social media surveillance—are included in the index. Enabling technologies that are critical to AI

functioning but not directly responsible for surveillance programs are not included in the index. Another data collection challenge is that governments (and many companies) purposely hide their surveillance capabilities. As such, it is difficult to precisely determine the extent to which states are deploying algorithms to support their surveillance objectives, or whether AI use is more speculative than real. The index does not differentiate between governments that expansively deploy AI surveillance techniques versus those that use AI surveillance to a much lesser degree (for example, the index does not include a standardized interval scale correlating to levels of AI surveillance). This is by design. Because this is a nascent field and there is scant information about how different countries are using AI surveillance techniques, attempting to score a country's relative use of AI surveillance would introduce a significant level of researcher bias. Instead, a basic variable was used: Is there documented presence of AI surveillance in a given country? If so, what types of AI surveillance technology is the state deploying? Future research may be able to assess and analyze levels of AI surveillance on a cross-comparative basis. Finally, instances of AI surveillance documented in the index are not specifically tied to harmful outcomes. The index does not differentiate between legitimate and illegitimate surveillance. In part, this is because it is exceedingly difficult to determine what specific governments are doing in the surveillance realm and what the associated impacts are; there is too much that is unknown and hidden.

69. "Freedom on the Net 2018: The Rise of Digital Authoritarianism," October 30, 2018, 9.
70. "Digital 2019: Internet Trends in Q3 2019," *DataReportal*, July 19, 2019, https://datareportal.com/reports/digital-2019-Internet-trends-in-q3.
71. My own research indicates that in at least eight African countries, Chinese companies are primarily or exclusively providing AI surveillance equipment to those respective governments. Feldstein, "Digital Authoritarianism."
72. Feldstein, "Digital Authoritarianism."
73. "Smart Cities," World Bank, January 8, 2015, https://www.worldbank.org/en/topic/digitaldevelopment/brief/smart-cities.
74. "Smart Cities: Utopian Vision, Dystopian Reality," Privacy International, October 2017, http://www.privacyinternational.org/report/638/smart-cities-utopian-vision-dystopian-reality.
75. "Huawei Smart City White Paper," Huawei Enterprise, 2016, https://e.huawei.com/en/material/onLineView?MaterialID=9b0000e57fa94a2dbc0e43f5817ca767.
76. "Huawei Smart City White Paper," Huawei Enterprise.
77. "The Road to Collaborative Public Safety," Huawei, 2017, http://e-file.huawei.com/~/media/EBG/Download_Files/Publications/en/Safe%20City%20Extra.pdf.
78. "Three Rules When Using AI to Add Value to Your IoT Smart Cities," Gartner, January 29, 2018, https://www.gartner.com/doc/reprints?id=1-4XYENKG&ct=180501&st=sb.
79. Bojan Stojkovski, "Big Brother Comes to Belgrade," *Foreign Policy*, June 18, 2019, https://foreignpolicy.com/2019/06/18/big-brother-comes-to-belgrade-huawei-china-facial-recognition-vucic/.
80. "Huawei Safe City Solution: Safeguards Serbia," Huawei Enterprise, August 23, 2018, http://archive.li/pZ9HO.
81. "A Layman's Guide: Facial Recognition in a Crowd," iOmniscient, 2018, https://iomniscient.com/wp-content/uploads/2018/01/Facial-Recognition-Book_LR.pdf.
82. Feldstein, "Road to Digital Unfreedom," 40.
83. Drew Harwell, "FBI, ICE Find State Driver's License Photos Are a Gold Mine for Facial-Recognition Searches," *Washington Post*, July 7, 2019, https://www.washingtonpost.com/technology/2019/07/07/fbi-ice-find-state-drivers-license-photos-are-gold-mine-facial-recognition-searches/.
84. Rowland Manthorpe and Alexander J. Martin, "81% of 'Suspects' Flagged by Met's Police Facial Recognition Technology Innocent, Independent Report Says," *Sky News*, July 4, 2019, https://news.sky.com/story/met-polices-facial-recognition-tech-has-81-error-rate-independent-report-says-11755941.
85. Charlie Warzel, "A Major Police Body Cam Company Just Banned Facial Recognition," *New York Times*, June 27, 2019, https://www.nytimes.com/2019/06/27/opinion/police-cam-facial-recognition.html.

86. "NIST Evaluation Shows Advance in Face Recognition Software's Capabilities," NIST, November 30, 2018, https://www.nist.gov/news-events/news/2018/11/nist-evaluation-shows-advance-face-recognition-softwares-capabilities.

87. Steve Lohr, "Facial Recognition Is Accurate, If You're a White Guy," New York Times, February 9, 2018, https://www.nytimes.com/2018/02/09/technology/facial-recognition-race-artificial-intelligence.html.

88. Randy Rieland, "Artificial Intelligence Is Now Used to Predict Crime. But Is It Biased?" Smithsonian, March 5, 2018, https://www.smithsonianmag.com/innovation/artificial-intelligence-is-now-used-predict-crime-is-it-biased-180968337/.

89. "Algorithms in the Criminal Justice System: Pre-trial Risk Assessment Tools," Electronic Privacy Information Center, 2020, https://epic.org/algorithmic-transparency/crim-justice/.

90. Caroline Haskins, "Revealed: This Is Palantir's Top-Secret User Manual for Cops," Vice, July 12, 2019, https://www.vice.com/en_us/article/9kx4z8/revealed-this-is-palantirs-top-secret-user-manual-for-cops.

91. "The Three Pillars of Predictive Policing," PredPol, 2018, https://www.predpol.com/law-enforcement/.

92. Brian Bergstein, "What AI Still Can't Do," MIT Technology Review, February 19, 2020, https://www.technologyreview.com/s/615189/what-ai-still-cant-do/.

93. Shahbaz and Funk, "Social Media Surveillance."

94. Shahbaz and Funk, "Social Media Surveillance."

95. Simon Denyer, "China's Watchful Eye," Washington Post, January 7, 2018, https://www.washingtonpost.com/news/world/wp/2018/01/07/feature/in-china-facial-recognition-is-sharp-end-of-a-drive-for-total-surveillance/.

96. Shahbaz and Funk, "Social Media Surveillance."

97. Shahbaz and Funk, "Social Media Surveillance."

98. Bryan Carney, "'Project Wide Awake': How the RCMP Watches You on Social Media," The Tyee, March 25, 2019, https://thetyee.ca/News/2019/03/25/Project-Wide-Awake/.

99. "Maintaining American Leadership in Artificial Intelligence," Executive Office of the President, February 14, 2019, https://www.federalregister.gov/documents/2019/02/14/2019-02544/maintaining-american-leadership-in-artificial-intelligence.

100. Minxin Pei, "China in Xi's 'New Era': A Play for Global Leadership," Journal of Democracy 29 (April 2018): 38.

101. See Jeffrey Ding, "Deciphering China's AI Dream," Future of Humanity Institute, University of Oxford, 2018, https://www.fhi.ox.ac.uk/wp-content/uploads/Deciphering_Chinas_AI-Dream.pdf.

102. See, for example, "China's Digital Authoritarianism: Surveillance, Influence, and Political Control," US House of Representatives, Permanent Select Committee on Intelligence, committee hearing, May 16, 2019, https://docs.house.gov/Committee/Calendar/ByEvent.aspx?EventID=109462; Robert Morgus and Justin Sherman, "Authoritarians Are Exporting Surveillance Tech, and with It Their Vision for the Internet," Council on Foreign Relations, December 5, 2018, https://www.cfr.org/blog/authoritarians-are-exporting-surveillance-tech-and-it-their-vision-Internet; "Freedom on the Net 2018: The Rise of Digital Authoritarianism," October 30, 2018; and Paul Mozur, Jonah M. Kessel, and Melissa Chan, "Made in China, Exported to the World: The Surveillance State," New York Times, April 24, 2019, https://www.nytimes.com/2019/04/24/technology/ecuador-surveillance-cameras-police-government.html.

103. Joe Parkinson, Nicholas Bariyo, and Josh Chin, "Huawei Technicians Helped African Governments Spy on Political Opponents," Wall Street Journal, August 14, 2019, https://www.wsj.com/articles/huawei-technicians-helped-african-governments-spy-on-political-opponents-11565793017.

104. Elias Biryabarema, "Uganda's Cash-Strapped Cops Spend $126 Million on CCTV from Huawei," Reuters, August 16, 2019, https://www.reuters.com/article/us-uganda-crime-idUSKCN1V50RF.

105. Danielle Cave Thomas, Samantha Hoffman, Alex Joske, and Fergus Ryan, Elise, "Mapping China's Tech Giants," Australian Strategic Policy Institute, Issues Paper, Report No. 15/2019, https://www.aspi.org.au/report/mapping-chinas-tech-giants.

106. "Building a Safe Mauritius, the Inspiration for Heaven," Huawei, 2019, https://web.archive. org/web/20200210040539/https://e.huawei.com/topic/leading-new-ict-en/mauritius-safecity-case.html.

107. Sheena Greitens describes another example of Chinese government subsidies of a Huawei surveillance project in the Philippines: "During Xi's visit, the two countries signed 29 agreements, one of which established a 'Safe Philippines Project,' in which the Philippines' Department of the Interior and Local Government agreed to partner with Huawei and China International Telecommunication and Construction Corporation to construct a 12,000-camera surveillance system aimed at public safety and security. The deal set targets of a 15% crime reduction and 25% improvement in response time, and was financed primarily by a loan from China Eximbank (19.11 billion Philippine pesos, PHP, of the 20.31 billion PHP project, close to $400 million)." Sheena Chestnut Greitens, "Dealing with demand for China's global surveillance exports," Brookings Institution, April 2020, https:// www.brookings.edu/wp-content/uploads/2020/04/FP_20200428_china_surveillance_ greitens_v3.pdf.

108. Anna Fifield, "Bloodthirsty Like a Wolf: Inside the Military Style Discipline at China's Tech Titan Huawei," *Washington Post*, December 13, 2018, https://www.washingtonpost. com/world/asia_pacific/bloodthirsty-like-a-wolf-inside-the-military-style-discipline-at-chinas-tech-titan-huawei/2018/12/12/76055116-fd85-11e8-a17e-162b712e8fc2_story. html?noredirect=on&utm_term=.fca5427820cf.

109. The EU's former top trade official, Karel De Gucht, is on record observing: "They [Huawei] get subsidies. If you have a line of a couple of tens of billions with the bank that you can use at your discretion this is a huge subsidy, no?" Shawn Donnan and Christian Oliver, "EU Commissioner Attacks China's Telecoms Subsidies," *Financial Times*, March 27, 2014, https://www.ft.com/content/d6d0bcc6-b5cb-11e3-b40e-00144feabdc0. Likewise, a 2012 US congressional report from the House Intelligence Committee noted that Huawei reaps the "benefit of billions of dollars in Chinese government financing," and that both Huawei and ZTE "provide a wealth of opportunities for Chinese intelligence agencies to insert malicious hardware or software implants into critical telecommunications components and systems." "Investigative Report on the U.S. National Security Issues Posed by Chinese Telecommunications Companies Huawei and ZTE," US House of Representatives, Permanent Select Committee on Intelligence, October 8, 2012, https://republicans-intelligence.house.gov/sites/intelligence.house.gov/files/documents/huawei-zte%20investigative%20report%20(final).pdf, 3.

110. Max Chafkin and Joshua Brustein, "Why America Is So Scared of China's Biggest Tech Company," *Bloomberg Businessweek*, March 23, 2018, https://www.bloomberg.com/news/ features/2018-03-22/why-america-is-so-scared-of-china-s-biggest-tech-company.

111. Chafkin and Brustein, "Why America Is So Scared."

112. Zhang Lin, "Chinese Communist Party Needs to Curtail Its Presence in Private Businesses," *South China Morning Post*, November 25, 2018, https://www.scmp.com/economy/ china-economy/article/2174811/chinese-communist-party-needs-curtail-its-presence-private.

113. Arjun Kharpal, "Huawei CEO: No Matter My Communist Party Ties, I'll 'Definitely' Refuse If Beijing Wants Our Customers' Data," *CNBC*, January 15, 2019, https://www.cnbc.com/ 2019/01/15/huawei-ceo-we-would-refuse-a-chinese-government-request-for-user-data. html.

114. Paul Mozur, "China's Internet Controls Will Get Stricter, to Dismay of Foreign Business," *New York Times*, November 7, 2016, https://www.nytimes.com/2016/11/08/business/in-ternational/china-cyber-security-regulations.html.

115. Christopher Balding and Donald C. Clarke, "Who Owns Huawei?," SSRN Scholarly Paper, Rochester, NY: Social Science Research Network, April 17, 2019, https://papers.ssrn.com/ abstract=3372669.

116. Since I first published these findings, at least one country, Armenia, has decided not to pro-ceed with its safe city partnership with Huawei. Conversely, more information has emerged that makes it likely that Iran is receiving some assistance in this area from Chinese firms. Feldstein, "Digital Authoritarianism."

117. "Rankings—the World Economy," *The Economist—World in Figures*, 2020, https://worldinfigures.com/rankings/topic/8.

118. "Rankings—the World Economy," *The Economist—World in Figures*.

119. Mailyn Fidler, "African Union Bugged by China: Cyber Espionage as Evidence of Strategic Shifts," Council on Foreign Relations—Net Politics (blog), March 7, 2018, https://www.cfr.org/blog/african-union-bugged-china-cyber-espionage-evidence-strategic-shifts.

120. See "Yanbu: A Smart Industrial Oil Kingdom City—Huawei Publications," Huawei, 2019, https://e.huawei.com/us/publications/global/ict_insights/201708310903/manufacturing/201712061133; Sebastian Moss, "Google Cloud Continues to Grow, Is Coming to Saudi Arabia," *DCD*, April 24, 2018, https://www.datacenterdynamics.com/news/google-cloud-continues-to-grow-is-coming-to-saudi-arabia/; Rob Evans, "BAE 'Secretly Sold Mass Surveillance Technology to Repressive Regimes,'" *The Guardian*, June 14, 2017, https://www.theguardian.com/business/2017/jun/15/bae-mass-surveillance-technology-repressive-regimes; Triska Hamid, "NEC Profits from Middle East Cyber Fears," *The National*, December 10, 2013, https://www.thenational.ae/business/nec-profits-from-middle-east-cyber-fears-1.267420; and Alaa Shahine, Erik Schatzker, Vivian Nereim, and Glen Carey, "Saudis Are Talking to Amazon, Alibaba about New City, Prince Says," *Bloomberg*, October 26, 2017, https://www.bloomberg.com/news/articles/2017-10-26/saudis-are-talking-to-amazon-alibaba-over-new-city-prince-says.

121. "Addition of Certain Entities to the Entity List," *Federal Register*, October 9, 2019, https://www.federalregister.gov/documents/2019/10/09/2019-22210/addition-of-certain-entities-to-the-entity-list.

122. Jon Bateman and Lyu Jinghua, "What Is the U.S. Ban on TikTok and WeChat All About?," Carnegie Endowment for International Peace, August 25, 2020, https://carnegieendowment.org/2020/08/25/what-is-u.s.-ban-on-tiktok-and-wechat-all-about-pub-82566. See also Josh Fruhlinger, "The CIA Triad: Definition, Components and Examples," *CSO*, February 10, 2020, https://www.csoonline.com/article/3519908/the-cia-triad-definition-components-and-examples.html.

123. Bateman and Jinghua, "US Ban."

124. "On Artificial Intelligence—a European Approach to Excellence and Trust—White Paper," European Commission, February 19, 2020, https://ec.europa.eu/info/sites/info/files/commission-white-paper-artificial-intelligence-feb2020_en.pdf.

125. "DOD Adopts Ethical Principles for Artificial Intelligence," US Department of Defense, February 24, 2020, https://www.defense.gov/Newsroom/Releases/Release/Article/2091996/dod-adopts-ethical-principles-for-artificial-intelligence/.

126. Eileen Donahoe and Megan MacDuffee Metzger, "Artificial Intelligence and Human Rights," *Journal of Democracy* 30, no. 2 (2019): 116. Some experts, such as Frank Pasquale, the author of *The Block Box Society*, call for deeper reforms. Pasquale introduces the concept of "second wave" of algorithmic accountability, writing, "Just as this 'first wave' of algorithmic accountability research and activism has targeted existing systems, an emerging 'second wave' of algorithmic accountability has begun to address more structural concerns." For Pasquale, the big question for policymakers is whether certain systems, such as facial recognition, should be employed at all, rather than how to best ensure ethical or responsible use. Frank Pasquale, "The Second Wave of Algorithmic Accountability," LPE Project, November 25, 2019, https://lpeproject.org/blog/the-second-wave-of-algorithmic-accountability/.

127. See Feldstein, "Beware the Implications."

128. Shashank Bengali and David Pierson, "How Singapore Has Kept the Coronavirus under Control," *LA Times*, March 11, 2020, https://www.latimes.com/world-nation/story/2020-03-11/a-singaporeans-view-of-the-coronavirus-its-surprising-to-see-the-u-s-so-messed-up.

129. Allie Funk and Isabel Linzer, "How the Coronavirus Could Trigger a Backslide on Freedom around the World," *Washington Post*, March 16, 2020, https://www.washingtonpost.com/opinions/2020/03/16/how-coronavirus-could-trigger-backslide-freedom-around-world/; Sam Ball, "100,000 Cameras: Moscow Uses Facial Recognition to Enforce Quarantine," *France24*, March 24, 2020, https://www.france24.com/en/20200324-100-000-cameras-moscow-uses-facial-recognition-to-enforce-quarantine.

130. "Request for Proposal to Procure National Automated Facial Recognition System," National Crime Records Bureau, Ministry of Home Affairs, Government of India, 2020, http://ncrb. gov.in/TENDERS/AFRS/RFP_NAFRS.pdf.

131. See Daniel Brinks and Michael Coppedge, "Diffusion Is No Illusion: Neighbor Emulation in the Third Wave of Democracy," *Comparative Political Studies* 39, no. 4 (2006): 463–489.

132. Tom Simonite, "AI License Plate Readers Are Cheaper—So Drive Carefully," *Wired*, January 27, 2020, https://www.wired.com/story/ai-license-plate-readers-cheaper-drive-carefully/.

133. Shoshana Zuboff, *The Age of Surveillance Capitalism: The Fight for a Human Future at the New Frontier of Power* (New York: Profile Books, 2019).

8

Responding to Digital Repression

This book has sought to explain how authoritarian leaders wield digital technologies to advance their repressive objectives. But the intersection of politics and digital technology is not a one-way street in which repressive states always have the advantage. This domain also offers opportunities for democracies, civil society groups, and political activists to fight back against digital repression trends.[1] In this final chapter, I present ideas and solutions for how civil society and democracies can combat such repressive strategies.

Revisiting an earlier question provides a useful starting point: how is digital technology reshaping the balance of power between government and civil society? For states with highly developed coercive capacity, the emergence of formidable technological tools presents new opportunities to cement their power. As more and more citizens gravitate online, governments' have gained crucial advantages by honing their ability to track individuals' movements, snoop on their conversations, and obtain unprecedented insights into what dissidents and potential rivals may be thinking or planning. In some places, particularly China, the balance of power has clearly shifted. The possibility that civic activists will be able to reverse the CCP's governance consolidation is remote.

But China is fairly unique in this respect. Even in authoritarian states like Russia and Iran, their governments are keenly aware that the same tools they use to manipulate public opinion, tar opponents, and rig elections can easily be turned against them. This is why so many regimes are fearful (and frequently resort to violence) when mass demonstrations occur—particularly in light of the turmoil stemming from the Arab Spring protests. In several important ways, digital technology has corroded such states' prior advantages even while providing them with new repressive tools.

First, the state's information advantage has weakened. Thirty years ago, state media wielded real influence over what citizens saw and heard. In fact, one of the first principles to undertaking a successful coup was to occupy state television and radio broadcast stations in order to control the transition narrative. Such

The Rise of Digital Repression. Steven Feldstein, Oxford University Press (2021). © Oxford University Press.
DOI: 10.1093/oso/9780190057497.003.0008

advice seems archaic in the new information age. While governments can still dominate the airwaves, the emergence of alternative information sources has changed the dynamic.

Second, barriers to political mobilization have decreased. Social media has lessened collective action problems that previously had prevented masses of people from taking to the streets. Even as governments have begun monitoring and manipulating mainstream platforms (responding to the examples of Facebook and Twitter revolutions in the Middle East, Ukraine, and elsewhere), activists have innovated. They have embraced new messaging apps like Telegram or Signal that feature end-to-end encryption and are more difficult for state agents to monitor and manipulate. Just look at the difference in technologies wielded by Hong Kong protestors in 2019 compared to those of the 2014 umbrella movement (discussed in this chapter).

Third, there are more resources to support digital movements that challenge a state's power and more opportunities to activate transnational networks, as well as to get companies and democratic governments to push back against oppressive governments. A digital playbook has emerged. Activist organizations are sharing lessons learned.[2] They are setting up how-to workshops to provide tips about spreading protest hashtags, safeguarding communications from government intrusion, and determining if devices have been hacked. When governments lash out—when they shut down the Internet, acquire spyware to break into journalists' smartphones, or enact information controls to block access to websites and apps, for instance—their actions do not go unheeded. A constellation of actors immediately respond. Take Internet shutdowns. Netblocks and OONI are usually the first to sound the alarm and provide data measurements documenting that connectivity has been cut off. Groups like Access Now, Human Rights Watch, Privacy International, or Article 19 then circulate online petitions and policy briefs demanding that the offending government cease its actions. Lawsuits are readied that are designed to force telecoms to stop blocking Internet connectivity. And finally, democratic governments are lobbied so that they will raise concerns bilaterally or in multilateral forums to further pressure India, Iran, or Sudan to restore digital access.

In other words, the employment of digital tools in civic and political struggles is not one-sided. Civil society organizations possess many such tools with which they can combat state repression.

This chapter begins by discussing strategies civil society groups can use to raise the costs of repression associated with the dictator's digital dilemma. It then examines specific innovations activists can pursue to counter state repression. Turning to the private sector, I then discuss companies' roles and responsibilities in relation to digital repression. Finally, I review methods that local groups could potentially use to confront transnational support from technologically sophisticated authoritarian states like China and Russia and reflect on what changes the Covid-19 pandemic may bring to this domain.

Raising the Costs of Repression: Shifting the Dictator's Digital Dilemma

In Chapter 2, I introduced the concept of the dictator's digital dilemma, the problem faced by repressive leaders who seek to benefit from the economic gains and political advantages of a digital society—without sacrificing political control. I offered China as a leading example of a country that has at least temporarily solved its digital dilemma, but noted that China's model is not applicable to most other countries. Instead, other authoritarian states or hybrid regimes have pursued alternative strategies: regional shutdowns targeting certain populations (Cameroon, Ethiopia), Internet restrictions designed to maximize state control while mitigating economic harm (Thailand), or social manipulation and disinformation tactics that supplement or replace Internet controls altogether (the Philippines, Myanmar). These tactics have been effective; many states have reaped considerable economic benefits from digital technology without paying a price for suppressing digital freedoms.

But this needn't be the case.

A strategic question civil society groups and their democratic partners should consider is how to raise the cost of digital repression so that solving the dictator's digital dilemma becomes prohibitively expensive for governments. As Table 8.1 summarizes, a successful strategy incorporates four points of pressure: reputational costs, economic costs, political factors, and supply-side considerations. In many respects, these actions reflect existing strategies rights activists use to push back against repression generally. But existing strategies must be extended to cover the new domains of digitally repressive technologies and actions.

First, governments pay attention to actions that affect their reputations. States spend inordinate amounts of time and political capital protecting their standing and pushing back against public criticism. During my time serving as a diplomat in the State Department, I saw this dynamic play out time and again in a variety of international forums. The UN Human Rights Council (HRC) is a good case in point. Despite absorbing a heavy dose of criticism for allowing countries with egregious human rights records to serve as members (current membership includes notorious abusers such as Cameroon, Pakistan, Qatar, and Venezuela), the HRC's resolutions and authorized investigations against alleged human rights violations carry significant weight. Governments go out of their way to water down human rights condemnations or to block embarrassing votes

Table 8.1 **Pressure Points Related to the Dictator's Digital Dilemma**

	Pressure Points		
Reputational	*Economic*	*Political*	*Supply side*
Naming and shaming in international forums	Economic pressure campaigns	Raising public awareness about the repressive effects of digital instruments	Pressure campaigns against companies
Media strategies (traditional and social media)	Corporate boycotts		Collaborating with companies on technical solutions and antirepression tools
	Sanctions		
Citizen documentation of repression		Electoral challenges to incumbents	Government restrictions (e.g., export controls)

that would expose them to public censure. I recall several HRC votes that were nail-biters despite involving situation such as targeted violence in Burundi authorized by its president, mass imprisonments of protestors in Ethiopia, and constitutional manipulation in the Congo. Country delegations vigorously opposed these resolutions. Even with airtight evidence of human rights transgressions, the offending states pushed the Africa regional bloc to withhold support for the resolutions and threatened to obstruct future multilateral priorities. These situations demonstrate that even the proceedings of a secondary UN body matter greatly to scores of countries. Smaller countries are particularly sensitive to international disproval and are very willing to offer concessions in order to delay or reduce international censure.

Thus, a key point of leverage against digitally repressive governments is to use international forums like the HRC to raise the reputational costs of continued bad behavior. As countries perceive that the ongoing suppression of political freedoms is leading to an increase in international criticism, this shift may cause internal rethinking about whether the benefits of maintaining censorship controls or instigating Internet shutdowns is worth the price.

In addition to leveraging international forums, advocates can also make use of simple technological tools to spread awareness (and outrage) about government repression. States no longer enjoy a monopoly on information—save for a few closed regimes like North Korea. As the Pew Research Center details, around five billion people globally own mobile devices, half of which are smartphones outfitted with cameras.[3] This widespread access to mobile technology means that victims, observers, and even wrongdoers can document human rights violations and quickly disseminate them. Governments comprehend that their citizens will eventually learn about coercive actions that they have undertaken. In response, they use counterstrategies such as filtering information their populations can access (this requires substantial resources and technical sophistication to sustain), or employing disinformation-flooding techniques to drown out unfavorable news. These tactics can be effective, but they also have limitations. On-the-ground documentation of repressive acts (such as violent crackdowns against protestors in Sudan and Iran in 2019) are difficult to suppress and have a powerful impact when they are exposed. Civil society groups that have established networks of individuals who can capture evidence of government repression and then publicize it to the outside world can galvanize internal dissent against a regime and generate critical shifts of opinion at home and abroad.

Correspondingly, it is important for groups to implement media broadcast strategies—using mainstream outlets and social media platforms—that will cut through obfuscation and disinformation generated by governments. No matter how egregious a regime's actions appear, it can be challenging for groups to disseminate a message that the public perceives as credible and that citizens will share widely. Governments are highly sophisticated when it comes to promoting narratives to delegitimize civil society (e.g., accusing groups of being foreign funded or antipatriotic). But when advocates' messages do break through, the reputational effects can be significant.

In Ethiopia's case, I saw such a reputational strategy pay off in relation to the imprisonment of members of an online collective known as the Zone 9 bloggers. In 2014, the government arrested this group on terrorism charges. While the US government pressed the Ethiopians for months to drop the charges and release the prisoners, a public pressure campaign led by groups such as the Committee to Protect Journalists, Global Voices, the Electronic Frontier Foundation, and Human Rights Watch gained steam.[4] They circulated international petitions, organized public events, and reinforced their messaging on social media. By 2015, prosecutors dropped charges and the journalists were freed. There was never any significant doubt about the Zone 9 bloggers' innocence. They had no known linkages to terrorist groups; their arrests were purely symbolic and meant as a warning to other dissenters. As long as the international community stayed quiet, Ethiopian authorities could get away with the imprisonments: the political costs were minimal, and the accrued benefits were high. Once external reputational costs to the regime began to rise, however, this dynamic changed their internal calculus and led to the bloggers' releases.

Second, imposing economic costs on state repression also contributes to changes in behavior. Many successful transnational movements—such as the Responsible Mineral Initiative or the antisweatshop movement (both of which generated economic boycotts)—sparked reforms in countries where there was little incentive to change the status quo. Financial penalties working in tandem with reputational costs can have a powerful effect. For example, if human rights groups convince democratic member states to offer a UN resolution condemning on-line censorship in Egypt, this action may embarrass the regime, but it is unlikely to alter policy. However, if the resolution is reinforced by corporate boycotts, economic pressure campaigns, or even sanctions that cause governments and companies to refrain from doing business with the offending government until it alleviates digital restrictions, the collective pushback provides a lot more bite. Such situations directly address a key aspect of the digital dilemma, changing economic considerations and placing public support for the regime at risk.

As discussed in Chapter 4, the Thai public displayed far greater sensitivity to the perceived economic costs of the government's Internet control plan than outrage over reductions in political freedoms. When the government tried to establish a single Internet gateway to regulate all information coming in or out of the country, their actions generated a middle-class backlash—citizens were alarmed by the proposal's potential harm to the economy.[5] We should note, however, that a fine line exists between targeted economic actions intended to change specific behaviors—such as getting a government to withdraw a punitive cyber libel law used to persecute civil society—versus actions intended to bring systemic change, such as demanding an end to all government surveillance. The former represents a concrete step that governments can straightforwardly carry out; the latter represents an unattainable demand.

The third element involves imposing political costs on digitally repressive actions carried out by the regime. A key step is to raise public awareness about the repressive consequences of specific systems or functions that the regime is deploying. For example, in 2019, journalists disclosed that the Serbian government had partnered with Huawei to install a mass surveillance system powered by facial recognition in Belgrade that encompassed one thousand cameras in eight hundred locations throughout the city, as I mentioned in Chapter 7. The announcement came at an inauspicious moment—coinciding with months of political protests against populist president Aleksandar Vucic. As *AP News* noted, "Some protesters began having second thoughts about joining anti-government demonstrations in the Serbian capital."[6] There were reports that the police had leaked videos of individual protestors to pro-government outlets, which published their images and identities. Journalists even documented joint patrols undertaken with Chinese police officers in Belgrade, ostensibly to assist Chinese tourists visiting the city (although many ascribed darker purposes for this intimidating show of force).[7] As the public has become aware of this technology, concern has grown. The civil society group SHARE Foundation explains, "Hundreds of people have submitted freedom of information requests asking the Ministry of Interior about said cameras, while public officials made contradictory statements and withheld crucial information."[8] SHARE has joined with other oversight groups to publish a detailed brief laying out why the surveillance system violates Serbia's Law on

Personal Data Protection. The next step for these groups is to translate public backlash into political repercussions at the ballot box.

Similarly, in Uganda, the *Wall Street Journal* disclosed that authorities had purchased a facial recognition surveillance system from Huawei for $126 million.[9] Until journalists exposed the contract, there was zero public recognition about the existence of this technology, how the government planned to use it, or its intended purpose (in the same article, reporters uncovered that Huawei technicians helped the government spy on political opponents by breaking into social media accounts—establishing a clear link between government hacking and the state's repression agenda).[10] Ugandan opposition lawmakers have subsequently criticized the project for its lack of transparency and potential security vulnerabilities: "There appears to be a policy to hand over the country's entire communications infrastructure to the Chinese, . . . It's unwise given our concerns about spying and creating backdoor channels."[11] It is vital that civil society groups not only monitor Uganda's system for abuse, but that they also levy a political cost on the government for allocating scarce resources in order to acquire this tool. Possible outcomes include (1) the government rescinds its purchase of the system due to public backlash (bringing a victory against digital repression), (2) the government continues using the system but pays a political price at the ballot box, or (3) authorities continue employing the system but cancel plans to install additional networks—representing a partial win against the spread of digital repression in Uganda. Raising the political cost of digital repression through public campaigns and electoral challenges at the ballot box can cause governments to reconsider their digital repression agendas.

While the first three elements focus on demand side factors, the fourth element shifts attention to supply-side considerations. Here, the goal is to pressure technology platforms, manufacturers, and service providers to restrict capabilities provided to repressive governments.

One approach is for groups to directly pressure companies to reduce repressive uses of their technology. Facebook's actions in the Philippines illustrate that companies will take concrete steps to limit exploitation of their platforms if they receive enough negative attention. The general consensus, as Maria Ressa describes it, is that either through benign neglect or by deliberately overlooking rampant disinformation, Facebook facilitated Duterte's rise and "broke democracy" in the Philippines.[12] The company has belatedly responded as public outrage has grown; in 2019, Facebook removed two hundred pages, groups, and accounts for undertaking "coordinated inauthentic behavior." Among those penalized was Nic Gabunada, Duterte's online campaign manager.[13] Facebook has suggested that it may implement further removals. More recently in Brazil, Facebook, Google, and Twitter simultaneously removed posts that had been shared by President Jair Bolsonaro that included misinformation related to the coronavirus. Facebook stated that the contents of Bolsonaro's posts violated their rules against sharing harmful content.[14] This action represented one of the first times that the company had chosen to deviate from stated policies of "not fact-checking politicians," and to specifically take down posts linked to a sitting head of state.[15] Subsequently, Twitter and Facebook revamped their rules ahead of the 2020 US elections and began attaching warning labels to misleading posts coming from US president Donald Trump and his allies.[16]

An important takeaway is that countering government disinformation by pressuring tech companies—who are themselves sensitive to reputational damage—can reap considerable dividends. Conversely, governments recognize the gatekeeping function that Facebook plays and are willing to employ their own hardball tactics as well. In Vietnam, Reuters reported that state-owned telecoms took Facebook's servers offline for nearly two months to pressure the company to censor antigovernment comments. During that period, Facebook "became unusable at times." The company caved to government demands, stating that it had decided to "restrict access to content which it has deemed to be illegal."[17]

Social manipulation and disinformation are not the only relevant digital repression techniques that governments use. Yet the same strategy also applies with regard to spyware providers or telecoms carrying out Internet shutdowns. For instance, when revelations first emerged about Sandvine's deep packet inspection technology enabling Belarus authorities to selectively block websites in response to mass protests, the company initially defended its conduct and bizarrely claimed that Internet content didn't count as "a part of human rights."[18] As outrage grew, Sandvine quickly changed its tune. Less than a week later, the company announced it had terminated its end-user license agreement with the Belarusian government, adding that the company "takes human rights abuses very seriously."[19]

Similarly, digital rights groups have pursued an increasingly active litigation strategy against telecoms that enact Internet shutdowns. In countries ranging from India and Zimbabwe to Sudan and Pakistan, advocates have scored courtroom victories where judges have ordered telecoms to restore Internet service. In Sudan, for instance, Abdelazeem Hassan sued telecommunications company Zain, arguing that depriving individuals of Internet access violated their consumer rights. He prevailed in the case (although Zain only restored service to his personal devices, contending that he filed the lawsuit in his personal capacity).[20] Hassan then went back to court and sued MTN and Sudatel to restore Internet access as well. In the second ruling, the court ordered the restoration of all Internet services in Sudan, not just for Hassan's devices.[21]

A second supply-side approach is for groups to work directly with technology companies to implement engineering safeguards or technological fixes that will constrain *ex ante* autocratic exploitation of products. In 2019, for example,

WhatsApp began imposing message-forwarding restrictions to stop misinformation. At first, the company reduced the number of groups users could forward messages to from 256 to 20. Then WhatsApp lowered the number to 5. Research suggested that these changes were having a positive effect in slowing down bad information.[22] In April 2020, WhatsApp imposed even more stringent controls in response to alarming levels of coronavirus misinformation, stipulating that messages flagged as "highly forwarded"—sent through a chain comprised of at least five people—could now only be forwarded to a single person.[23]

As a result of these changes, not only has WhatsApp slowed the spread of bad information, but it has also deprived autocrats of a key tool used to reinforce their political narratives. It's worth noting that WhatsApp's decisions have not come without cost. Far-right commentators in places like Brazil, Spain, the United States, Hungary, and the Philippines have blasted the company for engaging in Internet censorship, proving that, as one tech company official put it, "the right thing to do is oftentimes contested."[24]

A third supply-side approach is for advocates to pressure democratic governments to put export controls in place that limit the sales of certain technologies to repressive regimes. Currently, there are few formal mechanisms that exist, in part due to the newness of this field. The most applicable framework is the Wassenaar Arrangement, consisting of forty-two developed economies that coordinate export controls related to conventional arms and dual-use technology.[25] While the group added targeted surveillance tools to its list of technologies that require additional controls in 2013, this is the extent to which digital instruments face any sort of regulation.[26] Moreover, because Wassenaar is nonbinding and lacks an enforcement mechanism, it has not been effective in restricting unlawful software surveillance. (As Kaye observes: "It is insufficient to say that a comprehensive system for control and use of targeted surveillance technologies is broken. It hardly exists.")[27] This suggests that if groups hope to convince governments to restrict the exportation of digital tools to repressive regimes, they must rely on advocacy and ad hoc arrangements.

One of the most prominent recent efforts—intended to penalize Chinese companies responsible for providing repressive technology in Xinjiang— has borne some fruit. On October 9, 2019, the US Commerce Department announced it had added twenty-eight Chinese government and commercial firms to its "entity list" for human rights violations related to the "repression, mass arbitrary detention, and high-technology surveillance" against minority groups in Xinjiang.[28] Included among the twenty-eight entrants are leading Chinese AI companies such as Hikvision, iFlytek, SenseTime, Megvii, Yitu, and Dahua. The financial implications are considerable. Companies on the list are restricted from acquiring certain sensitive technologies and components from US firms pending specific licenses that the US government must approve (a time-consuming and laborious process that can effectively serve as a de facto ban). High-profile partnerships with leading US universities have been cancelled, including a five-year venture between iFlyTek and the Massachusetts Institute of Technology.[29]

While some experts maintain that the United States had its own strategic motives for adding these companies to the list—including protecting US interests in AI—this announcement centered around major human rights violations in Xinjiang.[30] Without persistent advocacy, it is highly unlikely that the government would have moved this designation forward. These examples illustrate that imposing supply-side costs on digitally repressive regimes is an effective lever, particularly when implemented in conjunction with the other three elements.[31]

Some policymakers argue that leaning too heavily on supply-side measures to influence policy brings unintended consequences. When I was in government, a common refrain I heard was that restricting US exports to repressive regimes would simply cause countries to procure this equipment from authoritarian sources—such as from China or Russia. Officials claimed that it was preferable for US companies to supply this technology and influence recipient governments to use it responsibly rather than cede the market to the Chinese or Russians. They argued that end-use agreements were effective ways to ensure human rights compliance. In truth, such claims are specious—the evidence shows that no matter where such technology originates, it tends to enable bad outcomes when placed in the hands of repressive regimes (as Sandvine's technology in Belarus illustrates).

One exception relates to social media platforms: US and Chinese companies exhibit major differences with respect to human rights and civil liberties concerns. Chinese firms like WeChat or Weibo are essentially walled off from advocacy groups and immune to outside pressure on politically sensitive issues. Moreover, China's system of intermediate liability forces its Internet companies to implement a broad array of filtering and censorship. As researchers from the Citizen Lab write, "Any Internet company operating in China is subject to laws and regulations that hold companies legally responsible for content on their platforms. Companies are expected to invest in staff and filtering technologies to moderate content and stay in compliance with government regulations. Failure to comply can lead to fines or revocation of operating licenses."[32] Such regulation means that Chinese platforms facilitate two repressive techniques for the price of one: government disinformation with minimal restraints and extensive censorship subject to the whims of the Chinese state. In contrast, even though Facebook may have "broken democracy" in places like the Philippines, it is better positioned to make amends for its past decisions.

Deconstructing the dictator's digital dilemma and identifying relevant pressure points can yield tangible democratic benefits. The right strategy implemented in the right contexts can be an important means to counter digital repression tactics. These methods are most effective in small or medium-sized countries where leaders' consent to govern is premised on solid economic growth. Countries like Kenya, Uganda, Brazil, Serbia, the Philippines, Thailand, Malaysia, and Ecuador are prone to using digital repression techniques. They fluctuate between autocratic and democratic periods of rule, have publics that are sensitive to economic conditions, and possess just enough political competition to keep the ruling coalition on edge. In such countries, well-timed interventions can make a difference. In contrast, larger states with more consistent patterns of digital repression (China, Russia, Iran, Turkey) or highly autocratic smaller states (Tajikistan, Oman) are less susceptible to these strategies.

Pushing back against discrete aspects of digital repression (punitive laws, egregious surveillance methods, persecutions of specific individuals) is much easier than effecting systemic change. Such is the difference between advocating for the release of the Zone 9 bloggers in Ethiopia versus pressuring Egypt to end mass surveillance and widespread suppression of dissent. An effective strategy provides offramps for change. It proposes achievable steps to alleviate the worst effects of digital repression, but is cautious about making excessive demands that would undercut the whole bargain.

Grassroots Strategies for Civil Society

The ideas above provide a macro framework for how civil society groups can leverage distinct points of pressure to shift government behavior and deter digital repression. It's useful to apply another layer of analysis to examine innovative local approaches that activists can pursue to counter state repression strategies.

First, there is a large investigative gap when it comes to adequately scrutinizing digital projects implemented in individual countries. Governments are able to get away with abusive tactics in part because of widespread public ignorance about which tools intelligence agencies are acquiring and how they are using those instruments. The good news is that exposing government secrets and enhancing accountability no longer requires a highly resourced media sector or established journalistic corps. Digital technology has changed the rules of the game. More than ever, citizen activists are able to employ open-source intelligence (OSINT) to expose government wrongdoing, publicize its impact, and catalyze reform.

The organization Bellingcat illustrates the rapidly changing nature of the field. Bellingcat was founded in 2014 by Eliot Higgins, an unemployed British journalist who had gained attention for his meticulous open-source investigation of 2013 chemical weapons attacks authorized by the Syrian government.[33] Higgins initially funded the organization from a Kickstarter campaign, which listed two objectives: bring together reporters and activists who have transformed journalism through the use of open-source tools, and attract others to learn how to use these same tools and technologies.[34] The results have been impressive. Bellingcat's investigations of the 2014 downing of Malaysian airliner MH17— as well as the 2018 poisoning of Sergei Skripal (a former Russian spy) and his daughter in England by two Russian military intelligence officers—have received wide acclaim. The MH17 investigation illustrates how Bellingcat used a full range of open-source intelligence tools to put together a convincing case against Russian authorities. The Bellingcat team combed through social media for relevant image postings during the time frame of the airline crash. As images were identified, the team geolocated crash sites using Google Earth. This process allowed Bellingcat to construct a course for a specific Russian missile launcher— which was used to shoot down the airplane—by placing images on a map corresponding with the time for each sighting.[35]

Bellingcat's success is reflected in a trove of similar investigative efforts.[36] As Muhammad Idrees Ahmad writes, other examples include "the New York Times's investigations into the killing of the Gaza medic Rouzan al-Najjar and identifying the killers of Jamal Khashoggi; Africa Eye's work on the Cameroon killings; DFRLab's work on Twitter trolls; and UC Berkeley Human Rights Center's contribution to Reuters's Pulitzer Prize-winning investigation in Myanmar."[37] These investigations typically rely on detailed online forensics work using social media platforms that connect inputs from multiple analytic sources.

Consequently, there are many opportunities for civil society groups to learn the basics of how to conduct open-source investigations. Bellingcat itself sponsors "how to" trainings for citizen activists.[38] The company also publishes detailed guides tailored for specific issues, such as monitoring Covid-19 economic slowdowns using open-source data, or methods to probe coronavirus disinformation.[39]

Second, civic organizations should consider making emergent learning strategies a central feature of how they operate. In Chapter 6, I discussed how Jawar Mohammed used emergent strategies to circumvent Ethiopian information controls and sustain a broad-based protest movement. Such strategies are especially relevant for groups that confront governments with superior capabilities under conditions they are unable to control. The only way for organizations to remedy this imbalance is to pursue adaptive and creative measures. As researcher Ionut C. Popescu describes it, emergent strategies are a process of "navigating through an unpredictable world by improvisation and continuous learning." While "deliberate" strategies focus on control and ensuring that managerial directives are fulfilled, "emergent strategy emphasizes learning—coming to understand through the taking of actions what those intentions should be in the first place."[40]

What are the strategy's implications in practice? For civil society groups, defining a common organizational vision is important (e.g., promoting free and open discourse on the Internet protected from government interference), but must be balanced with abundant flexibility so that individual members can best determine how to advance the vision. Applicable elements include the following:

- Recursive approaches that emphasize experimentation, learning, and iteration, removing the distinction between planning and implementation
- Flexible, horizontal structures that empower individuals to innovate as needed and as circumstances dictate
- Efficient actions undertaken without the benefit of substantial resources relative to a well-equipped opponent
- Leveraging peer-to-peer communications via social media and messaging apps, enabling new innovations to bubble up[41]

As it turns out, terrorist organizations like al-Qaeda and the Islamic State have been particularly successful in adopting these approaches. For example, Daveed Gartenstein-Ross and Madeleine Blackman describe how the Islamic State pioneered a "virtual planner model" to manage lone attackers:

> In this model, operatives who are part of ISIL's external operations division coordinate attacks online with supporters across the globe. Most of these supporters have never personally met the ISIL operatives they are conspiring with. Most of ISIL's prominent virtual planners appear to be based in the group's "caliphate" in Syria and Iraq, in large part due to proximity and access to ISIL's top leadership. But since the main equipment that virtual planners require is an Internet connection and good encryption, they could theoretically operate from other geographic locations. Being geographically dispersed carries greater risk of detection, but particularly as ISIL continues to decline as a territorial entity, the emergence of prominent virtual planners operating from outside the Syria-Iraq theater is likely.[42]

What made this plan so innovative is that the Islamic State had to use online techniques to overcome a major practical constraint: not being able to manage its operatives face to face. Not only did virtual planning solve the problem at hand, but iterations arguably made it more difficult for intelligence agencies to keep track of ISIL's movements and deter potential attacks. Thus, initial constraints can spur tactical iterations that may be more effective in the long run.

On a more positive note, Jawar's tactics in Ethiopia encapsulate how grassroots strategies deployed by civil society groups against government adversaries can have a significant impact. Jawar admits that "I really didn't know anything. I just posted on Facebook. I said, what is going to happen to us?" He goes on, "It would be a lie for me to think that I knew [what to do] about that. . . . People started dropping ideas. I said, okay, that's good. You have to be creative about it." Jawar mentions how the government set up mass internment camps to break the protests: "They [Ethiopian authorities] would take 20,000 people from one part of Oromia and put them in one military camp. That is networking. I created this training manual where they train, where they share experiences. They spent two months and they get out, well networked! And after that they don't even need Internet. They can just call each other."[43] This situation provides a textbook application of recursion theory. Rather than fall victim to the government's mass imprisonment program, the protestors turned the tables on their captors. They leveraged the fact that so many of them were detained in the same place and used that situation to their advantage. They emerged from prison considerably stronger and more cohesive.

In 2019, Hong Kong protesters provided another illustration of how iterative tactics helped level the playing field against a much stronger opponent. A critical tool was their incorporation of social media and messaging applications to facilitate collective decision-making while retaining an anonymous leadership structure. One of the most useful apps was LIHKG, which is similar to the online forum Reddit. It allows users to post new threads with various calls to action; the most popular threads were then pushed to the top. As one demonstrator described the app to the *New York Times,* "People will give responses or click push to make that specific thread a hot one. We can predict what's going to happen by which posts are the hottest."[44] This process allowed protestors to quickly move from place to place without substantial advance planning. For supporters providing aid and supplies, LIHKG enabled them to accurately determine where protestors were amassing.

The messaging app Telegram has also proven indispensable to protest movements worldwide (in fact several media outlets have begun hyping the platform's effect as the "Telegram Revolution").[45] Several design details offer unique benefits: one feature allows users to delete messages or set them to self-destruct after a certain period of time (meaning that if security agents force protestors to unlock their phones, they won't reveal their friends). A second design advantage is the ability to form groups with large memberships—which can number in the hundreds of thousands. This has not only facilitated rapid amplification of information, but when integrated with built-in polls, it has provided an easy way to collectively decide whether a mass of protestors should confront oncoming police or disperse.[46] Finally, it is much harder for governments to selectively block Telegram without shutting down the Internet completely. As Belarusian authorities learned in 2020, they could stop users from accessing

Twitter, Instagram, WhatsApp, or Facebook, but they were unable to take Telegram offline as well. (Telegram founder Pavel Durov tweeted: "We enabled our anti-censorship tools in Belarus so that Telegram remained available for most users there. However, the connection is still very unstable as Internet is at times shut off completely in the country.")[47] A defining legacy of these protests is their showcasing of new tactics and adaptive strategies to fight back against powerful state apparatuses.

Private Sector Responsibilities

Whether they desire it or not, companies increasingly stand at the forefront of digital rights struggles. Even corporations that seemingly have little to do with tech find themselves embroiled in digital controversy. The National Basketball Association's (NBA) dispute in China in October 2019 highlights how tensions can quickly erupt when two incongruous political systems—one open and permissive, the other closed and controlled—collide with one another. It began with a simple tweet: Daryl Morey, the Houston Rockets' general manager, sent out a short message of support for the Hong Kong protestors, commenting, "Fight for freedom, stand with Hong Kong." In rapid succession, the Chinese consulate in Houston denounced Morey, as did the Rockets' team owner. Morey deleted the offending tweet, but the controversy spiraled. The Chinese Basketball Association announced it was dropping its partnership with the NBA. Morey apologized and the NBA released a statement describing the tweet as "regrettable." The Rockets even considered firing Morey to appease the Chinese. Then US politicians got involved and the backlash began. Senator Ted Cruz, Texas representative Beto O'Rourke, and former HUD secretary Julián Castro—among many others—lambasted the NBA for caving to the Chinese.[48] Cruz released a blistering tweet: "We're better than this; human rights shouldn't be for sale & the NBA shouldn't be assisting Chinese communist censorship."[49] After many months, the situation slowly eased. But the economic damage to the NBA was significant. Sources estimate that Morey's tweet cost the NBA between $150 and $200 million in lost revenue.[50]

The larger lesson from the NBA-China controversy is that companies can be poor vehicles to carry messages concerning human rights and democracy. As researchers Jason Miklian, John E. Katsos, and Benedicte Bull write, "Even when companies want to support global democracy and human rights, they find it much harder than anticipated and trap themselves in unenviable choices."[51] At the same time, it is impossible to disaggregate corporate services and products from culture and politics. The NBA is part of the American zeitgeist, which markets itself as a force for individualism and free expression. It can't simply walk away from these values when the politics get too dicey. The takeaway from Miklian, Katsos, and Bull is that while companies "can't force social change upon recalcitrant regimes by themselves," if they focus on tangible goals and "act in parallel with governments that also support human rights and democracy," they're less likely to find themselves in hot water and their efforts will probably have greater effect.

A strong normative framework supported by a plurality of democracies can give cover to corporations to pursue policies responsive to democracy and human rights interests. This relationship applies widely, from social media platforms to firms that supply software or hardware used for surveillance. The more democracies set clear guidelines about acceptable corporate behavior, the better those standards are in providing a clear basis for companies to take difficult steps that may be incompatible with the political demands from nondemocratic states.

In general, companies inherently oriented to protect privacy or free expression face fewer complications. In the case of a company like Telegram, there can be strong alignment. Its messaging application is known for using very strong encryption and for protecting private communications no matter the content (it is used by protestors for democracy as well as by affiliates of the Islamic State and al-Qaeda). During the Hong Kong protests, Chinese authorities became increasingly frustrated by organizers' reliance on Telegram to coordinate demonstrations. In June 2019, the Chinese government launched a massive DDoS attack to disable the service.[52] Subsequently, concerns arose that Chinese and Hong Kong security forces might be exploiting a Telegram function that automatically matches usernames with phone numbers in a particular group. As Reuters reported, this would mean that authorities only needed to "request the owners of the phone numbers from the local telecom service in order to learn the users' true identities."[53] In response, Telegram changed its policies so that users can now "cloak" their phone numbers in order to prevent police monitoring. This situation clearly illustrates how a company that is primarily geared toward protecting user privacy is willing to take continuous proactive measures to thwart government actions.

But Telegram is an exception. Most companies have less clear-cut privacy or human rights interests. Facebook, for example, continually finds itself in hot water for making negligent if not reckless decisions enabling governments to propagate repressive content. A host of damaging revelations have emerged detailing how the company's leaders either ignored or failed to act against a variety of abuses. Sophie Zhang, a former data scientist at Facebook, detailed in a lengthy memo in September 2020 how the company deliberately overlooked mass harassment by Azerbaijan's ruling party against opposition parties, Covid-19 manipulation in Spain and later the United States, coordinated inauthentic activity in Bolivia and Ecuador, and "inauthentic scripted activity" around Ukraine's 2019 elections.[54]

In such cases, it is critical for democratic governments to take strong regulatory positions. When corporations debate whether to adhere to local laws or conform to international human rights norms, the degree to which democratic governments are willing to hold companies accountable to concrete standards can tip the scales when it comes to how strenuously a company will incorporate human rights protections in its operations. Norwegian telecommunications firm Telenor is a useful example. While Norway enjoys some of the strongest privacy protections in the world, Telenor runs mobile service providers in countries with high levels of repression, such as Pakistan, Bangladesh, Myanmar, and Thailand. The company faces constant pressure from those governments, rooted in local laws, to provide communications data, enact content restrictions, allow lawful interceptions, or enact Internet shutdowns.[55] As one international telecom executive told me, it is risky for companies to push back against government requests, no matter how problematic: "Noncompliance to authority requests can lead to risks to personnel security, license revocations, or forced shutdowns. There are also other reasons why it is not always helpful to alienate the authorities and to push back too hard."[56] Unless there is equivalent pressure coming from democracies to conform to human rights laws, the balance often tilts in favor of repressive governments. It is simpler for companies to accede to Thailand's or Pakistan's content restriction demands than to risk their ire. Companies have few incentives to shift their policies without counterbalancing pressure from democracies.

Some companies may not explicitly intend to violate human rights principles but employ business models that are reliant on exploiting user privacy and data. Scholars such as Tim Wu, Shoshanna Zuboff, Zeynep Tufekci, Ron Deibert, David Kaye, Tarleton Gillespie, Siva Vaidhyanathan, and Peter Pomerantsev have laid out public critiques of US social media platforms that employ sophisticated algorithms that purposefully peddle extreme content in order to keep users glued to their feeds (and then monetize this captured attention through microtargeted ads).[57] In other words, companies have their own revenue-seeking agendas that directly or indirectly enable a massive disinformation ecosystem to flourish.

When it comes to the role of algorithms in advancing disinformation and hateful speech, most of the focus has been on content moderation—to what extent algorithms are able to identify and suppress posts that break community standards and cross the line when it comes to spreading bad or false information. But an equally important and more troubling use of algorithms by social media companies is "content shaping" algorithms. Companies use algorithms such as Facebook's news feed, Twitter's timeline, and YouTube's recommendation engine to determine what users will see, what posts are queued up in their recommended viewing, and essentially which posts will "go viral."[58]

Thus, while many tech platforms argue that they are simply allowing users to say what they would like and are choosing not to interfere with their free speech rights, this is a mischaracterization. What platforms are really doing is quietly putting their fingers on the scale to determine which posts will be viewed and read by millions of individuals. At present, the overriding incentive that Facebook and other platforms follow is revenue and profit, even if the content in question spreads misinformation. In most cases, if the content increases user engagement, then the algorithm will bump up its visibility. Facebook's internal research reinforces this view. As the *Wall Street Journal* has reported, Facebook officials found that "64 percent of all extremist group joins are due to our recommendation tools" and that the majority came from Facebook's Groups You Should Join and Discover algorithms. They concluded that "our recommendation systems grow the problem."[59] It is not accurate for platforms to claim they are pursuing a hands-off policy regarding content; their algorithms are shaping what users see and react to.

While platforms have implemented some technical fixes in response to public outcries, these tend to be patchwork solutions whose effectiveness erodes over time. YouTube's "watch-next" algorithm is a good illustration. Of the more than one billion hours users spend watching videos on YouTube, its recommendations are responsible for 70 percent of watched content.[60] In January 2019, YouTube tweaked its algorithm to reduce its recommendations of conspiratorial videos. Initial reductions were significant—resulting in a 70 percent reduction in viewership of these clips. Eventually though, the proportion of conspiratorial recommendations crept up. As of February 2020, recommendations for such videos are now only 40 percent less common than when YouTube first announced its changes.[61] Without complementary policy shifts, engineering solutions on their own are unlikely to solve bad information problems and may bring diminishing effectiveness over time.

Because social media so profoundly affects political discourse and electoral outcomes, it follows that public officials should have more consistent input into policies that considerably impact the public domain.[62] As it stands, governments have delegated full responsibility for these decisions to private actors (who have a fiduciary duty to their shareholders). This is publicly irresponsible. As Pomerantsev asks in his book *This Is Not Propaganda*: "Could we even be empowered to take a stake in the decision-making process through which information all around us becomes shaped, with public input into the Internet companies who currently lord over how we perceive the world in darkness?"[63]

One proposal would be for regulators to mandate that companies provide a higher level of what David Kaye terms "decisional transparency"—disclosing why they make certain content decisions and what are the decision-making factors behind content-shaping algorithms and ad-targeting systems that determine who can pay to influence these algorithms.[64] While most social media platforms publish semi-annual transparency reports that provide country-by-country aggregated data about government takedown requests and demands for user data, these reports provide minimal information about why companies deny or agree to certain requests, the basis for their decisions, how they apply platform rules (e.g., Facebook's "community standards"), and how users can appeal certain decisions.

Regulators could also require platforms to conduct more systematic human rights due diligence in order to understand the social impact of their algorithms and targeted advertising strategies. At present, many companies claim they are upholding human rights principles or "do no harm" approaches without providing specific evidence of such actions. Companies should come up with quantifiable methods for assessing the impact of their products. For certain political events in which there are known disinformation risks, such as elections, platforms could even consider time-bound bans against political ads or promoted political content (this could be similar to French media rules that prohibit election coverage forty-four hours prior to every presidential and legislative election). Regardless of what mix of approaches regulators decide to pursue, it will be an improvement over an existing system of self-regulation that is clearly broken.

Some experts, such as danah boyd, head of Data & Society, have floated transforming Facebook, YouTube, Twitter, and Instagram into public utilities.[65] A more pragmatic option would be to set up co-regulation systems such as public-private oversight councils to influence aspects of platforms' governance.[66] There are many forms this could take; Article 19 has released a detailed consultation paper laying out possible solutions.[67] One of the most vexing issues is balancing legitimate concerns with how social media companies currently moderate content with proposals that lean too far in the opposite direction— giving governments a larger say in determining permissible content and potentially opening the door to censorship. As these ideas develop, it is important to keep the following principles in mind:

- Ensure that any regulatory structure reflects international standards of freedom of expression.
- Train technologists and engineers on the human rights implications of their products and instruct on international best practices for preventing abuse.
- Promote decentralized decision-making to appropriately reflect local contexts, and give local civil society advocates and users direct roles in shaping company policies.

- Incorporate a multistakeholder approach.
- Obtain participation and support from public authorities, but ensure this does not threaten the independence of the regulatory body.
- Emphasize transparency principles and tie them to effective remedies for individual users.

While social media companies receive the majority of negative attention for abuses linked to their products, just as concerning are private sector surveillance companies, which sell software intended to penetrate private communications and compromise personal information. Industry representatives claim that their technology is designed for legitimate law enforcement purposes only—to extract information to counter terrorist activities or to combat illicit criminal conduct. In reality, their most loyal clients are a who's who of repressive regimes, from Saudi Arabia and the UAE to Venezuela and Pakistan. As UN special rapporteur David Kaye notes, "Companies appear to be operating without constraint. . . . The private surveillance industry is a free-for-all."[68] Unsurprisingly, transparency in this sector is nonexistent. Experts have obtained most of their understanding about how these firms operate from leaked documents or detailed forensics studies linked to their products.

A starting point would be for democratic governments to require surveillance companies to publish annual transparency reports that included the following information: what human rights due diligence standards were implemented for sales to prospective clients, whether the firm enacted end-use agreements for their products and steps taken to monitor compliance, and actions taken by the firm when human rights violations linked to their products were disclosed.[69] Democracies could also require companies to include technical safeguards such as shutoff or claw-back provisions when there are documented abuses, firewalling products to prevent unauthorized law enforcement or intelligence agency access, limiting the duration of data records that are kept, or integrating data anonymization in algorithms.

Confronting Chinese and Russian Exports of Digital Repression Technology

The fundamental challenge associated with Chinese and Russian exports of digital repression technology and services is that there is a booming demand in autocratic countries for these tools. As data in Chapter 3 revealed, autocratic countries possess lower digital capacity than their actual rates of enacting digital repression. The implications are that countries should either adopt lower-capacity strategies to support their repressive agendas—such as implementing Internet shutdowns and locking up online users posting prohibited content—or they should seek to make up their capacity gaps through external suppliers. At present, companies based both in democracies and in autocracies provide powerful instruments to repressive regimes. In each of the case studies documented in this book, regimes in Thailand, the Philippines, and Ethiopia sourced from Chinese companies, but also from US, Israeli, and European firms. One way to constrain the technology spigot would be to put in place stricter controls for how companies in democracies do business. This would entail everything from instituting mandatory human rights due diligence requirements to drawing up blacklists of human rights-violating governments, which would be restricted from accessing certain capabilities (perhaps paralleling the spirit of the "Leahy Law," which prohibits arms sales to foreign security forces where there is credible information implicating a unit in gross violations of human rights).[70]

The problem with enacting restrictions on a broad array of digital technology is that because of the dual-use nature of this equipment, a policy intended to block surveillance or censorship could unintentionally harm unrelated parts of a country's economy. For example, a serious criticism of the Wassenaar Arrangement (in addition to its lack of enforcement capacity) is that it uses an overly broad definition of intrusion tools, thereby including legitimate programs such as endpoint security systems.[71] Moreover, a valid argument can be made that limiting the provision of US or European technology would simply open the door for greater market share by unscrupulous Chinese and Russian companies. Thus, a set of policies must do more than simply restrict US sales of equipment to bad regimes. It also needs to change the behavior of Chinese and Russian firms. How might democracies accomplish this task? Four strategies are worth considering.

First, it is possible to raise public awareness in specific countries about repressive uses of technology provided by Chinese or Russian firms. One way to increase public knowledge is to ramp up support for digital rights organizations, media outlets, and citizen activists to conduct investigations, highlight concerning issues, and spur national conversations about the negative impact of authoritarian-supplied technology. Another method is to leverage parliamentary oversight and investigations. Even in countries with highly centralized executives, legislatures have a limited ability to authorize independent investigations. To the extent that more and more parliaments decide to scrutinize how Chinese and Russian technology is being used in their countries, this will provide additional pressure. Citizens should also push their governments to provide heightened transparency regarding state use of Chinese and Russian technology, economic ties between the government and Chinese or Russian firms, and costs for specific digital projects (e.g., Uganda's government should be mandatorily required to disclose the cost of its Huawei safe city project rather than have this come to light following journalist inquiries).

Second, democratic countries must compete more vigorously against Chinese state-backed firms for crucial technology projects, such as building 5G networks. These systems will provide the foundation for critical network infrastructure, giving the underlying manufacturer a huge advantage. While the United States recognizes the risk posed by Huawei or ZTE dominating next-generation production of these systems, it has not satisfactorily addressed the principal advantage that Huawei or ZTE offers—considerably lower cost. In my conversation with Secretary Eliseo Rio, who was in charge of the Philippines' ICT department at the time, he indicated that 80 percent of the country's equipment consists of Huawei products: "We bid it out [network overhaul] and Huawei won. The next bidder, Ericsson, cost nearly twice that. And the quality of Huawei is just as good."[72] It is by design that Chinese firms are able to outbid their rivals. Chinese financial institutions provide conditional loans to countries that restrict tech purchases to Chinese companies. Chinese corporations are likewise subsidized at a heavy rate by the CCP; by one estimate, more than 3 percent of China's annual output goes toward direct and indirect business subsidies.[73] This cash infusion gives Chinese firms significant advantages vis-à-vis foreign rivals. They can access discounted loans from state banks, obtain low-cost inputs (cheap land, electricity), and receive direct cash infusions from government investment funds. This strategy enables firms like Huawei, ZTE, Hikvision, and others to consistently underbid rivals for digital technology contracts—from installing 5G networks and establishing data centers to building smart cities.

While it is neither practical nor desirable for democracies to compete head-on with China on subsidies, there are intermediate steps that democratic governments could take to level the playing field for their companies. For instance, in relation to high priority technologies, the US government could establish a digital technology infrastructure fund that would provide financial resources in the form of matching grants or low-interest loans to make US corporate bids more price competitive. Such a fund would offer several enhancements over existing mechanisms: upgrade the amount of resources available to companies, focus specifically on digital technology projects and reprioritize evaluation criteria so that strategic considerations become more important factors for determining whether financing is provided, and streamline lengthy administrative processes that US companies currently must undergo to obtain support.

Third, in addition to applying country-level strategies to counteract Chinese and Russian tech encroachment, democracies should continue to invest in building international norms and establishing standards that reflect democratic models of digital governance. Chinese and Russian delegations are making an all-out push to promote a cyber sovereignty vision of Internet governance that entitles governments to determine their own Internet regulations and standards, even if these directives contravene international law.[74] The censorship and surveillance implications are ominous. Thus, it behooves policymakers in the United States and Europe to actively push back against such efforts. This not only means blocking worrisome proposals from Chinese and Russian delegations, but also offering a compelling, democratic vision of digital governance, and a common language for setting policy, that will protect security while advancing human rights and political freedoms.

AI systems illustrate how pursuing a human rights-oriented approach in a nascent field can significantly improve outcomes. How online platforms use automated techniques, the role AI plays in displaying or moderating content, the degree to which companies access personal data to inform and refine algorithms, and to what extent racial and gender discrimination affects AI systems' inputs and outputs are outstanding questions. Individuals such as David Kaye, and groups such as Global Partners Digital, advocate for making human rights a central consideration when assessing AI impact.[75] For obvious reasons, such an approach would be anathema to Chinese or Russian interests. But this represents an opportunity for democracies to shape a fledgling technology and advance common principles to mitigate risks to human rights from AI systems, incentivize rights-respecting practice in public institutions and private entities, and incorporate grievance and remediation procedures for potential violations.

Fourth, export restrictions can be effective instruments when deployed sparingly and in a precise and consistent manner. In general, instituting blanket export controls linked to Chinese technology companies is not prudent either for the United States or other democracies. The economic consequences are damaging and there are real questions about whether such actions are actually effective. But that doesn't mean that Chinese companies directly linked to repressive activities shouldn't face penalties. This is why the US government's inclusion of twenty-eight Chinese companies on its Entity List for human rights violations committed in Xinjiang is symbolically important (even if imperfectly implemented). The United States and other like-minded democracies should seek concrete ways to build on such efforts. For example, the extent to which democracies act in concert when implementing these restrictions (e.g., coordinating US Entity List inclusions with parallel EU restrictions) leads to a better prospect of changing egregious Chinese behavior. In addition, democracies should consider imposing targeted penalties, such as visa bans or financial sanctions, on individuals responsible for carrying out digital repression activities (in the waning days of the Trump administration, the US government imposed sanctions on a slate of Chinese officials responsible for carrying out human rights violations in Xinjiang, as well as against Chinese officials authorizing the Hong Kong crackdown).[76] The United States already has an applicable law on the books, the Global Magnitsky Act, that is an appropriate vehicle for such sanctions. There is no reason the United States could not expand the law's use to include perpetrators of serious forms of digital repression. Democracies could also consider investment legislation that would restrict the provision of financing to Chinese or Russian technology companies that are building documented tools for repression. Finally, democratic governments should also scrutinize the conduct of their own companies. In the United States, for example, firms such as Sandvine, Thermo Fisher, and even Intel and Nvidia, have provided advanced technology to authoritarian governments to accomplish surveillance and censorship objectives.[77] Lawmakers would be wise to scrutinize the existing rules and determine how to tighten the export of intrusive US technology to repressive regimes.

Covid-19 Implications of Digital Technology

The Covid-19 pandemic has caused governments around the world to turn to digital tools to fight its spread.[78] While there are legitimate epidemiological reasons for states to deploy contact-tracing apps or use location-monitoring technology to track viral outbreaks, there are increasing reports of privacy violations and human rights abuses.[79] As governments deploy new tools in enlarged numbers, there has not been a corresponding debate to define protections, safeguards, and standards of use. Even more troubling, many governments have refused to set limits regarding how long they intend to use these tools. It is conceivable that for countries like Russia, China, Singapore, or Turkey, enhanced surveillance is here to stay.

This problem is not limited to autocratic governments; certain democracies have also embraced mass surveillance measures.[80] At least in democracies, there is some comfort that emergency measures will comply with basic human rights guarantees and include rudimentary safeguards to protect citizen data from public exposure and illegitimate use. But blanket authorizations of emergency powers taken in times of crisis can persist over time and lead to permanent erosions of political freedoms (as evidenced by the sharp curtailments of civil liberties in the United States after the 9/11 attacks, or elevated securitization measures imposed in Europe in response to Islamic State suicide attacks between 2014 and 2017). As the pandemic continues to rage, four emerging patterns are relevant.

First, the coronavirus has accelerated existing methods of repression. Governments already prone to using digital surveillance and censorship or peddling disinformation—such as China, Saudi Arabia, Turkey, and Thailand—have precipitously moved ahead to deploy facial recognition surveillance, contact-tracing apps, and social media monitoring, along with information controls.[81] However, there appears to be a gap between a broader array of countries carrying out general democratic violations linked to the pandemic (e.g., constraints on media freedom, legislative restrictions, abusive security enforcement), and a narrower set of countries specifically using digital repression tactics in response to Covid-19.

Second, states have become central in gathering and providing information. As analysts Nathan Brown, Intissar Fakir, and Yasmine Farouk write, "Technology may facilitate daily lives under lockdown, but it also aids in the official control of information."[82] The enduring implications of this shift are yet unclear, but they present flashing warning signs for citizens living in autocracies.

Third, arrests for violations of "fake news" laws linked to the pandemic are on the rise along with a corresponding increase in official disinformation on Covid-19. Governments are persecuting scores of individuals for spreading fake news about the coronavirus in countries such as Myanmar, Cambodia, Kenya, Uganda, China, and Morocco. Targets for arrest are often civil society activists and political opposition figures.[83] At the same time, many governments have ramped up their own disinformation efforts. The V-Dem project identifies 25 countries that have propagated government disinformation on Covid-19 along the following lines: *denialist* (authorities discredit or reject reports of Covid-19 outbreaks in their territories), *anti-science* (officials downplay Covid-19 dangers while disputing accepted medical recommendations), and *curist* (leaders promote unfounded treatments for the virus).[84]

Fourth, governments are implementing new surveillance techniques in a rushed and ad hoc manner. States have not yet established clear rules of the road regarding safeguards, data privacy protections, or remediations for abuse, even while launching intrusive health-monitoring applications. For example, Amnesty International revealed that contact-tracing apps launched by Bahrain, Kuwait, and Norway contained serious privacy and security risks for users. All three apps employ "live or near-live tracking of users' locations" through recurrent uploading of GPS data to a centralized server, signifying that state authorities can track an individual's movements at all times.[85] Norway subsequently retracted the app after Amnesty International published its report. Authorities in Bahrain and Kuwait continue to deploy their contact-tracing apps.

Concluding Thoughts

When it comes to the impact of digital technology on governance and repression, I am neither a techno-optimist nor a techno-pessimist. I do not believe there is anything inherently good or bad about the political impact wrought by technology. I remain inspired by spontaneous grassroots efforts that against all odds have deposed dictators in places like Tunisia, Sudan, and Burkina Faso. I have also been dismayed by the sinister effects of omniscient surveillance deployed in Xinjiang, state-sponsored hacking used by Saudi Arabia and the UAE to target independent journalists, and sophisticated disinformation campaigns in the Philippines and Russia. I foresee an unremitting struggle between specific regimes that will find clever ways to exploit technology to enhance their political control, and other places where digitally savvy civic activists will deploy innovative tactics to circumvent authoritarian governments, break the state's monopoly on information, and mobilize protests.

I am most concerned about the repressive impact of technology in contexts where the state already exercises an inordinate degree of control over people's daily lives—such as in China or Russia. There are few checks to limit how the Chinese state deploys increasingly intrusive technology and there are vast incentives for the CCP to invest heavily in surveillance and censorship methods. It has sufficient resources and capacity to sustain digital systems of control for the foreseeable future. Similarly, in Russia, a predatory regime distrustful of the broader public and possessing sufficient resources to maintain an elaborate monitoring and tracking apparatus doesn't auger well for Russians' future political freedoms—even when Putin departs from the scene.

I am also worried about contested states and illiberal regimes undergoing autocratization, where savvy leaders are using digital technology to enhance their political agendas and solidify control of formerly democratic systems. The Philippines, India, Hungary, and Sri Lanka, to name a few, all evince signs of serious political deterioration. While technology has not been the main impetus for democratic backsliding, it nonetheless plays an important role in assisting the rapid dismantlement of political rights. The Covid-19 epidemic adds another unexpected twist to digital repression trends. In the spirit of never letting a good crisis go to waste, many autocratic leaders (or autocratically inclined leaders) are shamelessly exploiting the pandemic. It just so happens that some of the most effective ways to combat the spread of the virus are through the deployment of digital surveillance technology that has the secondary effect of allowing governments to closely track their citizens' movements and communications. While I don't believe that the coronavirus's impact on repression will be politically transformative, the pandemic may considerably accelerate repressive trends by providing a suitable rationale for leaders to authorize new powers for the organs of the state.

I believe liberal democracies have faltered the most when it comes to delivering a compelling vision for how to balance innovative uses of technology while ensuring appropriate protections. In this respect, the United States has been particularly neglectful. The government has turned a blind eye while many Silicon Valley behemoths have violated public trust, run roughshod over privacy standards, and monetized personal data for commercial exploitation. Internationally, the United States continues to trot out repeated lines about supporting a free and open Internet. Meanwhile, it takes few steps to confront the viral dissemination of disinformation or to address the spread of polarized information polluted by extremist and conspiratorial narratives. The government's failure to adopt basic regulatory approaches to promote a healthy online ecosystem is a disservice to principles of free expression. Free speech does not mean that those who shout the loudest and spout the most polarizing rhetoric are the only ones who should be heard.

For democracies, solving the digital repression puzzle begins at home. Liberal democratic governments are obligated to ensure that privacy is safeguarded from corporate surveillance interests as well as from state intrusion. Freedom of speech must be protected, not only from prior constraints linked to the state, but also from disinformation agents who are weaponizing discourse to promote their agendas. And finally, economic competition must be reinvigorated through strengthened antitrust enforcement that allows new innovations to flourish and prevents oligopolistic accumulations of power by a small group of powerful companies.

Can we turn this state of affairs around?

In my conversation with *Rappler* head Maria Ressa, I asked her what steps democracies need to take to push back against the digital repression challenge. She responded, "Think about what happened post–World War II. There was Bretton Woods. There was NATO. There was the UN Declaration of Human Rights. These are the kinds of things we need now." She concluded, "Is this a fantasy?"[86]

Whatever the mechanism, the crucial question is this: Can democracies empower civic activists to reverse global digital repression trends while summoning requisite political will to undertake painfully needed reforms at home?

I believe this is a struggle and a story that is far from finished. Technology doesn't stand still. It exists in a constant state of iteration and advancement. This means that while digital technology has fueled a shift toward autocratization, I am certain that circumstances will change many times over in the future.

Notes

1. Portions of this chapter derive from previously published material by the author, including Steven Feldstein, "Testimony—Hearing on China's Strategic Aims in Africa," US-China Economic and Security Review Commission, May 8, 2020, https://www.uscc.gov/hearings/chinas-strategic-aims-africa; Feldstein, "Beware the Implications."

2. A good illustration of their enhanced organizing power is reflected in the numerous digital rights conferences and convenings that occur throughout the year, such as RightsCon (sponsored by Access Now) and the Internet Freedom Festival.

3. Laura Silver, "Smartphone Ownership Is Growing Rapidly around the World, but Not Always Equally," Pew Research Center, February 5, 2019, https://www.pewresearch.org/global/2019/02/05/smartphone-ownership-is-growing-rapidly-around-the-world-but-not-always-equally/.

4. See, for example, "Campaign to Free Ethiopia's Zone9 Bloggers," GlobalVoices Advox, 2020, https://advox.globalvoices.org/campaigns-research/behind-bars-in-ethiopia-campaign-to-free-the-zone9-bloggers/.

5. Janjira Sombatpoonsiri, "Growing Cyber Activism in Thailand," Carnegie Endowment for International Peace, 2017, https://carnegieendowment.org/2017/08/14/growing-cyber-activism-in-thailand-pub-72804.

6. Dusan Stojanovic, "Chinese Snooping Tech Spreads to Nations Vulnerable to Abuse," *AP News*, October 17, 2019, https://apnews.com/9fd1c38594444d44acfe25ef5f7d6ba0.

7. Stojanovic, "Chinese Snooping Tech Spreads."

8. "Serbia: Unlawful Facial Recognition Video Surveillance in Belgrade," SHARE Foundation, December 4, 2019, https://edri.org/serbia-unlawful-facial-recognition-video-surveillance-in-belgrade/.

9. Biryabarema, "Uganda's Cash-Strapped Cops."

10. Joe Parkinson, Nicholas Bariyo, and Josh Chin, "Huawei Technicians Helped African Governments Spy on Political Opponents," *Wall Street Journal*, August 15, 2019, https://www.wsj.com/articles/huawei-technicians-helped-african-governments-spy-on-political-opponents-11565793017.

11. Parkinson, Bariyo, and Chin, "Huawei Technicians."

12. Alexandra Stevenson, "Soldiers in Facebook's War on Fake News Are Feeling Overrun," *New York Times*, October 9, 2019, https://www.nytimes.com/2018/10/09/business/facebook-philippines-rappler-fake-news.html.

13. "Removing Coordinated Inauthentic Behavior from the Philippines," Facebook, March 28, 2019, https://about.fb.com/news/2019/03/cib-from-the-philippines/.

14. Kurt Wagner, "Facebook, Twitter, YouTube Remove Posts from Bolsonaro," *Bloomberg*, March 30, 2020, https://www.bloomberg.com/news/articles/2020-03-31/facebook-twitter-pull-misleading-posts-from-brazil-s-bolsonaro.

15. Josh Constine, "Facebook, Twitter, YouTube Remove Posts from Bolsonaro," *Techcrunch*, March 30, 2020, https://techcrunch.com/2020/03/30/facebook-removes-bolsonaro-video/.

16. Abby Ohlheiser, "Twitter Fact-Checks a Misleading Trump Tweet for the First Time," *MIT Technology Review*, May 26, 2020, https://www.technologyreview.com/2020/05/26/1002274/twitter-fact-checks-trump-mail-in-voting-tweet/.

17. James Pearson, "Exclusive: Facebook Agreed to Censor Posts after Vietnam Slowed Traffic—Sources," *Reuters*, April 21, 2020, https://www.reuters.com/article/us-vietnam-facebook-exclusive/exclusive-facebook-agreed-to-censor-posts-after-vietnam-slowed-traffic-sources-idUSKCN2232JX.

18. Ryan Gallagher, "U.S. Company Faces Backlash after Belarus Uses Its Tech to Block Internet," *Bloomberg*, September 11, 2020, https://www.bloomberg.com/news/articles/2020-09-11/sandvine-use-to-block-belarus-internet-rankles-staff-lawmakers?sref=QmOxnLFz.

19. Ryan Gallagher, "Francisco-Backed Sandvine Nixes Belarus Deal, Citing Abuses," *Bloomberg*, September 15, 2020, https://www.bloomberg.com/news/articles/2020-09-15/sandvine-says-it-will-no-longer-sell-its-products-in-belarus?sref=QmOxnLFz. Digital rights groups also initiated a pressure campaign against cybersecurity outfit NSO Group to limit the spread of its hacking tools that were used by repressive governments to target journalists, civil society activists, and political opponents. They have pursued a multipronged approach that includes publicly urging NSO Group's new private equity owner, London-based Novalpina Capital, to clamp down on abuses associated with NSO Group's products. Activists have also coordinated with WhatsApp to sue NSO Group in US federal court for harms linked to its hacking tools. Whether these actions will ultimately change NSO Group's behavior remains

to be seen, but at a minimum the company faces heightened public scrutiny, limiting its present and future client base. Sean Lyngaas, "Rights Groups Probe Investments in NSO Group's Private Equity Firm," *Cyberscoop*, May 29, 2019, https://www.cyberscoop.com/nso-group-novalpina-capital-pension-groups-investment/; Erik Manukyan, "Summary: WhatsApp Suit against NSO Group," *Lawfare*, November 7, 2019, https://www.lawfareblog.com/summary-whatsapp-suit-against-nso-group.

20. "Sudan Crisis: Internet Restored—but Only for Lawyer," *BBC*, June 24, 2019, https://www.bbc.com/news/world-africa-48744853.

21. "Judges Raise the Gavel to #KeepItOn around the World," Access Now, September 23, 2019, https://www.accessnow.org/judges-raise-the-gavel-to-keepiton-around-the-world/.

22. Angela Chen, "Limiting Message Forwarding on WhatsApp Helped Slow Disinformation," *MIT Technology Review*, September 26, 2019, https://www.technologyreview.com/2019/09/26/434/whatsapp-disinformation-message-forwarding-politics-technology-brazil-india-election/.

23. Casey Newton, "WhatsApp Puts New Limits on the Forwarding of Viral Messages," *The Verge*, April 7, 2020, https://www.theverge.com/2020/4/7/21211371/whatsapp-message-forwarding-limits-misinformation-coronavirus-india.

24. Author interview with a tech company official, April 27, 2020.

25. See Feldstein, "Can a U.N. Report Help Rein in Surveillance."

26. Garrett Hinck, "Wassenaar Export Controls on Surveillance Tools: New Exemptions for Vulnerability Research," *Lawfare*, January 5, 2018, https://www.lawfareblog.com/wassenaar-export-controls-surveillance-tools-new-exemptions-vulnerability-research.

27. Kaye, "Report of the Special Rapporteur."

28. "Addition of Certain Entities to the Entity List," U.S. Federal Register, October 9, 2019, https://www.federalregister.gov/documents/2019/10/09/2019-22210/addition-of-certain-entities-to-the-entity-list.

29. Will Knight, "MIT Cuts Ties with a Chinese AI Firm amid Human Rights Concerns," *Wired*, April 21, 2020, https://www.wired.com/story/mit-cuts-ties-chinese-ai-firm-human-rights/.

30. William A. Carter and William Crumpler, "Understanding the Entities Listing in the Context of U.S.-China AI Competition," CSIS, October 15, 2019, https://www.csis.org/analysis/understanding-entities-listing-context-us-china-ai-competition.

31. Similarly, in November 2020, the EU agreed to new export rules that governing the granting of licenses. It adds new controls for cyber surveillance tools and other dual use products contributing to human rights violations. "Dual use goods: Parliament and EU ministers agree on new EU export rules," European Parliament—News, November 9, 2020, https://www.europarl.europa.eu/news/en/press-room/20201105IPR90915/dual-use-goods-parliament-and-eu-ministers-agree-on-new-eu-export-rules.

32. Lotus Ruan et al., "One App, Two Systems: How WeChat Uses One Censorship Policy in China and Another Internationally," Citizen Lab, November 30, 2016, https://citizenlab.ca/2016/11/wechat-china-censorship-one-app-two-systems/.

33. Higgins was cited in a Human Rights Watch report on chemical weapons attacks in Ghouta, Syria, which helped establish government culpability. See "Attacks on Ghouta: Analysis of Alleged Use of Chemical Weapons in Syria," Human Rights Watch, September 10, 2013, https://www.hrw.org/report/2013/09/10/attacks-ghouta/analysis-alleged-use-chemical-weapons-syria.

34. "Brown Moses Announces Bellingcat—Open Source Investigations for All," Brown Moses (blog), July 1, 2014, https://brown-moses.blogspot.com/2014/07/brown-moses-announces-bellingcat-open.html.

35. Muhammad Idrees Ahmad, "Bellingcat and How Open Source Reinvented Investigative Journalism," *New York Review of Books*, June 10, 2019, https://www.nybooks.com/daily/2019/06/10/bellingcat-and-how-open-source-reinvented-investigative-journalism/.

36. Some efforts predate Bellingcat, such as the site 38 North (https://www.38north.org/), which provides analysis using street-level and satellite imagery of North Korea.

37. Ahmad, "Bellingcat."

38. Ned Beauman, "How to Conduct an Open-Source Investigation, According to the Founder of Bellingcat," *New Yorker*, August 30, 2018, https://www.newyorker.com/culture/culture-desk/how-to-conduct-an-open-source-investigation-according-to-the-founder-of-bellingcat.

39. See, for example, Charlotte Godart, "COVID-19: Monitoring the Global Slowdown," Bellingcat, April 10, 2020, https://www.bellingcat.com/news/2020/04/10/covid-19-monitoring-the-global-slowdown/; Natalia Antonova, "Investigating Coronavirus Fakes and Disinfo? Here Are Some Tools for You," Bellingcat, March 27, 2020, https://www.bellingcat.com/resources/2020/03/27/investigating-coronavirus-fakes-and-disinfo-here-are-some-tools-for-you/.

40. Ionut C. Popescu, "Grand Strategy vs. Emergent Strategy in the Conduct of Foreign Policy," *Journal of Strategic Studies* 41, no. 3 (2018): 446.

41. The Boston Consulting Group (BCG) has invested considerable resources in developing an in-depth curriculum focused on enhancing adaptive strategies for organizations. It defines three "R's" that are essential for surviving in an unpredictable environment: readiness (anticipating relevant trends affecting the organization), responsiveness (agilely confronting challenges as they arise), and resilience (ability to withstand obstacles and maintain organization cohesion). But BCG emphasizes that a fourth "R"—recursion—is perhaps the most important element. Recursion emphasizes experimentation, learning, iteration, and "modulation based on experience." It removes the distinction between planning and implementation, "since successful strategies emerge from practice rather than from analysis and design." Martin Reeves et al., "Adaptive Advantage," BCG, January 20, 2010, https://www.bcg.com/publications/2010/strategy-business-unit-adaptive-advantage.aspx.

42. Daveed Gartenstein-Ross and Madeleine Blackman, "ISIL's Virtual Planners: A Critical Terrorist Innovation," *War on the Rocks*, January 4, 2017, https://warontherocks.com/2017/01/isils-virtual-planners-a-critical-terrorist-innovation/.

43. Gartenstein-Ross and Blackman, "ISIL's Virtual Planners."

44. K. K. Rebecca Lai and Jin Wu, "Protesters in Hong Kong Have Changed Their Playbook. Here's How," *New York Times*, July 4, 2019, https://www.nytimes.com/interactive/2019/06/28/world/asia/hong-kong-protests.html.

45. Daria Litvinova, "'Telegram Revolution': App Helps Drive Belarus Protests," *AP*, August 21, 2020, https://apnews.com/823180da2b402f6a1dc9fbd76a6f476b.

46. Maciej Ceglowski, "Observations on Technology Use in Hong Kong Protests," remarks on the situation in Hong Kong at the Stanford Internet Observatory E2E Encryption Workshop, September 12, 2019, https://idlewords.com/talks/hk_stanford.html.

47. Pavel Durov, Twitter post, August 10, 2020, https://twitter.com/durov/status/1292912756233048064.

48. Matthew Yglesias, "The Raging Controversy over the NBA, China, and the Hong Kong Protests, Explained," *Vox*, October 7, 2019, https://www.vox.com/2019/10/7/20902700/daryl-morey-tweet-china-nba-hong-kong.

49. Ted Cruz, "tweet message," October 6, 2019, 8:16 p.m., https://twitter.com/tedcruz/status/1181030466247417861?lang=en.

50. Adrian Wojnarowski and Bobby Marks, "Sources: NBA Set to Release Revised 2020–21 Salary and Luxury Tax Projections," *ESPN*, January 29, 2020, https://www.espn.com/nba/story/_/id/28596920/sources-nba-set-release-revised-2020-21-salary-luxury-tax-projections.

51. Jason Miklian, John E. Katsos, and Benedicte Bull, "China's Conflict with the NBA Shows Why Companies Can't Force Social Change by Themselves," *Washington Post*, October 13, 2019, https://www.washingtonpost.com/politics/2019/10/13/chinas-conflict-with-nba-shows-why-companies-cant-force-social-change-by-themselves/.

52. Pavel Durvo, "tweet message," June 12, 2019, 4:54 p.m., https://twitter.com/durov/status/1138942773430804480.

53. Joel Schectman, "Exclusive: Messaging App Telegram Moves to Protect Identity of Hong Kong Protesters," *Reuters*, August 30, 2019, https://www.reuters.com/article/us-hongkong-telegram-exclusive/exclusive-messaging-app-telegram-moves-to-protect-identity-of-hong-kong-protesters-idUSKCN1VK2NI.

54. Craig Silverman, Ryan Mac, and Pranav Dixit, "'I Have Blood on My Hands;: A Whistleblower Says Facebook Ignored Global Political Manipulation," *Buzzfeed News*, September 14, 2020, https://www.buzzfeednews.com/article/craigsilverman/facebook-ignore-political-manipulation-whistleblower-memo.

55. See "Authority Requests Disclosure Report," Telenor Group, 2018, https://www.telenor.com/wp-content/uploads/2019/03/Telenor-Authority-request-report-2018.pdf.

56. Author interview with an international telecommunications official, July 9, 2019.
57. See for example, Tim Wu, *The Attention Merchants: The Epic Scramble to Get Inside Our Heads* (New York: Vintage Books, 2016); Ronald J. Deibert, "The Road to Digital Unfreedom: Three Painful Truths about Social Media," *Journal of Democracy* 30, no. 1 (2019): 25–39; Shoshana Zuboff, *The Age of Surveillance Capitalism: The Fight for a Human Future at the New Frontier of Power* (New York: Profile Books, 2019); Kaye, *Speech Police*; Tarleton Gillespie, *Custodians of the Internet: Platforms, Content Moderation, and the Hidden Decisions That Shape Social Media* (New Haven, CT: Yale University Press, 2018); Zeynep Tufekci, *Twitter and Tear Gas: The Power and Fragility of Networked Protest* (New Haven, CT: Yale University Press, 2017); Vaidhyanathan, *Antisocial Media*; Pomerantsev, *This Is Not Propaganda*.
58. Nathalie Maréchal and Ellery Roberts Biddle, "It's Not Just the Content, It's the Business Model: Democracy's Online Speech Challenge," New America—Ranking Digital Rights, March 17, 2020, https://www.newamerica.org/oti/reports/its-not-just-content-its-business-model/.
59. Jeff Horwitz and Deepa Seetharaman, "Facebook Executives Shut Down Efforts to Make the Site Less Divisive," *Wall Street Journal*, May 26, 2020, https://www.wsj.com/articles/facebook-knows-it-encourages-division-top-executives-nixed-solutions-11590507499?campaign_id=158.
60. Charlotte Jee, "YouTube Has Nearly Halved the Number of Conspiracy Theory Videos It Recommends," *MIT Technology Review*, March 3, 2020, https://www.technologyreview.com/2020/03/03/905565/youtube-halved-conspiracy-theory-videos-recommends/. There is some debate about the extent to which algorithms drive viewing patterns. A November 2020 study of YouTube concluded that recommendation algorithms led "only a fraction" of users to view far-right videos. Instead, most views originated from cross-platform traffic. The researchers also found consecutive sessions of video viewership showed no greater trend towards larger consumption of extreme content (a further indication about the dampened impact of recommendation algorithms). It is worth noting that this is a single study—yet to be peer reviewed—analyzing one particular type of content (extreme rightwing videos on YouTube), but it does reveal basic limitations to our current understanding about the dissemination of disinformation. Homa Hosseinmardi, Amir Ghasemian, Aaron Clauset, David M. Rothschild, Markus Mobius, and Duncan J. Watts, "Evaluating the scale, growth, and origins of right-wing echo chambers on YouTube," *arXiv preprint arXiv:2011.12843* (2020).
61. Marc Faddoul, Guillaume Chaslot, and Hany Farid, "A Longitudinal Analysis of YouTube's Promotion of Conspiracy Videos," *arXiv* preprint arXiv:2003.03318 (2020).
62. One thorny issue to guard against would be the removal of intermediate liability protection for social media companies. In the United States, Section 230 of the 1996 Communications Decency Act protects companies from responsibility for content posted by users. While there is growing public frustration with pervasive levels of misinformation and disinformation, removing the liability shield would likely have the perverse effect of increasing corporate surveillance to ensure user content conforms to legal requirements, and potentially instigating overcompliance (and de facto censorship) as platforms take down any speech that would expose them to liability. At the same time, the current system has left platforms unaccountable for egregious content and communications. An alternative could be for policymakers to consider adopting a "quid pro quo benefit." In exchange for being shielded from liability, platforms would be compelled to fulfill certain public interest obligations related to transparency, accountability, or ensuring their algorithms do not skew toward extreme or violent content. See Guy Rolnik et al., "Protecting Journalism in the Age of Digital Platforms," George J. Stigler Center for the Study of the Economy and the State, University of Chicago Booth School of Business, July 1, 2019, https://research.chicagobooth.edu/-/media/research/stigler/pdfs/media---report.pdf; Steven Feldstein, "How to tackle Europe's digital democracy challenges," Carnegie Endowment for International Peace, October 15, 2020, https://carnegieendowment.org/2020/10/15/how-to-tackle-europe-s-digital-democracy-challenges-pub-82960.
63. Pomerantsev, *This Is Not Propaganda*, 187.
64. Kaye, *Speech Police*, 121–22.

65. See danah boyd, "Facebook Is a Utility; Utilities Get Regulated," *Apophenia*, May 15, 2010, https://www.zephoria.org/thoughts/archives/2010/05/15/facebook-is-a-utility-utilities-get-regulated.html.

66. Facebook has taken fledgling steps in this regard. In November 2018, responding to numerous scandals regarding its content moderation practices, Zuckerberg announced the creation of an independent oversight board that would make binding decisions about whether to restore removed content and would explain its reasons for doing so. While this is a positive step, it leaves many concerns unaddressed. For one, the number of cases taken up by the body, which has been compared to a "supreme court" for content moderation, will be minuscule. More importantly, key parts of its operations will not be eligible for review. This includes " content posted through marketplace, fundraisers, Facebook dating, messages, and spam" or pertaining to services such as WhatsApp, Facebook Messenger, or Instagram. It is also unclear whether the board's decisions will have precedential effect and generate structural changes— such as modifying algorithmic content filtering. Finally, the board isn't mandated to address the proliferation of social manipulation and disinformation occurring on the platform. See "A Blueprint for Content Governance and Enforcement," Facebook, November 15, 2018, https://www.facebook.com/notes/mark-zuckerberg/a-blueprint-for-content-governance-and-enforcement/10156443129621634/?hc_location=ufi.

67. "The Social Media Councils: Consultation Paper," Article 19, June 2019, https://www.article19.org/wp-content/uploads/2019/06/A19-SMC-Consultation-paper-2019-v05.pdf.

68. "UN Expert Calls for Immediate Moratorium on the Sale, Transfer and Use of Surveillance Tools," United Nations Office of the High Commissioner on Human Rights, June 25, 2019, https://www.ohchr.org/EN/NewsEvents/Pages/DisplayNews.aspx?NewsID=24736.

69. For a more detailed list of potential questions surveillance firms should be obligated to disclose, see https://www.accessnow.org/open-letter-to-novalpina-capital/.

70. "Leahy Law Fact Sheet," US Department of State, January 22, 2019, https://www.state.gov/key-topics-bureau-of-democracy-human-rights-and-labor/human-rights/leahy-law-fact-sheet/.

71. Hinck, "Wassenaar Export Controls."

72. Eliseo Rio (acting secretary, Department of Information and Communications Technology), interview with the author, May 21, 2019.

73. David J. Lynch, "Initial U.S.-China Trade Deal Has Major Hole: Beijing's Massive Business Subsidies," *Washington Post*, December 31, 2019, https://www.washingtonpost.com/business/economy/initial-us-china-trade-deal-has-major-hole-beijings-massive-business-subsidies/2019/12/30/f4de4d14-22a3-11ea-86f3-3b5019d451db_story.html.

74. Many experts contend that China is leveraging forums like the International Telecommunication Union (ITU), a specialized agency of the United Nations, to push an alternative digital vision. At an ITU meeting in September 2019, for example, a large Chinese delegation that included Huawei representatives proposed establishing a "New IP" (Internet protocol) to replace the existing version. New IP would feature a "top-to-bottom design" and would potentially permit Internet service providers, many of which are state-owned, to have "control and oversight of every device connected to the network and be able to monitor and gate individual access." Madhumita Murgia and Anna Gross, "Inside China's Controversial Mission to Reinvent the Internet," *Financial Times*, March 27, 2020, https://www.ft.com/content/ba94c2bc-6e27-11ea-9bca-bf503995cd6f; Hascall Sharp, "Discussion Paper: An Analysis of the 'New IP' Proposal to the ITU-T," Internet Society, April 24, 2020, https://www.Internetsociety.org/resources/doc/2020/discussion-paper-an-analysis-of-the-new-ip-proposal-to-the-itu-t/.

75. David Kaye, "Report of the Special Rapporteur to the General Assembly on AI and Its Impact on Freedom of Opinion and Expression," UN A/73/348, August 29, 2018, https://undocs.org/A/73/348. See also Charles Bradley, Richard Wingfield, and Megan Metzger, "National Artificial Intelligence Strategies and Human Rights: A Review," Global Partners Digital, April 2020, https://www.gp-digital.org/wp-content/uploads/2020/04/National-Artifical-Intelligence-Strategies-and-Human-Rights%E2%80%94A-Review_April2020.pdf.

76. Demetri Sevastopulo and Christian Shepherd, "US sanctions top Chinese officials over Xinjiang detentions," *Financial Times*, July 10, 2020, https://www.ft.com/content/

c7c70bb0-00df-4a23-9126-d44ac4c99f02; Austin Ramzy and Tiffany May, "U.S. Imposes Sanctions on Chinese Officials Over Hong Kong Crackdown," *New York Times*, December 16, 2020, https://www.nytimes.com/2020/12/08/world/asia/hong-kong-china-us-sanctions. html.

77. Paul Mozur and Don Clark, "China's Surveillance State Sucks Up Data. U.S. Tech Is Key to Sorting It," *New York Times*, November 24, 2020, https://www.nytimes.com/2020/11/22/ technology/china-intel-nvidia-xinjiang.html.

78. See Steven Feldstein, "What Democracy Will Fall Next?," *Foreign Policy*, May 7, 2020, https:// foreignpolicy.com/2020/05/07/democracy-pandemic-coronavirus-hungary-populism/.

79. Several researchers and rights groups have compiled useful trackers to provide a global snapshot of digital measures countries are taking in response to COVID-19. See, for example, Woodhams, "COVID-19 Digital Rights Tracker"; "Tracking the Global Response to COVID-19," Privacy International, April 26, 2020, https://www.privacyinternational.org/examples/ tracking-global-response-covid-19.

80. Joshua Mitnick, "Better Health through Mass Surveillance," *Foreign Policy*, March 16, 2020, https://foreignpolicy.com/2020/03/16/israel-coronavirus-mass-surveillance-pandemic/.

81. Kareem Fahim, Min Joo Kim, and Steve Hendrix, "Cellphone Monitoring Is Spreading with the Coronavirus. So Is an Uneasy Tolerance of Surveillance," *Washington Post*, May 2, 2020, https://www.washingtonpost.com/world/cellphone-monitoring-is-spreading-with-the-coronavirus-so-is-an-uneasy-tolerance-of-surveillance/2020/05/02/56f14466-7b55-11ea-a311-adb1344719a9_story.html.

82. Nathan J. Brown, Intissar Fakir, and Yasmine Farouk, "Here to Stay?" Carnegie Endowment for International Peace, *Diwan*, April 22, 2020, https://carnegie-mec.org/diwan/81611.

83. In Niger, for example, authorities arrested prominent journalist Kaka Touda for his reporting on the virus. His arrest stemmed from a complaint from the General Reference Hospital alleging that Touda's posts about a potential coronavirus case was a threat to public order. Authorities have charged Touda under Niger's 2019 cybercrime law.
    "Journalist Kaka Touda Mamane Goni Arrested in Niger over COVID-19 Report," Committee to Protect Journalists, March 24, 2020, https://cpj.org/2020/03/journalist-kaka-touda-mamane-goni-arrested-in-nige.php.

84. Anna Lührmann, Jean Lachapelle, Sandra Grahn, and Amanda B. Edgell, "Pandemic Backsliding: Democracy and Disinformation Seven Months into the Covid-19 Pandemic," V-Dem Institute, 2020, https://www.v-dem.net/media/filer_public/37/de/37defb66-9457-4eeb-887a-f0c168dc4365/v-dem_policybrief-25_201002_v2.pdf.

85. "Bahrain, Kuwait and Norway Contact Tracing Apps a Danger for Privacy," Amnesty International, June 16, 2020, https://www.amnesty.org/en/latest/news/2020/06/bahrain-kuwait-norway-contact-tracing-apps-danger-for-privacy/.

86. Maria Ressa (cofounder, *Rappler*), interview with the author, August 27, 2019.

Appendix 1

Table A.1 **Digital Repression Index, 2019 Data**

Country	Region	Digital repression index	Digital repression capacity index	V-Dem electoral democracy score	V-Dem regime type	Social media penetration (2020)	Government social media monitoring	Government censorship filtering	Government social media censorship	Government disinformation	Political party disinformation	Government Internet shutdowns	Government blocking of social media	Arrests of online users
Afghanistan	SCA	0.324	-0.798	0.347	EA	0.094	-0.051	-0.13	0.41	0.034	0.192	0.715	0.517	0.781
Albania	EUR	-0.293	0.081	0.481	EA	0.49	0.318	0.13	-0.666	0.140	-0.008	-0.628	-1.348	-1.008
Algeria	MENA	1.369	0.622	0.3	EA	0.51	1.093	1.625	1.565	0.766	0.620	1.434	1.605	1.336
Angola	AFR	-0.081	0.283	0.386	EA	0.068	0.007	0.045	-1.477	0.011	0.122	0.515	-0.222	-0.294
Argentina	WHA	-1.147	-0.144	0.812	ED	0.76	-0.575	-1.662	-1.519	-0.850	-0.207	-1.435	-1.517	-1.396
Armenia	EUR	-0.870	0.026	0.805	EA	0.51	-0.618	-1.251	-1.428	-0.245	0.170	-1.417	-1.415	-1.166
Australia	EAP	-0.940	0.153	0.838	LD	0.71	-0.550	-1.596	-1.218	-0.286	-0.173	-1.262	-1.348	-1.576
Austria	EUR	-1.126	-0.151	0.809	LD	0.5	-0.520	-1.888	-1.709	-0.560	0.089	-1.309	-1.446	-2.153
Azerbaijan	EUR	1.204	1.134	0.206	EA	0.37	0.639	2.196	1.165	1.080	0.437	1.084	0.538	1.699
Bahrain	MENA	1.913	0.920	0.118	CA	0.84	1.475	2.691	1.268	1.924	1.483	2.166	0.618	2.738
Bangladesh	SCA	1.006	1.307	0.279	EA	0.22	0.457	1.01	1.898	0.260	0.259	1.596	0.98	1.639
Barbados	WHA	-1.133	-0.808	0.822	LD	0.66	-0.499	-1.51	-1.023	-1.262	-0.765	-1.369	-0.965	-1.618
Belarus	EUR	-0.310	0.930	0.257	EA	0.41	0.448	0.58	-1.321	0.042	-0.460	-0.879	-1.358	-0.111
Belgium	EUR	-1.298	0.382	0.882	LD	0.65	-0.575	-2.064	-1.365	-0.996	-0.274	-1.399	-1.471	-2.446
Benin	AFR	0.080	1.360	0.603	EA	0.092	0.039	-1.031	0.25	-0.087	0.018	0.818	0.267	0.352
Bhutan	SCA	0.531	-1.519	0.558	LD	0.56	0.550	1.1	1.036	-0.617	-0.562	1.132	0.804	1.044
Bolivia	WHA	0.355	-0.281	0.537	EA	0.65	0.562	-0.481	-0.577	1.192	0.694	-0.024	0.28	-0.534

Bosnia and Herzegovina	EUR	-0.594	-0.631	0.534	ED	0.52	-0.521	-1.455	-1.277	0.395	0.552	-1.37	-1.33	-0.249
Botswana	AFR	-1.110	-0.006	0.668	LD	0.43	-0.625	-1.976	-1.588	-0.439	-0.449	-1.285	-1.399	-1.454
Brazil	WHA	0.296	-0.334	0.674	ED	0.66	0.328	1.071	-0.425	1.261	1.315	-0.977	-1.453	0.069
Bulgaria	EUR	-0.787	-0.478	0.587	ED	0.56	-0.430	-1.573	-1.538	-0.273	0.814	-1.349	-1.149	-1.23
Burkina Faso	AFR	0.533	0.225	0.358	EA	0.078	0.051	0.408	-0.016	-0.062	-0.034	2.007	0.623	1.536
Burma/Myanmar	EAP	0.451	0.368	0.406	EA	0.41	0.563	0.437	0.552	-0.418	-0.517	1.459	0.753	0.893
Burundi	AFR	1.013	-0.930	0.162	EA	0.045	0.047	0.964	0.9	0.123	0.104	0.878	2.005	3.19
Cambodia	EAP	1.275	-1.177	0.238	EA	0.58	0.584	2.574	1.281	1.281	1.144	0.454	0.235	1.761
Cameroon	AFR	0.558	0.435	0.294	EA	0.14	0.068	0.257	1.508	-0.005	-0.020	0.689	0.412	2.083
Canada	WHA	-1.392	0.331	0.866	LD	0.67	-0.750	-1.684	-1.731	-1.410	-0.526	-1.387	-1.442	-2.074
Cape Verde	AFR	-0.916	-0.577	0.8	ED	0.49	-0.955	-1.257	-0.939	-0.568	-0.326	-0.933	-1.086	-1.513
Central African Republic	AFR	-0.079	-0.454	0.383	EA	0.025	-0.014	-0.213	-0.572	0.042	0.030	-0.057	-0.634	0.761
Chad	AFR	1.219	0.097	0.27	EA	0.02	0.014	1.694	1.383	0.028	0.022	2.609	2.35	1.254
Chile	WHA	-0.299	0.760	0.773	LD	0.79	0.310	-0.29	-0.239	0.215	-0.672	-1.278	-0.38	-1.411
China	EAP	2.589	1.592	0.083	CA	0.72	2.061	2.844	2.851	1.922	1.938	2.302	2.866	2.175
Colombia	WHA	0.235	-0.491	0.667	ED	0.69	0.831	0.648	-0.703	1.301	1.359	-1.385	-1.523	0.04
Comoros	AFR	0.195	-0.018	0.427	EA	0.2	0.095	0.128	0.502	-0.003	0.019	-0.076	0.113	0.547
Costa Rica	WHA	-1.244	-0.862	0.889	LD	0.73	-1.779	-0.89	-0.582	-1.499	-0.210	-1.298	-1.331	-1.872
Croatia	EUR	-0.599	-0.135	0.687	ED	0.51	-0.505	-1.054	-0.441	-0.156	-0.452	-1.293	-0.768	-0.505

(continued)

Table A.1 Continued

Country	Region	Digital repression index	Digital repression capacity index	V-Dem electoral democracy score	V-Dem regime type	Social media penetration (2020)	Government social media monitoring	Government censorship filtering	Government social media censorship	Government disinformation	Political party disinformation	Government Internet shutdowns	Government blocking of social media	Arrests of online users
Cuba	WHA	1.605	1.781	0.203	CA	0.55	1.420	3.277	1.276	1.365	1.134	0.67	1.105	0.775
Cyprus	EUR	-1.380	0.509	0.84	LD	0.83	-1.656	-1.768	-0.584	-1.092	-1.018	-1.326	-1.354	-2.142
Czech Republic	EUR	-0.997	-0.872	0.796	ED	0.53	-0.508	-1.235	-1.818	-0.086	-0.263	-1.385	-1.483	-2.226
Democratic Republic of the Congo	AFR	1.107	-0.640	0.327	EA	0.035	0.032	1.563	1.953	0.044	0.031	1.86	2.088	0.763
Denmark	EUR	-1.623	0.792	0.9	LD	0.71	-0.896	-1.997	-1.643	-1.867	-1.001	-1.419	-1.428	-2.318
Djibouti	AFR	0.859	-0.942	0.259	EA	0.2	0.232	0.777	1.979	0.201	0.218	0.813	1.224	1.179
Dominican Republic	WHA	-0.630	-0.374	0.598	ED	0.59	-0.518	-1.145	-1.004	0.273	0.750	-1.263	-1.353	-1.684
Ecuador	WHA	-0.450	-0.870	0.673	ED	0.69	0.372	-1.278	-0.327	-0.741	0.177	-0.482	-0.573	-0.631
Egypt	MENA	1.274	1.435	0.19	EA	0.41	0.429	1.825	1.166	0.875	0.729	1.599	1.06	1.992
El Salvador	WHA	-0.945	-1.220	0.631	ED	0.59	-1.104	-1.179	-0.584	-0.475	-0.164	-1.191	-1.284	-1.959
Equatorial Guinea	AFR	1.447	0.483	0.18	EA	0.072	0.136	2.544	2.389	0.104	0.097	1.909	1.87	2.728
Eritrea	AFR	1.381	-0.232	0.071	CA	0.006	0.011	1.867	2.766	0.018	0.018	2.419	2.233	1.725
Estonia	EUR	-1.207	1.995	0.892	LD	0.57	-0.893	-1.797	-1.586	-0.524	-0.481	-1.336	-1.361	-2.276
Eswatini	AFR	0.228	-0.135	0.149	CA	0.23	0.474	0.317	0.106	-0.025	0.224	0.327	-0.746	1.611
Ethiopia	AFR	1.070	-0.419	0.33	EA	0.055	0.012	2.022	1.62	0.110	0.103	1.572	1.865	0.499

Fiji	EAP	-0.001	-0.312	0.465	EA	0.63	0.231	-0.65	0.271	0.595	0.109	-0.68	-0.597	0.033
Finland	EUR	-1.508	0.427	0.87	LD	0.6	-1.180	-1.924	-1.573	-1.547	-0.563	-1.385	-1.377	-2.265
France	EUR	-0.746	1.806	0.879	LD	0.6	-0.568	-1.055	-0.342	-0.596	-0.456	-0.832	-0.927	-1.399
Gabon	AFR	0.864	0.547	0.367	EA	0.34	0.021	0.471	0.401	0.341	0.361	2.282	1.495	1.147
Georgia	EUR	-0.760	-0.160	0.642	ED	0.68	-0.386	-1.816	-1.411	0.621	0.507	-1.482	-1.534	-1.78
Germany	EUR	-1.062	0.329	0.834	LD	0.45	-0.368	-1.353	-0.729	-1.015	-0.447	-1.366	-1.412	-1.8
Ghana	AFR	-0.624	-0.339	0.718	LD	0.2	-0.325	-0.673	-0.662	-0.318	-0.007	-1.317	-1.179	-0.795
Greece	EUR	-0.866	1.078	0.86	ED	0.59	-0.696	-0.61	-1.661	-0.165	0.098	-1.324	-1.433	-2.043
Guatemala	WHA	-0.538	-0.825	0.594	ED	0.45	0.032	-1.51	-1.621	0.686	0.277	-0.645	-1.362	-1.283
Guinea	AFR	0.194	-0.819	0.442	EA	0.15	-0.099	0.783	-1.179	0.135	0.006	0.541	-0.253	1.552
Guinea-Bissau	AFR	-0.144	-1.859	0.507	ED	0.13	-0.081	-0.263	-1.597	-0.090	0.117	0.345	-0.229	0.329
Guyana	WHA	-0.532	-0.535	0.673	ED	0.55	-0.236	-1.629	-1.399	0.317	0.884	-1.149	-1.236	-0.23
Haiti	WHA	-0.656	-1.997	0.449	EA	0.18	-0.194	-1.819	-1.573	0.179	0.157	-0.466	-1.326	-0.579
Honduras	WHA	-0.461	-0.533	0.36	EA	0.42	0.325	-0.672	-0.862	0.245	0.315	-1.342	-1.271	-1.455
Hong Kong	EAP	1.156	0.158	0.318	CA	0.78	0.918	1.058	0.073	1.712	1.219	0.966	0.216	2.046
Hungary	EUR	-0.287	-0.021	0.485	EA	0.62	-0.206	-0.603	-0.743	0.840	1.161	-1.306	-1.341	-1.371
Iceland	EUR	-1.500	1.608	0.85	ED	0.82	-1.747	-1.678	-1.423	-1.785	-0.551	-1.089	-1.124	-2.077
India	SCA	1.213	1.069	0.507	ED	0.29	0.357	1.048	1.659	0.272	0.448	2.626	1.687	1.502
Indonesia	EAP	0.253	0.061	0.636	ED	0.59	-0.147	0.389	-0.111	0.437	0.351	0.382	0.156	-0.387
Iran	MENA	1.800	1.647	0.217	EA	0.4	0.882	2.509	2.212	0.726	0.862	2.047	2.69	1.327
Iraq	MENA	0.504	0.402	0.398	EA	0.53	-0.001	-0.168	0.112	0.591	0.755	0.883	0.757	0.295
Ireland	EUR	-1.357	-0.522	0.864	LD	0.65	-0.647	-1.956	-1.727	-1.216	-1.243	-1.304	-1.414	-1
Israel	MENA	-0.406	1.176	0.667	LD	0.7	0.348	0.225	-0.082	-0.597	0.369	-0.582	-1.398	-1.864

(continued)

Table A.1 Continued

Country	Region	Digital repression index	Digital repression capacity index	V-Dem electoral democracy score	V-Dem regime type	Social media penetration (2020)	Government social media monitoring	Government censorship filtering	Government social media censorship	Government disinformation	Political party disinformation	Government Internet shutdowns	Government blocking of social media	Arrests of online users
Italy	EUR	-0.845	-0.324	0.86	LD	0.58	-1.007	-1.014	-1.847	-0.234	0.617	-0.149	-1.403	-2.403
Ivory Coast	AFR	-0.336	0.785	0.58	ED	0.19	0.024	-0.343	-1.279	0.089	0.065	-1.284	-1.39	1.672
Jamaica	WHA	-1.027	-1.032	0.81	ED	0.44	-0.047	-1.81	-1.544	-0.670	-0.691	-1.278	-1.24	-1.136
Japan	EAP	-1.165	0.818	0.82	LD	0.65	-1.288	-1.402	-1.269	-0.517	-0.319	-1.42	-1.482	-2.048
Jordan	MENA	0.756	1.489	0.276	CA	0.56	0.573	1.022	1.684	0.641	0.239	0.459	0.444	0.076
Kazakhstan	SCA	1.146	0.906	0.231	EA	0.51	0.517	1.452	0.942	0.769	0.847	1.121	1.418	1.131
Kenya	AFR	-0.120	-0.168	0.429	EA	0.17	-0.007	-0.37	-0.395	0.204	0.143	-0.444	-0.434	-0.295
Kosovo	EUR	-0.370	-0.639	0.624	ED	0.61	0.583	-1.108	0.274	-0.432	0.027	-0.244	-0.833	-1.51
Kuwait	MENA	0.679	1.513	0.316	CA	0.99	1.234	0.951	1.523	0.616	0.127	0.122	-0.324	0.619
Kyrgyzstan	SCA	-0.257	-0.411	0.389	EA	0.39	-0.116	-0.125	-0.786	0.134	0.010	-0.976	-0.884	0.299
Laos	EAP	0.702	-1.258	0.122	CA	0.43	0.629	1.214	1.427	0.321	-0.449	0.286	0.084	2.233
Latvia	EUR	-1.263	-0.485	0.811	LD	0.53	-0.757	-1.537	-1.55	-1.189	-0.489	-1.272	-1.335	-1.993
Lebanon	MENA	0.938	0.452	0.465	EA	0.6	0.596	0.264	1.36	0.785	1.399	0.665	0.78	1.099
Lesotho	AFR	0.093	-0.567	0.568	ED	0.2	0.007	0.569	0.193	0.039	0.107	-0.073	-0.556	0.22
Liberia	AFR	0.125	-0.438	0.625	ED	0.11	-0.071	-0.921	-0.581	-0.013	-0.058	0.792	0.758	0.884
Libya	MENA	0.496	-1.355	0.25	CA	0.75	-0.088	-0.275	-0.045	0.661	1.172	0.88	0.46	0.612
Lithuania	EUR	-1.588	0.265	0.803	ED	0.66	-1.346	-2.187	-1.367	-1.263	-1.828	-1.337	-1.347	-1.9
Luxembourg	EUR	-1.255	1.224	0.879	LD	0.64	-0.845	-1.96	-1.608	-0.666	-0.614	-1.286	-1.303	-2.242

Madagascar	AFR	-0.198	-0.663	0.496	EA	0.084	0.033	-0.626	-0.605	-0.014	0.153	-0.978	-0.453	0.74
Malawi	AFR	-0.185	-0.983	0.5	EA	0.027	0.015	-0.883	-0.271	-0.023	0.001	0.274	-0.51	-0.326
Malaysia	EAP	-0.272	1.610	0.466	EA	0.81	0.754	-0.233	0.15	-1.091	0.293	-0.426	-0.935	-0.018
Maldives	SCA	0.174	0.518	0.49	EA	0.71	0.773	0.527	0.452	-1.238	0.619	0.274	0.384	-0.008
Mali	AFR	0.098	0.004	0.467	EA	0.085	0.016	-0.032	-0.618	-0.111	-0.049	-0.347	0.758	0.565
Malta	EUR	-0.751	-1.425	0.757	ED	0.91	-0.396	-1.732	-1.376	0.458	0.286	-1.225	-1.285	-1.942
Mauritania	AFR	0.718	0.227	0.368	EA	0.17	0.316	0.98	0.466	0.087	0.129	1.148	1.189	0.955
Mauritius	AFR	0.077	0.582	0.818	ED	0.68	0.843	0.565	-0.619	0.102	-0.092	-0.809	-0.236	-0.029
Mexico	WHA	-0.635	-0.181	0.71	ED	0.69	-0.367	-1.591	-0.787	0.382	0.932	-1.07	-1.416	-2.191
Moldova	EUR	-0.942	-0.018	0.586	ED	0.35	-0.240	-1.637	-1.337	-0.250	-0.393	-1.288	-1.333	-1.702
Mongolia	EAP	-0.884	-0.276	0.683	ED	0.68	-0.579	-1.438	0.213	-0.615	-0.014	-1.097	-1.481	-2.215
Montenegro	EUR	0.169	-0.530	0.455	EA	0.62	0.306	-0.53	0.4	0.774	0.764	-1.249	0.134	-0.647
Morocco	MENA	0.202	0.578	0.29	CA	0.49	-0.081	0.168	0.068	-0.221	-0.373	0.414	0.575	0.982
Mozambique	AFR	-0.400	-0.311	0.409	EA	0.081	-0.039	-1.178	-0.61	-0.005	0.093	-1.361	-0.346	-0.39
Namibia	AFR	-0.700	-0.278	0.7	ED	0.28	0.118	-1.13	-1.132	-0.276	-0.122	-0.972	-1.39	-1.043
Nepal	SCA	0.785	0.411	0.605	ED	0.35	0.172	0.819	1.852	0.143	0.109	0.881	1.02	1.125
Netherlands	EUR	-1.409	-0.067	0.83	LD	0.64	-0.835	-2.075	-1.683	-1.420	-0.443	-1.32	-1.374	-1.817
New Zealand	EAP	-1.391	1.046	0.873	LD	0.75	-1.253	-1.008	-1.441	-1.655	-0.867	-1.313	-1.287	-2.033
Nicaragua	WHA	1.089	-0.511	0.245	EA	0.47	0.142	2.638	1.374	0.509	0.561	1.125	1.018	0.357
Niger	AFR	0.783	-0.288	0.457	EA	0.021	0.006	1.412	0.753	0.025	0.031	0.99	1.354	1.344
Nigeria	AFR	0.237	-0.546	0.498	EA	0.13	0.183	1.17	0.319	0.024	0.120	-0.303	-0.412	0.494
North Korea	EAP	2.555	2.501	0.099	CA	0.006	0.022	4.192	5.158	0.019	0.013	4.13	4.077	3.039

(continued)

Table A.1 Continued

Country	Region	Digital repression index	Digital repression capacity index	V-Dem electoral democracy score	V-Dem regime type	Social media penetration (2020)	Government social media monitoring	Government censorship filtering	Government social media censorship	Government disinformation	Political party disinformation	Government Internet shutdowns	Government blocking of social media	Arrests of online users
North Macedonia	EUR	-0.374	-0.279	0.635	ED	0.53	0.274	-0.426	-0.37	-0.162	0.247	-1.092	-1.027	-0.95
Norway	EUR	-1.220	-0.284	0.874	LD	0.7	-1.352	-1.736	-1.448	-0.777	-0.445	-0.877	-1.274	-2.043
Oman	MENA	1.259	1.202	0.185	CA	0.56	1.589	2.336	1.674	0.314	-0.444	1.062	1.009	2.219
Pakistan	SCA	0.802	0.904	0.351	EA	0.17	0.253	1.322	1.168	0.151	0.222	1.302	1.069	0.325
Palestine/Gaza	MENA	0.545	-0.944	0.13	CA	0.54	0.847	-0.682	0.323	0.926	1.068	-0.429	-0.093	2.16
Palestine/West Bank	MENA	0.265	0.093	0.283	EA	0.54	0.649	1.064	-0.56	0.301	0.603	-0.647	-0.761	1.116
Panama	WHA	-1.013	-0.667	0.783	ED	0.56	-0.794	-1.189	-0.823	-0.912	-0.090	-1.362	-1.392	-1.435
Papua New Guinea	EAP	-0.715	-1.381	0.485	EA	0.086	-0.074	-1.637	-1.538	-0.113	0.051	-1.264	-1.325	0.106
Paraguay	WHA	-0.780	-1.514	0.601	ED	0.56	-0.922	-1.636	-1.21	-0.023	0.380	-0.889	-1.241	-1.062
Peru	WHA	-0.967	-0.118	0.784	ED	0.73	-1.013	-1.391	-0.962	-0.816	-0.162	-0.733	-0.987	-1.796
Philippines	EAP	0.627	-0.472	0.48	EA	0.67	0.894	-0.365	-0.445	1.057	1.110	0.673	0.609	0.121
Poland	EUR	-0.752	0.123	0.692	ED	0.5	-0.125	-1.849	-0.371	-0.026	-0.291	-1.256	-1.377	-1.1
Portugal	EUR	-1.394	0.729	0.87	LD	0.69	-1.604	-1.383	-1.138	-1.221	-1.159	-0.557	-1.516	-2.46
Qatar	MENA	1.413	1.939	0.091	CA	0.99	2.656	1.9	1.582	0.411	0.672	0.769	0.728	2.31
Republic of the Congo	AFR	1.038	-0.134	0.249	EA	0.13	0.121	1.541	1.651	0.232	0.228	1.346	1.39	1.562

Romania	EUR	-0.899	0.018	0.679	ED	0.57	-0.292	-1.325	-1.068	-0.418	-0.274	-0.83	-1.387	-2.168
Russia	EUR	1.193	1.597	0.246	EA	0.48	0.749	1.44	1.313	1.290	1.010	0.651	0.835	1.022
Rwanda	AFR	0.832	1.068	0.259	EA	0.048	0.105	1.223	1.974	-0.023	-0.048	0.072	1.588	1.462
Sao Tome and Principe	AFR	-0.796	-1.208	0.704	ED	0.29	-0.425	-1.581	-1.292	-0.560	-0.293	-0.854	-1.106	0.029
Saudi Arabia	MENA	1.981	1.662	0.023	CA	0.72	2.324	2.865	1.481	1.713	-0.453	2.388	1.7	2.207
Senegal	AFR	-0.361	0.100	0.708	ED	0.21	0.027	-0.216	-0.767	-0.254	-0.025	-1.337	-1.476	1.8
Serbia	EUR	0.088	-0.276	0.359	EA	0.42	0.252	0.055	0.437	0.931	1.097	-1.279	-1.313	-0.412
Seychelles	AFR	-0.554	-0.494	0.563	ED	0.74	-0.650	-0.574	-0.818	-0.122	-0.670	-1.265	-0.553	-0.331
Sierra Leone	AFR	-0.409	-0.617	0.624	ED	0.089	-0.162	-0.528	-1.101	0.004	0.049	-0.218	-1.434	0.119
Singapore	EAP	0.247	2.047	0.398	EA	0.79	1.342	1.103	1.019	-0.604	-0.340	-0.743	-0.821	1.68
Slovakia	EUR	-1.101	-1.105	0.813	ED	0.51	-0.780	-1.577	-1.544	-0.549	-0.131	-1.343	-1.348	-2.029
Slovenia	EUR	-1.147	-0.784	0.797	LD	0.53	-0.917	-1.928	-1.684	-0.664	0.795	-1.397	-1.453	-2.255
Solomon Islands	EAP	-0.637	-1.962	0.67	ED	0.14	-0.146	-1.543	-0.744	-0.091	0.152	-0.496	-1.156	-1.601
Somalia	AFR	0.567	-1.277	0.161	CA	0.1	0.049	0.605	0.165	0.173	0.177	0.901	0.81	1.433
Somaliland	AFR	0.318	-0.108	0.441	EA	0.1	0.093	0.429	0.45	0.083	0.041	0.485	0.169	0.508
South Africa	AFR	-0.466	0.211	0.678	ED	0.37	-0.195	-0.087	-1.538	-0.147	0.035	0.064	-1.097	-1.45
South Korea	EAP	-1.278	1.119	0.842	LD	0.87	-1.332	-0.392	-1.143	-1.543	-1.048	-1.343	-1.399	-1.725
South Sudan	AFR	1.568	-0.720	0.18	CA	0.025	0.072	1.749	3.262	0.078	0.078	2.938	2.416	2.238
Spain	EUR	-1.199	1.422	0.876	LD	0.62	-1.446	-0.514	-1.078	-1.327	-1.229	-1.386	-1.026	-1.486
Sri Lanka	SCA	0.537	0.768	0.612	ED	0.3	0.079	0.767	0.159	0.112	0.323	1.227	0.681	0.513
Sudan	AFR	1.232	0.159	0.213	CA	0.03	0.034	2.216	1.3	0.043	0.043	1.952	2.468	1.07

(continued)

Table A.1 Continued

Country	Region	Digital repression index	Digital repression capacity index	V-Dem electoral democracy score	V-Dem regime type	Social media penetration (2020)	Government social media monitoring	Government censorship filtering	Government social media censorship	Government disinformation	Political party disinformation	Government Internet shutdowns	Government blocking of social media	Arrests of online users
Suriname	WHA	-0.711	-0.625	0.736	ED	0.62	-0.970	-0.737	-0.295	-0.259	-0.643	-1.177	-1.328	-0.224
Sweden	EUR	-1.671	0.126	0.874	LD	0.73	-1.764	-1.917	-1.74	-1.532	-1.372	-1.343	-1.438	-1.886
Switzerland	EUR	-1.307	0.229	0.873	LD	0.52	-0.930	-1.816	-1.501	-1.115	-0.618	-1.249	-1.308	-1.916
Syria	MENA	1.681	0.621	0.145	CA	0.35	0.810	2.995	1.526	1.099	1.133	1.162	1.206	2.947
Taiwan	EAP	-0.562	0.315	0.811	LD	0.88	-0.197	-0.229	-1.029	-0.701	0.069	-0.438	-0.778	-1.607
Tajikistan	SCA	1.718	0.113	0.166	EA	0.07	0.093	2.132	3.183	0.178	0.108	2.424	3.101	2.364
Tanzania	AFR	0.094	0.408	0.43	EA	0.076	0.016	-0.913	0.56	0.027	0.032	-1.204	1.083	0.46
Thailand	EAP	0.582	0.765	0.166	CA	0.75	1.173	1.088	0.88	0.669	0.697	-0.698	-0.553	0.697
The Gambia	AFR	-0.257	0.545	0.568	ED	0.16	-0.152	-0.249	-0.474	-0.081	-0.090	-0.465	-0.637	-0.285
Timor-Leste	EAP	-0.497	-1.626	0.754	ED	0.31	-0.037	-1.205	-0.779	0.015	0.005	-0.447	-1.066	-0.916
Togo	AFR	0.795	1.065	0.359	EA	0.079	0.090	1.083	0.534	0.114	0.135	1.647	1.423	0.818
Trinidad and Tobago	WHA	-0.911	-1.054	0.744	LD	0.62	-0.138	-1.835	-1.562	-0.384	-0.024	-1.313	-1.363	-0.87
Tunisia	MENA	-0.460	0.516	0.723	LD	0.62	-1.191	-0.563	-0.888	-0.348	-0.151	-0.22	0.184	-1.178
Turkey	EUR	1.631	1.059	0.292	EA	0.64	1.400	2.469	2	1.155	0.716	1.052	1.475	1.56
Turkmenistan	SCA	1.945	1.321	0.154	EA	0.012	0.026	3.01	3.791	0.030	0.020	3.305	3.31	1.903
Uganda	AFR	0.371	0.883	0.307	EA	0.056	0.078	0.395	0.669	-0.033	-0.036	0.701	0.054	1.412
Ukraine	EUR	0.326	-0.136	0.469	EA	0.43	0.099	0.234	0.787	0.047	0.142	-0.626	1.209	-0.374

Country	Region													
United Arab Emirates	MENA	2.199	1.816	0.101	CA	0.99	2.427	3.841	2.175	1.254	0.622	1.461	1.865	2.717
United Kingdom	EUR	-0.666	0.871	0.859	LD	0.66	-0.411	-1.162	-0.509	-0.504	-0.553	-1.405	-0.355	-0.858
United States of America	WHA	-0.620	0.549	0.798	LD	0.7	0.421	-1.395	-0.341	0.166	0.006	-1.436	-1.517	-1.704
Uruguay	WHA	-1.129	1.505	0.858	LD	0.78	-0.778	-1.26	-1.067	-1.380	-0.116	-0.576	-1.409	-2.132
Uzbekistan	SCA	1.133	1.521	0.209	CA	0.096	0.212	1.779	1.982	0.170	0.090	1.799	1.502	1.269
Vanuatu	EAP	-0.967	-1.711	0.712	ED	0.31	-0.419	-1.375	-1.116	-0.539	-0.479	-1.312	-1.43	-1.281
Venezuela	WHA	1.745	1.009	0.229	EA	0.42	1.399	2.433	0.904	1.382	1.137	2.124	1.951	0.816
Vietnam	EAP	1.145	1.076	0.217	CA	0.67	0.824	2.063	1.836	0.926	-0.442	0.599	0.602	2.172
Yemen	MENA	1.393	0.731	0.123	CA	0.085	0.107	2.313	2.164	0.213	0.217	1.579	1.904	2.682
Zambia	AFR	0.302	0.563	0.372	EA	0.13	0.265	1.196	-0.264	0.053	0.230	-1.092	0.108	1.566
Zanzibar	AFR	0.414	0.582	0.245	EA	0.076	0.103	0.479	1.605	0.016	0.032	-0.4	-0.064	1.988
Zimbabwe	AFR	0.808	0.799	0.289	EA	0.066	0.179	0.93	1.197	0.095	0.140	1.245	0.923	1.904

N = 179 countries.

CA = closed autocracy; EA = electoral autocracy; ED = electoral democracy; LD = liberal democracy.

Appendix 2

QUANTITATIVE ANALYSIS METHODS AND STATISTICAL INFORMATION

Digital Repression Index: Notes

A useful analysis to evaluate the internal consistency of a composite indicator—how closely a set of variables can be grouped—is Cronbach's alpha. The Cronbach alpha coefficient for the eight variables making up the digital repression index is 0.96, which is a strong indication that they are evaluating the same latent aspect of digital repression. In addition, I applied an interitem association validity test that indicated a moderate to strong relationship among the eight variables, leading to the conclusion that they all measure a dimension of digital repression—and that, put together, they represent a valid composite measurement of digital repression. The last step I undertook was to use factor analysis to aggregate the eight variables into a composite digital repression score, which I then reversed so that higher values correspond to greater levels of digital repression (see Table A2.1 for factor loadings).

Table A2.1 **Digital Repression Index Factor Loadings**

Variable	Factor 1	Factor 2	Factor 3	Factor 4	Uniqueness
Gov SM monitoring	0.8523	−0.0201	−0.1904	−0.0115	0.2367
Gov Internet filtering	0.9327	−0.1072	−0.0452	−0.0014	0.1166
Gov SM censorship	0.9040	−0.1905	−0.0591	0.0309	0.1426
Gov disinformation	0.8070	0.4306	0.0096	0.0025	0.1632
Pol party disinformation	0.6458	0.5221	0.0798	0.0051	0.3039
Gov Internet Shutdown	0.9028	−0.1869	0.1675	−0.0214	0.1215
Gov SM Blocking	0.9117	−0.2392	0.1479	0.0097	0.0896
User Arrests	0.8902	−0.0097	−0.0982	−0.0131	0.1976

Table A2.2 **Digital Repression Capacity Index Factor Loadings**

Variable	Factor 1	Factor 2	Uniqueness
Gov Internet filtering capacity	0.8127	0.2055	0.2973
Gov Internet Shutdown capacity	0.6241	0.3922	0.4567
Gov cybersecurity capacity	0.7161	−0.3424	0.3699
Gov capacity to regulate online content	0.8014	−0.2078	0.3146

Table A2.3 **Linear Regression of Digital Repression Index by V-Dem Electoral Democracy Index**

Linear Regression		Number of obs	=	**1,788**	
		$F(1,1768)$	=	**4496.99**	
		Prob > F	=	**0.0000**	
		R-squared	=	**0.7258**	
		Root MSE	=	**.51609**	

Digital Repression Index	Coef.	Std. error	t	P>|t|	[95% conf. Interval]	
Electoral Democracy Index	−3.307524	0.493222	−67.06	0.000	−3.404259	−3.210789
_Cons	1.77191	0.338444	52.35	0.000	1.705531	1.838289

Table A2.4 **Standardized Coefficients for Pooled Time Series Random Effects Model**

Random-effects GLS regression			Number of obs	=	**1745**
Group Variable: **country 1**			Number of Groups	=	179
R-squared			Obs per group:		
within	= **0.5098**		min	=	8
between	= **0.7880**		avg	=	9.7
overall	= **0.7797**		max	=	10

DigitalRepressionIndexZ	Coef.	Std. error	Z	P > |z|	[95% Conf. Interval]	
PrivateCivLibZ	.1590327	.0203038	7.83	0.000	.1192379	.1988275
StatePhyViolenceZ	.11873	.0165101	7.19	0.000	.0863708	.1510891
PolCivLibZ	.4120509	.0218387	18.87	0.000	.3692479	.4548539
CivSocRepressionZ	.1517537	.0127298	11.92	0.000	.1268038	.1767035
_cons	−.0023549	.0309292	−0.08	0.939	−.062975	.0582653

Table A2.5 **Linear Regression of Social Media Surveillance by V-Dem Electoral Democracy Index**

Linear Regression			Number of obs	=	1,788
			F(1,1768)	=	2325.95
			Prob > F	=	0.0000
			R-squared	=	0.5756
			Root MSE	=	.88352

Gov SM Surveillance	Coef.	Std. error	t	P > |t|	[95% conf. Interval]	
Electoral Democracy Index	−4.053232	.0840429	−48.23	0.000	−4.218065	−3.888399
_Cons	2.230809	.0512364	43.54	0.000	2.13032	2.331299

Table A2.6 **Linear Regression of Online Censorship by V-Dem Electoral Democracy Index**

Linear Regression			Number of obs	=	1,788
			F(1,1768)	=	3114.96
			Prob > F	=	0.0000
			R-squared	=	0.6428
			Root MSE	=	.80397

Internet Censorship Avg	Coef.	Std. error	t	P>|t|	[95% conf. Interval]	
Electoral Democracy Index	−4.248376	0.761196	−55.81	0.000	−4.397669	−4.099083
_Cons	2.208659	.0514507	42.93	0.000	2.10775	2.309569

Table A2.7 **Linear Regression of Social Manipulation & Disinformation by V-Dem Electoral Democracy Index**

Linear Regression			Number of obs	=	1,788
			F(1,1768)	=	1591.13
			Prob > F	=	0.0000
			R-squared	=	0.5188
			Root MSE	=	.81954

Disinformation Avg	Coef.	Std. error	t	P > |t|	[95% conf. Interval]	
Electoral Democracy Index	−3.352203	0.840384	−39.89	0.000	−3.517027	−3.18738
_Cons	1.841936	.0541787	34.00	0.000	1.735675	1.948196

Table A2.8 **Linear Regression of Internet Shutdowns by V-Dem Electoral
             Democracy Index**

Linear Regression			Number of Obs		=	**1,788**
			F(1,1768)		=	**2306.68**
			Prob>F		=	**0.0000**
			R-squared		=	**0.5611**
			Root MSE		=	**.8134**

Internet Shutdown Avg	Coef.	Std. Err.	t	P>|t|	[95% conf. Interval]	
Electoral Democracy Index	−3.623276	0.75441	−48.03	0.000	−3.771238	−3.475314
_Cons	1.783277	.0532137	33.51	0.000	1.678909	1.887645

Table A2.9 **Linear Regression of Arrests of Users for Online Content by V-Dem
             Electoral Democracy Index**

Linear Regression			Number of Obs		=	**1,788**
			F(1,1768)		=	**5992.56**
			Prob>F		=	**0.0000**
			R-squared		=	**0.7160**
			Root MSE		=	**.8005**

Online User Arrests	Coef.	Std. Err.	t	P>|t|	[95% conf. Interval]	
Electoral Democracy Index	−5.007408	.0646855	−77.41	0.000	−5.134275	−4.880541
_Cons	2.593807	.0432813	59.93	0.000	2.508919	2.678694

To externally verify the index's validity, I compared country scores for the
digital repression indicator to Freedom on the Net scores for thirty-six countries from 2011 to 2019. The two indicators show a high degree of correlation
($r = 0.87$) and a robust linear regression coefficient ($r^2 = 0.76$). This provides
sufficient validation that the digital repression index accurately measures empirical digital trends.

Digital Repression Capacity Index: Notes

For the digital repression capacity index, Cronbach's alpha reveals a coefficient
value of 0.82. This measure suggests high internal consistency, and indicates
that the four variables are evaluating the same latent aspect of digital repression

capacity. The correlation matrix shows similar results, leading to the conclusion that the variables all measure a dimension of digital repression capacity, and that put together, they represent a valid measurement of digital repression capacity. Similar to the digital repression index, the last step I undertook was to use factor analysis to aggregate the four variables into a composite digital repression capacity score.

Appendix 3

Table A.3 **Commercial Spyware Used by Governments against Domestic Opponents**

Country	Regime Type	Commercial Spyware Vendor	Description
Angola	EA	Israeli firms, FinFisher	Hack/monitor regime critics
Azerbaijan	EA	Hacking Team	Systems to track LGBT population
Bahrain	CA	NSO Group, FinFisher, Verint	Violently repressed protests; purchased intel collection system
Bangladesh	EA	FinFisher	Used by intel agency linked to major HR abuses
Belarus	EA	Grayshift, Cellebrite	Confirmed hacking of activists/journalists
Botswana	LD	NSO Group/ Circles, Elbit Systems	Abuse of surveillance equipment to suppress reporting and public awareness of corruption
Brazil	ED	Hacking Team	History of surveillance abuses; infiltration of online platforms & political monitoring are common
Burma/ Myanmar	EA	Cellebrite	Cellebrite used to collect data from journalists' smartphones
Chile	LD	NSO Group/Circles, Hacking Team	Illegally intercepted calls of multiple journalists
China	CA	Fiberhome, Xi'an Tianhe Defense Technology, Multiple	Xinjiang visitors forced to download Fengcai spyware app which checks phone for items considered to be "suspicious"; Xinjiang spyware; Other
Colombia	ED	Hacking Team, Verint, Nice	Tech used to surveil opponents of the regime
Côte d'Ivoire	ED	Blue Coat	Bloggers arrested for online content
Ecuador	ED	Hacking Team, Israeli firms	Leaked documents have exposed illegal spying on politicians, journalists, and activists
Egypt	EA	Hacking Team, FinFisher	Malware campaigns against civil society
Eswatini	CA	Verint	Purchased systems relating to communications interception
Ethiopia	EA	Hacking Team, FinFisher, Cyberbit	Tech used to surveil opponents of the regime
Gabon	EA	FinFisher, Ames	Comms intercept & targeting of opposition/ civil society
Ghana	LD	Cellebrite, NSO Group	Possible use against journalists
Guatemala	ED	NSO Group/Circles, Pegasus	Govt procured spyware to monitor businessmen, politicians, journalists, diplomats and social leaders

Table A.3 **Continued**

Country	Regime Type	Commercial Spyware Vendor	Description
Honduras	EA	NSO Group, Israeli firms	Malware to spy on journalists, human rights defenders, and opposition groups
Hungary	EA	Hacking Team, Black Cube	Black Cube involved in campaign to discredit NGOs ahead of Hungary's April election
Indonesia	ED	FinFisher	Database of LGBT population; persecuted religious minorities
Iran	EA	Blue Coat	Numerous high-profile incidents of surveillance and targeted malware attacks
Italy	LD	Hacking Team, FinFisher	Concerns that intel agencies intercepting personal comms & employing hacking without statutory authorization or safeguards
Jordan	CA	FinFisher	Malware to spy on journalists, human rights defenders, and opposition groups
Kazakhstan	EA	Hacking Team, FinFisher, Israeli firms	Obtained software to monitor/interfere with online traffic & perform targeted cyberattacks against users and devices
Kenya	EA	FinFisher, NSO Group	Concerns about govt's use of surveillance to repress CSOs & HR defenders
Lebanon	EA	FinFisher, Dark Caracal	Developed unique mobile surveillance tool, Dark Caracal/Pallas, to extract hundreds of gigabytes of data from Android devices
Malaysia	EA	Hacking Team, FinFisher, Israeli firms	Extensive documentation of govt acquisition of spyware
Mexico	ED	Hacking Team, NSO Group, FinFisher, Ability	Malware to track civil society/opposition/journalists
Mongolia	ED	FinFisher	Linkages between FinFisher malware and State Special Security Dept
Morocco	CA	Hacking Team, NSO Group, FinFisher, Decision Group	Abusive use of spyware to target civil society
Nicaragua	EA	Israeli firms	Purchaser of intel-gathering software
Nigeria	EA	Hacking Team, FinFisher, Circles, Elbit, Cellebrite	Spied on politicians, regime opponents
Northern Macedonia	ED	Iskratel	Unlawful monitoring of activists, lawyers, opposition members, journalists, civil servants
Oman	CA	Hacking Team, FinFisher	Targeted surveillance linked to Oman's Ministry of Interior
Pakistan	EA	FinFisher	Malware used to infect PowerPoint documents & steal files from target computers

(*continued*)

Table A.3 **Continued**

Country	Regime Type	Commercial Spyware Vendor	Description
Panama	ED	Hacking Team, Israeli firms	Used software to track 150 people illegally
Paraguay	ED	FinFisher	Used software to spy on journalists
Peru	ED	Verint	Surveil regime opponents
Philippines	EA	Blue Coat, Rohde & Schwarz	Leaked documents indicate govt's intentions to procure tech for comms surveillance
Poland	ED	Hacking Team, NSO Group	Pegasus allegedly purchased by anticorruption police CBA
Qatar	CA	NSO Group, Blue Coat	Gain control of target's phone to obtain data and surveil surrounding activity
Russia	EA	Hacking Team, Multiple	Online accts of journalists & civil society activists often compromised suggesting coordinated campaign to access their data
Rwanda	EA	NSO Group	Security officials authorized to tap online comms; Pegasus software targeted Rwandan dissidents allegedly at the behest of the government
Saudi Arabia	CA	Hacking Team, NSO Group, FinFisher	Extensive documented abuse of spyware to target political opponents & civil society
Singapore	EA	FinFisher	Legal framework regulating comms interception falls short of international HR standards; oversight nonexistent
South Africa	ED	FinFisher	Reported surveillance of activists, journalists, and perceived political opponents
South Sudan	CA	Verint	Supplied espionage tech used in monitoring center
Spain	LD	NSO Group	Catalan politicians targeted by govt
Sudan	CA	Hacking Team, Blue Coat	Surveillance against regime opponents
Syria	CA	Blue Coat, repurposed crimeware	Spyware to target opposition; repurposed crimeware
Thailand	CA	Hacking Team, Blue Coat	Targeted surveillance against civil society, regime opponents
Togo	EA	NSO Group	Operator based in Togo using political websites to infect targets with spyware
Tunisia	LD	Blue Coat, Trovicor, BAE, Utimaco	Under Ben Ali regime widespread hacking & interception
Turkey	EA	Hacking Team, FinFisher, NSO Group	Most forms of telecommunication are tapped and intercepted
Turkmenistan	EA	FinFisher, Hacking Team	Targeted surveillance of citizens

Table A.3 **Continued**

Country	Regime Type	Commercial Spyware Vendor	Description
Uganda	EA	Israeli firms, Huawei, FinFisher	Arrested parliamentary members & charged w/ treason - linked to Huawei technicians
United Arab Emirates	CA	Hacking Team, NSO Group	Surveilled newspaper editor; tracked regime opponents
United States	LD	Cellebrite	CBP surveillance of journalists at border
Uzbekistan	EA	Hacking Team, Verint	Extensive deployment of invasive software used to hijack devices
Venezuela	CA	FinFisher	Widespread targeting of journalists, opposition groups
Vietnam	CA	Israeli firms	Deployment of FinSpy as part of ongoing campaign against bloggers who spoke out against the regime
Zambia	EA	NSO Group, Huawei	Huawei technicians helping govt monitor & intercept comms of criminal suspects, opposition supporters, activists, and journalists

N = 64 countries.

CA = closed autocracy; EA = electoral autocracy; ED = electoral democracy; LD = liberal democracy.

Appendix 4

Table A.4 **AI and Big-Data Global Surveillance Index**

Country	Regime type	Freedom on the Net 2019 status	Military spending rank (2018)	BRI	Safe city	Facial recognition	Smart policing	SM monitoring	Chinese tech	Tech primarily from Chinese firms	US tech	Frequently mentioned companies
Algeria	EA		25				··	··	··	··		BAE, Huawei
Argentina	ED	Free	43			··	··	··	··		··	Huawei, ZTE, NEC, Bosch, Oracle
Australia	LD	Free	13		··	··	··	··	··		··	Palantir, NEC, CrowdOptic, iOmniscient, Hikvision, Dahua
Bahrain	CA	Not free	65	··		··	··	··	··		··	iOmniscient, Pelcom, LSS
Bangladesh	EA	Partly free	44	··	··	··	··	··	··	··	··	Huawei, Snaptrends
Bolivia	ED		79	··	··	··	··		··	··		Huawei, ZTE, CEIEC
Botswana	ED		86		··	··	··		··	··		Huawei
Brazil	ED	Partly free	12		··	··	··	··	··		··	Dahua, Verint
Burma/ Myanmar	EA	Not free	58	··		··			··	··		Hikvision, Huawei
Cambodia	EA	Partly free	84	··				··				
Canada	LD	Free	14			··	··	··			··	Avigilon, Palantir, Salesforce, Sightline Innovation

												Vendors
Chile	LD		34		⋮		⋮	⋮		⋮		Huawei
China	CA	Not free	2		⋮	⋮	⋮	⋮			⋮	Multiple; Semptian, Megvii, SenseTime, Huawei, ZTE, Hikvision, Dahua, Face++, iFlyTek, Yitu, CEIEC, Yixin, Meiya Pico, Knowlesys
Colombia	ED	Partly free	24			⋮	⋮		⋮			NEC
Czech Republic	LD		53	⋮								
Denmark	LD		42		⋮	⋮	⋮		⋮	⋮		Palantir, BrainChip, Hikvision, Leapcraft, Cisco
Ecuador	ED	Partly free	55			⋮	⋮	⋮		⋮		CEIEC, Huawei
Egypt	EA	Not free	51	⋮	⋮	⋮	⋮	⋮				Honeywell, Huawei
France	LD	Free	5	⋮	⋮	⋮	⋮	⋮				Huawei, Palantir, Teleste, Thales, ZTE
Georgia	ED	Free	100		⋮	⋮	⋮					NEC
Germany	LD	Free	8	⋮	⋮	⋮	⋮	⋮				Huawei, Palantir, IfmPt, Secunet

(*continued*)

Country	Regime type	Freedom on the Net 2019 status	Military spending rank (2018)	BRI	Safe city	Facial recognition	Smart policing	SM monitoring	Chinese tech	Tech primarily from Chinese firms	US tech	Frequently mentioned companies
Ghana	ED		110		::		::		::	::		Huawei
Hong Kong	ED		110			::	::	::	::	::		iOmniscient, Huawei
Hungary	ED	Free	63	::		::		::				
India	ED				::	::	::	::	::		::	NEC, ADRIN, Infinova, Hikvision, Microsoft, Qognify
Indonesia	ED	Partly free	4		::	::	::	::	::		::	NEC, PT Industri Telekomunikasi Indonesia, Huawei
Iran	ED	Partly free	26	::	::	::	::	::	::	::		ZTE, CETC
Iraq	EA	Not free	18	::	::	::	::		::	::		Huawei
Israel	EA		32	::	::	::	::	::			::	Verint, NICE, AnyVision, Elbit, BriefCam, Microsoft, ZenCity

Country				Vendors
Italy	ED		17	Huawei, Parsec, Axxonsoft, Hanwha Techwin
Ivory Coast	LD	Free	11	Huawei
Jamaica	ED		112	
Japan	ED		82	NEC
Kazakhstan	LD	Free	9	Analytical Business Solutions, Huawei, Speech Technology Center
Kenya	EA	Not free	64	Huawei, Webintpro, NEC, Safaricom
Kyrgyzstan	EA	Partly free	69	Huawei
Laos	EA	Partly free	118	Huawei
Lebanon	CA			Crestron, Guardia
Malaysia	EA	Partly free	52	Huawei, NEC, Yitu
Malta	ED	Partly free	49	Huawei
Mauritius	LD		128	Huawei
Mexico	LD		141	Dahua, InfiNet, Telmex, Thales, Axxonsoft

(continued)

Country	Regime type	Freedom on the Net 2019 status	Military spending rank (2018)	BRI	Safe city	Facial recognition	Smart policing	SM monitoring	Chinese tech	Tech primarily from Chinese firms	US tech	Frequently mentioned companies
Mongolia	ED	Partly free	31			••	••		••			Dahua
Morocco	ED		122	••	••	••	••	••	••	••		BAE, Huawei
Namibia	ED	Partly free	47	••	••	••	••		••			Otesa
Netherlands	ED		89		••	••	••		••			Huawei, IDEMIA, Hikvision
New Zealand	LD		21	••	••	••	••		••		••	Palantir, Hikvision
Pakistan	CA		30	••	••	••	••	••	••	••		Huawei, Sandvine
Panama	EA	Not free	20	••	••	••	••		••		••	FaceFirst, Huawei
Paraguay	ED		45		••	••						
Peru	ED		54		••	••	••		••			Desarrollos Terrestres Perú
Philippines	ED			••	••	••	••	••	••		••	Huawei, CITCC, Boeing, Verint, Integrated Computer Systems
Qatar	CA			••	••	••	••					BAE, Orange, Axxonsoft

Country		Freedom	No.								Companies
Romania	ED		40			⋮			⋮		NEC
Russia	EA	Not free	6			⋮			⋮		Multiple; NTechLab, Ladakom-Service, Speech Technology Center, Analytical Business Solutions, Cisco, Axxonsoft, Huawei
Saudi Arabia	CA	Not free	3			⋮			⋮		Multiple; NEC, Hikvision, BriefCam, Hugslock, Gatekeeper, BAE, Huawei
Serbia	ED		73		⋮	⋮		⋮	⋮		Huawei
Singapore	ED	Partly free	22		⋮	⋮		⋮	⋮		Huawei, Yitu, Tascent, Dassault, Accenture, Airbus, AGT, NEC
South Africa	ED	Free	48		⋮	⋮		⋮	⋮		Huawei
South Korea	LD	Free	10		⋮	⋮	⋮	⋮	⋮		Hanwha Techwin, Korea Telecom, SK Telecom, LG Uplus, Axxonsoft
Spain	LD		16			⋮			⋮		Herta, Huawei, SICE

(continued)

Table A.4 **Continued**

Country	Regime type	Freedom on the Net 2019 status	Military spending rank (2018)	BRI	Safe city	Facial recognition	Smart policing	SM monitoring	Chinese tech	Tech primarily from Chinese firms	US tech	Frequently mentioned companies
Switzerland	LD		38		··	··						Ekin
Taiwan	LD		23			··						Gorilla, Lilin, NEC
Tajikistan	CA			··	··	··			··	··		Huawei
Thailand	EA	Not free	29	··	··	··			··			Huawei; Megvii, Panasonic, ZTE
Turkey	EA	Partly free	15	··	··	··	··	··	··			HAVESLAN, Dahua, Hanwha Techwin
Uganda	EA	Partly free	94		··	··			··	··		Huawei
Ukraine	ED	Partly free	39	··	··	··			··		··	Hikvision, Huawei, Microsoft
United Arab Emirates	CA	Not free		··	··	··	··	··	··		··	Huawei, Hikvsion, NEC, BriefCam, GateKeeper, BAE, AGT, Circinus
United Kingdom	LD	Free	7		··	··	··	··			··	Hikvision, NEC, Palantir

Country	Regime	Freedom status	Score						Company
United States	LD	Free	1	..	..	..	..	..	Multiple; Cognitec, Palantir, PredPol, Amazon, BriefCam, Axis, Avigilon, Honeywell, Anduril, Elbit, NEC, Panasonic, Qognify, Genetec
Uruguay	LD		68	..	..	..	..	..	Palantir, Herta, ZTE
Uzbekistan	CA	Not free			..	..	..	..	Huawei, Infinova, Speech Technology Center
Venezuela	CA	Not free			..	..	..	..	CEIEC, Huawei, ZTE
Vietnam	CA	Not free	30			..	..	..	
Zambia	EA	Partly free	98		..	..	..	..	Hikvision, Huawei, ZTE
Zimbabwe	EA	Partly free	91		..	..	..	..	CloudWalk, Hikvision, Huawei

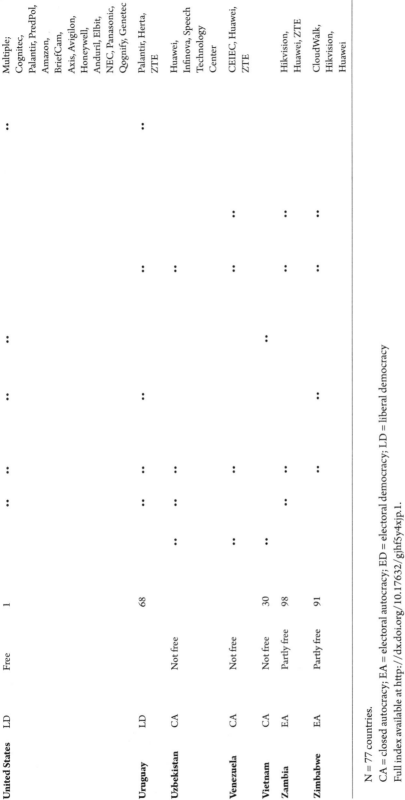

N = 77 countries.

CA = closed autocracy; EA = electoral autocracy; ED = electoral democracy; LD = liberal democracy

Full index available at http://dx.doi.org/10.17632/gjhf5y4xjp.1.

Zotero Source Library https://www.zotero.org/groups/2347403/global_ai_surveillance/items.

INDEX